Two Faces of **EXCLUSION**

Two Faces of **EXCLUSION**

THE UNTOLD HISTORY OF ANTI-ASIAN RACISM

IN THE UNITED STATES

Lon Kurashige

THE UNIVERSITY OF

NORTH CAROLINA PRESS

Chapel Hill

The University of North Carolina Press has been a
member of the Green Press Initiative since 2003.

Cover illustration: *Shimomura Crossing the Delaware* by Roger Shimomura.
Used by permission of the artist.

Library of Congress Cataloging-in-Publication Data
Names: Kurashige, Lon, 1964– author.
Title: Two faces of exclusion : the untold history of anti-Asian racism in the
United States / Lon Kurashige.
Description: Chapel Hill : The University of North Carolina Press, [2016] |
Includes bibliographical references and index.
Identifiers: LCCN 2016018925| ISBN 9781469629438 (cloth : alk. paper) |
ISBN 9781469659138 (pbk. : alk. paper) | ISBN 9781469629445 (ebook)
Subjects: LCSH: Racism—United States—History. | Asian Americans—History. | Asians—
United States—History. | United States—Race relations—History. | United States—
Emigration and immigration—History. | Asia—Emigration and immigration—History.
Classification: LCC E184.A75 K87 2016 | DDC 305.800973—dc23
LC record available at https://lccn.loc.gov/2016018925

Portions of chapters 3 and 7 and chapter 5 were previously published in
somewhat different form, respectively, in Lon Kurashige, "Transpacific
Accommodation and the Defense of Asian Immigrants," *Pacific Historical
Review* 83, no. 2 (May 2014): 294–313; and Lon Kurashige, "Rethinking Anti-
Immigrant Racism Lessons from the Los Angeles Vote on the 1920 Alien Land
Law," *Southern California Quarterly* 95, no. 3 (Fall 2013): 265–83.

For Cole and Reid

CONTENTS

ILLUSTRATIONS

A section of illustrations follows page 110

PREFACE

IIIIIIIIIIIIIIIIIIIIIIIIIIIIIIIIIIIIIIIIIIIIIIIIIIIIIIIIIIIIIIIIIIIIIIIIIIIIIIIIIIIIIIIIIIIIIIIIIIIIIIIIIIIIIIIIIIIIIIIIIIIIIIIIIIIIIIIII

This book studies racial politics—the crass, overt, in-your-face kind that discriminates against groups of human beings based upon supposedly objective criteria such as nationality, heredity, culture, and skin color. This type of racism, once the norm, is now ostracized to the fringes of most societies, including the United States. As a result, when studying contemporary America scholars tend to focus on more subtle, less visible, or what some call polite forms of racism that perpetuate racial discrimination and inequality stealthily and often without intention. There is much to appreciate about this kind of analysis, but it can be taken too far such that the historical distinction between vulgar and polite racism gets fuzzy and we lack understanding of the sometimes surprising process through which vulgar racism was overcome in law and politics, if not totally eliminated. A case in point is the history of anti-Asian racism in the United States, the subject of this book.

The idea for this investigation began in the archives, like so many works of history do. While reading through documents by a seemingly notorious anti-Asian racist, I discovered that later in life he curiously changed his views about race. After his conversion, he struggled to end the exclusion of Japanese immigrants and later was a rare leader of public opinion to oppose the internment of Japanese Americans to concentration camps during World War II.[1] In researching this man's transformation, I found many other influential whites who had fought against anti-Asian discrimination. I also turned my gaze inward. After publishing two books and numerous articles on Asian American history and after teaching university courses on the subject for more than a decade, how could I have missed this persistent and robust opposition? It turned out that my ignorance had less to do with me than with an intriguing blind spot in historical knowledge. I started writing *Two Faces of Exclusion* to explore this collective amnesia and ended up rethinking the larger history of anti-Asian politics.

What has emerged is a story about an intense and shifting political conflict over the discrimination of Asian immigrants and ethnics, whom I refer to inclusively as "Asian Americans." Before writing this book, I had assumed that the Japanese American internment, as well as immigration exclusion and other acts of prejudice, derived from an ongoing national consensus of opinion that considered Asians inferior to whites and antithetical to American institutions. But I have learned that these expressions of racism never went uncontested within the policy-making community and that even those who upheld whites as the superior race could oppose discrimination against Asian Americans. For more than three decades, from the middle to late nineteenth century, this opposition prevented Californians bent on excluding the Chinese from ending the nation's immigration policy welcoming all peoples irrespective of race.

Yet from 1882 to 1924, a perfect storm of historical circumstances converged to enable lawmakers to shut America's gates to Asian immigrants and further discriminate against those already in the country. While the Chinese had faced harassment in California since first coming in the 1850s, as well as the handicap preventing Asians from becoming U.S. citizens, they retained the same rights of entry as any immigrant until Congress in 1882 placed laborers from China in a special category for restriction. From that time, restriction turned into exclusion for nearly all but elite classes of Chinese, as the number of new arrivals dwindled. The ban spread to latter migrations from Japan, India, and Korea—and by statute any Asian with the exception of Filipinos, who, when they became U.S. colonial subjects, gained free right of entry to the imperial homeland. The Immigration Act of 1924 codified Asian exclusion. In establishing quotas for all nations outside the Americas, Congress prevented only the peoples of Asia from using them.

But historical conditions began to change again after 1924. Slowly, almost imperceptibly, the forty-two-year storm of exclusion weakened. While institutional racism persisted, and while Filipinos lost their right of entry and were summarily excluded, rays of sunlight appeared, such as the granting of naturalization rights to Asian immigrant veterans and the rise of support for Asian American workers in the house of labor. After exerting a powerful last gasp with the internment of Japanese Americans during World War II, the storm abated with surprising pace. Chinese exclusion lifted in 1943, and three years later so did the policies against Filipino and Indian immigration. By 1952 all Asians had access to national origins quotas and could become U.S. citizens. Consequently, the regime of institutional racism that was built on the denial of naturalization came crashing down with a suddenness that no one expected. Hawai'i statehood (1959), which established a lasting and influential Asian American voice on Capitol Hill, and comprehensive immigration reform (1965), which equalized immigration quotas for everyone outside the Americas, produced the final end to the exclusion era. Since then the nation has witnessed its largest and most diverse influx of newcomers from Asia—the foundation of today's vibrant and growing Asian American population. While remnants of exclusion era racism remain and new storms have appeared, the mother of all storms is over. Given equal rights and opportunities, Asian Americans have attained dramatic social mobility and mainstream acceptance; and by taking advantage of a new era of relatively open (though highly selective and in their own way discriminatory) immigration and refugee policies, they were able to increase the group's overall population from fewer than 330,000 in 1950 to well over 17 million by 2010.

This, in a nutshell, is the book's narrative. The pages that follow flesh out its details and contingencies through analysis of the societal fears and Asian immigrant vulnerabilities that lined up to create the perfect storm of exclusion. The findings reveal that lacking one or more of these factors left exclusion, along with attendant forms of institutional racism, politically weakened. While the proponents of exclusionary policies command much attention in this book, so too do their political adversaries. For exclusion was not a rout; it was a debate. There were always two sides to the question. Even during the height of anti-Asian policies, when exclusionists won a series of victories, the organized and well-funded opposition included some of the most powerful leaders in fields of American politics, business, religion, academia, and culture. Exclusionists remained watchful and wary of their respected opponents; they never underestimated them.

While the exclusion debate focused on Asian Americans, it was at the same time connected to a constellation of issues, interests, and ideas in American politics and international relations. The debate touched nearly every major political theme in modern U.S. history. At the center was the division between East and West of which exclusionists, following Rudyard Kipling's famous line, said, "Never the twain shall meet." But also key was the regional divide between East Coast and West Coast, as well as familiar conflicts between North and South, black and white, free and unfree labor, Republicans and Democrats, president and Congress, workers and owners, feminists and gender traditionalists, farmers and monopoly capital, isolationists and internationalists, town and country, Communists and capitalists, and peace advocates and supporters of war preparedness. Exploring the exclusion debate requires heeding the advice of a well-respected historian of American slavery. "To understand people's attitudes about race," he cautioned, "you have to understand their attitudes about everything."[2]

The story traces the exclusion debate as it spilled beyond the boundaries of what we have come to think of as Asian American issues to merge with broad concerns about immigration, race relations, sectional interests, industrial relations, international relations, and national security. In fleshing out this expansive context, the research has relied upon sources that, although commonly used in studies of political history, are often overlooked in the analysis of Asian Americans. These include congressional roll-call voting, electoral voting returns, and other forms of historical data. Wherever possible, I have used basic quantitative analysis to ground the study of political debate.[3] In handling discourse, I have put a premium on using the words of the main actors, especially as expressed in public forums like congressional hearings and speeches, legal decisions, and executive decrees. I also have relied upon existing studies, especially on subjects where the literature is particularly strong, while adding my own substantial research to fill gaps of knowledge and shore up areas thinly studied. What results is neither a monograph nor a work of historical synthesis but a hybrid of these two genres that one scholar aptly calls a "research survey."[4] For the specialist, this book offers a fresh interpretation of familiar sources. For the newcomer to Asian American history, it provides a political and intellectual framework that can serve as the foundation for further reading on social, cultural, intellectual, gender, sexual, religious, legal, global, and other dimensions to this experience.[5]

In order to cover more than a century of anti-Asian politics within a study of reasonable length, I have concentrated on groups that excited the greatest concern and whose proposed and real discrimination catalyzed the most powerful opposition. As such, the narrative centers on the earliest and largest groups, Chinese and Japanese Americans, whose homelands remained central to U.S. interests in the Asia-Pacific region throughout the book's narrative. The analysis also focuses on Filipino and Indian Americans, but Korean Americans are only briefly mentioned because their migration ended before the U.S. government could get involved in stopping it. Also largely absent in this story are the voices of everyday actors (agricultural and industrial workers, farmers, small business operatives, mothers, and children) who cared deeply about the exclusion debate but whose actions within the United States and Hawai'i had at best an indirect impact upon the policy-making process.[6]

Like many historians, I have explored the past with one eye on the present. For more than a decade while I was conducting research for this book, there occurred numerous debates in the United States and around the world about the discrimination and restriction of immigrants. While the most dramatic conflicts no longer involve Asian Americans, they testify to the ongoing issues studied here. Sometimes I have been struck by the uncanny similarities between present and past; yet at other times I am equally impressed by the great changes that have occurred that make the past seem like a truly strange place. What, then, is the exclusion debate's contemporary relevance? This is the toughest and most urgent question addressed in this book. The introduction opens with it, and the conclusion provides answers that may be surprising to those who see anti-Asian racism as simply a blemish on the nation's historical record. If you read this book carefully and grasp its meaning, then you will be prepared to offer your own answers. My greatest hope is that it encourages us all to work together in resolving current and future storms of exclusionary politics.

ACKNOWLEDGMENTS

IIIIIIIIIIIIIIIIIIIIIIIIIIIIIIIIIIIIIIIIIIIIIIIIIIIIIIIIIIIIIIIIIIIIIIIIIIIIIIIIIIIIIIIIIIIIIIIIIIIIIIIIIIIIIIIIIIIIIIIIIIIIII

This book project started before my two sons went to school and has finished as the oldest is getting ready for college. In a sense, working on it has been like raising another child. It was born of great hope and enthusiasm; developed in fulfilling, humbling, and at times uncomfortable ways; and ended up becoming something that was both expected and yet wonderfully surprising. I'm happy and grateful to acknowledge the village of support that I enjoyed in raising this third child.

Let me begin by recognizing support from the Abe Fellowship (2012–13), administered by the Social Science Research Council. Nicole Levit, her staff at the SSRC, Ellis Krauss, Eiji Kawabata, and other affiliated scholars made my year as an Abe Fellow productive and quite enjoyable. Research funding from the University of Southern California constituted the backbone of support for this project. This includes the USC Dornsife Dean's Office for a generous book subvention; Provost Immigration and Integration Initiative Fellowship; Provost Undergraduate Research Program Award, which at the outset of this project enabled me to hire four undergraduate researchers (Katie Gibelyou, Lauren Nakamura, Victor Lee, and Hannah Buerano); and Advancing Scholarship in the Social Sciences and Humanities award, which gave me an early sabbatical to finish writing this book. Additional funding provided by USC's Center for Japanese Religions and Cultures and a short-term research fellowship from Hannan University came at an important time. While in Japan conducting research, I affiliated with three schools: University of Tokyo, where it was quite special to be connected with Yujin Yaguchi and his graduate students; Sophia University, where I enjoyed discussions with Kazuto Oshiro, Mariko Iijima, and Yuko Konno, as well as the companionship of Mika Minoura and Naoko Suzuki at the Center for American and Canadian Studies; and Hannan University, where Tomoe Moriya was ever the gracious and intelligent host.

Many pieces of this book grew out of my participation in panels at professional conferences for Organization of American Historians, American Historical Association as well as its Pacific Coast Branch, Association for Asian American Studies, and Society for Historians of American Foreign Relations. The research also benefitted from my involvement in a series of symposiums run by Yasuko Takezawa (Kyoto University) and in invited talks for Wesleyan University, Simon Fraser University, Portland State University, Purdue University, UC Berkeley, UC Santa Barbara, University of

Nevada, University of Tokyo, Hannan University, Sophia University, Imin Kenkyukai (Study group for Immigration History), Historical Society of Southern California, and the University of Southern California. Sections of this book were previously published in *Pacific Historical Review* and *Southern California Quarterly*. I want to thank David Johnson and Carl Abbott, and Merry Ovnick for my engagement with their journals and for granting permission to reproduce parts of my articles in this book. I'm also grateful to Roger Shimomura for allowing me to reproduce his amazing and provocative art on the book cover.

It is particularly rewarding to recognize the teachers and mentors who continue to speak to me, in person and in spirit, long after my undergraduate and graduate years. The late Robert Kelley (UC Santa Barbara) stands out for his personal support and model of scholarship, which taught me to appreciate far-reaching patterns in American politics, as well as the importance a historical lens can bring to policy analysis. Allan G. Bogue and Tom Archdeacon introduced me to quantitative historical analysis when I was in graduate school, and long after I left Wisconsin, Professor Bogue went out of his way to assist me with roll-call voting analysis. In Los Angeles, Carole Shammas has been my inspiration and go-to source for quantitative history. As a teacher and mentor myself, I enjoyed interactions with hundreds of students who engaged with ideas and pedagogy related to this book; one of these was Vivian Yan, who also provided research assistance. I take particular delight in acknowledging the graduate students (now esteemed colleagues) whose questions, comments, and research interests not only improved this book but also changed the way I see the world. They are Phuong Nguyen, Mark Padoongpatt, Yuko Konno, Go Oyagi, and Yu Tokunaga. Yuko provided the added bonus of skilled translations, archival assistance, and companionship while I was conducting research in Japan.

As partly a work of historical synthesis, this book relies especially on the research of others. I am fortunate to be part of the first generation of scholars to have benefited from the establishment of Asian American history as a legitimate field of study. How wonderful it has been to draw upon the ideas of so many brilliant, innovative, and courageous thinkers—the most relevant of whom are acknowledged not only in the endnotes but also in the bibliographic essay. Past and present colleagues at USC who have contributed to this book include Philippa Levine, Bill Deverell, Jason Glenn, Duncan Williams, Jane Iwamura, Jane Junn, Josh Goldstein, George Sanchez, Saori Katada, Carole Shammas, John E. Wills, Phil Ethington, Steve Ross, and Lois Banner. The librarians and staff members at USC offering much appreciated support for this project were Katharin Peter, Sherry Mosely,

Beth Namei, and Sue Tyson. And crucial to my analysis of precinct voting in Los Angeles were Yao-Yi Chiang (USC Spatial Sciences Institute), for his technical assistance; Todd Gaydowski (Los Angeles city archivist), for finding and digitizing a large map upon which the analysis was based; and my research assistants John Tan and Evelyn Sanchez.

An extended community of scholars and friends who commented on parts of the book manuscript at various stages or otherwise supported this research was another invaluable resource. Thank you to Mari Yoshihara, Gordon Chang, Sarah Griffith, Meredith Oda, Shelley Sang-Hee Lee, Yujin Yaguchi, Augusto Espiritu, Rick Baldoz, Madeline Hsu, Maddalena Marinari, Michael Block, Gary Gerstle, Michael Omi, Dana Takagi, Eric Muller, Yasuko Takezawa, Greg Robinson, Nadia Kim, Reverend John Iwohara, Richard Modiano, and Eiichiro Azuma. I can't thank enough Brian Hayashi and Naoko Shibusawa for taking time away from their own pathbreaking research to critique the entire book manuscript at an advanced stage. It was Brian who helped me see that the perfect storm metaphor could be extended to chapter titles. I also was very fortunate to receive feedback from Paul Spickard and Erika Lee as official referees for the University of North Carolina Press and even profited from an anonymous report that failed to meet the standards for peer review. Chuck Grench, my editor at UNC Press, has been a rock of support for me and my work, and Jad Adkins, Mary Caviness, and others at the Press have been both friendly and professional. And then there was Julie Bush's masterful copyediting, which saved me from more inconsistencies and mistakes than I care to remember. As convention has it, none of the persons listed in these acknowledgments bears responsibility for errors in this book. That burden is mine alone.

Finally, there is no way I would have completed this project without a stable and supportive family and home environment. That my extended family history in California, Hawai'i, the Pacific Northwest, and Japan is embedded in the stories told in this book has made this project all the more meaningful to me. In the end, my own family—Anne, Cole, and Reid— deserve the ultimate credit for creating a fulfilling household from which I could work, and for which I have been happy to do so.

CHRONOLOGY

|||||||||||||||||||||||||||||||||||||||||||||||||||||||||||||||||||||||||||||||||||||||||||||||||||||||||||||||||||||||||||||||||||

1842	Treaty of Nanking ends First Opium War
1844	Treaty of Wanghia launches formal U.S.-China relations
1848	California and Oregon (up to Puget Sound) become U.S. territories
1850	California imposes foreign miners' tax targeting the Chinese
1853	U.S. forces Japan to end isolation from global relations and trade
1858	Treaty of Amity and Commerce launches formal U.S.-Japan relations
1860–65	U.S. Civil War
1862	Anti-coolie trade law
1865–77	Reconstruction era
1868	Fourteenth Amendment; Burlingame Treaty guarantees Chinese immigration
1870	San Francisco approves anti-Chinese Cubic Air Ordinance
1871	Massacre of Chinese in Los Angeles
1879	Anti-Chinese Fifteen Passenger Act vetoed by President Hayes
1881	Angell Treaty revises liberal Burlingame Treaty
1882	Chinese exclusion law bans laborers for ten-year period
1886	American Federation of Labor (AFL) founded
1892	Geary Act renews Chinese labor exclusion for another ten years
1894	Revision of unequal U.S.-Japan treaty; Immigration Restriction League founded
1898	Hawai'i and Philippines annexed by the United States
1904	Exclusion Act makes ban on Chinese laborers permanent
1906	President Theodore Roosevelt's message to Congress favors Japanese immigration
1907	Japan Society of New York founded
1910	Korea becomes a Japanese colony; Carnegie Endowment for International Peace founded
1913	Alien land law enacted in California; Rockefeller Foundation established
1916	Philippines Autonomy Act (Jones Law)
1917	Immigration Act excludes Indian immigrants
1920	California voters strengthen alien land law (Proposition 1 approved); United States refuses to join the League of Nations

1922	Washington Conference arms limitation treaties; *Ozawa* decision confirms ineligibility for U.S. citizenship to nonwhite Asian immigrants
1923	Survey of Race Relations begins; *Thind* decision confirms Indian immigrants' ineligibility for U.S. citizenship
1924	Immigration Act excludes Japanese immigrants and calls for national origins quotas
1925	Institute of Pacific Relations (IPR) founded in Hawai'i
1930	Watsonville anti-Filipino riots
1934	Philippine Independence Act (Tydings-Duffie Act) excludes Filipino immigrants
1935	Nye-Lea Act grants U.S. citizenship to Asian veterans; Congress of Industrial Organizations (CIO) established
1937	International Longshoremen's and Warehousemen's Union established
1941–45	United States in World War II
1942–45	Evacuation and internment of Japanese Americans
1943	Revision of unequal U.S.-China treaty; Chinese exclusion repealed; all-nisei 442nd Regimental Combat Team established
1945	United Nations founded
1946	Luce-Celler Act repeals Indian and Filipino exclusion; Philippine independence
1948	Evacuation Claims Act provides nominal payment for internee losses
1949	Peoples Republic of China founded
1950–53	Korean War
1952	McCarran-Walter Act ends Japanese exclusion
1954	Hawai'i "Democratic Revolution"
1955	AFL and CIO merge
1956	Alien land law repealed by California voters
1959	Hawai'i statehood
1964	Civil Rights Act; United States escalates troops in Vietnam War
1965	Immigration and Nationality Act (Hart-Celler Act) ends national origin system
1968	Asian American movement established
1988	Civil Liberties Act pays reparations for Japanese American internment
2012	House of Representatives expresses regret for Chinese exclusion

Two Faces of **EXCLUSION**

INTRODUCTION

RACISM AND THE MAKING
OF A PACIFIC NATION

IIIIIIIIIIIIIIIIIIIIIIIIIIIIIIIIIIIIIIIIIIIIIIIIIIIIIIIIIIIIIIIIIIIIIIIIIIIIIIIIIIIIIIIIIIIIIIIIIIIIIIIIIIIIIIIIIIIIIIIIIIIIII

Visitors to Los Angeles's historic center, if they look carefully, will find information about the city's original Chinatown not far from Our Lady Queen of Angels Catholic Church, Avila Adobe, a monument to Latino American war veterans, and the Mexican-themed commercial district of Olvera Street. One sidewalk placard marks the location on Calle de los Negros where on October 24, 1871, a mob of "500 locals shot, hung, and stabbed innocent Chinese residents." This "massacre," the marker reads, erupted during a period when "anti-Chinese legislation and social discrimination greatly affected Chinese American families and their community life" and "left them without legal protection."

How do denizens of the twenty-first century make sense of this all-too-true image of Asian helplessness and victimization on the American frontier? Two answers present themselves. First, the hostility is seen as a reflection of more recent racism that has plagued Asian Americans. The murder of Vincent Chin in 1982 by two unemployed white automobile workers in Detroit, Michigan, is a bracing example of the reoccurrence of anti-Asian violence. Ronald Ebens and his nephew Michael Nitz got into a fight with Chin, mistook the Chinese American man for being Japanese, and beat him to death, motivated in part by vengeance against Japanese automakers for competing so successfully against their American rivals. The attackers used racial epithets, calling the victim "Chink" and "Jap," and before the fight began one of them decried, "It's because of you little motherfuckers that we're out of work."[1]

In the recent past, Filipinos, Vietnamese, and other Asian Americans have been the victims of similar outbursts of racially motivated killing. More common are less violent and more subtle forms of hostility expressed through hate speech, accent discrimination, and "glass ceilings" in employment. Stereotypes are the most banal, but hardly innocuous, form of anti-Asian prejudice. One type assumes that Asian Americans are uniformly smart and successful "model minorities," while another questions their ability to become truly American. Such nonviolent racism was central to the case of Wen Ho Lee, a naturalized Taiwanese American scientist who in 1999 was fired from a research position at the Los Alamos National Labo-

1

ratory. A federal judge charged Lee with selling nuclear weapons secrets to China and placed him in solitary confinement for nine months. It turned out that the scientist was innocent on all counts of espionage and that FBI investigators had leaped to conclusions in part due to his ancestry. The presiding judge, as well as President Bill Clinton, publicly apologized to Lee for his unnecessary ordeal while reprimanding overzealous law enforcement.[2]

The murder of Vincent Chin and case of Wen Ho Lee testify to the often misrecognized fact that Asian Americans continue to face discrimination, stereotypes, and violence, but the persistence of anti-Asian racism is too easily forgotten in today's "post-racial" America. That said, the degree of helplessness and victimization experienced by the Chinese on Calle de los Negros in 1871 seems strangely remote from our world today. If the first response to the Chinatown massacre is to view it as a "distant mirror" from which to understand the continuation of racism today, the second is to see it as a kind of circus mirror projecting a grossly exaggerated picture with little contemporary relevance. From this second perspective, the vigilante killings appear like a historical artifact from the "Wild West," when pioneers crossed the country on horse-powered wagons, engaged in pistol-spinning duels, and took "scalps" as war trophies. It goes without saying that Southern California's current Asian American community—consisting of Chinatowns, Little Tokyo, Koreatown, historic Filipinotown, Little India, Little Saigon, Thai Town, Cambodia Town, and massive populations dispersed within the region's sprawling suburbs—looks nothing like it did on that fateful night in October 1871.

In striking contrast to the nineteenth century, Asian immigrants now enjoy the same legal protections as any U.S. citizen or permanent resident. Social discrimination receives sanction by neither government nor normative understandings of race or community standards. All anti-Asian laws and legal precedents have been expunged from the books or rendered moot. Congress officially apologized for Chinese exclusion and authorized payment of $20,000 as restitution to every living survivor of the Japanese American internment. The impressive ascent in socioeconomic status for Asian Americans has inverted the exclusion era meaning of "Chinaman's chance," which had meant having no chance at all. Today, as writer Eric Liu puts it, "Chinaman's chance" means being afforded the great opportunity, enjoyed by millions of new immigrants, to achieve the American dream.[3] To borrow a phrase from activists in the 1960s, the yellow peril has become the "yellow pearl" as Asian Americans have infused the United States with millions of dollars of foreign capital, not to mention priceless contributions to the nation's human capital, economy, culture, and universities. Asian

Americans are even making noticeable inroads into such arenas as enter-
tainment and politics in which they have been woefully underrepresented.
Their influence across many fields of endeavor is so powerful that one won-
ders why and how American society changed so dramatically since the days
of the Chinese massacre.

How did a nation that once singled out Asian Americans for discrimination and scorn end up becoming the world's magnet for today's migrations from Asia? The burden of this book is to explain the long-term
process through which U.S. leaders overcame hostility toward Asian Americans in order to embrace the country's "Pacific destiny," which in the mid-
nineteenth century foretold a golden age of U.S.-Asian commerce and
civilization. More than 150 years later, the vast majority of American policy
makers accept the country's identity as a Pacific nation that celebrates its
interconnections with the vast Asia-Pacific region. To explain this historical transformation, many scholars have studied America's Pacific history
through a wide-angle lens capturing the evolution of economic, geopolitical, and cultural trends over long periods of time.[4] In contrast, *Two Faces
of Exclusion* sheds light on this story of global integration by narrowing
the focus to institutional racism in the United States because discriminatory legislation, treaties, diplomatic agreements, legal rulings, and administrative decisions were critical bellwethers for America's development
as a Pacific nation.[5] The analysis pays close attention to the movers and
shakers of anti-Asian policies, including public officials (presidents, members of Congress, justices, cabinet members, and foreign diplomats) as well
as groups and individuals with direct interests in public policies, such as
scholars, labor organizers, missionaries, business leaders, peace advocates,
and other nonstate actors. While today Asian Americans play leading roles
in any discussion of anti-Asian racism, this was not the case in the nineteenth and early twentieth centuries when Asian immigrants were disen-
franchised and thus forced to exert what policy influence they could leverage through sympathetic whites and officials from their home countries.
The actions and perspectives of Asian Americans, with a few exceptions,
became influential during and after World War II when these groups overcame the handicaps that had marginalized them from the political arena.

Exclusion Debate

What, then, explains the rise, persistence, and fall of anti-Asian institutional racism? Answering this question requires focusing on a core
political conflict between *exclusionists*, who used the state to discriminate
against Asian Americans, and the opposition to this discrimination from

groups and individuals whom I call *egalitarians*. Exclusionists are not hard to imagine as antagonists who perpetrated conceptions and practices of white supremacy during a time when race had much more ominous, hierarchical, and explicit meanings than it does today. It is important to note, however, that exclusionists were not demons. While some evinced a disturbing cold-heartedness and lack of universal empathy, most expressed a commendable compassion for the underdog, even though this did not extend to Asian Americans. Egalitarians are more difficult to envision than exclusionists because the century in which the exclusion debate took place is fixed in our minds as overwhelmingly, if not monolithically, racist. From today's perspective, it is hard to imagine many policy actors back then who embodied the dictionary definition of egalitarian: "relating to, or believing in the principle that *all people* are equal and deserve equal rights and opportunities." So how do we to explain the significant opposition to anti-Asian racism?[6]

This book defines egalitarians as those who opposed exclusionist demands through language rooted in America's Declaration of Independence, which famously claims that "all men are created equal." As a foundational political discourse, egalitarianism was malleable—so much so that even exclusionists justified racial discrimination as necessary for egalitarian purposes, including equal opportunities for working-class whites. But this was a racial discourse rooted in an *exclusive* vision of a white republic or classless society. In contrast, those I call egalitarians projected an *inclusive* view of the nation in which Asian Americans were accorded equal treatment. In opposing Chinese exclusion in 1882, Senator George Frisbee Hoar argued, "Nothing is more in conflict with the genius of American institutions than legal distinctions between individuals based upon race or upon occupation. The framers of our Constitution . . . meant that their laws should make no distinction between men except such as were required by personal conduct and character."[7]

President Theodore Roosevelt also used the language of inclusive equality in 1906 when defending Japanese immigrants. "The Japanese," he said in that year's State of the Union address, "have won in a single generation the right to stand abreast of the foremost and most enlightened peoples of Europe and America; they have won on their own merits and by their own exertions the right to treatment on a basis of full and frank equality."[8] During World War II, the photographer Ansel Adams extended this nondiscriminatory language of equality to Japanese Americans confined in concentration camps. His book of photographs *Born Free and Equal: The Story of Loyal Japanese-Americans* affirmed the good citizenship he found among the internees at the Manzanar camp and contained this affirming quote from President Franklin D. Roosevelt: "In vindication of the very ideals for which we are fighting this war, it is important to us to maintain the high standard of fair, considerate, and equal treatment for the people of this minority, as of all other minorities."[9]

FDR's statement reveals complexities and contradictions within the egalitarian position, for the wartime confinement of Japanese Americans stemmed from his own racial suspicions and willingness to discriminate members of this group from among other "enemy aliens" and U.S. citizens. Theodore Roosevelt, too, could uphold Japanese equality on one hand while undermining it on the other by pledging allegiance to the white race. Even George Hoar, who remained steadfast in his opposition to Chinese exclusion, was not beyond voting for the exclusion of French Canadians and others deemed a labor and civilizational threat to his home state of Massachusetts. As a result, it is important to see egalitarians not simply as righteous antiracists but rather as historical actors driven by interests that often perpetuated the racial status quo as well as the domestic and global capitalist order. Egalitarians were not saints; even the many missionaries who defended Asian Americans possessed their own cultural biases and saw discrimination as a threat not just to their religious principles but also to their material and political interests in spreading the Gospel. In this way, the egalitarian defense of Asian Americans was limited by both a pragmatic sense of what was politically possible in an imperfect society as well as by judgments based in religion, race, class, nation, gender, and other ideological constructs that deemed only certain types of Asian Americans worthy of protection, such as merchants, students, Christians, and others who were not laborers, Communists, or prostitutes.[10]

Egalitarians were also diverse and situated in time and place. In addition to missionaries, Radical Republicans included Asian immigrants within their attempt to reconstruct southern race relations after the Civil War. Conservative business leaders focused on a crucial labor supply embraced egalitarianism, as did peace advocates and racial liberals who were the forerunners of civil rights activism that came to include Asian American issues after World War II. But here is the crucial point about egalitarians: regardless of their different, antithetical, and imperfect motives, they, as a coalition of interests invested in the nondiscrimination of Asian Americans, played a crucial role in the history of anti-Asian racism. Their combined efforts impeded, moderated, and eventually overturned exclusionary laws that significantly influenced the lives of millions of people within and outside the United States. Such actions also shaped the nation's race, labor, and international relations, as well as the development of what has been called the Pacific World. If we are to understand the trajectory of anti-Asian policies, then we must grasp the core conflict between exclusionists and egalitarians.[11]

The assertion that anti-Asian racism was debated, rather than simply imposed, is at odds with conventional historical understanding. Scholars for the past half century have been preoccupied with the exclusionist side of the story. These studies have revolutionized our understanding of U.S. policies and practices by revealing, with increasing originality and sophistication, the centrality of race in the historical experiences of Asian Americans.[12] But in so doing they have played down, if not overlooked, the significance of the egalitarian opposition to anti-Asian racism. What results is a picture of American racial consensus that emphasizes discrimination, abuse, indifference, and the compromising of democratic ideals.[13] The pragmatic, historically contingent conception of egalitarians used in this book presents an opportunity to explore beneath the surface of this apparent racial consensus by interrogating the conflicting positions taken by policy makers on Asian American issues.[14]

One reason why the relevant scholarship has ignored the robust egalitarian opposition has to do with the field's preoccupation with "racial formation," the making of race as a material and ideological structure of inequality and domination. In this way, the sphere of formal politics has been understood as an arena of race making, and in so doing a wide variety of forces that have influenced anti-Asian policies (including diplomacy, national security, labor relations, and imperial expansion) have not been appreciated on their own terms. Rather, they are seen as determined by racial discourse, if they are discussed at all.[15] A related factor that has obscured the importance of the exclusion debate has stemmed from the separation of diplomatic relations from the analysis of exclusion era politics. Before the 1960s, the study of anti-Asian politics in the United States fell into two main research areas: one focusing on U.S. relations with East Asia and the Pacific, and the other on processes of assimilation, including the formation of racial attitudes by dominant groups as well as the social, cultural, and psychological adaptations made by minorities. The current scholarship on anti-Asian policies derives from the second type of research while largely neglecting the first.[16] A telling sign that the earlier diplomatic studies have been forgotten is that the latest research on Asian Americans has embraced international experiences and contexts as if these were brand-new trends in the study of Asian immigration. To be sure, the recent focus on transnationalism has opened up fresh questions regarding migration and diaspora that were not anticipated by the earlier diplomatic studies. But these earlier studies of diplomatic and trade relations remain indispensable for understanding the history of anti-Asian politics, a process that shaped, and was shaped by, the formation of the larger Pacific World.[17]

The shortcomings of the conventional approach demand a new framework that can account for both sides of the exclusion debate as it enveloped all major Asian immigrant groups. It is tempting to see such a framework as revealing a past that although still replete with racism was not as bad as we have thought. But this is not how I see it because such a perception implies that the history of racism exists on a continuum, with some viewing it as really oppressive (say a 9 on a 1–10 scale) and others viewing it less so (a 6 out of 10). The continuum implies judgment of historical approaches usually based on their utility for a contemporary political or ideological project (e.g., advancing a cause or a conditioned ideal of objectivity). The framework used in this book is designed to *understand* the conflict between exclusionists and egalitarians rather than to judge or rank how bad the past was. Its operating assumption is that persons on either side of the exclusion debate had more in common than they realized. All of these historical actors believed in the righteousness of their cause and cast aspersions on their opponents, and in so doing enacted social, political, and racial divisions that perpetuated rather than ended conflict. The fact that recent scholarship has focused on exclusion without addressing the centrality of the exclusion debate is indicative of the persistence of these divisions, albeit in very different circumstances.

The narrative in this book takes a long-term view of the rise and fall of institutional racism in order to understand the way in which the United States became a Pacific nation. In particular, the exclusion debate is historicized within the confluence of four independent yet conjoined policy issues that each generated a stable community of interest across space and time. The main policy communities centered on immigration and labor, race relations, foreign relations, and national security. Each community has had its own internal debates, constituencies, policy-making processes, and historical trajectories. Egalitarians typically consisted of immigration expansionists, race liberals, internationalists, and civil libertarians. Exclusionists, on the other hand, were often immigration restrictionists, race conservatives, isolationists, and security hawks. Each side of the exclusion debate represented a historically specific alliance of ideologically and materially heterogeneous actors, some of whom made rather strange bedfellows.[18]

The alignments were remarkably stable over time, but some groups and individuals within the policy communities changed positions in ways that had a major impact on the exclusion debate. A good example is when the American Federation of Labor, a stalwart exclusionist, switched to the egalitarian camp in the 1950s, becoming a leading supporter of ending discrimination against Asian Americans as part of its newfound commitment to civil and immigrant rights. Individual actors also switched sides in a given policy community and in so doing changed their minds about Asian Americans. In this way, the California journalist and Progressive Party leader Chester H. Rowell—the notorious racist whose surprising transformation launched the research for this book—came to embrace Asian Americans when after World War I he became allied with internationalists seeking to prevent war between the United States and Japan.[19]

Individual actors also straddled the line between exclusionist and egalitarian camps. Theodore Roosevelt, for example, was claimed by both sides of the exclusion debate. His respect for Japanese civilization already has been acknowledged. As an imperialist internationalist and security hawk, Roosevelt could only applaud Japan's military power and conquests as the mark of a superior people on a par with the greatest Western civilizations. But as a president seeking reelection, he bowed to political pressures from organized labor, nativists, and fellow progressive reformers in negotiating the restriction of Japanese labor migration. He also supported the principle, enactment, and enforcement of racial segregation. Thus it would be wrong to think of actors within the four policy communities as static and predictable figures who marched through time unchanged by shifting circumstances. Such an assumption would deny historical contingency, as well as the contradictions and unexpected outcomes that distinguish "neat and clean" theorizing from messy historical realities. The policy community framework provides guidelines for explanation, rather than all-encompassing predictions of human behavior or historical change. If the contest between exclusionists and egalitarians was a sporting event, then this framework would provide the rules of the game, while the perfect storm narrative would address the gameplay as it unfolded between the mid-nineteenth and mid-twentieth centuries.

Perfect Storm Narrative

When the first migrations of Chinese to the United States began in the 1850s, exclusionists ruled the political debate in California, though not throughout the nation. They were backed by popular fears in the West that foreigners would dominate the gold fields and overwhelm the newly incorporated territory. While Mexicans and other peoples from Latin America faced racial hardships in the Golden State, they were considered white by law, unlike Asians, blacks, "mulattoes," and Native Americans, who confronted special discrimination due to their lack of legal standing. In determining the grounds for American citizenship, the nation's first Congress in 1790 elected to limit naturalization to "free white persons" of "good character." These phrases signified groups considered to be unprepared or unable to perform the duties of citizenship.[20] While Asian subjects were not mentioned in the debate over the Naturalization Act, federal courts, in response to cases spurred by the arrival of Chinese migrants, confirmed that the law's white standard excluded them from citizenship. After the Fourteenth Amendment (1868) granted citizenship to free blacks and newly freed slaves during Reconstruction, and after the Dawes Act (1887) did the same for certain Native American peoples, Asians remained one of the most defenseless targets for discriminatory policies in California.

The inability of Asians to become American citizens constituted the most important of the group's vulnerabilities in the United States. This handicap not only enabled a host of laws and ordinances discriminating against "aliens ineligible to citizenship" but also prevented Asian immigrants from becoming key players in electoral politics. Free and easy access to citizenship for European groups encouraged the growth of political parties investing in the quick naturalization of potential voters, including quasi-white groups such as the "wild Irish" and the "tribe of Israel."[21] In the nineteenth century, the Democratic Party attracted large waves of German and Irish immigrants, and Republicans competed with it for the loyalties of Jews, Hungarians, Italians, Poles, and other so called new immigrants. In this way, the Naturalization Act made possible a "possessive investment in whiteness" by political parties inclined to support the prejudices and economic and cultural interests of European immigrants at the expense of politically castrated Asian immigrants.[22]

Legal handicaps made it exceedingly difficult for Asian immigrants to prove loyalty to the United States. For many, the bar to citizenship foreclosed the option of permanent settlement, prolonging sojourner mentality even for those who remained in the United States for the rest of their lives. Ineligibility for citizenship also discouraged many from joining the U.S. military, contributing to the nation's civic life, adopting American culture and values, and learning English. Thus legal handicaps set many Asian immigrants on a different course of Americanization from their European counterparts. The opportunity costs for being ineligible for citizenship were revealed through the experience of Armenian immigrants, a relatively small, non-European group who concentrated in California's Central Valley at the same time and in the same locations as Japanese immigrants.

Because they could become U.S. citizens, Armenians were not subjected to institutional racism and were able to develop a strong footing in local and state politics. An intriguing counterfactual question asks, Would the discrimination and internment of Japanese Americans have occurred if, like Armenians, they were eligible to citizenship? Such a question highlights the significance of ethnic voting blocs in protecting the interests of Armenians, as well as Irish immigrants, black freedmen and freedwomen under Reconstruction, and other immigrant and racial groups.[23]

Three more vulnerabilities reinforced the notion that Asians would not make good citizens. The first centered on the lack of understanding and familiarity growing out of the long period of East-West isolation that was reinforced when China's Ming emperor in 1433 ended the nation's short-lived ocean explorations that reached as far as Africa and the Persian Gulf.[24] China, one of the world's most economically powerful nations for most of human history, sealed itself off from global economic developments, such as Europe's exploitation of New World resources. Japan and Korea also remained apart from the "ocean world" opened up by Portuguese and Spanish explorers. What resulted was a deep civilizational divide in which both Asians and Europeans failed to appreciate their common humanity. The situation gave rise to the orientalist sentiment behind Rudyard Kipling's famous lines "Oh, East is East, and West is West, and never the twain shall meet." Asian immigrants were at a disadvantage from the very start of their venture to the United States because they were seen as utterly strange and different from Europeans.[25]

Another consequence of extended East-West separation concerned the loss of economic parity between these two regions after 1800, when impact of the Industrial Revolution generated historic levels of wealth and economic development in Europe and North America but not Asia. By the time Chinese immigrants began arriving in California in the middle of the nineteenth century, East Asia had become a "Third World" region compared with the rapidly rising technology, military power, and standards of living in western Europe. This transformation seemed to confirm the racial backwardness and inferiority of Asian immigrants. Further confirmation came in the form of Western imperialism through which the United States, Great Britain, and many European powers established unequal treaties in China and Japan while colonizing much of the rest of Asia. The imperial conquest began in earnest after 1842 when the British defeated China in the First Opium War.[26]

Thus in addition to the legal handicap of ineligibility for citizenship (the first vulnerability), Asian immigrants suffered from the deep stigma placed on Eastern peoples and civilization (second vulnerability), which was reinforced by the economic inferiority of Asian nations vis-à-vis the West and Western colonization (third and fourth vulnerabilities). These last two vulnerabilities made it difficult for Asian nations, as subordinated powers, to exert much leverage over U.S. officials in negotiating and defending the rights of their citizens in the United States. In this way, the vulnerabilities of Asian immigrants made it possible for California to enact a host of discriminatory policies, but before 1882 this racism remained fixed in the Far West and held little hold over Washington, D.C., or the nation's centers of finance and economic power in the Northeast.

As chapter 1 illustrates, the prolonged exclusion era was not possible until five fears related to immigration became national obsessions and in so doing conjoined with the Asian vulnerabilities to produce the perfect storm of exclusion. The first and most important of the fears grew out of anxiety about a flood of foreigners overwhelming the American population. Until the 1890s, most Americans welcomed immigrants as vehicles of economic growth for a developing nation with chronic labor shortages. This ended abruptly, however, with the symbolic closing of the frontier (1890) combined with concomitant fears of labor unrest and dangerous overcrowding in the nation's cities. Many Americans now called for immigration restriction, and given their vulnerabilities, Asians became their first victims.

Four other broad-based fears emerging in the late nineteenth and early twentieth centuries were contingent on the first. Fear of human flooding provoked increasingly powerful craft labor unions to prevent competition from foreign workers with low standards of living. Union organizers argued that unchecked immigration induced cutthroat competition that damaged the livelihoods of American workers. Population pressures also gave rise to the fear of "mongrelization" that scientists said resulted when people with inferior blood mixed with "Anglo-Saxons" and the fear of social disorder pitting recent immigrants (largely southeastern Europeans) against white society. And, finally, radical political ideologies carried disproportionately by foreigners sparked national security fears regarding espionage, sabotage, assassination, and other acts of terror. As with the fear of human flooding, none of the four other fears implicated only Asian immigrants, but given their vulnerabilities, they became particularly susceptible targets. Chapters 2–5 reveal how the conditions fueling the perfect storm of exclusion, as listed in table I.1, played out during the height of the exclusion era.

A key turning point in the storm of exclusion came in 1924 when Congress passed comprehensive immigration reform to restrict the numbers of newcomers. The Johnson-Reed Act, and subsequent legislation, estab-

Table I.1. Asian vulnerabilities and U.S. immigration fears

Asian vulnerabilities	U.S. immigration fears
Ineligible for citizenship	Human flood
Civilizational stigma	Labor competition
Economic inferiority of Asian nations	Mongrelization
Western colonization of Asia	Racial disruption of social order
	Espionage, sabotage, and terrorism

lished a quota system to safeguard the nation from overwhelming numbers of European immigrants while subjecting Asians to near total exclusion. Thus was established a form of human flood control that calmed the primary fear of inundation by foreigners, even though select exclusionists would continue to complain about possible holes in the dike. Feelings of security gave rise to a period of "late exclusionism," as detailed in chapter 6, when the perfect storm moderated but by no means ended. This period also saw the emergence of Asian subjects with legal standing, whose assimilation and proof of loyalty to the United States overcame the first vulnerability related to "aliens ineligible to citizenship." Chapter 7 shows how even more actors with legal standing emerged during World War II, as second-generation Japanese Americans, in particular, earned widespread respect as soldiers in the U.S. Army. With human flood control in place and immigration fears trumped by the greater fear of losing the war against Japan, Congress repealed the exclusion of Chinese, Indians, and Filipinos, while granting each long-sought naturalization rights. This Great Transformation calmed the perfect storm of exclusion. The end of exclusion also moderated the wartime treatment of Japanese Americans, who were interned in concentration camps during the war amid the apex of national security fears. By 1952, the federal government had admitted the terrible mistake of the interment (though did not adequately atone for it) and included Japanese immigrants in egalitarian reforms that all but ended the exclusion debate.

The book's final chapter addresses Hawai'i statehood and comprehensive immigration reform that brought a final end to the exclusion era. No longer did Asian Americans lack significant representation in the U.S. Congress, nor did they (or any race or national group) appear as targets for overtly discriminatory immigration and naturalization policies. The egalitarians won the exclusion debate, but at the same time conflict between different types of egalitarians erupted over the interpretation of Asian American achievement. Did the ultimate egalitarian victory mean that America had moved beyond race and no longer needed to keep fighting against racism? This question remained unsettled in the late twentieth and early twenty-first centuries as historians and policy makers reflected on the history of anti-Asian racism as a monolithic expression of racial consensus. The memory of the 1871 Chinese massacre is but one example of the historical amnesia we confront today that erases the egalitarian side of the exclusion debate. The book's conclusion explores the costs of forgetting the significance of egalitarianism and why we should remember the history of anti-Asian racism as a critical debate. The beginning of our story will reveal that today's notion of Asian American equality and racial inclusion, far from being a product of recent history, has its origins in the mid-nineteenth century, at the start of mass migration from Asia.

1 BEFORE THE STORM

RACE FOR COMMERCIAL EMPIRE, 1846–1876

‖‖‖

In July 1852 Senator William H. Seward projected an expansive vision of the young United States as a global power surpassing even the great British Empire. The growing importance of transpacific trade, Seward emphasized, marked a turning point in which Europe "will sink in importance; while the Pacific Ocean, its shores, its islands, and the vast regions beyond, will become the chief theatre of events." Given that the recent statehood of California and claiming of the Oregon Territory had put America onto the shores of the Pacific, the young nation in Seward's eyes was poised to complete its "emancipation from what remains of European influence and prejudice, and in turn develop the American opinion and influence which shall remould constitutions, laws, and customs, in the land that is first greeted by the rising sun." The democratization of Asian nations, he proposed, would emerge as a natural result of East-West commercial relations. In this way, transpacific commerce would enable the United States to become an empire "greater than any that has ever existed."[1]

Immigration was integral to Seward's dreams of global expansion. Not only would commerce transform the Pacific basin but also the region's surplus populations would be relied upon to develop America's fledging West Coast cities, industries, and economic infrastructure. Seward highlighted the recent migration of Chinese laborers to California and the Caribbean, calculating that the North American continent had the ability to absorb at least two hundred million people from China alone! Aware of America's anti-Chinese sentiment, which was already producing discriminatory policies in California, Seward assured that Asian immigrants were no different from the nation's millions of European foreigners: "As for those who doubt that this great movement [of Chinese migrants] will quicken activity and create wealth and power in California and Oregon, I leave them to consider what changes the movements [of European immigrants], similar in nature but inferior in force and slower in effect, have produced already on the Atlantic coast of America."[2]

Seward's vision met stiff opposition in Congress. The notion of hundreds of millions of Asians in North America was a nonstarter on Capitol Hill, notwithstanding the many Californians who were already calling for Chinese exclusion. In addition to conflict over immigration, the senator's florid dreams faced opposition from entrenched regional, party, and ideological interests. The Civil War, however, boosted his chances, as Seward became secretary of state under President Abraham Lincoln, while the secession of the South left the business-friendly Republican Party firmly in power. Secretary Seward improved relations with China and Japan in order to increase transpacific commerce and migration. His actions, as much as anyone else's at the time, fixed a positive construction of Asian immigrants firmly within the federal government. Even after his death in 1872, an expansionist immigration constituency, with deep roots among Republicans and bipartisan congressional support, managed to hold off increasingly strong attempts to exclude Chinese immigrants.

This chapter explores the exclusion debate during the first three decades of America's engagement as a Pacific nation. While most Americans in the middle of the nineteenth century celebrated expansion from "sea to shining sea," few grasped what Seward had already known: unencumbered commercial relations with Asia meant the beginning of free-flowing transpacific migration. Joining Seward were fellow Republicans friendly to the maritime interests of New England and the Mid-Atlantic states. Missionaries, too, championed Chinese immigrants as a sign of healthy U.S.-China relations, as did proponents of mining, railroads, and other western industries that came to rely on Chinese labor. After the Civil War, Radical Republicans, who opposed slavery and defended the freedmen's and freewomen's rights, added a racial egalitarian element to the expansionist constituency in seeking to include Chinese immigrants as part of sweeping civil rights protections designed to empower African Americans in the defeated South. The exclusionists, on the other hand, wanted to reap the benefits of becoming a Pacific nation without having to pay the price of Asian immigration. They were concerned about the economic opportunities for everyday Americans that West Coast expansion made possible. Exclusionists opposed Chinese immigrants as a tool of western capitalists and northeastern financiers leveled against the economic rights and racial privileges of the nation's landless poor, growing industrial workforce, and downtrodden European immigrant groups. Often—though not always—foes of Radical Republicans, exclusionists also viewed the Chinese as a threat to the nation's whiteness, as well as to its European-based culture and institutions.

Expansionism and Divergent Notions of Empire

America's Pacific adventures grew out of the thriving China trade that, beginning in the early Republic, involved scores of merchant houses and clipper ships based largely in Boston, New York, and other northeastern ports. American vessels brought items such as sea otter skins, seal pelts, ginseng root, Hawaiian sandalwood, Mexican silver, and eventually opium to China in return for teas, silks, porcelain, and refined cotton cloth. Starting in the 1820s the trading ships would also carry an increasing number of missionaries on their way to China, Hawai'i, and other Asia-Pacific outposts. Yet it was not until the 1840s that the U.S. government became directly engaged in transpacific commerce. During this crucial decade the nation claimed its first territories on the Pacific coast and also signed its first commercial treaty with China. American traders and missionaries welcomed President James K. Polk's support for their endeavors. In settling the Oregon boundary dispute with Great Britain and wresting California from Mexico, the president put the country in a prime position to forge a transpacific commercial empire—something he, Seward, and numerous other public figures and private profit seekers had long desired. Most Americans mistook the grabbing of western ports in California and the Puget Sound as the nation's "manifest destiny," as if God, rather than the calculating designs of American statesmen, had ordained the course of expansion.[3]

The establishment of U.S. states and territories on the Pacific Ocean followed on the heels of continental expansion to Texas. In 1836 American settlers, who two decades earlier had been invited by Mexican officials to develop lands north of the Rio Grande River, fomented a revolution that launched Texas as an independent republic. The plan all along was for the vast southwestern territory to be annexed by the United States, but many U.S. policy makers feared this would provoke war with Mexico, which disputed the new Lone Star republic's boundaries. More important, Texans' embrace of slavery induced bitter sectional and partisan conflict in Congress. Northerners and members of the Whig Party opposed annexation as a plot by southerners to expand slavery. While Whigs and northeastern commercial interests favored the old nationalist economic vision of Alexander Hamilton, their rivals—Democrats and southern slave owners—shared Thomas Jefferson's and, more immediately, Andrew Jackson's suspicions of federal authority.

In the 1844 presidential election, Hamiltonians rallied around the Whig Henry Clay's protectionist "American system" that emphasized high tariffs and infrastructural improvements, while Jeffersonians remained true to the laissez-faire tradition of Andrew Jackson and his fellow Tennessean Democrat James Polk. Polk won the presidency as a dark horse candidate mainly because he embraced the annexation of Texas and an expansive Oregon claim, while Clay equivocated on both issues. Even before Polk entered the White House, Congress welcomed Texas into the Union. Oregon followed in 1846 when President Polk pressured Great Britain to cede its land claims below the forty-ninth parallel and to set this longitude as the territory's northern border. Meanwhile, the annexation of Texas provoked the feared war with Mexico in which the victorious Americans in 1848 confirmed its hold on Texas while acquiring the rest of Mexico's northern territories, including the prize of California.[4]

Expansion to the West Coast united the U.S. policy makers in a way that had been impossible just a few years earlier regarding the annexation of Texas. Polk's election proved that expansionism had become popular, and the Mexican war only raised the appeal of the Democrats' cry for manifest destiny. But the boost to Pacific commerce made possible by expansion was more important to Hamiltonian Whigs and Yankees. This time they joined with Jeffersonian Democrats and southerners in celebrating the inclusion of vast western territories. Spacious dreams about the China market bridged partisan, sectional, and ideological divides. It was not just Yankees like Seward who championed Pacific commerce. In his day, Thomas Jefferson himself had stressed the importance of Oregon as the entry point to the vast riches of the Orient. So too did the inveterate southern Democrat John C. Calhoun, who well before Seward saw the opening up of ports in China, and potentially Japan and across East Asia, as marking a new day in world history. "These ports," Calhoun predicted, "will be opened; and the whole of that portion of Asia, containing nearly half the population and wealth of the globe, will be thrown open to the commerce of the world and be placed within the pales of European and American intercourse and civilization."[5]

Thomas Hart Benton was one of the most outspoken Democrats touting America's Pacific destiny. Benton was a lion among western senators, who with his peers Stephen Douglas (Illinois) and Lewis Cass (Michigan) repeatedly stood for continental expansion. The Missouri senator's fantasies about China's riches and America's commercial prospects in the Pacific matched those of his Whig rival William Seward. Benton, too, underscored the importance of Chinese labor migration to develop the American West, while couching his vision of U.S.-China commerce within a broad understanding of the transition from the Atlantic to the Pacific World. The Missourian portrayed Europeans, and now Americans, as the vanguard race that was destined to revive the once-great civilization of China through East-West commercial and racial integration. In defending the importance of the Oregon Territory in 1846, he proclaimed that the "sun of civilization must shine across the sea: socially and commercially, the van of the Caucasians, and the rear of the Mongolians, must intermix. They must talk together, and trade together, and marry together. Commerce is a great civilizer—social intercourse as great—and marriage greater. The white and yellow races can marry together, as well as eat and trade together."[6]

Caleb Cushing was another American who epitomized the bipartisan appeal of Pacific commerce. The scion of a wealthy Massachusetts shipping magnate, Cushing graduated Harvard College in 1817 and eventually won election to the Bay State legislature and then to the U.S. Congress. He distinguished himself by serving, at different times, both the Democratic and Whig Parties. In 1843 President John Tyler, a lapsed Whig, appointed the New Englander to lead the first U.S. diplomatic mission to China, where a year later Cushing gained privileges for the United States that took advantage of Britain's wedge into the China market introduced after its victory in the First Opium War. This war concluded in 1842 with the Treaty of Nanking, in which defeated China agreed to replace the Canton system of highly restricted international trade with one much more favorable to the foreign "barbarians." Following Britain's lead, Cushing in 1844 negotiated the Treaty of Wanghia that accorded to Americans the same privileges enjoyed by the British or any other favored nation in China. Such rights rested on access to, and equal privileges within, five "treaty ports" newly opened up by the British. They also included protections for foreign missionaries as well as the controversial privilege of extraterritoriality, which granted foreigners immunity from Chinese law. Whether led by Democrats or Whigs, America's China policy (if it can be called that) was essentially to follow Britain's lead as it continued the pattern of military victory over Chinese forces leading to expanded trading rights and opportunities. By the end of the Arrow War (Second Opium War) in 1860, American merchants and missionaries were able to practice their trades and preach the Gospel across a wide swath of a nation that for centuries had been off-limits to foreigners.[7]

Despite bipartisan interests in China, Americans projected different visions of national development onto the nation's Pacific destiny. To Democrats, the promise of Chinese markets justified the kind of continental expansion that Jefferson believed was necessary to maintain access to landholding for a growing republic of independent farmers. Benton typified the Jeffersonian vision while including not just yeoman farmers but also urban workers, artisans, and even manufacturers. Democrats embraced what Benton called the "productive and burthen-bearing classes" as the backbone to a developmental model that valued economic opportunity and social mobility as bulwarks against Old World concentrations of wealth and power. This Jacksonian "producer ethic" was at odds with bankers and other agents of monopoly capital that in the eyes of Democrats threatened to diminish the freedoms of the common man. Party members applauded the inclusion of California and Oregon because it not only expanded the nation but also, more importantly, enabled the long-term economic viability of their "Empire of Liberty." Ever since Jefferson's day, proponents of this kind of land-based empire celebrated westerners and the frontier as the taproot for American democracy. At the same time, they looked with dismay at the settled and "civilized" East Coast that was said to resemble the traditional and undemocratic ways of Europe.[8]

Whigs and Yankees, on the other hand, were less troubled by East Coast civilization or its Old World progenitors. Seward and other Hamiltonians were particularly impressed with the commercial power of the British Empire, using it as a model for America's economic development. The three Whig goals of American development were to increase manufacturing, speed up movement of goods and crops to market, and open up and ensure overseas trade. Protective tariffs were to take care of the first goal and internal improvements the second. The final goal of overseas trade was to be met principally by the promise of Pacific commerce. Unlike Jeffersonians, Hamiltonians were more concerned with catching up and surpassing the global power of the British Empire than with access to landholding. While Democrats and westerners saw the China trade as means for maintaining land-based social equality at home, Whigs and Yankees saw the inclusion of Pacific ports as a means for transforming America into a global maritime empire.[9]

A crucial instrument for controlling the seas was the permanent placement of U.S. gunboats in China. Begun in 1835, the Navy's Asiatic squadron anchored two ships in Chinese waters after the opening of treaty ports, and with the expansion of U.S.-China trading and the establishment of formal diplomatic relations, the force increased by 1860 to thirty-one vessels. The squadron, like those from Britain, France, Holland, and other imperial powers, escorted diplomats, protected the nation's citizens, and served as a constant reminder to Chinese officials of its weakness vis-à-vis foreign powers. While America was not yet an imperial power like these other nations, its "gunboat diplomacy" in China revealed that it was not opposed to using military pressure to gain international advantages. The emerging outlines of American empire could also be detected after the inclusion of California and Oregon spurred northeastern financiers to explore plans for a transcontinental railroad, as well as an isthmian canal connecting the Atlantic and Pacific Oceans. Moreover, in 1853 U.S. commodore Matthew C. Perry, upon threat of force, opened up Japan, which for two hundred years had isolated itself from world affairs. Perry's naval steamships, known to the Japanese as "black ships" because of the soot they billowed, were a marvel of transoceanic technology that would transform the Pacific into a busy commercial thoroughfare. In 1858 the Treaty of Amity and Commerce established formal U.S.-Japan relations and guaranteed trading rights for the United States, as well as a coaling station in Japan and extraterritoriality for its citizens.[10]

Concurrent developments in the Kingdom of Hawai'i foretold the nation's imperial future as well. In 1848 the Hawaiian king initiated a process of land reform (*mahele*) that, in addition to creating legal claims to land, made it possible for foreigners to own property. This proved a great boon to American investment in the islands' nascent sugar industry, which would experience an astronomical rate of growth and launch the political ascent of a handful of American planter families that would establish a kind of plantation-based oligarchy. The "Big Five" companies that came to control Hawai'i's political-economy were C. Brewer & Co., Castle & Cooke, American Factors, Alexander & Baldwin, and Theo. H. Davies & Company. But the *mahele*, for native Hawaiians, risked empowering acquisitive foreigners who placed profits and saving souls above local sovereignty.[11]

All of the above proposed or actual components of Pacific commerce in the middle of the nineteenth century had one thing in common: they were northeastern, Yankee endeavors. The China trade at this point held little promise for the agrarian southern economy. While Chinese merchants bought manufactured cotton from New England factories, they had little use for the South's raw cotton crop. The sectional difference regarding the China trade was evident in congressional voting on transpacific mail service. In 1851 congressmen representing California and the major Atlantic ports pushed the federal government to take over a struggling private steamship company with routes to China. The move was deemed necessary for the United States to compete with Great Britain, which subsidized its own steamships to the Far East. But one Ohio senator criticized the "obnoxious" sectional benefits of transpacific mail service, which, according to him, were reserved for the East and West Coasts. A roll-call vote in the House asking whether or not the measure should be killed by tabling it confirmed the significance of sectional interests. Representatives from states involved in oceanic trade, largely in the Northeast but including Virginia and California, overwhelmingly opposed tabling the bill for transpacific mail service. But their colleagues from interior states were far less likely to join them. Partisanship was also a factor as the vast majority of Free-Soilers (most former Whigs) opposed killing the bill, while Democrats were far more likely to vote the other way.[12]

Three years later, in 1854, the sectional and partisan conflict erupted again during another failed attempt to subsidize transpacific mail steamers in light of the opening up of Japan. In this case, the South was the only region in the Senate to oppose the measure. Whigs overwhelming favored it, while Democrats split.[13] William Seward spoke for the Whig majority in championing the government-sponsored steamers so as to take advantage of the historic moment when "the East and the West, after a separation of three thousand years, are to be fraternally reunited." But Mississippi senator Albert G. Brown countered the New Yorker in arguing that such "schemes" favored the northeast maritime trade by creating better mail service to China than currently existed in his part of the South. Brown proclaimed that "whenever justice is done to the section of country whence I come[,] I may look with a little more liberal eye on these schemes for carrying the mail to Shanghai and Hong Kong, and all over creation."[14]

The Rise of Mass Politics

If the expanding frontier and the nation's Pacific dreams opened the door to relations with China, then the simultaneous emergence of mass politics established the infrastructure through which newly mobilized voters increasingly would demand that door be shut. The election of Andrew Jackson as president in 1828 democratized the nation's politics whereby common people no longer would simply defer to their social betters. Instead, the masses began to vote and hold their congressional representatives accountable to their interests. They found a home in Jackson's newly created Democratic Party. Condemning the "corrupt bargain" that prevented him from becoming president in 1824, Jackson took politics beyond educated circles in holding mass rallies, parades, and celebrations that forever ended the old politics of deference. Migrants from Ireland and Germany, pouring into the nation during the 1840s and 1850s, became Democratic stalwarts as political "machines" in the nation's major urban centers cultivated the ethnic vote. Immigrants, small farmers, mechanics, and agricultural and industrial workers formed the Democratic base. Many of these groups were bitterly opposed to African slaves and other forms of unfree labor such as coerced Chinese "coolies," who were seen as unfair competition that threatened both Jefferson's yeoman farmers and Jackson's producer classes.[15]

In the meantime, free Chinese immigrants began to settle on the nation's western frontier. When the United States and China launched formal relations in 1844, America had yet to witness a significant influx of Chinese immigrants. But this changed in a hurry after the discovery of gold in California attracted migrants from around the world. The establishment of a discriminatory foreign miners' tax, victimizing Chinese and other non-white peoples, soon followed. The subsequent push within the newly christened California state legislature to exclude Chinese from the mining districts grew out of the call to protect the "free white labor of our state" from the negative consequences of competition with Chinese workers. But such efforts failed in 1853 when mining companies defended the Chinese as an important component of U.S.-China trade relations. Equally important to the defense of Chinese immigrants were their large payments to the state's foreign miners' tax. "If we exclude Chinamen and other foreigners from the mines of California," a state committee on mines reported, "we lose an important part of the source from whence we might derive our revenue." At that time the young state was running a deficit; by 1855 more than 25 percent of its coffers were filled by the foreign miners' tax.[16]

Californians were torn between their overwhelming hostility toward Chinese immigrants and the state's dire need for revenue. But even when they put their financial house in order, the U.S. Constitution prevented them from direct attempts to exclude the Chinese. In 1855 the Sacramento legislature imposed a steep fifty-dollar head tax on each migrant from China, only to have it struck down two years later by the U.S. Supreme Court. In 1858 the state legislature passed an act prohibiting Chinese immigrants and setting fines for anyone caught smuggling them into the state. But the victory was short-lived as the Court set aside this exclusion act for violating the Constitution's commerce clause, which gave to Congress the exclusive right to regulate immigration as a form of foreign trade. This ruling established a pattern in which many of California's anti-Asian policies failed to meet legal challenges, thus prompting the state's exclusionists to become increasingly expert at writing legislation that would withstand judicial review.[17]

The anti-Chinese actions in California prompted efforts at self-defense. Chinese immigrants organized mutual aid societies (*huiguan*) based on their hometown regions in China. These organizations assisted with housing, employment, health care, conflict resolution, and homeland ties, including returning the bones of deceased immigrants for burial in China. From early on, *huiguan* leaders discouraged large waves of Chinese immigrants because they generated racial and labor conflict in California. Leaders also sought to control prostitution, gambling, and other vices among Chinese migrants. In May 1852, Norman Asing, founder of the Yanghe *huiguan*, published an open letter to the California governor in which he professed love for "free institutions" and the "principles of the Government of the United States" in pointing out that the discrimination and abuses suffered by the

Chinese in the state violated these American ideals. Opposing the governor's support for anti-Chinese legislation, Asing maintained, "The declaration of your independence, and all the acts of your government, your people, and your history, are against you." Asing went on to extol the greatness of Chinese civilization. When America was a wilderness, he said, China "exercised most of the arts and virtues of civilized life," was "possessed of a language and literature, and men skilled in science and arts," and had "no small share of the commerce of the world." Although the skin color of the Chinese might differ from many of the European races, Asing stressed, he did not "consider that your Excellency, as a Democrat, will make us believe that the framers of your declaration of rights ever suggested the propriety of establishing an aristocracy of skin."[18]

American missionaries worked closely with Chinese immigrant leaders to defend the ethnic community. One of the earliest was William Speer, who had served the Presbyterian mission in China before catering to the Chinese in San Francisco. In 1856 he delivered a "humble plea" on behalf of Chinese immigrants to the state legislature in Sacramento. Echoing pronouncements made by Asing and other ethnic leaders, Speer asked the legislators to limit Chinese immigration, to lower significantly taxes placed on foreign miners and the "heads" of incoming Chinese immigrants, and to protect the ethnic community from discrimination and violence. Speer argued that treating the Chinese fairly was not merely a question of brotherly love. Rather, "the interests of California forbid a policy calculated to exclude or debase Chinese immigration here." Sounding like Seward, the missionary maintained that the recent incorporation of the West Coast into the United States created a golden opportunity to greatly increase America's China trade. In addition to the gold, silver, and other precious minerals that California currently exported to China, the state, explained Speer, could reap a fortune by growing cotton, tea, silk, and other commodities highly sought in the Chinese market. In the end, he celebrated the contributions of the nation's three great sections, North, South, and now West. Unlike the North and South, the West's mission was to fulfill America's Pacific destiny by making connections with Asia: "The spread of the Chinese race, going on in an astonishing manner within a few years, over the whole globe, makes it of incalculable importance to improve our opportunity. But it becomes us, in whose hands are the interests of this western shore, to notice the changes now going on in the Pacific world."[19]

Meanwhile, the Whig Party collapsed in the early 1850s under the weight of the bitterly contested slavery issue. While Democrats managed to maintain cross-sectional ties, the Republican Party, established in 1854, came to cater exclusively to Yankee fears regarding the southern "Slave Power." The GOP inherited most of the northern Whigs as well as attracted abolitionists and some northern Democrats seeking to prevent homesteaders and laborers from seemingly unfair competition with southern slave owners. The Republican cry "free soil, free labor, free men" received its strongest support among the Protestant reformers and Hamiltonian nationalists in New England and the adjacent "burned-over" district extending from upstate New York west through the upper Midwest. The large populations of Irish and German Catholics in New York City and other northern urban communities remained Democratic terrain even after 1860, when Lincoln's election as president induced eleven southern states to secede from the Union, which began the Civil War. The GOP inherited the nativist hostility toward Irish and German immigrants that had animated the spectacular rise and fall of the Know-Nothing Party, which for a few eventful years had stepped into the political vacuum left by the Whigs.[20]

William Seward, himself considered a leading Republican presidential candidate for the 1860 election, became Lincoln's secretary of state. Seward's attempt to build a commercial empire, however, had to wait until the Civil War ended, and even after that he failed to sustain interest in foreign affairs from a nation consumed with postwar Reconstruction. Another obstacle was the reluctance of Congress to support U.S. expansion in the tropics. Secretary Seward was unable to purchase Denmark's West Indies (what would later become the U.S. Virgin Islands) because congressmen from both parties were convinced that whites would not thrive in warm, tropical climates and that darker-skinned peoples of the region would not make good Americans. Despite the secretary's expansive plans to cover the oceans with U.S. territories, the only properties he could add were the deserted Midway Islands in the Pacific and the vast frozen tundra of Alaska. The latter purchase, known to his many critics as "Seward's Folly," gained much-needed congressional support as a means for American expansion to decidedly non-tropical Canada.[21]

Seward's failures are often attributed to the fact that his ideas of imperial expansion were before their time. But if one looks beyond the acquisition of territory to transpacific commercial relations, then a better picture of Seward's, and the Republican Party's, accomplishments emerges. After southern legislators left Capitol Hill to join the Confederacy, Yankee congressmen adopted an "American system" of high tariffs and internal improvements that encouraged western economic development. Important to these efforts was a series of Pacific Railroad Acts that starting in 1862 provided generous grants of public lands and monies to build a transcontinental railroad extending from the Missouri River to the Pacific Ocean. Two companies, Union Pacific working westward from Iowa and the Central Pacific eastward from California, completed the historic project in 1869. By this time, 90 percent of the Central Pacific workers were Chinese, but in a typical nod to western racism, none were evident at the festivities celebrating the railroad's completion at Promontory Summit in the Utah Territory.[22]

To extend the nation's transportation system from California to China, the Republican-dominated Congress finally put the government into the business of transpacific mail service in establishing a $500,000 annual contract with the Pacific Mail Steamship Company, a private firm based in San Francisco. The government also agreed to fund four high-quality side-wheel wooden steamships. The Senate vote revealed the same pattern of northeastern and western support for transpacific mail service; Republicans were firmly on board while Democrats were split.[23] The business-friendly and internationally oriented *New York Times* called this achievement "one of the most important events of the day . . . [that] inaugurates a new era in the commerce of the country." The newspaper noted that "with this line of steamships regularly established, and the completion of the Pacific Railway . . . we become the masters of commerce, and New York becomes the greatest commercial emporium of the world." The excitement continued in 1867 when the Republican governor of California hosted a banquet in San Francisco to honor the company's first transpacific voyage. After noting the strange sounding names of Chinese who spoke at the celebration, the *New York Tribune* predicted that "such things will not seem odd much longer, and that our intercourse will soon be as free and as common with Peking and Yeddo [Edo, the old name for Tokyo] as with London and Paris." In this way, the newspaper heralded the steamship line as benefiting not just trade but also emigration from China that promised to "increase the rate of development of . . . labor-lacking regions." The *Chicago Tribune,* in praising the steamship line, was even more blatant about the nation's need for workers: "We want labor . . . and if we cannot get American and European labor fast enough, we will have Asiatic as the next best thing."[24]

Labor shortages, not just in the West but throughout the North, were a major problem during the Civil War as the conflict drew workers and farmers away from economic production and war industries suffered. Consequently, Republicans boosted emigration from Europe by making sure that aliens were eligible to settle free western lands under the Homestead Act of 1862. Seward and President Lincoln took matters further in getting Congress to put the government into the business of labor recruitment.

Passed in 1864, the Contract Labor Act established a bureau of immigration within the State Department that contracted with various private companies to recruit immigrant labor by providing money for their passage in return for a lien on their future wages. The most prominent of these profitable firms, American Emigrant Company, was backed financially by such leading Republicans as Massachusetts senator Charles Sumner, Secretary of the Navy Gideon Welles, and famed antislavery newspaper editor and pastor Henry Ward Beecher. In addition to supplying much-needed labor, the emigration companies also served as a vehicle to suppress the emergence of labor organizing among American workers. Contract laborers at times were recruited specifically to replace striking workers. Not surprisingly, the National Labor Union, an early instance of large-scale labor organizing in the United States, protested the Contract Labor Act. The increasing power of the labor vote, combined with the ending of labor shortages in the North after the war, spelled the demise of the contract labor law in 1868—but not other forms of federal inducements to immigration.[25]

Republicans made a key distinction between contract labor, seen as a benefit to the American economy, and Chinese "coolie" labor, which was deemed a moral outrage akin to the slave trade. Based on a centuries-old practice of importing Chinese and East Indian labor, the coolie trade attracted increasing attention during the first half of the nineteenth century as an alternative to the increasingly banned African slave trade. Coolies technically were "free laborers" who had consented to long-term labor contracts, but the brutality of their passage and treatment as plantation laborers in the Caribbean and Latin America struck most Republicans as involuntary servitude. In 1862 Congress made it a crime for American ships to participate in the Chinese coolie trade and six years later extended this to include Japanese coolies. Both acts received overwhelming bipartisan support, as well as the blessings of Chinese immigrant leaders preoccupied with the ethnic group's good image. But the definition of "coolie" remained ambiguous as exclusionists cast the net broadly to include all Asian immigrants, while immigration expansionists distinguished between useful contract laborers and imported coolies.[26]

Expansionists held the upper hand in Washington, D.C., and during the height of Reconstruction established crucial federal protections for Chinese immigrants. The first came with the approval of the Fourteenth Amendment, designed to establish citizenship and guarantee equal rights for the newly freed African American slaves. During congressional debate on the proposed amendment, one senator sought to erect race limitations to birthright citizenship that would include African Americans while excluding Chinese, Gypsies, and other seemingly inferior races. His proposal, however, ran aground when California senator John Conness—surprisingly, given the state's anti-Chinese bent—opposed such a limitation as adding an unnecessary complication to the amendment. Conness, a Radical Republican who distinguished between useful Chinese contract laborers and imported coolies, also assured that there was no fear of his state being overrun by Chinese American citizens because of the paucity of Chinese immigrant women.[27] In the end, the exclusionist threat was defeated and the amendment included vague and expansive criteria for birthright citizenship that said nothing about race: "All persons born or naturalized in the United States, and subject to the jurisdiction thereof, are citizens of the United States and of the State wherein they reside." The Fourteenth Amendment also provided legal protections for Chinese immigrants through its "equal protection" clause. Since most African Americans were not yet citizens, the amendment was cast broadly to prevent state action depriving "any *person* within its jurisdiction the equal protection of the laws." This clause, on its surface, appeared to include Chinese immigrants as well as black noncitizens.[28]

Republican interests in Pacific commerce, immigration expansion, and constitutional protections produced a radically new U.S.-China accord in 1868—the Burlingame Treaty. Brokered on the U.S. side by Seward and on China's side by American and former U.S. congressman Anson Burlingame, the treaty sought to elevate America's position in China by offering to the Chinese emperor more favorable diplomatic relations than he had experienced with Britain and the European powers. As a result, the Burlingame Treaty was the first international accord to place China on equal terms with the West. Signed in Washington during the height of Radical Reconstruction, it was apiece with the broader postwar Yankee regime. Burlingame, after all, was an antislavery Republican who in touting China's modernity to Americans relied upon strong support from Seward and leading radicals like Massachusetts senator Charles Sumner.[29] Signed on the same day that the Senate ratified the Fourteenth Amendment, the Burlingame Treaty too was a powerful antiracist statement. Five of the treaty's eight articles sought to ameliorate discriminatory policies that Chinese immigrants faced on the West Coast, while another distinguished Chinese free contract laborers from the infamous coolie trade. The treaty's key feature placed them on the same legal footing as foreigners from "most favored nations," including Britain, France, Russia, and Prussia; another guaranteed Chinese subjects the right to immigrate without restriction to the United States. In Burlingame's words, the treaty "strikes down and reprobates—that is the word—reprobates the infamous Coolie trade. . . . It invites free immigration into the country of those sober and industrious people by whose quiet labor we have been enabled to push the Pacific railroad over the summits of the Sierra Nevada. . . . I am glad the United States had the courage to apply her great principles of equality. I am glad that while she applies her doctrines to the swarming millions of Europe, she is not afraid to apply them to the tawny race of Tamerlane and of Genghis Khan."[30]

Republicans, along with much of the nation, celebrated the dawn of a new day in U.S.-China relations as it had done the year before with the inauguration of the nation's China steamers. The *New York Tribune* noted the treaty's respect for the "equality and brotherhood of nations" and that the results of this "wonderful revolution . . . can hardly fail to be magnificent." The *San Francisco Alta*, a Republican stronghold, delighted in China's trust in Burlingame, noting that the emperor had "converted a citizen of the youngest nation of the world into the Ambassador of the oldest." In a partisan shot to southern Democrats, the *Alta* praised China as a friend of the Union who during the Civil War had denied the Confederate navy access to its ports.[31]

Democratic newspapers, as can be expected, attacked the Burlingame mission and treaty as a part of a conspiracy by the "Mongrel" Republican Party to doom the white race by elevating the status of blacks and now Chinese. The *New York World* scoffed at the treaty's foundation of racial equality in asserting that "Fleas are not Lobsters. Mongolians are not Europeans." The *San Francisco Examiner* turned the focus on Radical Republicans as bigoted hypocrites who saw racial equality with Chinese as more important than ethnic equality with America's European immigrants. The radicals, wrote the *Examiner*, were "the lineal descendants of those Puritans, who like the Chinese, looked upon all others as kind of outside barbarians, whipped women for religious opinion, burned witches and expelled quakers from their society." The newspaper further proclaimed that New Englanders were "the originators of the prejudice against foreigners [chiefly Irish Catholic immigrants] which culminated in the Know Nothing party of latter times."[32]

Such ethno-cultural conflict, extending back before the Civil War, exacerbated partisan and ideological differences within the North itself. During the war, conflict concerning recent European immigrants erupted in days of rioting in New York in which largely Irish immigrants protested against the Union's policy of war conscription that gave wealthier native-born Americans a better chance than they had to avoid the draft. Given that the Irish were part of the powerful Democratic machine of Boss Tweed, the

Draft Riots highlighted a partisan rift with the Republican draft policy. But Republicans themselves were hardly unified on the issue of European immigration as leaders like Seward had long opposed nativism, while many of his partisans retained their Know-Nothing leanings.

Another division among Republicans became evident in the ratification of the Burlingame Treaty when Senator Conness struck a discordant note by opposing one aspect of the treaty's equal treatment of Chinese immigrants. Conness managed to insert a clause exempting naturalization to U.S. citizenship from the list of most favored nation rights enjoyed by the Chinese in America. While the Californian had not worried about second-generation Chinese becoming citizens during the debate over the Fourteenth Amendment, he did fear granting the same privilege to the immigrant generation. Thus despite its rousing popularity within the GOP, the Burlingame Treaty revealed limits of Yankee egalitarianism. The treaty would mark the peak of the Republican consensus regarding the fair treatment of Chinese immigrants.[33]

The Burlingame Constituency

The Burlingame Treaty's restriction of naturalization rights for Chinese revealed that even at the height of his power, and with radicalism eliminating the legal basis of racism in the defeated South, Seward was unable to place the status of Pacific immigration on a par with Atlantic immigration. The most receptive to full equality for the Chinese were missionaries like William Speer as well as radicals from northeastern states with entrenched maritime interests, ties to the China trade, and concerns about shortages of western labor. Most notably, these included Seward, Burlingame, and Sumner. Next in line were business leaders, like those of the western railroad interests who counted on Chinese labor, as well as Republicans from the Midwest and the Great Plains. These people supported the Burlingame Treaty but for various reasons, including racism and labor politics, balked at the prospect of full equality for the Chinese. Western Republicans like Senator Conness made up the most unstable part of the Burlingame constituency. Their support for the treaty would be tested the most as anti-Chinese movements on the West Coast demanded Chinese exclusion with growing insistence and political force.

An early challenge to the Burlingame constituency came in 1869 during the House debate over the proposed Fifteenth Amendment, designed to protect the voting rights of newly enfranchised African Americans. James A. Johnson, a California Democrat and transplanted southerner, proposed a resolution stating that the House never intended for the Fifteenth Amendment to enfranchise "Chinese or Mongolians." His resolution was soundly defeated on a party-line vote in which House radicals revealed the strength of the Burlingame constituency. The next year congressional egalitarians extended civil and voting rights protections to Chinese through legislation designed to prevent southern states from getting around the Fourteenth and Fifteenth Amendments. Nevada radical William M. Stewart was the main force behind the insertion of section 16 into the 1870 Civil Rights Act that gave aliens the same protections as citizens. As if directly addressing California's anti-Chinese head taxes, such protections included this line: "No tax or charge shall be imposed and enforced by any State upon any person emigrating thereto from a foreign country that is not equally imposed and enforced upon every person emigrating to such State from any foreign country."[34]

A few months later, during debate over the illegal naturalization of European aliens, Senator Charles Sumner saw an opportunity to address the missing piece of Burlingame egalitarianism by proposing to strike the word "white" from the nation's naturalization laws. The Massachusetts senator defended his proposition by evoking Lincoln's commitment to the universal principles of equality proclaimed in the Declaration of Independence. While able to win temporary Senate approval for the measure, Sumner's plan backfired by pushing many radicals too far on the Chinese issue. Stewart, fresh off championing the civil rights of Chinese immigrants, took a strong stand against the notion of naturalizing them. Many other Republicans rallied to his side by articulating anti-Chinese arguments that sounded more like Democratic Party platforms than Burlingame egalitarianism. In the end, the Senate retracted support for Sumner's proposition, deciding to grant naturalization to African immigrants but not to the Chinese.[35]

While citizenship rights would continue to elude Chinese immigrants, sufficient progress had been made over the past two decades for William Seward to remain hopeful about the future of America's Pacific commerce. After leaving public life in 1869 and before his death three years later, Seward embarked on a trip around the world that revealed the fruits of his and his generation's expansionist labors. His trip included riding west on the transcontinental railroad and then across the ocean to Japan on a Pacific Mail steamship. How much had changed since Seward first won election to the Senate in 1848! At that time California, which had just become a U.S. territory, possessed more Mexicans than Americans and nary a Chinese. Japan, moreover, was closed to the world, and the idea of traveling there from New York by railroad and steamship was merely a pipedream.

On board the steamer to Japan, Seward's observations of the ship as well as its passengers and storage items revealed how the Pacific had become transformed into an accessible commercial highway. He noted strolling along the ship's expansive seven-hundred-foot upper deck and listed fellow travelers: a Russian diplomat, British civil servants returning to posts in East Asia, U.S. naval officers of the Asiatic Squadron, and American missionaries and their families. Below deck in the steerage hold were five hundred "invariably successful" Chinese immigrants returning home with their California savings. The ship was also carrying exports to China, Mexican silver dollars, and American manufactured goods, agricultural machines, carriages, flour, butter, fruits, drugs, and medicines. In the middle of the Pacific the ship stopped with great fanfare as its crew exchanged mail, newspapers, and other items with a sister steamship going in the opposite direction toward San Francisco. That ship, while carrying a similar load of first-class passengers and steerage Chinese, was doubtlessly also packed with teas, silks, rice, and other Chinese export goods.[36]

As excited as he was to experience transpacific travel for himself, Seward was under no illusions about how much ground Asian nations had to cover in order to catch up to westerners. In terms of political economy, he learned firsthand that American society was superior to them in every way. Still, he remained convinced upon visiting China that if the Chinese continued to learn from the West, they could eventually rid themselves of the "obnoxious" system of domination they currently experienced at the hands of foreign powers. To him, the Chinese had the same political, social, and moral capabilities as whites; race in no way prevented them from gaining the benefits of westernization. Seward also remained sanguine about Chinese immigrants as a crucial feature of transpacific commerce and western development. To him, immigration and expansionism were inevitable features of the shrinking modern world that Americans rejected at their peril.[37]

But Seward also was well aware of the rising political power of anti-Chinese protests in the United States. While the Burlingame Treaty and subsequent legislation secured the supply of Chinese immigrant labor for western development, it also produced a backlash from political forces on the West Coast and increasingly across the nation that sought to exclude the Chinese. Fearful of being accosted by crowds of anti-Chinese protesters, Seward kept a low profile as he passed through San Francisco on his world travels.[38] White workers especially bemoaned the city's surplus of Chinese labor that resulted from the completion of the transcontinental railroad as well as from increased Chinese arrivals stimulated by the liberal Burlingame Treaty and the initiation of transpacific steamship passage. Beginning in 1870, unemployed whites gathered in the city's vacant "sandlots" blaming the Chinese and their "robber baron" employers for the lack of jobs. Smaller businessmen who competed against Chinese-headed companies joined the white workers in a chorus of Sinophobic sentiment. It was during this time that down south in Los Angeles some five hundred vigilantes (including the chief of police) massacred nineteen Chinese immigrants and destroyed their residences and businesses in a fit of rage against organized crime in Chinatown. A severe downswing in the nation's business cycle starting in 1873 made California's dangerously anti-Chinese situation even worse.

Within this charged atmosphere, exclusionists in the Golden State labored to undermine federal protections of Chinese immigrants and other persons of color. The Burlingame Treaty, Fourteenth and Fifteenth Amendments, and Civil Rights Act of 1870 in various ways led to court decisions banning California's long-standing policies discriminating against foreign miners, taxing new arrivals from China, and preventing nonwhites from testifying in court. Not to be denied, exclusionists on the San Francisco Board of Supervisors passed a series of ordinances designed to harass Chinese businesses and residents. The "cubic air" policy discriminated against lodging houses that catered to Chinese immigrants by requiring that their rooms be of adequate size for proper ventilation. Another posed a tax on laundry businesses, which was especially harsh on smaller operations favored by the Chinese. And perhaps the most offensive empowered the county sheriff, who was in the habit of detaining Chinese for violating the above two ordinances, to cut off their long, braided queue—a hairstyle mandated by the Chinese emperor. The San Francisco mayor acknowledged that the last two ordinances were in violation of the Burlingame Treaty and thus vetoed them, but the board managed to salvage the laundry tax by overriding the mayor's veto.[39]

Legislators in Sacramento also responded to new federal protections for the Chinese by enacting laws meant to get around them. In 1870 they focused on the exclusion of prostitutes, coolies, and others who were engaged in federally recognized criminal activity and four years later expanded the enforcement of this act by empowering the state immigration commissioner to detain and question all new arrivals suspected of being either a coolie or a prostitute. By this time the state's Republican Party had abandoned its egalitarianism in order to appease the growing labor vote. Thus it was left to Stephen J. Field, a U.S. Supreme Court justice who also presided over the circuit court of appeals for California, to uphold the rights of Chinese immigrants. Field overturned a decision in which the California Supreme Court upheld the constitutionality of the measure excluding prostitutes and coolies. His 1874 ruling admonished California for overstepping its authority in restricting immigration and for violating the protections granted to Chinese based on the Burlingame Treaty's most favored nation rights, as well as on the Fourteenth Amendment and Civil Rights Act of 1870. Field's egalitarianism, it is important to note, was based in his reading of federal law rather than on ideological or practical concerns about anti-Chinese discrimination or the nation's political economy. It turns out he had no qualms with the idea of Congress excluding the Chinese.[40]

On the heels of Field's decision, congressmen in Washington, D.C., did in fact take up the issue of smuggling prostitutes and coolies into the United States. In 1875 California Republican representative Horace Page followed up on Field's reading of federal law by sponsoring an act enhancing the enforcement of laws against such illegal immigrants, particularly from China. Like the anti-coolie trade law in 1862, the Page Act received overwhelming support and passed without controversy as a means for restricting entry to unworthy and unwanted types of immigrants. Consistent with their earlier campaigns for moral reform among the Chinese, *huiguan* leaders (now combined into the "Six Companies") and missionaries who advocated on behalf of Chinese immigrants applauded the crackdown on prostitution.[41] This type of moral outrage added a layer of complexity to Republican expansionism that was evident not just in their earlier campaigns against slavery and coolie labor but also in sexually charged congressional attempts to ban polygamy among Mormons, who before the war had migrated en masse to the Utah territory in order to escape religious persecution back East. In theory, the Page Act did not conflict with Burlingame egalitarianism because it targeted illegal types of immigrants. But overzealous attempts by American consular and immigration officials to identify disguised prostitutes inevitably harassed and discouraged legitimate female migrants, some of whom were second wives of Chinese immigrant businessmen. Consequently, while the number of men arriving from China increased throughout the 1870s, the arrival of women declined, and Chinatowns were to remain largely bachelor societies with few wives and children.

Historians often regard the Page Act as the first major step in the political process that would lead to the exclusion of Chinese labor migration in 1882. Some trace the inevitability of exclusion further back in time to the rejection of Sumner's proposal for Chinese naturalization (1870), or even to the first anti-Chinese measure emerging in gold rush–era California. But none of these accounts fully appreciate the political, economic, and legal authority of the Burlingame constituency. That Republican egalitarians banned entry to Chinese prostitutes and coolies for moral reasons was not inconsistent with the spirit or letter of the Burlingame Treaty that focused on free and legal migration. Nor was their balking at Chinese naturalization, which many believed was an unnecessary complication to Reconstruction policy, while others, like Seward, argued that the Chinese were not yet westernized enough to handle the franchise. Moreover, California's increasing hostility, which was now bipartisan, by itself had never enjoyed much clout in Congress given the tiny size of its delegation—four House seats in 1875. Recognizing the power of the Burlingame constituency, exclusionists were not totally wrong when they cast themselves as David battling against the egalitarian Goliath.

More important than the Page Act for challenging the Burlingame constituency was the return of the Democratic Party as a serious challenger to Republican rule. A Democratic landslide in the 1874 midterm elections overturned the two-thirds Republican majority in the House, enabling Democrats to control a branch of federal government for the first time since the Civil War. The change, induced by the lingering effects of economic depression and widespread charges of corruption in the Grant administration, galvanized exclusionist forces. At this point William Seward had been dead for two years. His vision of commercial empire in the Pacific, however, remained alive among American policy makers, maritime interests, business leaders, Protestant missionaries, and others who over the next two decades would extend the nation's control of new territories much further than the former secretary of state could in his lifetime. In this way, the past three decades proved a crucial prologue to America's Pacific destiny. The nation had expanded from "sea to shining sea," established formal diplomatic relations with China and Japan, built a viable transportation infrastructure from the East Coast to the Far East, and secured the civil and treaty rights of Chinese immigrants, who were counted on to literally and figuratively build bridges between the United States and China. But regional, labor, and partisan interests that had opposed Chinese immigration since the start of Seward's Pacific endeavors were gaining strength not just on the West Coast but also across the nation and especially in Congress. Republican hegemony that materialized during the Civil War collapsed in the midterm elections of 1874 and in the presidential election two years later would be confirmed dead. Thus would begin a new chapter in the ongoing exclusion debate.

2 FIRST DOWNPOUR

CHINESE IMMIGRANTS AND GILDED AGE POLITICS,
1876–1882

||||||||||||||||||||||||||||||||||||||||||||||||||||||||||||||||||||||||||||||||||||||||||||||||||||||||||||||||||||||||||||||

On March 1, 1882, George Frisbee Hoar opened debate in the U.S. Senate for a measure intending to exclude the immigration of Chinese laborers. The Massachusetts senator criticized the bill for violating the "genius of American institutions" that judged men by their conduct and character rather than by race or occupation. The proponents of exclusion, he contended, disgraced the nation's founders by "invoking the old race prejudice which has so often played its hateful and bloody part in history" by victimizing "the negro, the Irishman, and the [American] Indian." That the exclusionists held the upper hand in Congress added to Hoar's frustration. Bitter and defensive, he ended his statement with a dire warning: "As surely as the path on which our fathers entered a hundred years ago led to safety, to strength, to glory, so surely will the path on to which we now propose to enter bring us to shame, to weakness, and to peril."[1]

Hoar was not alone in attacking the exclusion of Chinese laborers. Almost the entire New England contingent on Capitol Hill voted against it, many of whom registered their own equally eloquent remarks against racial discrimination. They had reacted the same way three years before when an earlier version of exclusion passed both houses of Congress, only to be killed by presidential veto.[2] In this way, the New England delegation continued the constituency for the liberal Burlingame Treaty in which William Seward ensured the free flow of people and goods from China. But historical conditions had changed considerably since 1868, when the entire nation celebrated the ratification of this U.S.-China accord. Reconstruction was over, and as a result, the Republican dominance of Congress gave way to the return of a balanced party system in which southern Democrats challenged Yankee hegemony. In addition, the industrial age emerged in full force as America experienced an alarming polarization between rich and poor that threatened to harden into permanent hierarchies of privilege and class that were anathema to the nation's republican experiment. It was during this "gilded age" of disillusionment that Americans targeted immigrants as both cause and symptom of the decline in the nation's promises of economic opportunity and social mobility. The rising social fears coincided with Asian vulnerabilities in the United States to enable exclusionism to gain an audience outside the West Coast and transform the nation's immigration laws.

This chapter examines the start of the perfect storm of exclusion through revision of the Burlingame Treaty and the ultimately successful effort in Congress to exclude Chinese laborers. It follows the story of how a regional issue found a place on the nation's political agenda amid highly competitive partisan and sectional conflicts exacerbated by prolonged economic depression. Crucial to the nationalization of the exclusion debate was the decline and fall of the northeastern political and economic hegemony that emerged during the Civil War and remained through most of Reconstruction. Chinese exclusion was part of a series of legislation that challenged Yankee rule through combined interests from the Midwest, South, and West — regions that made up the nation's economic periphery. In this sense, exclusion was part of dramatic Gilded Age protests and political campaigns waged by workers, farmers, and consumers against monopoly capitalism.

Congress and the West

While Congress had passed laws prohibiting coolies and prostitutes, it stayed away from action that would directly challenge the Burlingame Treaty's guarantees of unrestricted immigration. This changed in the fall of 1876 when a joint congressional committee, tasked to investigate the "character, extent, and effect of Chinese immigration," conducted month-long public hearings in San Francisco. Oliver Morton, Republican senator from Indiana, chaired the committee and was joined by two openly anti-Chinese Californians, Republican senator Aaron A. Sargent and Democratic representative William A. Piper. Morton ran the hearings like a criminal trial; exclusionists and egalitarians each had turns to call and question 128 witnesses, none of whom were Chinese. The majority report written about the proceedings was an exclusionist document condemning Chinese immigration and calling for revision of the Burlingame Treaty. Morton, however, disagreed with these findings. Because he died shortly after the hearings ended, egalitarians compiled his notes and published them as a minority report favoring the liberal status quo. Morton's views were consistent with extensive testimony from many leading Californians. One historian notes that "nearly half of the witnesses who testified supported Chinese immigration, a group that included not just ministers and large-scale employers but also lawyers, doctors, farmers, merchants, and laborers."[3]

The offsetting committee reports, however, were a bad omen for the Burlingame constituency, which until then had dominated congressional debate. Testimony at the San Francisco hearings by leading exclusion-

ists revealed what the egalitarians were up against. California state senator Frank McCoppin opened the case for exclusion by reporting the findings of the state legislature's own investigation into Chinese immigration
conducted earlier in 1876. The senator noted that population pressures
in China pushed its citizens "to seek an outlet in foreign lands, and this
[west] coast, being the most accessible to them, is in danger of being overrun by this pagan horde, unless their coming be checked by legislation and
a modification of existing treaties." McCoppin maintained that unlike the
European, "the Chinaman, under all circumstances and changes, retains
his distinctive national traits, and when abroad lives in hope of securing a
competence and returning to the land of Confucius." Consequently, Chinatown in San Francisco stood apart from any place in North America, "as
foreign as any quarter of Canton or Peking," and its residents obeyed the
dictates not of city officials but of their own ethnic leaders, who governed
through the alliance of mutual aid organizations known as the Six Companies. Most important to the exclusionist argument was the claim that
Chinese, because of their low standard of living, could always work for less
wages than "the American or European mechanic or laborer" who "appre-
ciates the decencies of life, and wants a home having separate apartments
[from relatives] for himself and wife and children." The Chinese, in contrast, were a "very frugal people" who could exist on a "little rice" and sleep
in a "portion of a shelf fifteen to thirty inches wide." McCoppin concluded,
"In the struggle for bread, for existence in fact, this man has an advantage
over the American or European."[4]

Among the many exclusionists at the hearings, none offered a more au-
thoritative economic analysis than Henry George, a San Francisco news-
paperman and state gas meter reader. George, who would soon be heralded
as a national prophet of social reform, studied the Chinese issue from the
perspective of Adam Smith and other mainstays of classical liberal economics. The San Franciscan reasoned that competition from Chinese immigrants lowered the wages of white workers, thus displacing many from
jobs and making California less attractive to prospective migrants from
Europe or the eastern United States. On top of this, paying lower wages for
Chinese workers did not, as egalitarians claimed, reduce consumer prices.
George compared cheap labor to the use of labor-saving machines. Because
mechanization increased worker productivity, the resulting higher production of goods allowed owners of firms to lower prices and still increase
profits. This was not true, he said, of cheap labor, which did not increase
worker productivity and thus did not increase production. In this way, large
manufacturers who hired the Chinese could not pass along the savings in

labor costs to consumers. From George's perspective, Chinese immigrants damaged the livelihood of white workers without providing anything positive for the public good in return.[5] The main beneficiaries were large industrialists and growers who cared more about their own fortunes than democratic institutions: "The ultimate effect of an immigration such as the Chinese would be to have a community composed of the very rich and the very poor. It would be a condition of a society such as exists to-day in British India, where the few white men who are there ride in palanquins, and are waited on by dozens of servants, while all the work is performed by an inferior class. It would be the same state of things that existed in the southern States, prior to the war."[6]

George's analysis rested on prejudiced assumptions about Chinese civilization and racial characteristics that reflected and perpetuated the great East-West divide. The San Franciscan saw Italians as better immigrants than the Chinese because they were a different race: "The Italians are of the same stock that we are, and have come to their present pitch by a slow course of development for thousands of years." The high level of European civilization, said George, enabled not just Italians but also Germans and Irish to intermarry and breed (assimilate) with Americans. In contrast, the Chinese were deemed less intelligent than whites and were compared to blacks, who "up to a certain point . . . learn very fast, but beyond that point it is very difficult for them to go." Further, Chinese immigrants lacked the ability to become good citizens and voters because "they have been stationary for so many thousands of years" and because they are "deficient in all those qualities that have given us our institutions—regard for personal liberty, dislike of arbitrary power, regard for law, and personal independence." While the Burlingame constituency celebrated the awakening of China from years of supposed slumber, George preferred to see the Chinese as sleepwalking automatons controlled by plutocratic masters. His was a perspective that knew little, if anything, about Asian and Pacific peoples or transpacific relations and commerce. It was not a maritime vision bent on commercial empire, like Seward's, but a continental one focused on domestic class relations. A typical exclusionist, George was more interested in perfecting liberty at home than in spreading it abroad.[7]

Given the power of the Burlingame constituency, the exclusionists at the San Francisco hearings realized that a total ban on immigration, let alone deportation of Chinese in the United States, was politically impossible. Instead, they focused on imposing federal regulations to significantly reduce the number of new immigrants while respecting the treaty rights of those already in the country. In this way, exclusionists called for the prompt revision of the Burlingame Treaty so that Congress could pass such a restriction act. Given the overwhelming popularity of exclusionism in California, as well its growing strength across the nation, many egalitarians conceded the idea of restriction. The Chinese Six Companies, reported Colonel Frederick A. Bee, its white representative, long had sent letters "discouraging our people from coming to this country, but the people have not believed us, and have continued to come." These attempts were undermined by "the capitalists of this honorable country [who] are constantly calling for Chinese cheap labor." Consequently, the "white laboring men of this country are very angry because the Chinese obtain employment which they claim belongs to white men alone, and so they hate the Chinamen, sometimes throw stones at them, sometimes strike them on the street, and constantly curse them."[8]

The situation was so intolerable to the Six Companies that it welcomed intervention by the federal government to permit the restriction of the laboring classes. A letter from the immigrant alliance included in the transcript of the San Francisco congressional hearings stated that if the Burlingame Treaty was altered and Chinese were excluded entirely, "then shall we Chinese forever remain at home and enjoy the happiness of fathers, mothers, wives, and children, and no longer remain strangers in a strange land. Then the white laborers of this country shall no longer be troubled by the competition of the Chinese, and our Chinese people no longer be subjected to the abuses and indignities now daily heaped upon them in the open streets of this so-called Christian land. If this can be accomplished, we Chinese will continually offer to the virtue of this honorable country our deepest gratitude and thanks." Colonel Bee reiterated the fact that the Chinese in the United States were "just as desirous of getting back to their old home as those parties are to have them do so." On this score, he introduced the novel idea to have the U.S. Navy repatriate the Chinese free of charge, which would no doubt increase already high demand in returning home.[9]

In conceding restriction, the Six Companies were in no way giving up the egalitarian struggle, for most Chinese immigrants remained in the United States and their rights needed protection. Colonel Bee pleaded their case to the congressional committee, emphasizing the invaluable contributions Chinese workers were making to the economic development of the West Coast. He reminded the members that when it was signed, the Burlingame Treaty was considered a huge economic gain for the nation that all Americans, regardless of party, region, or class, applauded—including one of the California exclusionists on the congressional committee.[10] While Bee challenged exclusionist depictions of Chinatown as a den of iniquity and disease, he asserted that economic development was the ultimate standard by which Chinese immigration must be judged, and by that measure it had profited the country immensely. "I care nothing about the filth of Chinatown," he testified. "I care nothing about the prostitutes who are bought there. Look at the stern facts as they exist. We do more farming than any State in the Union. We are now becoming the first wheat State in the Union. This class of laborers, these mudsills, are at the bottom of our success, and I challenge contradiction. We have reclaimed a million acres and more of swamp, overflowed, and tule lands where the Chinamen stand up to their waist in soft tule marsh throwing up this dirt. . . . Where is the white man who will go into that ditch and work? He is not here; you cannot find him."[11]

Charles Crocker, a leading figure in the Central Pacific Railroad, confirmed Bee's assessment of Chinese labor in testimony about his experience building the transcontinental railroad, where he saw firsthand that Chinese workers outperformed their white counterparts. Crocker was convinced that "if I had a big job of work that I wanted to get through quick with, and had a limited time to do it, I should take Chinese labor to do it with, because of its greater reliability and steadiness, and their aptitude and capacity for hard work." He added, "They are very trusty, they are very intelligent, and they live up to their contracts." In this way, Chinese labor benefited the nation's economic development, and without it "we would be thrown back in all branches of industry, farming, mining, reclaiming lands, and everything else." Chinese workers, moreover, benefited, not hurt, "every white laborer who is intelligent and able to work, who is more than a digger in ditch, or a man with a pick and shovel, who has the capacity of being something else." This was so because the Chinese took the jobs at the bottom of the labor market that elevated "intelligent" whites to a higher level of work. The only class of white workers who were degraded by the Chinese were those lacking ambition and intelligence, who "will work just long enough to get something to buy liquor with, and then they will spend their time drinking it up." In the end, Crocker argued, excluding the Chinese would not help this class of workers because "those men, no matter whether the Chinamen are here or whether they are not here, never will be anything else but what they are."[12]

Crocker, who rose from moderate beginnings to become a titan of industry, gave voice to the "self-made man" ideology that carried widespread currency during the Gilded Age. The notion was that America afforded any man worth his salt the opportunity to climb the social ladder as high as his abilities would take him. Chinese labor, to Crocker, was an invaluable tool for making such a climb on the western frontier. But he did not think it right that the Chinese themselves make this climb. They were merely a "mighty good substitute for white labor" when none was to be found. Crocker made clear his racial preference for whites in stating that a "homogeneous population is better than a heterogeneous population." He also preferred to hire white workers and claimed that they made better immigrants because they could assimilate to American institutions in a way that the Chinese could not. He opposed giving the Chinese U.S. citizenship for the same reason. Crocker's system for paying Chinese workers revealed that his views of them were influenced by the great East-West civilizational divide. The Central Pacific paid the Chinese in a lump sum to a labor broker, which was different from the direct, individual relationship the company had with its white employees. According to Crocker, it was "impossible" to keep track of Chinese names. "We would not know Ah Sin, Ah You, Kong Won, and all such names. We cannot keep the names in the usual way, because it is a different language." In recognizing seemingly immutable civilizational differences between Chinese and whites, Crocker agreed that Chinese immigrants must be regulated so that they remained no more than 10 percent of California's total population. Since he believed the state had space for twelve to fifteen million people, this meant that up to one million Chinese could reside there to provide a ready supply of good workers. While this conception of a "homogeneous population" clashed with that of exclusionists—who, if they had their druthers, would put the number of Chinese much lower—Crocker's expansionist views on immigration revealed how labor market exigencies could trump exclusionary racism.[13]

It was not surprising that Protestant missionaries who inherited from William Speer the cause of protecting the Chinese provided some of the most unqualified support for Chinese immigrants at the San Francisco hearings. The commanding voice here was Otis Gibson, who served the Methodist mission in China for ten years. For a six-month period while in China, the bilingual missionary interpreted for the American consul and, in this capacity, ran consulate business. After returning to the United States, he was posted in 1868 to the home mission in San Francisco's Chinatown, from which he advocated on behalf of the persecuted ethnic community. Like the Six Companies, Gibson called for the restriction of Chinese immigrants so as to calm labor and racial tensions in California. The missionary, however, went beyond the Six Companies in opposing "a large and rapid influx of immigration from any foreign country whatever." In this way, he called for an across-the-board limitation because "immigration from both Europe and Asia has been stimulated to an unhealthy degree." Gibson flatly stated that the Chinese were not racially inferior to whites. He maintained, "In simple brain power and possibilities of culture, the Chinese race is equal to any other people in the world. They are capable of learning our language, laws, customs, principles of government, our theories and practices. We know of nothing which the Chinese are incapable of learning." Gibson's estimate of Chinese racial characteristics stemmed in part from his esteem for China's civilization. He understood well why the Chinese looked down on Western civilization and had such excessive pride in their country's achievements: "With a people more numerous, a government more powerful, and a history of greater antiquity, a literature more extensive and refined, a better system of philosophy, and a purer standard of morals, a general civilization, in fact, quite in advance of all the peoples with which they had as yet come in contact, it is not so very strange, after all, that Christian civilization has found the Chinese thinking of themselves as standing at the head of the human race."[14]

Gibson also emphasized the economic contribution made by Chinese workers. "Capital and industries," he testified, "would not invest in industrial pursuits in the State if it were not for the presence of Chinese to compete with white labor." He assured that Chinese labor provided healthy economic competition for Irish workers and that neither group held a monopoly on vice or crime. Fellow missionary August W. Loomis carried the jab at the Irish even further in stating that the Chinese were "less dangerous than Roman Catholics." Unlike Catholics, the Chinese "do not purpose to intermeddle with our religious rights; they have no hierarchy; they are not sworn to support any religious system; they are mixed up at home; they have no one religion." B. S. Brooks, who joined Colonel Bee in representing the Six Companies, also criticized the largely Irish immigrants who led anti-Chinese hostility in San Francisco. A longtime resident of California, Brooks argued that Kearneyism (Denis Kearney was the leader of anti-Chinese crowds) was much more threatening to American institutions than the Chinese were. The Californian resented the fact that immigrants, such as Irish and Germans, who themselves were not truly American in spirit, heaped abuses on the Chinese for being antithetical to American institutions. "I have no sympathy," he testified, "for the argument made by an Irishman, a German, or a foreigner of any nation, who has come here and been naturalized and been made a citizen and allowed to hold land, when he talks about *our* land being land for the white man, and says that this yellow-colored man comes in competition with the white man." In this way, egalitarians like Brooks, Gibson, and Loomis continued the ethno-cultural conflicts that had been a hallmark of Republican politics since the Know-Nothing nativism of the 1840s and 1850s.[15]

The final element of egalitarian testimony in San Francisco cast Chinese immigration as a major step forward in advancing America's Pacific destiny. Brooks praised visionaries like Seward for being able to see beyond the narrow, parochial interests expressed by those opposing Chinese immigrants: "If such arguments had been listened to, and if such views had prevailed, all the elements of progress, or wealth, and of comfort to the people of the present century, which is brighter than all that has preceded it in its great progress—its telegrams, its railroads, its steam engines, its printing-machines, the cotton gin, would never have existed at all." Former California governor Frederick Low echoed this point. Upon leaving the governorship, Low served as President Ulysses S. Grant's minister to China from 1869 until 1873 and was thus imbued with Sewardian faith in U.S. commercial empire in the Pacific. While admitting that Asians could not "assimilate, amalgamate, and become part and parcel of this Government and its people," Low maintained that preventing "such immigration, with the world lessened in size, as it is practically, by railroads, telegraphs, and steam-communication, and with the intelligence that is diffused throughout the world, is practically impossible, unless we would go back to the darker ages of China and isolate ourselves, and build up a great wall, perhaps, to keep the people from coming from the North, and blockade our ports to keep people coming in from the East and West." While egalitarians, like Low and Brooks, could accept the exclusion of Chinese laborers as a necessary pause in the breakneck pace of global integration, they chided exclusionists for seeking naively to return to a time when oceans divided, rather than united, East and West. To them, the exclusionists were fighting a losing battle against inexorable forces of Pacific integration.[16]

Yet just three years after the San Francisco hearings closed, the anti-globalization forces seized command of the exclusion debate. During that spell, Reconstruction had ended and an increasing number of southern Democrats found themselves back in Congress; race relations in the South took a turn for the worse, while the exclusion cause turned for the better. Helping the exclusionists was the continuation of economic depression throughout the nation. In August 1879 a select House committee ventured west as part of national investigations into the causes of the depression. In coming to San Francisco, the committee focused on two seemingly crucial factors to that region: Chinese immigration and land monopolies. While Henry George did not testify this time, his magnum opus, *Progress and Poverty*, was just being published and would offer a broadly influential analysis of the causes of the depression that would become famous for pointing to the unequal distribution of land. Yet even without George's economic evaluation, the exclusionists dominated the hearings. Out of twenty-eight persons testifying (none of whom were Chinese), only two defended the Chinese—and one was the missionary and stalwart egalitarian Otis Gibson, who reiterated most of the points made in 1876, such as the need to restrict European and Asian immigrants equally. Much of the testimony blamed the depression on the Chinese. As a detriment to both white labor and capital investment, they were seen as curbing economic growth in California. Moreover, their harmful presence in agriculture contributed to land monopolies by wealthy owners to prevent the healthy formation of small family farms. In this way, the Chinese question merged with the land question in California.[17]

Challenging the Burlingame Constituency

With the return of southern Democrats to Congress, Radical Republicans like Charles Sumner were forced to abandon the notion of naturalizing Chinese immigrants and instead engaged in a rear-guard struggle to preserve the spirit, if not the letter, of the Burlingame Treaty. This was a difficult challenge given the growing national awareness of the Chinese issue as evidenced by the congressional hearings in 1876 and 1879. The rise of the Workingmen's Party in California on the slogan "The Chinese must go!" furthered the national exposure as its leader Denis Kearney toured the East speaking about the evils of Chinese immigration. Another factor involved in the spread of the Chinese issue beyond the West was the resumption of a balanced two-party system that produced the closest series of presidential elections in American history. Because the margins of victory were so thin, Republican and Democratic presidential candidates for the first time took California's small number of electoral votes seriously by jumping on the anti-Chinese bandwagon.[18]

Each of these developments—the end of Reconstruction, the nationalization of the Chinese issue, the rise of labor protests, and the return of the two-party system—occurred against the backdrop of a new historical era in which the promise and problems of the nation's unprecedented acceleration of industrialization took center stage. Political priorities shifted in response to spectacular clashes that pitted workers, farmers, and consumers against industrialists, bankers, and other defenders of monopoly capitalism. Bitter memories of Civil War and Reconstruction were replaced by fears that massive poverty and unregulated corporate greed were giving rise to class warfare during the extended period of depression. The era's two greatest economic theorists were Henry George and Karl Marx. George called for a "single tax" on excessive land ownership to redistribute income from the rich renter class to the landless poor, while Marx advanced a radical alternative to capitalism where workers, not the wealthy, would own the core parts of the economy, what he called the "means of production."

Pushed by fears of class warfare, a critical mass of Republicans joined Democrats in viewing Chinese immigration as a detriment to American society and the nation's ethno-racial cohesiveness rather than as a benefit for economic development and international relations. In this way West Coast anti-Chinese antagonism gained a national audience, and by 1879 the exclusionists were poised for victory. That year Congress approved a bill that restricted all ships landing at U.S. ports from carrying more than fifteen Chinese passengers. The measure was designed to choke off accessible transpacific travel to the Chinese. President Rutherford B. Hayes dashed exclusionist hopes by vetoing the Fifteen Passenger Act. But this proved only a temporary setback. Hayes was no racial radical and blocked restriction only because it conflicted with the Burlingame Treaty. He soon made up for his veto by dispatching James Angell, president of the University of Michigan and egalitarian sympathizer, along with two exclusionist congressmen, to negotiate a new treaty with Qing officials that explicitly permitted the restriction of Chinese laborers. The Angell Treaty, ratified in 1881, was truly a work of diplomacy as both exclusionists and egalitarians claimed victory. Its key clause stated that the United States may "regulate, limit, or suspend [Chinese labor migration] . . . but may not absolutely prohibit it." The treaty also established teachers, students, merchants, and their household servants as classes of Chinese exempt from exclusion.[19]

The Angell revisions permitted another exclusion measure to sail through the next session of Congress in 1882—which induced Senator Hoar's diatribe described at the start of this chapter. Exclusionists brought the bill in line with the new treaty by limiting its duration to twenty years and by targeting only Chinese laborers (the bulk of migrants), not merchants, students, or other classes. Yet these limitations failed to prevent President Chester A. Arthur's veto. His rationale resonated with the Burlingame constituency's embrace of the China trade.

"Experience has shown," wrote Arthur, "that the trade of the East is the key to national wealth and influence." He worried that imposing a harsh twenty-year ban on immigration would "repel Oriental nations from us and . . . drive their trade and commerce into more friendly lands." The president's veto explanation also gave voice to egalitarian arguments about the value of Chinese labor for America's economic development. "No one can say," he wrote, that the country has not profited by their work. They were largely instrumental in constructing the railways which connect the Atlantic with the Pacific. The States of the Pacific Slope are full of evidences of their industry. Enterprises profitable alike to the capitalist and to the laborer of Caucasian origin would have lain dormant but for them. A time has now come when it is supposed that they are not needed, and when it is thought by Congress and by those most acquainted with the subject that it is best to try to get along without them. There may, however, be other sections of the country where this species of labor may be advantageously employed without interfering with the laborers of our own race.[20]

While exclusionists were up in arms over Arthur's veto, the president indicated that he would support exclusion if its duration were shortened to ten years. Disappointed though not defeated, the exclusionists reluctantly agreed. Congress approved a revised ten-year bill that Arthur signed into law on May 6, 1882. Given the strength of the opposition, as evident in Arthur's veto and the balanced language of the Angell Treaty, not even the most hopeful exclusionist could have imagined that the ten-year experiment barring Chinese laborers would remain in place for over six decades. But everyone knew that the time had come for exclusion after nearly a generation of Yankee rule. By 1879 the Burlingame constituency could stop neither the political resurgence of the Democratic Party nor the increasing number of Republicans who echoed the Democrats' anti-Chinese program.[21]

Table 2.1 reveals the partisan significance of exclusion with respect to the House of Representatives.[22] In 1879 the House had a Democratic majority, and that year 84 percent of Democrats voting on Chinese immigration measures were exclusionists, while only 17 percent supported the status quo. This gap increased three years later as almost all House Democrats backed exclusion, while the small Democratic opposition all but vanished. The overwhelming Democratic vote for exclusion revealed that the return of a balanced two-party system dramatically challenged the Burlingame constituency. Longtime opponents of Chinese immigrants and African Americans, Democrats saw each group as a threat to the party's core constituencies, urban white ethnics in the North and white southerners. Since 1867, Democratic national platforms consistently followed California exclusionists in casting Chinese as an unassimilable race used by monopolist corporations to undermine the livelihood of white workers.

The Republican pattern of voting on exclusion, however, was more com-

Table 2.1. Party vote on Chinese labor exclusion, 1879 and 1882

Vote	1879		1882	
	Republican	Democrat	Republican	Democrat
Egalitarian	60%	17	39	2
Exclusionist	40	84	61	98
N =	116	127	124	103

Source: ICPSR, votes 303, 347, and 373, 45th Cong., House; and votes 82–83 and 93, 47th Cong., House.

plicated. In 1879 more than 60 percent of GOP House members voting on the anti-Chinese measures sided with egalitarians, while 40 percent supported exclusion. This ratio transposed three years later when a clear majority of Republicans voted for exclusion, while nearly 40 percent opposed it. Even though Republicans controlled the Senate in 1879, the party's division in that chamber enabled the approval of the Fifteen Passenger bill as well as the 1882 ten-year measure, when Democrats controlled the upper chamber. Given the size and near unanimity of the Democratic vote on both sides of Capitol Hill, it is unlikely that Republicans could have stopped exclusion even if they retained party discipline. In this sense, it is clear that exclusion was made possible by the "redemption" of the South that returned the historically anti-Chinese Democrats to power in Congress. But given the earlier hegemony of the Burlingame constituency, the decline in Republican solidarity was an important contributing factor. Why did a large number of Republicans outside the anti-Chinese West break party ranks to vote with the Democrats on exclusion?

The Possessive Investment of Regions

One way to understand the splintering Republican opposition to exclusion is to examine where it did and did not occur. Table 2.2 breaks down exclusion votes into seven regions, revealing that New England was the only one from which a majority of its House delegation opposed exclusion in both 1879 and 1882. A large majority of Mid-Atlantic members (71 percent) supported egalitarians in 1879 but three years later switched to exclusionists. Even so, when the percentages for both years are averaged, New England and the Mid-Atlantic ranked as the top two regions most likely to oppose exclusion. The strength of this northeast opposition was evident even among the regions' Democrats, who in 1879 were almost four times more likely to oppose exclusion than partisan allies in the Midwest or South (not

Table 2.2. Republican votes on Chinese labor exclusion by region, 1879 and 1882

Region	1879 Egalitarian	Exclusion	1882 Egalitarian	Exclusion
New England	86% (n = 12)	14 (2)	70 (14)	30 (6)
Mid-Atlantic	71 (25)	29 (10)	42 (13)	58 (18)
E. Midwest	45 (18)	55 (22)	29 (13)	71 (32)
W. Midwest	59 (10)	41 (7)	44 (7)	56 (9)
South	80 (4)	20 (1)	0 (0)	100 (4)
Border states	100 (1)	0 (0)	20 (1)	80 (4)
West/mountain	0 (0)	100 (4)	0 (0)	100 (3)
Total	60 (70)	40 (46)	39 (48)	61 (76)

Source: ICPSR, votes 303, 347, and 373, 45th Cong., House; and votes 82–83 and 93, 47th Cong., House.

shown in table). The Midwest, divided by the Mississippi River into eastern and western halves, differed significantly from the Northeast, especially the much larger eastern House contingent that comprised states carved out of the Northwest Territory. In both years a majority of members in the eastern Midwest were exclusionist. Table 2.2 adds the small Republican contingent in other regions for context, but in themselves these contingents had little impact on the exclusion votes.[23]

The regional variance in exclusion voting fits the pattern of the pre-existing cleavage regarding transpacific commerce, pitting the Northeast against the rest of the country, with the exception of the West Coast (see maps 2.1 and 2.2). The distinctiveness of the Northeast for the China trade was based in the region's role as the nation's manufacturing and financial center. The leading U.S. imports from China in 1880 were tea and raw silk, which together made up around 70 percent of all Chinese imports. Most of the trade in tea was handled by New England merchant houses that had long-standing ties to the China market. Table 2.3 shows that New England also enjoyed the nation's second-largest silk economy, while the largest silk manufacturers were in the Mid-Atlantic. Together New Jersey, New York, and Pennsylvania controlled 80 percent of the nation's silk manufacturers and 78 percent of industry employees and also held nearly 70 percent of industry capital. The leading U.S. export to China in 1880 was manufactured cotton. Table 2.3 reveals that the Northeast dominated this business as well. New England possessed nearly 60 percent of the nation's cotton manufacturing firms and more than 70 percent of this industry's capital and employees. Given the dominance of New England and the Mid-Atlantic on key

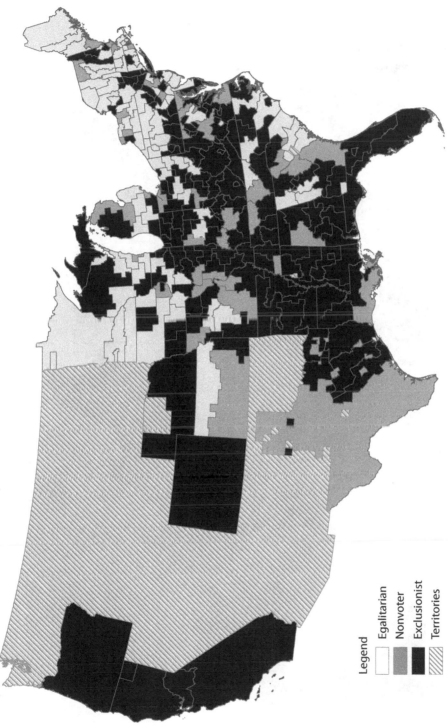

Map 2.1. Chinese labor exclusion voting by congressional district, 1879. Although Congress approved Chinese labor exclusion (vetoed by President Hayes), the map reveals significant pockets of egalitarian opposition, especially in New England, upstate and western New York, and the western Midwest. *Source:* ICPSR, votes 303, 347, and 373, 45th Cong., House; and votes 82–83 and 93, 47th Cong., House.

Legend

☐ Egalitarian
■ (gray) Nonvoter
■ (black) Exclusionist
▨ Territories

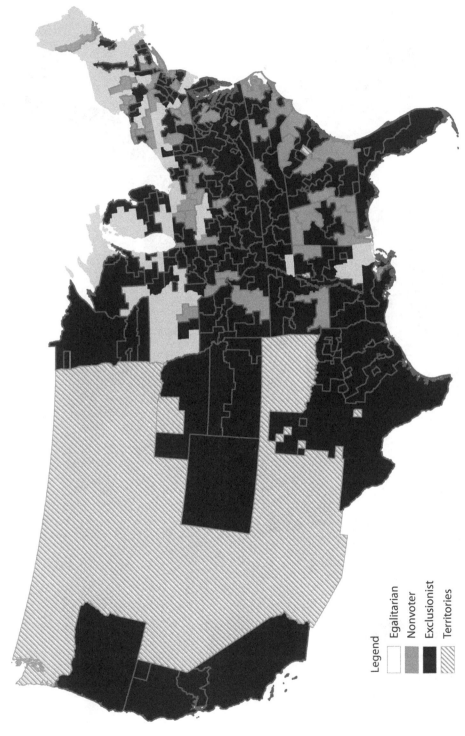

Map 2.2. Chinese labor exclusion voting by congressional district, 1882. The pockets of egalitarian opposition in 1879 diminished in 1882, save for New England and parts of the western Midwest. *Source:* ICPSR, votes 303, 347, and 373, 45th Cong., House; and votes 82–83 and 93, 47th Cong., House.

Legend

Egalitarian
Nonvoter
Exclusionist
Territories

Table 2.3. U.S. cotton and silk manufacturing by region, 1880

Region	Cotton mfg. firms	Cotton mfg. capital ($)	Cotton mfg. workers	Silk mfg. firms	Silk mfg. capital ($)	Silk mfg. workers
New England	430 (57%)	154,754,690 (74%)	127,185 (73%)	54 (14%)	5,790,000 (30%)	5,866 (17%)
Mid-Atlantic	120 (16)	26,413,943 (13)	24,281 (14)	306 (80)	13,028,100 (68)	26,875 (78)
All Other Regions	206 (27)	27,111,713 (13)	23,193 (13)	22 (6)	307,200 (2)	1,780 (5)
Total United States	756 (100%)	208,280,346 (100)	174,659 (100)	382 (100)	19,125,300 (100)	34,521 (100)

Sources: Edward Atkinson, "Report on Cotton Manufactures of the United States," 15, and Wm. C. Wyckoff, "Report on the Silk Manufacturing Industry in the United States," in U.S. Census Office, *Report on the Manufactures of the United States* (Washington: Government Printing Office, 1883).

Chinese imports as well as on U.S. exports to China, it is clear that these two sections controlled America's China trade.

Northeast dominance in the China trade was consistent with the region's overall position as the nation's leading industrial area. According to political scientist Richard Franklin Bensel, this region in 1900 claimed the top six states with the highest per capita ratio of manufactured goods compare to agricultural products. Of these, Rhode Island and Massachusetts were by far the most intensively industrial states, followed by New Jersey and Connecticut and then New York and Pennsylvania.[24] Another sign of the Northeast's centrality to the nation's economy was the uneven distribution of wealth in the late nineteenth century. Bensel has compiled lists of the most and least developed counties in the United States in 1890. He found forty-seven counties scored in the highest level of his developmental index while twenty-five scored in the lowest level of this index. More than 70 percent of the most developed counties were in New England or the Mid-Atlantic states, followed by less than 20 percent in the Old Northwest. The border states claimed three of the most developed counties and the South had one, with none for either the western Midwest or the Far West. The list of least developed counties confirmed the regional concentration of wealth: all twenty-five were in the South. Here is clear evidence for distinguishing between a dominant northeast metropole and an economic periphery running through the Midwest, South, and West.[25]

Given the Northeast's economic interests and egalitarianism, it was not surprising that prominent business leaders in Massachusetts and New York sent petitions to Congress urging members of Congress to oppose exclusion. The New York Board of Trade provoked the greatest response in 1882 with a petition signed not only by firms conducting business with China but also by those "engaged in the sale of dry goods, by persons engaged in the iron trade, by banks and bankers to a very large amount and extent, by the insurance companies of the city, by persons engaged in the cotton trade, and others, remonstrating against the passage of any law to prohibit Chinese immigration." The New York senator who introduced the petition stated that these "gentlemen are animated by that spirit which I remember so universally prevailed in my boyhood and which was expressed in one stanza in the song of 'Jefferson and Liberty,' with which we are all so familiar." The song proclaimed:

> Her strangers from a thousand shores
> Compelled by tyranny to roam,
> Shall find amid abundant stores
> A freer and a happier home.[26]

The New York petition, submitted after President Arthur's veto of exclusion in 1882 already had aroused West Coast tempers, sparked a minor firestorm in California. The *Sacramento Daily Union* responded by condemning in the harshest terms well over one hundred firms. "In the eyes of the sordid traders whose names are signed to this petition," the newspaper editorialized, it does not matter "whether the Pacific States are Mongolianized, so long as the trade with China is not interfered with." The *Union* tarred these "greedy money grubbers" with the brush of anti-Americanism, reminding readers that during the Civil War era these very same New York merchants had been more interested in business relations with the South than in opposing slavery. In this way, they were no different from the dreaded British, whose "lust for gain" generated an empire through which "the most indefensible outrages have been perpetuated upon weak nations."[27]

Implied in the *Union*'s comparison between the New York merchants and British imperialists was recognition that California was in a weak economic position vis-à-vis the Northeast, just like the American colonies had been against the British Empire. Much like any colonized people, Californians were at the mercy of the northeast business community, dependent upon them for manufactured goods and, more importantly, for much-needed capital to engage in economic development. Within the framework of this colonial relationship, people on the West Coast had no ability either to overthrow the northeast metropole or to go it alone by severing economic ties to it. But they could alter their consumption, and so California newspapers called for concerned citizens and firms of the Golden State to boycott the companies that had signed the petition. Newspapers published the names of the signees, and within a week the *San Francisco Bulletin* reported the cancelation of "several policies" with "Eastern insurance companies doing business in this city." This caused the *New York Times* to warn its readers that California merchants, who typically relied on businesses in New York and Boston, were proposing to look to Philadelphia and other cities "where they meet with sympathy on the Chinese question."[28]

As it turned out, the boycott exposed the nation's regionally based political economy more than it damaged it. The protest did not last long since within a month of vetoing the twenty-year exclusion bill, President Arthur worked out an agreement cutting the period in half, paving the way for Chinese labor exclusion. It is doubtful that the boycott had any real effect on the targeted New York merchants. But it did reveal that the fight over exclusion was connected to western concerns regarding the dominance of the northeast metropole as the engine of the nation's industrial growth. Such concerns also were evident in newspaper editorials. While the existing scholarship on Chinese exclusion registers extensive and diverse political discourse about the issue, it does not rank the popularity of arguments in the debate to reveal their relative impact. Recent database search engines, however, make it possible to study a particular newspaper's views on exclusion by counting the number of editorials that contain politically loaded keywords used in the exclusion debate. The frequency with which certain keywords appeared lays bare economic tensions between exclusionists and egalitarians that were reflected in a sample of newspapers on the East and West Coasts.

Table 2.4 compares the appearance of the same keywords in the *San Francisco Chronicle*, an exclusionist newspaper in California, with that of a set of three egalitarian newspapers, the *New York Times*, the *New York Tribune*, and the *Hartford Courant*.[29] Listed on the left side are five terms that were more likely to appear in the San Francisco paper's editorials than in the northeast ones during the peak push for Chinese exclusion (1876–82). The numbers represent the degree of difference, which would be zero if the keywords appeared equally as often in publications on both sides of the exclusion debate and would be 100 if they appeared on one side but not the other. In this sense, "coolie" appeared 19 percent more often and "labor" 14 percent more often in the *San Francisco Chronicle* than in the other three papers. This is significant because the terms with the highest number are in accord with the exclusionist view that Chinese immigration was at heart a

Table 2.4. Chinese exclusion keywords in select newspapers, 1876–1882

Keyword	San Francisco Chronicle	Keyword	Egalitarian newspapers*
coolie	19	rights	19
labor	14	trade	17
union	8	goods	15
importation	7	republican	8
monopoly	7	treaty	6

New York Times, New York Tribune, Hartford Courant

labor market issue in which imported Chinese coolies were seen as undermining the livelihood of white labor. Listed on the right side of table 2.4 are five terms that were more likely to appear in the northeast papers by order of magnitude such that "rights," "trade," and "goods" were more likely to appear at rates of 19, 17, and 15 percent, respectively. This is significant because it confirms the great egalitarian interest in commercial relations and in upholding U.S.-China treaties. In this way, keyword analysis supports the notion that the northeast newspapers supported the Burlingame constituency's long-standing agenda of western economic development and transpacific trade relations.[30]

Beyond the division between the East and West Coasts, the economic basis for the exclusion vote was also evident in the South. While only 17 percent of the southern House delegation in 1879 opposed exclusion, members from this group (both Democrats and Republicans) came overwhelmingly from areas rich in cotton manufacturing. The southern opposition to exclusion was over three times more likely to come from districts with a relatively high degree of cotton manufacturing, while the reverse was true for low-level areas. This opposition vanished in 1882, but at that time Georgia senator Joseph Brown broke with the solid South to oppose exclusion. His reasons for doing so matched the Northeast's economic rationale. Like Hoar and others who stood against exclusion, Brown defended the Chinese as a civilized people who, if not treated as badly as they had been in the United States, would assimilate to American customs and labor standards. More important, Brown did not worry about Chinese immigrants because they represented a "mere fractional part" of the massive number of newcomers to the nation. "The Chinese Empire," he figured, "is in a great deal more danger to-day of being overrun and subverted by Yankee energy and Yankee enterprise . . . than this country is of being overrun by Chinamen."[31]

What Brown did worry about was violating the Burlingame Treaty. He made it plain that the success of the South's fledgling cotton manufacturers relied upon the treaty's promise to transform China into a massive export market for American goods. "We produce 60% of the cotton of the world," he said, and the "400,000,000 people of the Chinese empire . . . use cotton almost exclusively for clothing." The Georgian cited figures from the Census Bureau to prove that his hope for a yearly bonanza of U.S.-China commerce was not wishful thinking. According to the bureau chief, the value of America's China trade almost doubled, from $15.3 to $27.7 million, since the Burlingame Treaty's ratification. Thus Brown contended that exclusion posed a serious economic risk not just to the South but to the country as a whole. Furthermore, the Georgia senator maintained that exclusion undermined the historic investment already made by the American government to reach the China market. This included huge land grants to develop the West Coast, building transcontinental railroads to move goods from east to west, and funding a fleet of expensive steamers to deliver them across the Pacific Ocean. "In view of all these important considerations," Brown asked his fellow senators if they were "prepared to sacrifice the investments we have made, and the vast advantages opening to us for the future, by giving unnecessary and unjustifiable offense to China by a flagrant violation of our treaty stipulations with that government, when there is not even a plausible pretext for the act, as we can amply protect ourselves against the evils of any dangerous influx of Chinese laborers, and still keep within both the letter and spirit of the treaty."[aa]

Thus the political economy of Chinese exclusion in Congress pitted the regional interests of New England and the Mid-Atlantic against the West and South with a minority of new economy southerners siding with the northeast metropole. Missing from this framework, however, was the Midwest. It is important to understand the midwestern vote because this region, the largest Republican contingent in the House, shared neither the Northeast's maritime interests nor the West's preoccupation with the Chinese question. Given the polarization of Republicans on both sides of the country, what explained the Midwest's support for exclusion, especially the strong exclusionist vote by the Old Northwest (71 percent) in 1882?

Midwest Periphery

While there are no studies examining the Republican vote in the Midwest, three possible reasons can be identified from the relevant scholarship. The first suggests that Republicans sought to appease California voters. Scholars have long known that the end of Reconstruction boosted the political clout of California exclusionists, who, during an era of tightly contested presidential elections, could deliver the state's six electoral votes to a particular candidate, potentially the margin of victory. This fact encouraged Maine Republican and presidential aspirant James Blaine to lead the exclusion movement in the East. Moreover, when President Arthur upset exclusionists by vetoing the twenty-year exclusion bill in 1882, it was widely predicted in the press that in so doing he had lost California for Republican candidates.[33] Yet the problem with the "California thesis" is that it cannot explain New England's staunch opposition to exclusion; not even Blaine could get fellow New England congressmen to support exclusion. So if the California thesis cannot explain voting patterns among Republicans in New England, then why should it be trusted to explain those in the eastern Midwest? Another problem with the California thesis is the dearth of evidence proving that it actually influenced the votes by individual members of Congress. Because it cannot account for the New England opposition or prove its direct impact on congressional voting, the California thesis, while capturing the growing national awareness of the Chinese issue, cannot in itself explain why a majority of midwestern Republicans broke ranks to vote with Democrats on exclusion.[34]

Second, it is possible that midwestern Republicans supported exclusion in order to win the increasingly important labor vote. While historians debate whether union workers east of the Mississippi River were adamant for or indifferent to Chinese exclusion, it is clear that office seekers from both parties were inclined to portray Chinese immigrants as a threat to American workers.[35] By the 1880 presidential election, Republicans included an anti-Chinese plank in their national platform, thus putting both parties on record in support of exclusion. Democrats reached out to labor through urban ethnic machines that mobilized particularly Irish and German immigrant voters in northern cities. But Republicans, with their tradition of "free soil, free labor, free men," also had strong ties to working-class voters. In fact, northern Republicans won considerable support from the working classes through their ideology and practice of high tariffs, which claimed to protect American workers from competing against low-wage overseas labor. Republicans insisted that the tariff benefited both American workers and manufacturers by increasing the cost of foreign-made goods.

But like the California thesis, the labor factor is troubled by comparison with New England. If midwestern Republicans joined the Democrats on exclusion in order to appease the labor vote, then why did their New England colleagues not do the same? It does not seem likely that the midwestern Republicans would care more about labor issues than would their New

England colleagues, who represented the most industrialized parts of the country. Another problem with the labor thesis is that it is not supported by quantitative evidence. A study of midwestern Republican congressional districts shows no relationship between a congressman's vote on exclusion and the proportion of industrial workers in his constituency. There was also no connection between exclusion voting and districts with large cities like Chicago, Detroit, Cincinnati, and Cleveland—where most industrial workers lived. If the labor vote pushed midwestern Republicans to support exclusion, then one would expect to see a solid block of exclusionists coming from districts with high concentrations of industrial workers. This, however, was not the case.[36]

Third, midwestern Republicans may have voted for exclusion due to racist and nativist concerns about Asians and new European immigrants. Here it is important to recall that egalitarians like Charles Crocker, Frederick Low, and other Republicans in the Burlingame constituency shared with Democrats core assumptions about the superiority of Europeans, especially "Anglo-Saxons," over all other peoples.[37] But such personal views were at odds with Republican political goals of expansionist immigration, maritime interests, and harmonious U.S.-China relations that continued to dictate Republican voting in the New England. There is no evidence to indicate that Republicans in the Midwest were more prone than their colleagues in the Northeast, the home of Know-Nothingism and Anglo-Saxon supremacy theories, to back the Democrats' white supremacist agenda. In addition, quantitative analysis shows no connection between the vote on exclusion and congressional districts with high proportions of foreign-born residents. But what about the conflict between European immigrants and the Chinese, as expressed by Otis Gibson and August Loomis at the San Francisco hearings in 1876? Since some scholars have argued that persecuted immigrants from Europe sought to become "white" by casting aspersions on the Chinese, blacks, and other non-European groups, could it be that mobilized immigrant voters pushed Republicans of the Midwest to the exclusionist camp? Quantitative evidence suggests not. If nativism, either from native-born Americans or from old immigrants such as Irish and German Americans, caused midwestern Republicans to support the Democrats on exclusion, then one would expect solid exclusionism from districts with lots of native-born or old immigrant residents. Again, this was not the case.[38]

The reason why the three major explanations for exclusion (the California thesis, the labor vote, and nativism/racism) fail upon closer look is because the relevant scholarship has not carefully analyzed congressional voting patterns or connected exclusion votes to the demographic characteristics of congressional districts. In deeply probing the pervasive anti-Chinese discourse, existing studies have ignored the lateral connections between exclusionist measures and congressional voting on many seemingly unrelated issues. In this way, scholarship has assumed that exclusion votes were sui generis, as if they remained outside normative congressional voting patterns. The error of this assumption is apparent when exclusion votes are examined within the context of 348 House roll-call votes taken in the Forty-Seventh Congress (March 4, 1881, to March 4, 1883). What emerges is a picture of exclusion that highlights none of its three conventional explanations.

Contextualizing the exclusion votes with the totality of roll-call voting reveals they were part of a trend in which members from regions peripheral to the nation's industrial economy opposed the interests of the northeastern core. While Republicans showed tremendous party discipline in the vast majority of roll-call votes, they split significantly on a handful of votes pertaining to their various regions. Table 2.5 lists eight of the votes that produced the greatest division between House Republicans in the Northeast (New England and the Mid-Atlantic combined) and Midwest (East and West Midwest combined). The table reveals that the vote on the twenty-year Chinese exclusion bill was part of a broader division between the Northeast (sixty-two members) and Midwest (sixty-seven members), which together made up 90 percent of House Republicans. Noted in the table is the percentage of "No" votes for each regional contingent and the difference in percentage points between them (higher numbers mean larger division).[39]

Two of the votes in table 2.5 reflect the division between the ocean-looking Northeast and the land-locked Midwest seen in the earlier conflict over transpacific mail service to China. Nearly 60 percent of Midwest Republicans, compared to only 30 percent of those in the Northeast, opposed increased funding to improve the nation's revenue marine service, which acted as a coast guard to enforce maritime laws and collect customs duties. The second measure concerned an amendment to a major bill designed to boost the nation's overseas shipping. The amendment proposed to eliminate a clause favored by the Northeast that gave incentive to overseas shipping by exempting vessels from state taxation. Not surprisingly, the overwhelming majority (85 percent) of Northeast Republicans opposed the amendment, while only a slim majority (51 percent) of Midwest Republicans did so.[40]

Three of the votes in table 2.5 addressed clear western interests. The vote on the rivers and harbor appropriation bill was consistent with a long-standing regional conflict between the Northeast and rest of the nation about the development of internal waterways, which usually dispropor-tionately benefited the West. In this case 73 percent of Northeast Republi-cans opposed the measure, compared to only 44 percent of Midwest Re-publicans. In the same vein, the midwesterners supported easy railroad access through western lands by opposing a proposed amendment to a bill granting the St. Louis & San Francisco Railroad access through Indian land. The amendment intended to make it more difficult for the United States to use eminent domain to appropriate Choctaw and Chickasaw lands. While Republicans in both regions opposed the amendment, the midwestern opposition (85 percent) was much stronger than the northeastern (61 per-cent) with the most vocal proponents of the amendment coming from New England. The final western issue concerned pensions for veterans of the Mexican-American War and various Indian wars, who disproportionately lived in western regions. Northeast Republicans (85 percent) strongly op-posed a motion to set the date to vote on this issue, compared to only tepid opposition from their Midwest colleagues (36 percent).[41]

The final two votes (not including the Chinese exclusion bill) represented in table 2.5 sought to check the power of monopoly capitalism that was rooted in the northeast metropole. The bill on patents protected farmers from corporate lawsuits seeking reparations for purchasing agricultural products that allegedly violated corporate patents. The regional difference was particularly striking on this vote: 57 percent of Northeast Republicans opposed it, compared to only 8 percent of their Midwest colleagues. In a similar vein, the midwesterners approved a bill seeking to lessen the ability of corporations to win lawsuits against private citizens. This measure, con-cerning the jurisdiction of federal and state courts, removed such lawsuits from federal circuit courts, leaving them in the hands of more consumer-friendly state courts. Northeast Republicans strongly opposed this bill (89 percent), compared to only 40 percent of those from the Midwest.[42]

Thus table 2.5 shows that the regional response to Chinese labor exclu-sion fits the pattern revealed in the other seven votes that induced Midwest Republicans to split with their northeastern peers. This analysis provides more evidence that the political economy of Chinese exclusion during the Gilded Age, as in previous eras, featured a core conflict between land-based exclusionists in the South, Midwest, and Far West and maritime-based egalitarians in the Northeast. Democrats were the party of the periphery and of urban white ethnics who distinguished themselves from the Repub-lican connection to northeastern corporations, Reconstruction, and mari-time commerce and its attendant treaties and foreign commitments. But

Table 2.5. Regional difference in House Republican votes in the Forty-Seventh Congress

Vote	Republican Northeast	Republican Midwest	Difference (percentage points)
Patents	57%	8%	49
Mexican/Indian war pensions	85	36	49
Courts	89	40	49
Shipping	85	51	34
Revenue marines	30	59	29
Rivers and harbors	73	44	29
Railroad via Indian land	61	85	24
Chinese exclusion 20 years	67	45	22

Source: ICPSR, votes 123, 298, 300, 292, 207, 341, 250, 83, 47th Cong., House

Republicans were also part of the periphery because they were divided by regions, such that those based outside the northeastern metropole disproportionately crossed the aisle to vote with Democrats on a handful of issues important to their regions. In this way, Chinese exclusion involved not just presidential electioneering, the labor vote, and racial nativism but also, and perhaps mainly, simultaneous struggles centered in the nation's economic periphery over economic development as well as the moral economy of land values, agriculture, and industrialization. The groundswell of critiques raised against monopoly capitalism during the Gilded Age made it possible for exclusionists to merge the Chinese question with the "social question" and thus appeal to a national audience. Democrats, and Republicans outside the northeastern core, were especially receptive to Chinese exclusion as part of their larger opposition to Northeast interests.

What caused the exclusion of Chinese laborers has been the subject of much analysis and varying opinion. Generally agreed upon, and sustained in this chapter, is the crucial role played by Democrats, who had long pushed for exclusion as a safeguard against an apparent labor and racial menace to white Americans. In this way, the return of southern Democrats to federal office after the end of Reconstruction sealed the fate of Chinese labor migration. Exclusion was largely a partisan victory. But it also received support from over half of the Republicans in Congress and was signed by a Republican president. Various explanations for the waning influence of the Burlingame constituency have looked to electoral politics, the labor vote, and race-based nativism as the cause. None, however, has focused analysis on congressional voting patterns in order to explain the significant regional variance in the Republican vote, in which the northeastern members stood firm in support of Chinese immigration while midwestern members cast their votes with the Democrats. Quantitative analysis of roll-call voting in the Forty-Seventh Congress suggests that the exclusion of Chinese laborers fit a pattern of congressional opposition to Northeast interests that was rooted in the Midwest, South, and Far West. This opposition was in step with the western framing of Chinese exclusion as an issue that pitted besieged Californians against powerful northeast monopoly capitalists. Thus the bipartisan support for exclusion was part and parcel of attempts by peripheral regions to challenge the hegemony of the nation's economic core, which had enjoyed unprecedented growth and political power for nearly two decades during the Civil War party system. Exclusion signaled the end of this party system as well as the beginning of a new era in which bipartisanship would increase and extend the nation's discrimination against Chinese immigrants.

3 EYE OF THE STORM

THE LABORING OF EXCLUSION,

1882–1904

||||||||||||||||||||||||||||||||||||||||||||||||||||||||||||||||||||||||||||||||||||||||||||||||||||||||||||||||||||||||||||||||||||||||||||||||||||||

In August 1885 Samuel Gompers, a cigar-makers' union leader from New York City, testified at Senate hearings investigating relations between labor and capital in the United States. Gompers criticized a Wisconsin firm for recruiting people in Germany to replace striking workers. While opposing this type of imported labor, he had "no objection to the people of any country coming to America, Chinese excepted (I am not so sentimental as all that), provided they come here of their own free will, and not influenced by deception." The exception made for Chinese immigrants, Gompers said, expressed the opinion of the "American workmen" who "were not going to be trodden down by the Chinese undermining them." Exclusion was necessary because "it is a question whether the working men of America shall eat rats, rice, or beefsteak."[1]

The discrimination against immigrants from China testified to America's deep-seated racism that had been, and would continue to be, a major factor fueling exclusionism. The bipartisan coalition behind the exclusion of Chinese laborers in 1882 gained momentum in the struggle against "sentimentalists," whom Gompers dismissed as stuck in the past (referring to Radical Reconstruction) fighting for the lost cause of interracial brotherhood. In 1886 he became president of the American Federation of Labor (AFL)—the nation's most powerful union advocate during the entire exclusion era—and played a major role in enacting a series of draconian anti-Chinese federal policies that transformed restriction of laborers into exclusion for nearly all peoples from China. At the same time, the AFL joined a nationwide campaign to exclude migrations from other parts of Asia as well as from southern and eastern Europe. These "new immigrants" too were seen as harmful not just to organized labor but also to America's racial heritage and institutions.

But closing the nation's gates, as the Chinese case had revealed, was filled with egalitarian roadblocks and detours that stymied exclusionist goals and forced compromise. While Democrats and Republicans, as well as congressmen from all regions including the Northeast, came to agree on Chinese exclusion, they disagreed sharply about restricting other groups. Much to the exclusionists' chagrin, egalitarians were able to hold the gates open to the vast majority of seemingly unassimilable immigrants. Consequently, Gompers was convinced that the AFL was losing the fight against capital. He blamed railroad and shipping interests for the nation's inability to stop the influx of European "pauper labor" as well as for the smuggling of Chinese immigrants. Such egalitarians, Gompers bemoaned, were also behind the nation's new age of imperialism and empire that spawned constituencies supporting the free migration of Japanese and Filipinos to the United States and its recently acquired territory of Hawai'i.

This chapter follows the evolution of the exclusion debate as regional protests against monopoly capitalism were absorbed into mainstream politics through labor struggles as well as through campaigns for progressive reforms. In so doing, the congressional opposition to Chinese exclusion all but collapsed as a bipartisan exclusionist coalition enacted further legislation and ratified treaties that renewed the exclusion of Chinese laborers and limited the freedoms of the exempt classes, as well as of those immigrants already resident in the United States. In this way, exclusionism triumphed. But the debate continued as egalitarians fought for class-based exclusion that maintained the rights of the exempt classes, while exclusionists like Gompers supported expanding exclusion to include all Chinese. The conflict also extended to new immigrants from Europe and Asia as egalitarians thwarted attempts to exclude these groups. The exclusion debate was also a factor in discourse and policy regarding American imperial expansion in the Pacific.

"Chinee-ize the American People"

The 1882 act excluding Chinese laborers from the United States for ten years did more than displace the egalitarian spirit of the Burlingame and Angell Treaties; it placed an increasingly anti-Chinese Congress in the driver's seat to set immigration policy. The result was a series of acts, each building onto the exclusion of Chinese laborers an increasingly discriminatory system of restriction, regulation, and surveillance. In 1884 Congress broadened the definition of excluded laborers by denying entry to them on the basis of race, even if they were not citizens of China, and making more burdensome the registration system required of all Chinese immigrants in America under the 1882 act. In response, Qing officials negotiated a new U.S.-China treaty in which China agreed to self-imposed immigration restrictions. Self-restriction was seen as a way to establish a treaty basis for exclusion that would limit Congress's freedom to further tighten the screws.

Negotiations of the Bayard-Zhang Treaty in 1888 revealed a newly assertive Chinese diplomatic corps, which, after establishing a legation in Washington, D.C., and the San Francisco consulate, became actively engaged in immigration politics. This was welcomed by the merchants of the Six Companies, who until then had shouldered the burden of defending overseas Chinese. While the merchants embraced the principle of self-restriction, they objected to the proposed treaty's length of exclusion (twenty years), causing an uproar against it from egalitarians in the United States and southern China that led the Qing government to back away from ratification. The treaty's failure pushed Congress, with President Grover Cleveland's blessing, to deny Chinese laborers already in the United States reentry into the country after traveling abroad to visit family in China.[2] Four years later Congress renewed the 1882 act as well as all supplements to it for another ten years. The renewal act, known by its California sponsor, Thomas Geary, also included the dreaded "dog tag law" requiring all Chinese immigrants to carry a certificate testifying to their legal right of residence, without which they risked being thrown in jail and subsequently deported.[3]

These were gloomy days for egalitarians within and outside of Chinatown. During the 1880s Chinese immigrants in the Pacific Northwest faced racist pogroms in nearly two hundred towns.[4] In 1885 mobs of angry whites killed forty Chinese and caused half a million dollars in property damage in separate attacks in Seattle and in Rock Springs, Wyoming Territory. A year and a half later Congress agreed to pay $148,000 to the relatives of Rock Springs victims in lieu of an official apology or punishment of the murderers. The Six Companies, now backed by the Chinese legation and consulate, continued to rely on paid white American employees such as Colonel Frederick Bee, now consul general of San Francisco, to sway public opinion. But as lobbyists they found few allies on Capitol Hill as the once-dominant Burlingame constituency had all but evaporated. While Senator George Hoar continued to stand against exclusionists until he died in 1904, the New England congressional delegation no longer put up much of a fight as it shrank in size and became increasingly Democratic.[5]

Ironically, it was a Democratic president who offered a silver lining for the downtrodden egalitarians. After Chinese immigrants boycotted the Geary Act's "dog tag" regulations, President Cleveland calmed U.S.-China tensions by halting the implementation of this type of surveillance. His action prevented the arrest and deportation of tens of thousands who were encouraged by China's foreign ministry and the Six Companies to violate the registration law.[6] Cleveland also earned praise from egalitarians (and the wrath of exclusionists) by being party to the rejuvenation of the failed

Bayard-Zhang Treaty. The new treaty, approved in 1894 by Secretary of State Walter Gresham and China's foreign minister Yang-ju, established the principle of China's self-restriction while finally placing exclusion on a treaty basis. In a party-line vote, Democrats in the Senate approved the Gresham-Yang Treaty, while the Republican minority opposed it along with all but one western senator.[7]

The branch of government that gave egalitarians the most hope was the judicial branch because exclusion laws did not restrict the right to a fair trial. Those barred from entering the United States received legal consul from some of the best white attorneys in San Francisco, such as Thomas Riordan, who was retained by the San Francisco consulate. As one historian notes, "By far, Chinese immigrants' most valuable resource during the exclusion era was an organized network of immigration lawyers who facilitated Chinese entry and reentry by keeping track of necessary paperwork and lobbying on behalf of clients, tasks that would have been extremely difficult for Chinese to accomplish on their own."[8] Such attorneys also launched test cases challenging the constitutionality of anti-Chinese laws and ordinances, including *Yick Wo v. Hopkins* (1886), in which the U.S. Supreme Court struck down a San Francisco measure imposed against Chinese laundries that violated the Fourteenth Amendment's equal protection clause. In another precedent-setting decision, the Court in 1898 granted an American-born Chinese the right to reenter the United States. Exclusionists had argued that the children of Chinese immigrants were not automatically granted U.S. citizenship because their parents themselves lacked the right of naturalization. Yet the *Wong Kim Ark* decision rejected this claim in favor of a broad interpretation of birthright citizenship (jus soli).[9]

As the exclusionist campaign picked up steam after 1882, it also broadened to target European immigrants. Congress led the way in 1884 when it excluded contract laborers from Europe in legislation sponsored by Martin Foran, the first congressman to openly identify with organized labor. Samuel Gompers's testimony against German imported labor—addressed at the start of this chapter—was in support of Foran's bill. But the main focus of the legislation was southern and eastern Europeans, as well as French Canadians. As with the Chinese, exclusionists saw these newcomers as tools of big business who lowered the standard of living for union workers. These new immigrants were considered nonwhite because they were not Protestant and lacked prized Anglo-Saxon racial traits. Congressman Foran decried the character of Italian and Hungarian immigrants: "They know nothing of our institutions, our customs, or of the habits and characteristics of our people. . . . They are brought here precisely in the same manner as the Chinese were brought here. . . . Very many of them have no conception of freedom. . . . They seldom sleep in beds. . . . They do not know to purchase any of the luxuries which tend to elevate and enlighten people. . . . Being low in the scale of intelligence, they are willing slaves."[10]

Like Foran, Gompers saw new migrants from Europe as part of capital's attempt to "Chinee-ize the American people."[11] While Terence Powderly and the Knights of Labor in the 1870s had called for the exclusion of Italians and Hungarians (along with Chinese), Gompers was better able to follow through on this demand because his newly formed AFL was an exclusive bastion for skilled workers.[12] An organization of craft unions, the AFL, unlike the Knights, rejected membership for the vast majority of workers in America, who were unskilled and not organized into unions. Excluding new immigrants from entry to the United States was merely an extension of preventing them from entering the AFL. The radicalization of class conflict amid the depression of the 1890s further separated the AFL from the masses of new immigrants, who were seen as breeders of socialism, anarchism, syndicalism, and other dangerous "foreign" traditions. Because the Foran Act failed to stem the influx of new immigrants, AFL leaders advocated harsher forms of gatekeeping that mirrored anti-Chinese efforts. The line that Gompers once drew between free migrants and imported labor became increasingly fuzzy as he began explicitly to use race as the basis for excluding a broad array of unwarranted groups. Whatever power the AFL wielded grew out of a "split labor market" in which skilled craft workers separated themselves from the mass of unskilled and unorganized workers. To Gompers, the livelihood of skilled workers was threatened by management above them as well as by unskilled workers below, as these two groups were prone to conspire against the best interests of skilled workers through strikebreaking and the replacement of skilled jobs with low-wage tasks.[13]

As the "aristocracy of labor," the AFL joined with blue-blooded New Englanders of the Immigration Restriction League in lobbying Congress to reduce significantly the migration of "inferior" racial stocks from Europe. Founded in 1894 by a trio of Harvard University graduates, the league fashioned itself as the savior of the nation's Yankee heritage and gene pool, which, its leaders argued, were being recklessly supplanted through unchecked immigration. To resolve this problem, league members looked to the imposition of a literacy test to be given to all potential immigrants. Fellow leaguer Senator Henry Cabot Lodge of Massachusetts sponsored literacy test legislation in 1897 that passed both houses of Congress only to be vetoed by Democratic president Cleveland, who expressed an egalitarian faith in the country's ability to assimilate newcomers.[14]

Nevertheless, the House vote revealed a stunning change from earlier ones regarding Chinese exclusion. New Englanders overwhelmingly favored restriction, while southerners and representatives from border states made up the major opposition to it. The regional opposition had less to do with concerns about immigrant rights than with partisanship and the labor needs of the newly industrializing South. The minority of new economy southerners who had welcomed Chinese immigrants in 1882 (and before) now morphed into the region's majority stance on European immigration. Meanwhile, New England found itself in a similar position as pre-1882 California; it confronted a flood of new European and French Canadian immigrants challenging the livelihoods of union workers. The region's Republicans also faced a resurgent Democratic Party that demanded broad-based exclusion. George Hoar, while standing up for Chinese immigration, opposed new immigrants in New England and favored using the literacy test to restrict them.[15] In advice given to Lodge, his junior colleague in the Senate, Hoar warned, "Unless we can break this compact foreign vote, we are gone, and the grand chapter of the old Massachusetts history is closed."[16]

The collapse of New England's opposition to immigration restriction marked a major turning point in which the majority of Americans, not just organized labor, switched from welcoming immigrants as a national asset to despising them as an all-around liability. This change can be witnessed in the perspectives of Francis Amasa Walker, head of the U.S. Census Bureau and president of the Massachusetts Institute of Technology.[17] Like most New England intellectuals, Walker grew up embracing immigration as an unquestioned benefit for the nation's economic development, and like William H. Seward, he strongly opposed Chinese exclusion while eschewing the doomsday warnings of the Know-Nothing tradition.[18] But fears about the rise of organized labor, which he attributed to foreigners, started to shake his faith in immigration. Even more important was the demographic picture emerging from the census. Walker paid close attention to the alarming trend of decreasing Yankee birthrates and dramatically increasing numbers of immigrants that by the early 1890s convinced him that immigration was now a detriment to the nation. As a result, he openly called for restricting new immigrants to prevent Yankees from becoming strangers in their own country. Despite deep reservations about the assimilability of Germans and Irish, he backed off for pragmatic reasons from targeting these older and more politically powerful immigrant groups.[19]

While Walker was one of the Immigration Restriction League's senior statesmen, Henry Cabot Lodge was more typical of the younger generation of New Englanders who launched it. Son of a wealthy China merchant,

Lodge earned a bachelor's and law degree from Harvard and went on to receive the school's first Ph.D. in political science. His dissertation was a pioneering study into the racial origins of representative democracy through the "genius" of Anglo-Saxon peoples. Though steeped in race theory, Lodge was not a race purist who believed that different peoples must be separated into homogeneous nations.[20] After all, he was a skilled politician who embraced his Irish constituents by broadening the celebration of Anglo-Saxons to include all peoples of the "English-speaking race." He was also a New England Republican who together with George Hoar fought for the civil and voting rights of African Americans in the South and was optimistic that the nation could assimilate them. Lodge, like Walker and Gompers, targeted new immigrants in part because they were politically vulnerable. But as in everything he did as a public servant, he was motivated by a duty to strengthen, protect, and champion the nation's moral and physical character, which he equated with the New England tradition. Like his good friend Theodore Roosevelt, Lodge was alarmed by the Gilded Age's rampant materialism; immigration restriction was a means to reform the hard edges of capitalism while taking back the nation from plutocrats who would sacrifice the county's prized Yankee spirit and blood for economic gain.[21]

Christian leaders and reformers came to the politics of immigration restriction with even loftier goals than Lodge's nationalism. While missionaries like Otis Gibson had agreed to the policy of Chinese exclusion and self-restriction, they continued to speak out, typically in concert with the consulate and Six Companies, against continuing anti-Chinese abuses as an affront to treaty rights, the intelligence and assimilability of their flock, and God's will.[22] But the nature of Gilded Age reform spurred broad and increasingly urgent calls for gatekeeping from the nation's Christian leadership. Josiah Strong, a founder of the influential Social Gospel movement, updated the educational and charity work traditions of missionaries with new scientific theories from Charles Darwin and Herbert Spencer, as well as with research from the first generation of American professional social scientists, like Henry Cabot Lodge, who applied and adapted these theories. Strong became well known for his 1885 revision of *Our Country: Its Possible Future and Its Present Crisis*, a manual first published by a different author in 1842 for home missionaries ministering to Chinese immigrants, African Americans, Native Americans, European immigrants, and settlers on the western frontier. Strong's version justified the manifest destiny ideology undergirding American expansionism by resorting not only to Christian theology but also to fresh conceptions of the "mighty Anglo-Saxon race." Like Walker, he used the census as a crystal ball to predict the ruination of America through a flood of new immigrants: "In view of the fact that Europe is able to send us six times as many immigrants during the next thirty years as during the thirty years past, without any diminution of her population, and in view of all the powerful influences co-operating to stimulate the movement, is it not reasonable to expect a rising tide of immigration unless Congress takes effective measures to check it?"[23]

Missionaries, however, did not hold monolithic views on immigrants and exclusion. Women home missionaries rescuing Chinese prostitutes in San Francisco rejected the notion of biological racism, arguing that immigrants were capable of becoming good Christians and Americans. In many ways, Strong's Anglo-Saxon determinism was anathema to the missionary endeavor, at home or abroad, which was based on hope, uplift, and enlightenment rather than on dismal predictions about the decline of Western civilization. For the rescue missionaries in San Francisco, this faith was crucial to proving women's moral authority over men, which justified their quest to get beyond the separate sphere of domesticity.[24]

In many ways the exclusion debate in 1882 foreshadowed the broader anti-immigrant movement arising in the 1890s to prevent the "Chineeizing" of the American people. From the perspective of today's multicultural era, it is tempting to see progressive, forward-thinking reformers such as Strong, Walker, and Lodge in the same mold as the western labor nativists who led the anti-Chinese movement. But this would misunderstand the rise of a new element in the immigration debate: a generation of largely middle-class, native-born Americans who participated in the efflorescence of innovative and earnest efforts to humanize the hazardous effects of industrialization. The progressive nature of this element needs to be understood against the background of the era's true conservatives, such as the Yale sociologist William Graham Sumner, who resisted social reforms as interrupting the natural flow of Darwinian competition. So while laissez-faire purists like Sumner were conservative exclusionists, reformers like Strong, Walker, and Lodge were progressive exclusionists who, as will become evident in this and subsequent chapters, were better able to adapt and soften their views with changing international circumstances.[25]

The New Expansionism

In addition to progressive reform, a second new element entering the immigration debate at the end of the nineteenth century was territorial expansion. After the Civil War, Seward considered the acquisition of territory and free-flowing Chinese immigration to be parts of an expansive vision of commercial empire in the Pacific. This dream never materialized.

The public did not warm to his territorial ambitions, Congress eventually stopped Chinese labor migration, and U.S.-China trade failed to live up to its hype. Yet thirty years after the Burlingame Treaty stoked the nation's Pacific fantasies, Americans followed through on Seward's expansionism when the country gained possession of the Hawaiian Islands in 1898 and, soon thereafter, the Philippines, Guam, Puerto Rico, and Samoa. The United States joined the ranks of Britain, Germany, Japan, and other imperialist nations. The new insular territories, in turn, stimulated immigration fears about how to keep dark-skinned colonial subjects from entering the metropole and how to prevent the colonies themselves from becoming a backdoor entrance to the United States for the dreaded Chinese.

Imperial expansionism resembled earlier continental expansionism that had brought California, Texas, and Oregon into the nation. Both were backed by pro-business Republicans and justified as the outcome of America's manifest destiny to civilize savage places and people. But the industrial age and the concomitant closing of the frontier compromised the Jeffersonian notion of land-based expansion to promote an empire of liberty. While U.S. imperialism retained the language of freedom, it denied to colonial subjects the reality of American citizenship and democracy. The new possessions, with the exception of Hawai'i, would not be put on a path to statehood and thus would be treated as subordinated political units, much like Britain and other European powers administered its colonies. While paying lip service to Jeffersonian freedoms, the men behind the imperialist surge knew that European Americans would never settle in large numbers in the new possessions, and they believed that the nonwhite peoples living there were racially and culturally incapable of becoming good Americans. In this way, the imperialists were Hamiltonians taking part in a naked grab to gain national power, security, and prestige on the backs of weaker nations and peoples. Gone was Seward's pretense that America sought an "empire of commerce." In its place came the mantra that new possessions would provide markets for the surplus of manufactured goods resulting from the nation's massive industrialization.[26]

Hawai'i was the first of the new territories claimed by the United States. Since foreigners were allowed to own land within the kingdom, American sugar planters and shipping firms had gained increasing political and economic power in the islands. In 1875 the U.S. formalized ties with Hawai'i through a reciprocity treaty that allowed sugar to enter the American market without tariff. This huge boon to the islands' economy was of a piece with the aims of the Burlingame constituency that had promoted transpacific trade and opposed Chinese exclusion. In 1887 American business leaders were instrumental in limiting the power of the Hawaiian monarch, and six years later they overthrew the monarchy itself in a bloodless coup d'état. Much like the Americans who tore Texas away from Mexico, the Hawai'i provisional government lobbied for the United States to annex the islands. Negotiations with President Benjamin Harrison were promising. Aware of the prevalence of anti-Chinese sentiment in Congress, the provisional government assured the United States that Chinese immigrants would be excluded from entering Hawai'i, a practice begun under the monarchy in 1887. The planters further promised to prevent its resident Chinese from venturing to America's West Coast. Yet the return of the Democratic and anti-imperialist Cleveland to the White House ended talk of annexation, forcing Hawai'i to become an independent republic with neither monarch nor guarantees of U.S. embrace.[27]

Led by an oligarchy of plantation owner and managers, the new Hawai'i republic bided its time waiting for Republicans to return to the White House. In the meantime, to emphasize Hawai'i's racial compatibility with the United States, Governor Sanford Dole recruited settlers from the United States as well as "white" migrants from Portugal's Atlantic islands in order to offset Hawai'i's preponderance of Chinese and Japanese immigrants. Dole's government also maintained bars to citizenship and voting rights against Asian immigrants. When Japanese officials protested these restrictions as treaty rights violations, annexationists in the islands misconstrued these as a threat by Japan to claim Hawai'i for itself. The election of William McKinley in 1896 stirred Hawai'i annexationists' hopes as the longtime Republican congressman and former Ohio governor was accompanied by GOP majorities on Capitol Hill. A year and a half later, amid a wave of nationalism generated by the Spanish-American War, Hawai'i officially joined the United States as a territory.[28]

McKinley was an unlikely initiator of the nation's imperialist age. With little interest in foreign affairs, he got drawn into a revolutionary struggle threatening American business interests in the Spanish colony of Cuba. The suspicious sinking of a U.S. battleship in Havana Harbor pushed him to declare war against Spain. America's military plan then expanded to the Philippines, another Spanish colony confronting an organized independence movement. In conjunction with local freedom fighters, U.S. troops overwhelmed Spanish forces in both the Caribbean and Pacific. After a quick and relatively painless victory in the Spanish-American War, McKinley granted conditional independence to Cuba but not the Philippines. Spanish forces in Manila surrendered to U.S. admiral George Dewey rather than to Filipino rebels, and in this way America took the Philippines, along with Puerto Rico and Guam, away from the Spanish crown.[29]

Like the push for immigration exclusion, America's imperial endeavors emerged as part of the nation's adjustment to the industrial age. Historians have identified three factors driving American imperialism: economics, race, and geopolitical interests. First, the acquisition of new territories derived from the search for overseas markets to absorb America's troubling overproduction of manufactured goods. The classic study of the economic foundations of America's acquisition of new territories after the Spanish-American War concludes, "The United States obtained these areas not to fulfill a colonial policy, but to use these holdings as a means to acquire markets for the glut of goods pouring out of highly mechanized factories and farms."[30]

Second, new frontiers were considered essential to renewing a racialized notion of the nation's democratic spirit. In Theodore Roosevelt's eyes, America's greatness stemmed from fighting Indians and interacting with the harsh environment of the American West. New frontiers in the Pacific, as well as in the Caribbean, said Roosevelt, were needed to re-masculinize a people made soft and dull when they traded farm life for civilized urban lifestyles. While immigration exclusion would save the "English-speaking race" from inundation by foreign peoples, imperialism would rejuvenate it through conquest and interaction with savage peoples.[31]

Third, American imperialism resulted from changing geopolitical circumstances. While Seward negotiated the Burlingame Treaty from a position of weakness vis-à-vis the British, the nation's economic might and enlarged naval fleet had dramatically improved its global standing by the time it became an imperialist power. Victory over Spain placed the Americans in a position of strength. Now that the nation had caught up to British trade and power in the Pacific, it sought to protect its competitive advantages amid a host of new imperial players in the Pacific, namely Germany, Russia, and Japan. In this context, Seward's dream of a peaceful empire of commerce was a quaint and distant memory. The new militarized Pacific vision came from Alfred Thayer Mahan, the U.S. naval officer whose study of sea power as the generative force of history guided imperialists like McKinley, Lodge, and Theodore Roosevelt. Mahan's was one of the earliest and most respected voices pushing for the annexation of Hawai'i. To him, a naval base and a coaling station in the islands were crucial for defending America's West Coast. Although less certain about taking the Philippines, Mahan came to accept the colony, and its naval base and coaling station, as crucial to stabilizing increasingly fractious interimperial conflict in East Asia.

The Mahanian vision not only injected national security into America's Pacific dreams but also overturned the Sewardian faith in Chinese immigration. In a letter to the *New York Times* in January 1893, Mahan pointed to Hawai'i's sizable Chinese population as an important, though unaddressed, reason for the United States to annex the islands. "It is a question," he warned, "for the whole civilized world and not for the United States only, whether the Sandwich Islands, with their geographical and military importance, unrivalled by that of any other position in the North Pacific, shall in the future be an outpost of European civilization, or of the comparative barbarism of China."[32] After China lost the Sino-Japanese War in 1895, Mahan's calls for annexing Hawai'i switched to the threat of Japan and its immigrants. He warned Roosevelt, assistant secretary of the U.S. Navy, about Japan's increasingly powerful navy and designs on Hawai'i and the Philippines while urging him to counter Japanese moves by fortifying the Pacific fleet.[33]

Imperialists and exclusionists were born out of the same circumstances of rapid industrialization, immigration, and the shrinking of time and space across the Pacific. But there was a key difference between America's empire building and its gatekeeping that had direct implications for the exclusion debate. Acquiring new territories created new constituencies for managing colonized populations that often opposed outright immigration exclusion. The most obvious example was Hawai'i's plantation oligarchy, which one historian described as a kind of white aristocracy that saw itself as "generous, benevolent, and wise, loving the Islands more than outsiders could know, and . . . [assuming] there was no question but that they knew what was best for Hawaii." Despite platitudes concerning Anglo-Saxon superiority and fears of Asian foreigners, the planter elite, along with their nonvoting representative to the U.S. Congress, were bound by the labor needs of the sugar plantations to oppose hardline exclusionism. In 1901 Hawai'i's acting governor warned that the islands' acute labor shortage would lead to "disastrous results" because it was impossible for the "Anglo-Saxon race" to perform the arduous work done so well by Asian workers. "Hawaii, therefore, is entitled to [immigration] legislation favorable to its greatest prosperity," he stated. Yet beyond material interests, the planter elite were also paternalists who sought to uplift the "lesser races" through education, the church, hospitals, and a host of social service agencies, especially the Young Men's Christian Association.[34]

Hawai'i planters shared the same paternalism of mainland imperialists, which pushed both into the egalitarian camp regarding Asian immigration. Like missionaries, imperialists were bound by a racial logic and aspiration to uplift "savage" peoples and bestow upon them the blessings of civilization, if not salvation. In this way, the "white man's burden" to educate and civilize dark-skinned peoples in newly acquired territories contrasted with the exclusionist's duty to repel and expel the unassimilable Chinese and "Chinee-ized" immigrants. Imperialism was a creed of education and rehabilitation, while exclusionism was one of irredeemable difference and religious and racial damnation. This distinction was not always apparent because both imperialists and exclusionists assumed that Anglo-Saxons were the superior race. The difference, however, was clearly embedded in policies regarding the Philippines.[35] While the American military cast Filipinos as racial enemies and threats, civilian officials, such as President McKinley and the colony's first civil-governor, William Howard Taft, embraced them as "little Brown brothers" who were capable of becoming good Americans. To further this goal, the president, starting in 1901, opened the U.S. Navy to Filipinos. In addition, thousands of American teachers and civil servants came to uplift the Philippines, motivated by the same combination of idealism and opportunism that drove northerners to the South during Reconstruction.[36]

The nation's assimilationist agenda for the Philippines established new egalitarian constituencies for the immigration debate. The most important of these was the Philippine Commission, the legislative body for the islands headed by Taft from 1900 to 1904. During this time the commission began a scholarship program that would send three hundred Filipino students to American universities. The pensionados were to learn important skills that upon their return home could be used to develop the Philippines. These bright youth from the elite *ilustrado* class were also deployed as exemplars of America's benevolent assimilation of their homeland, as well as of the impressive capacity of Filipinos to become American. In recommending pensionados to the University of Michigan, Taft wrote, "I hope that it is the beginning of the education of a great number of young Filipinos in America where they can breathe in the air of Anglo-Saxon individual liberty and Anglo-Saxon civilization."[37] The program's first supervisor recalled that the goal was "to make a favorable impression" on Americans "who mostly thought theretofore that Filipinos wore gee strings and slept in trees." In 1904 the commission ensured that smartly dressed, English-speaking pensionados were showcased at the St. Louis World's Fair, which featured a huge exhibit about America's colony.[38]

Legal decisions bolstered the egalitarian support for Filipino migration to the metropole. With the exception of Hawai'i, none of the residents of the new territories received American citizenship. It was left to the Supreme Court to specify the rights of colonial subjects through a series of decisions known as the Insular Cases. The Court developed the legal concept of "American nationals" to distinguish them from being either aliens or citizens. Egalitarian lawyers like Frederic Coudert invoked the Fourteenth Amendment and *Yick Wo v. Hopkins* in pushing for a broad definition of American nationals as peoples living under U.S. jurisdiction who should be fully protected by the Constitution and Bill of Rights, save for receiving the right to vote. But the Court, Congress, and the Philippine Commission fleshed out a legal position for Filipinos that fell far short of Coudert's definition, with one major exception: Filipinos were deemed to possess the same rights of migration and travel as American citizens and, thus, as bearers of U.S. passports were neither barred from entering the United States like Chinese laborers nor harassed as suspected smuggled laborers or prostitutes like permitted Chinese immigrants.[39]

Another egalitarian constituency entering the exclusion debate was religious groups who sought to uplift Filipinos. The leading organization here was the Lake Mohonk Conference on Friends of the Indian. Begun in 1883 by Quaker and Social Gospeler Albert Smiley, this conference gathered together a wide range of policy makers, scholars, business and religious leaders, and other public figures to discuss and propose humanitarian solutions for the "Indian problem." Senator Henry Dawes was an early attendee who was inspired at Lake Mohonk to draw up the well-known act that bears his name designed to uplift Native Americans by granting them American citizenship and encouraging their assimilation.[40] In 1895, Smiley added a second conference on peace and arbitration to which Josiah Strong, Theodore Roosevelt, Henry Cabot Lodge, and other leading imperialists regularly attended.[41] And with the annexation of new territories, the Indian conference broadened to focus on uplifting different races. Lyman Abbott, the president of the newly named Conference on Friends of the Indian and Other Dependent Peoples, addressed this changed name and the circumstances of imperialism that shaped it:

It was only about a quarter of a century ago that we began to realize that our problem was to civilize the Indians. We had hardly gotten that problem fairly before us before God said to us: "Here are the Porto Ricans . . . and the Filipinos; take them also." And our problem for our insular peoples is the same. It is curious how, when we are just beginning to comprehend a typical problem, that we have been puzzling over for a quarter of a century, God does not take it away from us, but gives us another that is still harder. This is our problem respecting them: it is not to develop Porto Rico . . . or the Philippines; it is to develop Porto Ricans, [and] Filipinos. It is not to get labor to make sugar or fell forests or dig canals or furnish coffee or give us a better livelihood at a cheaper price, it is to make men out of those who are yet but stunted or dwarfed or just beginning to be made.[42]

Like the conference itself, Lyman Abbott represented a connection between nineteenth-century religious reformers and the twentieth-century exclusion debate. He assumed the editorship of the *Christian Union* (which would become the *Outlook*) as well as the pastorship of the Plymouth Church in Brooklyn, New York, from the famous antislavery advocate Henry Ward Beecher. Abbott advanced causes supporting immigrants and racial minorities by serializing pathbreaking books such as Helen Hunt Jackson's *Ramona*, Jacob Riis's *Making of an American*, and Booker T. Washington's *Up from Slavery*. In turning to the nation's latest "dependent peoples," Abbott and the *Outlook* objected to the racial assumptions and harsh treatment proposed by exclusionists in favor of humanitarian uplift toward Anglo-Saxon standards. In this way, the gatherings at Lake Mohonk carried on the egalitarian spirit of the missionaries who defended the Chinese as an assimilable race and protected the treaty rights of permitted Chinese immigrants while at the same time agreeing to the exclusion of laborers, criminals, and prostitutes. Such was the selective nature of turn-of-the-century Christian egalitarianism.[43]

All told, American imperialism brought new players to the exclusion debate who injected into it issues of national security, colonization, and the uplift and rights of colonial subjects. While egalitarians no longer subscribed to the Sewardian notion of free migration, their moderate position on immigration exclusion remained distinct from the hard stance taken by exclusionists, who often sided with the vocal opposition to American imperialism. Indeed, there was a great deal of overlap in the rosters of exclusionists and anti-imperialists. Congressional roll-call votes on annexing Hawai'i and the Philippines were partisan affairs with the overwhelming majority of Democrats opposing the Republican majorities in both houses. Democrats, who feared a powerful federal government and its military, and southerners, who opposed the inclusion of millions of nonwhites into the nation, were allies against American colonization as they were against Chinese immigration. Another carryover from the immigration debate was the AFL and other labor aristocrats. While he backed the war effort in Cuba,

Samuel Gompers vociferously opposed taking territory. He paid particular attention to Hawai'i and the Philippines because of their large populations of potential Asian immigrants. If Hawai'i continues "a species of labor repugnant to the free institutions of our country," he argued in a letter to the Speaker of the House of Representatives, "there is no safeguard against the extension of the same species of contract slave labor to the sugar industry of Louisiana and the cotton fields of the southern states." Gompers went on to assert that annexing Hawai'i was tantamount to ending Chinese exclusion: "It required more than twenty years of constant organization, agitation, and education to legislatively close the gates of our country to the Chinese. The wisdom of that legislation had been demonstrated until there are few, if any, who advocate its repeal. The annexation of Hawai'i would, with one stroke of the pen, obliterate that beneficent legislation and open wide our gates, which would threaten an inundation of Mongolians to overwhelm the free laborers of our country."[44]

Gompers invoked the Chinese again in a speech denouncing annexation of the Philippines. To him, colonization meant increasing the nation's standing army, which could potentially be used to suppress strikes. It also would lead to raising taxes on workers to pay for military and colonial expenses and, worst of all, the migration of millions of Filipino workers, which would result in the "Chineizing of our people, the degeneracy of our institutions, and the possible decadence of our Republic."[45]

Open Door and Closed Gate

Fresh off their victory over Spain and acquisitions of Hawai'i, Guam, and the Philippines, American officials felt entitled to play a leading role in resolving conflict in the northern Pacific. In 1899 Secretary of State John Hay issued the first series of diplomatic notes about America's intention to save China from foreign threats by preserving broad commercial access to its markets. This "Open Door" policy opposed efforts by Russia, Germany, France, Japan, and other imperial powers to carve up China into separate colonial spheres, which would not only impinge on its sovereignty but also impede America's Pacific ambitions. Given U.S. economic might, it was in the nation's best interests to preserve the commercial status quo. Senator Lodge emphasized the urgency of American action: "All Europe is seizing on China and if we do not establish ourselves in the East that vast trade, from which we must draw our future prosperity, and the great region in which alone we can hope to find the new markets so essential to us, will be practically closed to us forever."[46] The Open Door policy also opposed the Qing government's long-standing reluctance to allow foreigners, "white devils," access to its markets, as well as to its peoples through the expanding push by missionaries into the nation's interior regions. The Chinese, in turn, would test the Open Door policy. Faced with severe drought and increasing humiliation by foreign powers, a secret society known to outsiders as "Boxers" launched a rebellion in 1899 whose slogan was "Support the Qing, exterminate the foreigners." The Chinese government split over the Boxer Rebellion, with the dowager empress lending military support to the violent uprising that killed hundreds of foreign missionaries and their native converts. McKinley responded by diverting five thousand troops from America's war in the Philippines to join an international force from eight countries to suppress the rebellion. China was forced to pay a huge indemnity to the victorious powers and on top of that faced an even stronger foreign presence, especially in the north where Russian and Japanese troops remained.

The heightening of imperial rivalries after the Boxer Rebellion pushed American officials to strengthen the Open Door policy. For the first time, they began to back up the nation's commercial interests in China with bold diplomatic and military moves that transformed America's role from interested bystander to enforcer of the commercial status quo. The Open Door, said McKinley, Hay, and a growing chorus of imperialist popularizers like Lodge, Roosevelt, Strong, and Mahan, was not only crucial for America's economic health and national security. It was also consistent with the nation's larger moral responsibility to uplift backward peoples — Chinese no less than Filipinos or native Hawaiians.

America's deepening involvement in China increased the international stakes of the exclusion debate. Well-organized and well-funded interest groups like the business-friendly American Asiatic Association sprang up to lobby for the fair treatment of Chinese immigrants. Led by the indefatigable John Foord, the association consisted of America's leading manufacturers and financiers who were seeking to not only expand U.S.-China trade but also secure lucrative infrastructure contracts, especially from the Chinese government. Combined with traditional egalitarians (missionaries, diplomats, and China traders), the association joined Qing officials and the Six Companies in protesting the harsh treatment meted out to permitted Chinese immigrants from classes exempted from the exclusion policy. Congress had subjected them to increasing scrutiny and discrimination until 1894 when the Gresham-Yang Treaty seemed to take the matter out of its hands. But the situation took a turn for the worse when the U.S. Immigration Bureau assumed administrative control over Chinese immigration in 1900. Under the leadership of Terence Powderly, longtime union organizer and former president of the Knights of Labor, the bureau conducted an all-out campaign against the smuggling of Chinese laborers. Powderly interpreted exclusion law so broadly and capriciously that his campaign ended up preventing nearly all Chinese from entering the country. In addition, the Powderly regime raided Chinese immigrant communities searching for smuggled immigrants and on one occasion in Boston arrested over two hundred people.[47]

Foord galvanized the Open Door constituency to press Congress to stop the bureau's anti-Chinese practices. In 1902 he testified at hearings on Capitol Hill addressing the 1882 act's renewal for a third ten-year period. Foord documented the abuses committed against permitted Chinese immigrants and urged Congress to return to the 1882 act's original intent, which he said was to create a class basis for immigration that denied entry to laborers while admitting middle- and upper-class Chinese. Exclusionists, led by Gompers and skilled labor, countered by rallying bipartisan congressional troops to once again resist the specter of Chinese immigration. In addition to renewing exclusion, Gompers called for the writing into law of Powderly's administrative practices, as well as for extending the ban on Chinese laborers to those coming from Hawai'i and the Philippines. According to one historian, the showdown between exclusionists and egalitarians "ended in a near draw," which amounted to the "first show of strength" for the Open Door constituency. While the Geary Act was renewed and extended to deny entry to Chinese from the new territories, Congress refused to codify into law Powderly's discriminatory practices.[10]

Meanwhile, a showdown on Japanese immigrants was brewing, as their presence in California grew. Already a concern in Hawai'i to Mahan and others involved in the annexation debate, Japanese plantation workers, after completing three-year contracts, often left the islands for better pay and opportunities in California's booming agricultural industry. When needing workers for its new sugar beet operation in Salinas, the Spreckels Sugar Company simply recruited them from its Maui plantation while advancing passage to the Golden State on a company-friendly shipping line. Direct migration from Japan to the West Coast supplemented the Hawai'i pipeline.[49]

Exclusionists took careful note of the rising level of Japanese immigration. The year 1900 marked a major turning point for anti-Japanese activism when unions of skilled workers from the building trades took control of San Francisco government. An early sign was a "monster rally" in the city where attention was drawn to the harmful impact that Japanese immigrants had on the wages and standard of living of white workingmen. Mayor James D.

Phelan warned that "these Asiatic laborers will undermine our civilization and we will repeat the terrible experience of Rome." Stanford University economist and labor union sympathizer Edward Alsworth Ross pushed for Japanese exclusion by explaining that laws of economics foretold that hordes of "cheap labor" from Japan would doom hard-fought efforts by American workers to combat exploitation by capitalists. Ross struck a particularly strident note in proclaiming that "should the worst come to the worst, it would be better for us if we were to turn our guns upon every vessel bringing Japanese to our shore rather than permit them to land." The Japanese Foreign Ministry (Gaimusho) responded to the ruckus in California by voluntarily restricting its labor migrants to the U.S. mainland. Like the Six Companies, Japanese officials sought to nip anti-Japanese protests in the bud before they could blossom into a full-bodied political movement.[50]

Both Phelan and Ross were early California progressives who connected Japanese exclusion to concerns about corporate greed and political corruption. They were joined by newspaper editor and publisher Chester H. Rowell. On the first day of the new millennium in 1901, Rowell warned that America faced two problems that, unless resolved through enlightened, humanitarian means, would ruin the nation's cherished democratic institutions. One was the rising power of Asian nations like Japan, who would increasingly demand (and get) their fair share of the world's riches, resources, and respect. The other was the growth of socialism, which Rowell saw as leading to economic stagnation and political anarchy. In this way, the problem of the twentieth century involved both the color line between whites and Asians as well as the class division between haves and have-nots.[51] In Rowell's mind, the two problems were intertwined in a zero-sum game where resolving one exacerbated the other. Consequently, his calls for Japanese exclusion, in contrast to Phelan's or Ross's, were overlaid with egalitarian concerns for preserving favorable U.S.-Japan relations by respecting Japanese civilization and racial characteristics. "As nations come more and more into contact," he warned, "the question of social equality between them will become a serious problem," because even though Japanese and Americans were biologically incompatible, they were equally civilized.[52]

Rowell's concerns about international relations matched those of the U.S. State Department and other parts of what Californians saw as the "Eastern Establishment." Japan, after all, was an imperialist power with a sizable and battle-tested navy fresh off victory in the Sino-Japanese War. Like European empires, Japan plucked territory from China, including the Ryukyu Islands (Okinawa), Taiwan, and the Liaodong Peninsula in the northern Chinese province of Manchuria. In 1895 Russia, Germany, and

France combined to pressure Japan to forfeit its Manchurian stake, an act exacerbating imperial tension in northern China and neighboring Korea. In contrast, Japan's relations with Britain and the United States were improving after signing commercial treaties with both countries that placed the rising Asian power on equal footing with the most favored nation. This crucial step allowed Japan to become the first non-European country to overcome the handicap and stigma of unequal treaties, the kind that continued to bedevil China. Japan's deepening friendship with Britain and the United States was one reason why these nations did not join the "triple intervention" forcing Japan to give up Manchurian territory. By 1902 Japan cemented its relations with Britain by forging the Anglo-Japanese Alliance, while both the United States and Britain looked to their Asian friend to offset Czarist Russia's threat to the Open Door and China's territorial integrity.

The equalizing of U.S. relations with Japan put a damper on exclusionism. During the ratification of the U.S.-Japan commercial treaty in 1895, a California senator tried to insert a clause permitting the exclusion of Japanese immigration. His amendment, however, was defeated when southern Democrats, focused on the cotton trade with Japan, joined with northeast Republicans to oppose western interests.[53] The good feelings for Japan even extended to craft unions. Gompers became interested in the plight of workers in Japan and as such developed close personal contacts with pioneers of the Japanese labor movement, such as Fusataro Takano. In writing to Takano after the Sino-Japanese War, Gompers showed his respect for Japan (and disdain for China) by suggesting that it would have been better for the liberation of the downtrodden Chinese people had Japan "dismembered" China and "dethroned" the royal family. Takano also corresponded with George Gunton, a prominent American labor writer and editor of the AFL's *Federationist*, which Gompers had sent to Takano. In a letter to the Japanese labor leader, Gunton confirmed that "there is very strong friendly feeling here towards Japan. The truth is, I think, Americans have a higher opinion of the progress Japan has made during the last twenty years than they have of any other country."[54]

Thus while labor unions and progressives in San Francisco were loudly decrying the menace of Japanese immigration, Gompers, Gunton, and the AFL remained uncommitted on the issue of Japanese exclusion. In 1901 at the AFL's national convention in Scranton, Pennsylvania, the organization resolved to consider Japanese immigration separately from its pronouncements against the Chinese. Faced with opposition by some members, Gompers postponed action on Japanese immigration by referring the matter to the AFL's executive council. In support of Gompers's move, the president of the Chicago Federation of Labor noted his opposition to Japanese exclusion because "they are entirely superior to the Chinese . . . and should be elevated." The chair of AFL's Chinese exclusion committee also supported Gompers's decision so as not to divert attention to his cause.[55]

While the AFL hesitated to oppose Japanese immigrants, egalitarians came rushing to their defense. At the front of the line was the Japanese Foreign Ministry, which in the 1890s had established a legation in Washington, D.C., along with consulates in San Francisco, Chicago, and New York. Like China, Japan's foreign ministry employed white Americans for key positions on its consular staff and retained American lawyers to research and write briefs to support the treaty rights of Japanese immigrants. The foreign ministry worked in concert with friends of U.S.-Japan relations, consisting of diplomats, business leaders, scholars, missionaries, and internationalists who in many ways overlapped with the Open Door constituency seeking to protect Chinese immigrants. One friend of Japan was Jane Stanford, widow of Leland Stanford, railroad magnate, former California governor, and major donor to Stanford University. In response to Edward Alsworth Ross's speech denouncing Japanese immigration, Mrs. Stanford had the economics professor fired for his radical views that not only gave credence to dreaded labor unions but threatened to cut off the supply of cheap labor like the kind that built her husband's transcontinental railroad.

Stanford University president David Starr Jordan, the man whom Mrs. Stanford counted on to fire Professor Ross, epitomized another type of friend of Japan.[56] Jordan's pro-Japan sympathies were based in large part on personal experiences and relationships. He had a special fondness for the Japanese, whom, his biographer notes, he "idolized more than . . . any foreign people, with the possible exception of the British." This fascination with Japan grew out of his first trip to the country in 1900 to conduct research on fish species. A well-known ichthyologist, Jordan spent the summer recording the various types of fish inhabiting Japan's waters. In so doing he received crucial assistance from local villagers, whose courtesy and intelligence deeply impressed him. He was also fascinated by the remarkable level of civilization found in rural Japan, where "all towns of 10,000 people or more had a natural history museum, and usually an art gallery as well." This trip, Jordan recalled, proved to be the "most interesting and instructive of all my scientific excursions."[57]

An even more important source of Jordan's Japanophilia was international students from Japan who studied in the United States. Of course, those who went to Stanford were first in his mind. He recounted meeting many of these former students during his first trip to Japan and a subsequent one in 1911. They not only welcomed him to their country but also served him ably as translators, guides, research assistants, and members of Stanford's alumni club. Jordan was quite intimate with these students, and they returned his fatherly affection by bestowing upon him the exalted respect for a "dear teacher." But Jordan's positive encounters with Japanese international students were not limited to Stanford alums. He called all students educated in England and the United States the best examples of Japan's remarkable modernization; they were the natural enemies of militarism and thus essential to maintaining peaceful relations in the Pacific region.[58]

A consummate scholar, Jordan was under no illusion that every Japanese was elite, educated, and peace-minded. He admitted to paying little attention during his first Japan trip to the "grinding poverty of unskilled urban workmen," "long hours of factory hands, both women and men," and the "treadmill of child labor." He also consistently argued that Japan's caste system and treatment of women inhibited its democratic progress. Most important for our purposes, Jordan distinguished sharply between much-despised Japanese "coolie" laborers and his beloved international students. The former, to him, were clannish and unassimilable and threatened to become a permanent underclass in California. But he differentiated undesirable and desirable Asian immigrants by opposing the exclusion of international students and other types of Japanese elites.[59]

Jordan created scientific justifications for his defense of Japanese immigrants that intertwined with his personal rationales. Important here was his unorthodox interpretation of race theory. Jordan was a confirmed social Darwinist who, like the vast majority of scientists around the world, believed that separate and distinct races (or types of people) were a biological fact of nature. By applying lessons learned from his research on fish to humans, he was convinced that some races needed to be protected and encouraged to flourish by excluding others. Following the evolutionary theory of Charles Darwin and the social applications of evolutionism by Herbert Spencer, he agreed that out of hundreds of races, some, through the process of natural selection, developed superior traits through which they gained an advantage in the world. The superior races, including Aryans, Nordics, Anglo-Saxons, and Teutons, established the most civilized and militarily powerful nations. In this way, a nation's fate was determined by its biological composition; a healthy mixture of "superior" races pointed toward a great future, while too many "inferior" ones led to stagnation and disaster.[60] The science of distinguishing superior and inferior races and identifying the conditions under which the superior could flourish was called "eugenics." It followed then that eugenicists paid a great deal of attention to issues of immigration policy so as to have a mechanism for calibrating the right racial mixture of a society. After leaving Stanford, Ross joined with Harry Laughlin, Charles Davenport, Madison Grant, and other leading eugenics scholars in creating rationales for broad-based immigration exclusion rooted in race science. Their research provided intellectual justification for exclusionary immigration policies that restricted Asians as well as Europeans and other immigrants in nations across the globe.[61]

While Jordan's support for the exclusion of Japanese laborers derived from his practice of eugenics, his defense of international students and other elites from Japan ran contrary to conventional wisdom among eugenicists. Here is where his unorthodox view of race comes in. Jordan disagreed with Spencer's conclusion that the racial mixture of Japanese and Europeans would be a "bad one." In Japan he had met and approved of many elite Japanese men married to European or American women, including the world-renowned writer and eventually undersecretary of the League of Nations Inazo Nitobe. Jordan also saw for himself that the Eurasian wife of Tokyo's mayor was hardly the bad result of a mixed marriage. All of this supported Jordan's theory that the Japanese made up a "white" race. He was convinced that "fundamentally the Japanese, perhaps primitively of the Aryan race, with large admixtures of Chinese, Malay, and Manchu blood, are not so different from the western peoples."[62]

More important to Jordan than tracing bloodlines were "superior" Japanese racial characteristics. Blood mattered to Jordan, but not pure blood, and so despite their small drop of Aryan blood, he included the "Samurai" with the "Greek, Roman, Frank, Saxon, Norman, Dane, Celt, Scot, and Goth" as "free men" endowed with the biological propensity for democracy. What mattered most was that each of these groups possessed the "good virtues and morals" of self-restraint, abstinence, efficiency, initiative, and frugality. In other words, as Jordan's biographer argues, the Japanese were compatible with the spirit of puritanism that was so important for establishing the American Republic.[63]

Jordan and Mrs. Stanford represented an emerging constituency to prevent Japanese exclusion, an issue that in the early twentieth century would move to the center of the exclusion debate. It is tempting to view the emerging conflict over Japanese immigration as a reenactment of the earlier clash over Chinese exclusion. Such a view, one the one hand, correctly compares U.S.-Japan commercial agreements to the Burlingame Treaty as historic treaties creating a wave of good feeling and economic aspirations that kept West Coast exclusionists in check. But, on the other hand, it ignores two historical changes that set off the 1890s from the 1870s. By the latter decade, exclusionism had become the law of the land backed by a solid bipartisan consensus and a powerful nativist movement to expand Chinese exclusion to include new migrants from Europe and Canada. The dawning of America's imperial age proved the second major change. Acquiring new Pacific territories with sizable Asian populations created new pipelines for Asian immigration to the U.S. mainland that galvanized both egalitarians and exclusionists. The Open Door policy, coupled with the increasing centrality of U.S. involvement in the Pacific and East Asia, would create new political barriers and opportunities for the exclusionist cause and, in the process, propel the exclusion debate into the new century.

4 RISING TIDE OF FEAR

WHITE AND YELLOW PERILS, 1904–1919

|||||||||||||||||||||||||||||||||||||||||||||||||||||||||||||||||||||||||||||||||||||||||||||||||||||||||||||||||||||||||||||||||||

In December 1906, the exclusion debate returned to the center of American politics as a major topic in President Theodore Roosevelt's sixth State of the Union address to Congress. Echoing his earlier presidential addresses as well as those by his predecessor William McKinley, Roosevelt pronounced the crucial importance of the nation's East Asian trade. "The countries bordering the Pacific Ocean," he noted, "have a population more numerous than that of all the countries of Europe; their annual foreign commerce amounts to over three billions of dollars, of which the share of the United States is some seven hundred millions of dollars." The president urged Americans to increase their share of this trade so that the nation, including West Coast industries and cotton manufacturing states, could reap a tremendous windfall. But, he warned, "in order to get these benefits, we must treat fairly the countries with which we trade."[1]

Roosevelt followed these remarks with a lengthy discourse about mutually respectful international relations that was reminiscent of William H. Seward's defense of Chinese immigrants at the height of the Burlingame constituency. Without saying so directly, the president condemned anti-Japanese hostility in California, shaking his "big stick" against that "very small body of our citizens that act badly." He contradicted racial rationales for exclusion by reading a long list of Japan's achievements as "one of the greatest of civilized nations; great in the arts of war and in the arts of peace; great in military, in industrial, in artistic development and achievement." He also proposed two recommendations for resolving the conflict. First was to amend the nation's naturalization law so that Japanese immigrants could become U.S. citizens. Next was to grant the federal government more powers over localities so as to prevent the "mob of a single city" from performing "acts of lawless violence against some class of foreigners which would plunge us into war." Here Roosevelt came to the crux of the matter. Unlike with Chinese immigrants, racist acts committed against the Japanese threatened to push the United States into an unwanted military conflict with Japan.[2]

This chapter addresses the militarization of the exclusion debate when national security fears merged with preexisting anxieties about immigration and labor. Given the weakness of China, such military fears were largely absent in a final showdown over Chinese exclusion, in which Roosevelt's worries about the disruption of U.S.-China trade did not prompt him to stand up for Chinese immigrants. But national security issues took on a heightened role in the immigration debate after Japan's stunning victory in the Russo-Japanese War. Exclusionists warned that Japanese immigrants were infiltrating the United States in order to pave the way for Japan's conquest of California and America's Pacific territories. On the contrary, egalitarians condemned such yellow peril fear, as well as the discrimination it justified, as itself the main threat to peace. In this way, Roosevelt viewed American racism as a white peril that could lead the country into war. Such a threat pushed him, and later President Woodrow Wilson, to play an active role in major international crises emerging from California's anti-Japanese movement. Yet neither president could derail the West Coast determination for Japanese exclusion. When Roosevelt died in 1919, the debate remained unresolved as exclusionists stood firmly behind discriminatory state and local policies, while egalitarians sought to maintain world peace by preventing Congress from an outright ban on Japanese immigration.

Threats to the Open Door

In speaking out forcefully against anti-Japanese hostility, Roosevelt did for Japan what he was unwilling to do for China. He had supported exclusionism in the 1890s and in his first presidential address to Congress in 1901 called "to re-enact immediately the law excluding Chinese laborers and to strengthen it wherever necessary in order to make its enforcement entirely effective."[3] In addition, he kept exclusionists in control of the Immigration Bureau by replacing Terence Powderly with Frank P. Sargent, a westerner and close associate of Samuel Gompers. When Qing officials refused to renew the Gresham-Yang Treaty in protest against the bureau's discrimination of Chinese immigrants, the president showed little interest in negotiating a new accord and instead allowed Congress to pass legislation that removed exclusion from existing treaties. The resulting 1904 act made the exclusion of Chinese laborers permanent and no longer subject to ten-year renewal.[4]

Apart from its standard racist rationales, Roosevelt's exclusionism paid heed to political realities. As a candidate for president, Roosevelt played up anti-Chinese policies in order to woo western voters. At the same time, he played down immigration issues elsewhere in the country because they divided Republicans between business expansionists, who welcomed cheap labor, and progressives, who opposed it as an element of plutocratic rule. After winning the presidency in 1904 (in which he swept the West), Roosevelt was in a better position to listen to egalitarians in his party as they sought to reform the Immigration Bureau's discrimination against Chinese immigrants by restoring rights of entry to the exempt classes. But drawing his attention even more was a major international boycott of American goods that spread from overseas Chinese communities to China's major cities and towns. A response to the Exclusion Act of 1904, this protest spurred nationalist fervor as propagandists throughout China used immigration grievances to generate what the boycott's historian calls "one of the earliest and largest urban popular movements in modern China."[5]

As American trade and investment in China suffered, and as American missionaries became increasingly unnerved by the return of antiforeign hostility reminiscent of the Boxer Rebellion, the president sprang to action. He started an investigation of the Immigration Bureau's Chinese Service while also replacing the secretary overseeing the agency, an anti-Chinese Californian, with a Jewish immigrant from New York who was more concerned with excluding anarchists than Chinese. At the same time, John Foord and the American Asiatic Association lobbied Congress for a bill that would repudiate the Powderly-Sargent regime of anti-Chinese regulations. The end of the Chinese boycott in 1906, however, took the wind out of egalitarian sails, as the president allowed exclusionists in Congress to kill the Asiatic Association's bill and failed to come to terms on a new U.S.-China treaty that would protect the rights of entry for the exempt classes. Another sign of Roosevelt's retreat was his appointment of another prolabor sympathizer to replace Sargent as head of the Immigration Bureau. In the end, the president, like most progressive egalitarians, was unwilling to expend much political capital to defend the rights of the Chinese exempt classes. Despite the persistent allure of the China market, U.S. trade and investment there was still in its infancy and thus did not persuade Roosevelt to jump off the exclusionist bandwagon.[6]

The situation was different with respect to Japan. Due to the lack of compelling national interests in China, the United States was unwilling to fight to maintain that country's territorial integrity. In this way, Roosevelt looked to Japan as an ally to thwart what he believed to be the greatest threat to the Open Door, the Russian Empire. Clashing Russian and Japanese interests in northeast Asia pushed the two countries into war in 1904. Although the United States remained neutral, Roosevelt cheered for Japan and warned Germany and France that if they joined with Russia, his country would take up arms against them. The preponderance of American public opinion sided with Japan as a progressive nation in step with modern times, unlike the barbaric Russian Empire. Lyman Abbott's editorial in the *Outlook* characterized the Russo-Japanese War as one "between the twentieth century and the sixteenth."[7]

During the heyday of Anglo-Saxon race theories, it was unusual for Americans to side with an Asian nation over a seemingly white, Christian people. But Japan was exceptional, and as a result its emergence as a world power caused American supporters to do much twisting of conventional racial logic. For Roosevelt, Japan's defeat of Russia only heightened his already strong respect for the island nation. As vice president, he had applauded Japanese troops as the best fighters among the eight powers suppressing the Boxer Rebellion. "What extraordinary soldiers those little Japs are," he had exclaimed to close friend and English diplomat Cecil Spring-Rice. After Japan's stunning naval victory over Russia in 1905, Roosevelt, now president, "grew so excited that I myself became almost like a Japanese, and I could not attend to official duties."[8]

But celebrating naval victories and conveying the kind of deep respect for Japan that Roosevelt displayed in his sixth message to Congress were not the same as embracing the Japanese as kin. While Roosevelt felt closer to the Japanese than he did to Russians and other "Aryan races," he commented to Spring-Rice that "their thoughts are not our thoughts." The difference was not biological, as Herbert Spencer, the famous social Darwinist, argued in opposing race mixing between whites and Japanese. Rather, based on his extensive knowledge of history, Roosevelt believed that it resulted from centuries of cultural separation between Europe and Asia that could not be erased by a generation of Japanese modernization. While Thomas Hart Benton, the mid-nineteenth-century expansionist senator whom Roosevelt lionized in a well-regarded biography, had been optimistic that Americans and Chinese could intermarry and thus bridge the East-West divide, the president saw the much-vaunted melting pot as applying only to Europeans. The Japanese, he was convinced, were racially equal to whites but so culturally different that there should be no mass intermingling between the two, lest there be disastrous conflict leading to race warfare.[9]

Alfred Thayer Mahan, another one of Roosevelt's heroes, also walked a fine line between identifying Japan as a member of the "European family" while at the same time recognizing clear racial limitations between whites and Japanese. In the debate over Hawai'i annexation, Mahan warned about Japan's designs on the islands and how these were being manifest through the invasion of immigrants. With the start of America's Open Door policy, however, he turned his attention from the Pacific to continental Asia. His explanation of the racial characteristics of the Japanese, laid out in 1900, provides a fuller perspective than Roosevelt's of the impact that Japan's rise of world power had on American leaders. Mahan embraced Japan as a "Teutonic power" committed, along with other Teutons (Americans, British, and Germans) to maintaining the Open Door against the threat of the "Slavic peril" from Russia. In this way, the Japanese were the first "Asiatic" race to be undergoing a long-term evolutionary process in which it was taking on not just the material trappings of the West but, more important, the intellectual and moral traditions of Western civilization: "In Japan, and as yet in Japan alone, do we find the Asiatic welcoming European culture, in which, if a tree may fairly be judged by its fruit, is to be found the best prospect for the human race to realize the conditions most conducive to its happiness,—personal liberty, in due combination with restraints of law sufficient to, but not in excess of, the requirements of the general welfare." If Seward was right that steamship commerce broke the barrier between East and West, then Mahan was arguing that Japan's commitment to the Open Door marked the first sign that Asians and Europeans were assimilating in ways that Seward had only fantasized.[10]

But, like Roosevelt, Mahan equivocated about the degree to which the Japanese were similar to Europeans. When comparing them to the dreaded Slavs, the Japanese appeared in a positive light. Yet Mahan grew more cautious when geopolitical considerations in China were not his main concern. In presenting Japan's westernization as a young tree, he was careful to point out that the sapling had yet to develop deep roots. He wrote, "Japan is still under the disadvantage, by no means irretrievable, that the exterior and material characteristics of European civilization have been received too recently and rapidly for entire assimilation. In the short time that has elapsed since national political conversion began, it is not possible that chance can have penetrated far below the surface, modifying essential traits and modes of thought."[11] The shallowness of Japan's westernization became an increasing worry for Mahan after the outcome of the Russo-Japanese War allayed his fears about Russian incursions in China. Now, in his mind, Japan presented the major threat to the Open Door.[12]

Mahan was not alone in his fears about Japan's intentions in China. Roosevelt too worried about Japan getting a "big head" after the war and wanted Russia to remain a viable power in Asia so as to check Japanese influence. In brokering the peace treaty between Japan and Russia, the president moderated Japan's demands in seeing to it that Russia did not have to pay a crippling war indemnity. This provoked outrage from the Japanese press, which decried Roosevelt's duplicity in pretending to be the nation's great friend. At the same time, critical views of Japan began to capture public opinion in the United States. While the idea of Japan as a yellow peril bent on world conquest had been introduced by Kaiser Wilhelm in 1892, this notion did not gain traction within the American mainstream until after the Russo-Japanese War. American war correspondents played a crucial role in spreading yellow peril fears. While some, like George Kennan, who reported for the *Outlook*, cast Japan in a positive light, the vast majority of correspondents, perhaps due to their mistreatment by the Japanese military, stoked the flames of race hatred.[13]

The best example of these fearmongers was Jack London, novelist, Californian, and war correspondent for the *Oakland Tribune*. London operated from the same basic race principles as Roosevelt and Mahan: that the Japanese had materially caught up to the West but still remained fundamentally different from Europeans. The Californian, however, treated race difference as a brute fact of nature rather than as part of a hopeful evolutionary process in which the Japanese were becoming Western. "The leopard cannot change his spots," London stated, "nor can the Japanese, nor can we." While Roosevelt was reluctant to place a judgment on the differences between Japanese and Americans, London had no problem in declaring the Japanese to be the religiously and ethically inferior race. Unlike Americans, a "religious race" committed to social righteousness and personal salvation, the Japanese were blind worshippers of the emperor and his government. "He relates himself to the State as, amongst bees, the worker is related to the hive; himself nothing, the State everything; his reasons for existence the exaltation and glorification of the State," London pointed out. Lacking a Christian soul, Japan could never be trusted to do the right thing in keeping the peace in China. London maintained that the real yellow peril came not from the Japanese alone but from their ability as Asians to manage four hundred thousand Chinese in a joint effort to overthrow the West.[14]

Such racialized fears provoked defense of the Japanese from egalitarians who joined the Open Door constituency in condemning America's shoddy treatment of Asian peoples. Some of the first aroused were American missionaries in Japan, who, like their counterparts in China and American Chinatowns, viewed race through the lens of Christian theology, self-interest, and years of intimate experiences with "the Other." As experts on foreign cultures, often with bilingual skills, missionaries played an important role as America's eyes and ears on the world at a time before there were extensive diplomatic corps, foreign correspondents, and international relations scholars. So it was that Sidney Gulick, a forty-five-year-old bilingual

American missionary who had been assigned to Japan since 1888, entered the policy discussion about the Japanese threat to the Open Door. Gulick sought to turn the yellow peril discourse on its head by publishing a book arguing that this peril, though very real, was in fact a reaction to the "white man's" bad behavior in Asia and his sense of superiority over its peoples, institutions, and cultures. Gulick used Japan's military victories over Russia as an occasion to warn Americans that the "yellow man" would no longer tolerate abuse by Westerners and that if these resentments remained, they would boil over into a race war far worse than the Boxer Rebellion in which Asians "will destroy the white man's banks, railroads, factories and all his enterprises and drive him with curses and bloodshed from his land."[15] The only way to stop the yellow peril was to address the white peril of racism and imperialism, without which there would be no real Asian threat. The "white race," he concluded, "must abandon its cherished conviction of essential racial superiority and of its inherent right to dominate the earth, and to subordinate all coloured races to its own economic interests. So long as this conviction is held as an ideal, *so long is the white race to continue a peril to the peace and welfare of the earth.*"[16]

Movement in California

Racism in California, and not just in Asia, would provide another source of white peril. The state's anti-Japanese hostility in 1900, which prompted Japan to stop issuing passports to laborers seeking to migrate to the U.S. mainland, continued to gain momentum so that five years later the idea of Japanese exclusion moved onto the agenda of California politics. The state's anti-Japanese movement grew out of the same social and political conditions that produced the long-standing hostility against Chinese immigrants. Led by politically powerful skilled labor unions and influential San Francisco newspapers, local hostility against Japanese immigration became a statewide cause to guarantee economic opportunity for aspiring whites by limiting access to the state's labor market and natural resources. At the same time, the anti-Japanese movement sought to restrict the ability of big businesses to undercut labor unions by relying on cheap foreign workers. In these ways, fears of racial dispossession continued to grease the wheels of exclusionism, although with the Japanese they took on military overtones. And, as with the Chinese, California's protest rang true throughout the American West with states such as Nevada, Montana, and Idaho also submitting early warnings to Congress about the menace of Japanese immigration.[17]

A key catalyst for the resurgence of exclusionist protests in the West was the Japanese and Korean Exclusion League, an interest group established in May 1905 with deep roots in San Francisco politics and organized labor, particularly its Building Trades Council. The league's president, Olaf Tveitmoe, an ex-convict and veteran of violent business-labor clashes, took an aggressive stance against the Japanese that was reminiscent of Denis Kearney and his anti-Chinese "sandlot" supporters. Tveitmoe led a boycott against Japanese restaurants in San Francisco, ostensibly for reasons of labor equity, and he called on league members to pressure school board officials to remove the small number of Japanese students from classrooms shared with whites by requiring that they attend the city's segregated Chinese school. The anti-Japanese movement thrived amid the chaos of the great earthquake and fire that destroyed much of San Francisco in April 1906. Assaults against Japanese immigrants increased dramatically, and even two distinguished scientists from Japan studying the effects of the massive quake were victimized by repeated racial abuse. Adding insult to injury, San Francisco school officials in November 1906, despite vigorous objections by President Roosevelt and Japanese officials, enacted the segregation policy for Japanese students.[18]

Thus was the immediate context for President Roosevelt's sixth message to Congress in which he championed the greatness of Japan and threatened to use his big stick to thwart racism in California. Just before delivering the speech in December 1906, Roosevelt read with great approval a report submitted by Secretary of Commerce and Labor Victor Metcalf, whom he personally had sent to San Francisco to investigate the anti-Japanese situation. A Californian with a track record of exclusionism, Metcalf was caught between filial duty to Roosevelt and duty to his home state. The report represented a compromise in which the author simply listed facts, offering no interpretations or judgments. But Metcalf's findings convinced the president that there was no credible basis for segregating Japanese students or for the myriad other forms of anti-Japanese hostility and discrimination. Consequently, Roosevelt condemned in his address the "wicked absurdity" of segregating Japanese students and in private referred to Californians as "infernal fools" who would put at risk America's national security by needlessly provoking Japan. The message to Congress was his attempt "to let not only the Californians but the rest of the my countrymen know that no political considerations would interfere for a moment with my using the armed forces of the country to protect the Japanese if they were molested in their persons and property."[19]

Roosevelt's show of force, which pleased the Japanese greatly, failed to resolve the problem in San Francisco. The threat of using federal troops to block the segregation order only steeled the exclusionists' resolve while arousing calls from them to impeach the president. Metcalf was denounced as a traitor and Roosevelt as a stooge; the secretary's report was ignored. The California legislature retaliated by proposing a bill to prevent Japanese immigrants from owning farmland. Roosevelt's big stick had become a boomerang that came back to inflict political harm. In the face of California intransigence, as well as the constitutional reality of states' rights, the president sought compromise. He invited the entire San Francisco school board to Washington, D.C., where he got members to rescind the segregation order in exchange for his stopping the steady influx of Japanese migrants from Hawai'i, as well as his securing a Gentlemen's Agreement with Japan to make formal its self-imposed prohibition against Japanese laborers migrating to the U.S. mainland. In the face of this compromise, Roosevelt also got California's governor to halt pending alien land legislation. In this way, the two major sources of Japanese labor migration, from Hawai'i and straight from Japan, would cease, and the California problem, for the time being, disappeared from the headlines.[20]

Although in many ways a sequel to conflicts over Chinese immigration, the segregation crisis revealed a largely new cast of characters in the exclusion debate. Holdovers on the exclusion side were Samuel Gompers and the American Federation of Labor. While hesitant to back Japanese exclusion at the AFL's national convention in 1901, and while maintaining friendly ties to the nascent labor movement in Japan, Gompers encouraged California exclusionists. In 1904 the AFL joined the anti-Japanese campaign by passing a resolution calling for Japanese exclusion. Such cooperation was consistent with labor struggles in California in which the AFL and Olaf Tveitmoe's San Francisco Building Trades Council worked together in the face of employers' open shop movement to ban unions. To understand the perspective of mainstream labor leaders and exclusionists like Tveitmoe and Gompers, it is crucial to see their antagonism against Japanese immigrants in the context of the nation's violent industrial relations.

The state's major battle was raging in Los Angeles, where employer organizations, with vociferous support from the *Los Angeles Times*, were transforming Southern California into a stalwart opponent of the labor-friendly North. So it was that two brothers, with extensive ties to organized labor and assistance from San Francisco unionists, committed the "crime of the century" in bombing the *Los Angeles Times* building in 1910. Twenty-one people died, and in addition to the perpetrators of the violence, Tveitmoe and other labor activists were arrested. Gompers stood behind the bombers and committed significant AFL resources in a failed bid to win their freedom. The Socialist Party, too, supported the bombers, as its leader Eugene V. Debs explained: "It is easy enough for a gentleman of education and refinement to sit at his typewriter and point out the crimes of the workers. But let him be one of them himself, reared in hard poverty, denied education, thrown into the brute struggle for existence from childhood, oppressed, exploited, forced to strike, clubbed by the police, jailed while his family is evicted, and his wife and children are hungry, and he will hesitate to condemn these as criminals who fight against the crimes of which they are the victims of such savage methods as have been forced upon them by their masters." Given the state of class warfare at the time, Socialists joined with the AFL and the San Francisco Building Trades Council in condemning the seeming importation of Japanese immigrants as yet another weapon for victimizing American workers.[21]

Progressives, unlike labor activists, were a relatively new element in the exclusion debate, and in California they came in two varieties. One was urban Democrats like James D. Phelan, mayor of San Francisco and son of an Irish Catholic immigrant who made a fortune in the gold rush. Though sympathetic to labor, Phelan was cut from a different cloth from the likes of Tveitmoe and the greater membership of his Japanese and Korean Exclusion League. The mayor was a patron of the arts and high culture who entertained celebrities at his magisterial Italianate estate. Treating California as if it was one of his treasured antiquities, Phelan sought to restore and preserve its "European" heritage by excluding nonwhite foreigners like the Japanese. This is why at San Francisco's monster rally in 1900 he warned that "these Asiatic laborers will undermine our civilization and we will repeat the terrible experience of Rome." Phelan's nativism merged with his progressivism as the reform mayor sought to clean up corruption in San Francisco politics. A darling of the exclusionist Hearst press, which included the *San Francisco Examiner*, the mayor would play a powerful role in advancing the anti-Japanese movement long after he left city government in 1902.[22]

Chester Rowell represented the Republican side of progressive exclusionism. A reformer who watched San Francisco politics carefully from the Fresno hinterlands, Rowell, like Phelan, was committed to cleaning up corrupt politics in the Golden State. As editor of the *Fresno Republican*, he spearheaded a campaign to regulate gambling and prostitution in the Central Valley city's Chinatown. In 1907 he set his sights on Sacramento in gathering progressive Republicans into the Lincoln-Roosevelt League, which in three years opened a new chapter in California politics by breaking the long-standing political hegemony of the Southern Pacific Railroad.

Rowell was the mastermind behind the state's Progressive Party and the election of its candidate, Hiram Johnson, as governor in 1910. Like Phelan, Rowell's anti-Japanese position was not born out of class struggle or Socialist or other radical ideologies. Rather, it grew out of a critique of the greed and corruption of big business. If employers had their way, he argued, California would become "Orientalized" as a civilization "based on white aristocracy and coolie servility." To prevent such a "calamity," Rowell asserted that "it is better that the [state's] fruit industry be destroyed than that imported servile labor be made a permanent part of our population and a permanent element in our industrial system."[23]

Rowell's first editorial on the Japanese immigration question, written in September 1904, agreed with plans by San Francisco school officials to remove to segregated schools adult Japanese studying alongside children and adolescents in the city's public schools. But, unlike the school officials, he had no objection to Japanese school-age children staying in the public schools. Rowell maintained that the Japanese were racially different from but equal to whites, and they acquired "our civilization as rapidly as any foreigners not of our own immediate kindred." One sign of this was how Japanese immigrants had shown the "very faults of the white men" in breaking labor contracts in order to "get the better of the bargain." Rowell also attributed to Japanese immigrants the greatness of their home country, which was "now demonstrating in [the Russo-Japanese] war what . . . [it] had already demonstrated in the arts of peace, that they are anybody's equals." After Russia's defeat, Rowell sounded like Theodore Roosevelt in issuing this fulsome praise: "By the test of war, by which we measure ourselves, the Japanese have done better than we could do." In this critical way, Rowell differed markedly from Phelan and organized labor in moderating his support of Japanese exclusion due to concerns about its negative effect on U.S.-Japan relations.[24]

David Starr Jordan, the eugenicist president of Stanford University, provided another leading voice in California on the issue of Japanese immigration, but, unlike Phelan and Rowell, he opposed the exclusion movement. Jordan, a great friend of Japan who received two special awards from the Japanese emperor, distinguished between acceptable and unacceptable Japanese immigrants. While agreeing that laborers should be banned from entering the United States because they were unassimilable, he felt strongly that this was not the case for better classes of Japanese (like international students at Stanford) who displayed race characteristics on a par with the greatest of Europeans. Another basis for Jordan's egalitarianism was his active involvement in bettering international relations. What distinguished him, as well as Roosevelt and Rowell, from the vast majority of Americans was his recognition that America's fate as a nation was inextricably bound with those of East Asian nations. While most Americans either denied or dreaded the nation's Pacific destiny, Jordan embraced this historic moment by encouraging Californians in particular to work closely with peoples across the Pacific. Because "Japan and China must be our neighbors for the next thousand years, it is above all vital that the [nation's] frontier be guarded with courtesy and friendship."[25]

Western Exclusionism versus Eastern Egalitarianism

Jordan's and even Rowell's recognition of the primacy of international relations in the local conflict over Japanese immigration put them in good stead with America's eastern establishment. As was the case with the Chinese, the nation's business elite supported the president and his administration in seeking to prevent western racial policies from jeopardizing Pacific investment and trade. An important sign of this eastern egalitarianism was the creation in 1907 of the Japan Society of New York, the first organization in the United States solely focused on U.S.-Japan relations. Here was a response by American and Japanese elites to counteract the damage done by the segregation crisis. The moment was ripe for this new kind of transpacific organization as American international lawyers, like Roosevelt's secretary of state Elihu Root and the Japan Society's director Lindsay Russell, became increasingly invested in the movement for global arbitration catalyzed by a series of conferences at The Hague in the Netherlands. Others, such as publicist Hamilton Holt, a founding member of the Japan Society, went even further to promote international peace by seeking to create the framework for world government, an early conception of the League of Nations. A leading voice of American opinion, Holt was editor of the *Independent*, a thriving Social Gospel publication that rivaled (although on the issue of Asian immigration often agreed with) Lyman Abbott's *Outlook*. Theodore Roosevelt, in a belated lecture for the Nobel Peace Prize he won in 1906, embraced Holt's movement for world government.[26]

Even more important to the formation of a U.S.-Japan constituency was the industrialist Andrew Carnegie, who by this time had retired from the steel business to become a full-time philanthropist dedicated especially to the cause of world peace. A letter from Carnegie was read at an early Japan Society banquet that cheered the wisdom of American and Japanese leaders for resolving the segregation conflict. The philanthropist's greetings revealed an optimistic faith that nations were giving up on war and that the long-standing U.S.-Japan friendship provided "special reasons why the people of Japan and America should never kill each other like wild beasts on the field of battle." After providing funds to build the "peace palace" for the permanent court of arbitration at The Hague, Carnegie outdid himself in 1910 by granting $10 million to create the Carnegie Endowment for International Peace, headquartered in Washington and New York City and led by Elihu Root, who had served as secretary of state under Roosevelt. Three years later John D. Rockefeller donated even more money than Carnegie to set up his own foundation dedicated to improving the world through the sciences, public health, and medical education. Such massive undertakings as the Carnegie Endowment and Rockefeller Foundation created a new infrastructure for a class of elite and educated Americans to engage in global affairs.[27]

The rise of international organizations, on the one hand, facilitated the replacement of missionaries with secular, university-trained specialists as America's eyes and ears on the world. But, on the other hand, missionaries and Social Gospelers themselves transformed into ostensibly secular specialists to become active at all levels of these internationalist endeavors. Hamilton Holt exemplified the latter mode of international engagement. Like Lyman Abbott, Holt came from a family steeped in the Congregationalist Church, which had been home to staunch abolitionists and, after the Civil War, supporters of African American civil rights and social uplift. While in graduate school in sociology and economics at Columbia University, Holt took over the *Independent*, a journal founded by his grandfather, and transformed it into a secular fount of liberal opinion about urban and labor problems, as well as about issues of immigration and international affairs. Consistent with his involvement in the Japan Society, Holt worked with the Carnegie Endowment to establish a U.S.-Japan scholarly exchange that began in 1912 with Inazo Nitobe coming to the United States. Nitobe was well regarded by Roosevelt as well as by many other Americans through his book *Bushido* (about the way of the samurai). The following year, Holt would send to Japan Hamilton Mabie, who had replaced Lyman Abbott as the editor of his rival journal, the *Outlook*. This scholarly exchange was the extent of the endowment's engagement with Japan until another international crisis in California compelled Carnegie to do more to promote U.S.-Japan peace.[28]

To western exclusionists, the Japanese problem did not end with the resolution of the school segregation issue. A devil lurked in the details of the Gentlemen's Agreement: entry was allowed for the immediate relatives of Japanese immigrants already in the United States. This meant that while Japanese laborers were barred from entering the U.S. mainland, the wives and children of those who had arrived before the agreement took effect were free to come—and so too were merchants, students, teachers, diplomatic personnel, missionaries, and others who did not fall into the "laborers" category. As with the Chinese, exclusionists suspected widespread fraud in the admission of tens of thousands of persons from these exempt classes. The practice of "picture brides," in which immigrant men married in absentia through the exchange of photographs, was especially alarming because it generated a new wave of female immigrants to America, who then proceeded to give birth to a sizable second generation of American citizens. If the "Orientalization" of California servile labor was bad enough, the idea of large, self-perpetuating colonies of unassimilable Japanese was considered an even worse threat to California's democratic institutions.

Exclusionists ignored class differences among the Japanese, just as they ignored differences between first-generation immigrants (issei) and second-generation U.S. citizens (nisei). Soon after the Gentlemen's Agreement began, an increasing number of issei started to climb the social ladder by moving out of agricultural labor and into small farming. The shining example was George Shima (Kinji Ushijima), an early Japanese immigrant millionaire, who built an agricultural empire growing potatoes and other crops on reclaimed wastelands. But for every "potato king," there were tens of thousands of Japanese family farms that struggled to earn a living by growing high-risk specialty crops like strawberries on small plots of leased land. The issei shift from migrant labor to farming prompted exclusionists to move away from the argument that Japanese laborers posed a threat to white workers and instead to decry that the Japanese posed a threat to white farmers by monopolizing large tracts of productive farmland. While San Francisco unionists and politicians continued to push for exclusion, the anti-Japanese movement gained momentum in the agricultural regions in the Sacramento delta that were undergoing massive flood control and land reclamation projects. One of the rationales for these projects was to open up affordable farmland that would counter the state's entrenched tradition of aristocratic, absentee landholding. To progressives like *Sacramento Bee* publisher V. S. McClatchy, who headed the state's Board of Land Reclamation, the Japanese were anathema to the white yeoman farmers with whom the board wanted to populate the Sacramento Valley.[29]

Consequently, the idea that Roosevelt once had quashed of restricting Japanese from owning and leasing land returned to center stage in California politics. While President William Howard Taft, too, was able to get California governors to keep alien land bills in check, the election of Woodrow Wilson in 1912 changed the equation. A Democratic southerner and racial conservative, the new president was put in the ironic position of seeking to deny a state's right to discriminate against a racial minority group. But with Governor Hiram Johnson and the Progressive Party controlling Sacramento, Wilson lacked important partisan ties that previously had boosted Roosevelt's and Taft's influence in California. The solid anti-Japanese position of the state's Democrats—epitomized by James Phelan, San Francisco mainstream labor leaders, and the Hearst press—took away from Wilson reliable partisan allies that could be used to discourage alien land legislation. An important force of moderation in the anti-Japanese crisis came from exclusionist Chester Rowell, Johnson's good friend and the founder of the state's Progressive Party. Rowell urged Johnson to support a general bill preventing any and all aliens from owning land. Other states, and even Japan itself, had this kind of alien land legislation, and as such Rowell assured that it would not offend Tokyo officials.[30]

While Rowell was concerned about international relations in general, he was particularly worried that a harsh alien land law would deter Japanese participation in California's upcoming Panama-Pacific Exposition, a world's fair to be held in 1915 celebrating the opening of the Panama Canal. Rowell joined with fellow exposition board members to persuade the state legislature against passing legislation offensive to the Japanese. But, as it turned out, the board was upstaged by a group of local farmers who highlighted the bogeyman of interracial sex that had long justified intense anti-black violence and murder in the American South. In a particularly moving address to the legislature, one farmer declared: "Near my home is an eighty-acre tract of as fine land as there is in California. On that land lives a Japanese. With that Japanese lives a white woman. In that woman's arms is a baby. What is that baby? It isn't a Japanese. It isn't white. I'll tell you what that baby is. It is a germ of the mightiest problem that ever faced this State; a problem that will make the black problem of the South look white."[31]

In late April 1913, President Wilson sent Secretary of State William Jennings Bryan to Sacramento in a last-ditch effort to postpone passage of an alien land law that was offensive to Japan. The legislature received the "Great Commoner" with the respect due his role as the president's emissary, as well as Bryan's own substantial reputation as the champion of Populism and two-time presidential candidate. Yet the secretary's visit had no real impact. Soon after he left, the legislature adopted a measure preventing aliens ineligible for citizenship from owning land while limiting leases to no more than three years. Governor Johnson did not hesitate to sign the measure since even Rowell admitted it had overwhelming popular support. While the president and other egalitarians had fought to the limits of federal influence, California exclusionists won this round in the ongoing exclusion debate.[32]

The news of the alien land law was a bitter pill to swallow in Tokyo, let alone in Japanese immigrant communities. The jingoist press in Japan called for war to avenge this insult to national pride, an action that in turn stoked yellow peril fears among Americans. Such a threat to harmonious U.S.-Japan relations prompted the Carnegie Endowment in late 1913 to dispatch former State Department official Francis Loomis to quietly report on the anti-Japanese situation in California. Loomis conveyed his findings and recommendations to Nicholas Murray Butler, president of Columbia University and director of the endowment's powerful committee on international education and communication.[33] After interviewing Governor Johnson, Chester Rowell, and a host of other major players in California politics, Loomis alerted Butler that the governor intended to introduce an even harsher alien land law in the next legislative session in 1915 that would remove the leasing allowance and close loopholes that allowed Japanese to control land buy purchasing it in the names of American citizens. Both men knew that such a measure would exacerbate already strained U.S.-Japan relations. Loomis blamed the problem on "organized labor miscreants and . . . interested politicians" who spread lies and half-truths about the Japanese that the general public consumed due to the lack of alternative, truthful information. At the same time, he was optimistic that the people of the state would be receptive to an aggressive education campaign run by Californians of "high character" who were leaders in the public and private sectors, universities, and religious organizations. He singled out Chester Rowell as one of these possible egalitarians who was "perhaps the most enlightened and highly cultivated person in the Progressive Movement in California." Rowell told Loomis that the anti-Japanese movement had gone far enough and that although he still wanted Japanese exclusion, he opposed further offending Japan by strengthening the alien land law.[34]

Loomis was further encouraged by a large sum of money ($35,000–45,000) pledged by Japanese immigrants to fund a campaign to educate whites in California about their presence in the state. The catch was that this money could be used only if the Carnegie Endowment provided $50,000 in matching funds. Loomis proposed an education program consisting of lectures by Californians of "high character," support for a Japan Society–like organization that he had already established in San Francisco, and a major research survey on the facts and contributions of Japanese immigrants in the state. He recommended as the director of the education campaign Dr. Harvey Guy, professor at the Pacific School of Religion and a bilingual missionary who had served in Japan.[35] The Carnegie Endowment, however, balked at Loomis's proposal. Though sympathetic, Elihu Root and the board feared Andrew Carnegie's name being associated with a campaign that could be seen as opposing the interests of organized labor. Butler, who strongly backed Loomis's plan to counteract the influence of the "wretched demagogues" in California, proposed funneling Carnegie money through the New York Japan Society. Yet neither his nor Loomis's assurances that the money could be given anonymously changed the board's mind.[36] It is likely that Root and others were influenced by the *Los Angeles Times* bombing, in which the two men arrested, along with Olaf Tveitmoe of the Japanese and Korean Exclusion League, were active in the iron workers' union that was engaged in violent struggles against Carnegie's U.S. Steel corporation. From the endowment's perspective, it would be unwise to confront California labor unions on the Japanese issue while the wounds from the *Times* bombing were still fresh.

Yet the conviction, idealism, and resources with which the eastern establishment sought to resolve the U.S.-Japan conflict were truly remarkable, for after the Carnegie Endowment rejected the education campaign proposal, a group of internationalists and religious leaders (including Frederick Lynch, Hamilton Holt, and the missionary Sidney Gulick) convinced Andrew Carnegie to open up his purse strings once again to endow a new kind of internationalist endeavor, the Church Peace Union.[37] Embracing a wide variety of Western faiths (including Protestantism, Catholicism, and Judaism), the Peace Union funded liberal Social Gospel organizations like the Federal Council of Churches of Christ in America. This organization in turn implemented much of Loomis's proposed education campaign in California. Gulick, who during a leave from Japan in 1913 took a job with the Federal Council of Churches, was at the center of this campaign and many other religious-based programs for international peace. His latest book, *The American Japanese Problem*, echoed themes from his earlier *White Peril in the Far East* in asserting the dangers inherent in American racism and misunderstanding of modern Japan. The latter book, however, offered a solution for the U.S.-Japan conflict that Gulick said would be acceptable to Tokyo. This involved Congress reducing the influx of all immigrants (not just those from Japan) and then allowing entrance to individuals based on the proportion of their compatriots who were naturalized American citizens. In short, Gulick proposed establishing an immigration system in which entrance quotas would differ by nation depending on the size of its naturalized immigrants in the United States. While in theory the quota for Japan would be tiny given the ban against the naturalization of Asian immigrants, it is quite likely that Gulick was already thinking ahead to the time when they could become American citizens.[38]

With Gulick running the education campaign from New York under the auspices of the Federal Council of Churches, the transpacific nature of the egalitarian movement took off. The bilingual missionary (he did not resign his position) was intimately connected to officials in the Japanese Foreign Ministry (Gaimusho), influential Japanese peace advocates such as the banking tycoon Baron Eiichi Shibusawa, and a network of missionaries and former missionaries from Japan—some, like Harvey Guy, who already were working for the Gaimusho and the leading association of Japanese immigrants to resolve the California situation. Prompted by the alien land law crisis, a triumvirate of mutually supportive private and public egalitarian interests from New York, Tokyo, and California (and eventually the entire West Coast) was engaged in a wide variety of programs to derail the anti-Japanese movement. Some of the highlights included maintaining lobbyists in California, mobilizing white churches to support U.S.-Japan friendship, launching a committee of the San Francisco Chamber of Commerce devoted to improving relations with Japan, establishing press bureaus to promote favorable public opinion for Japan, and clearing up misunderstandings of Japan at the Panama-Pacific Exposition, which, in the end, Tokyo officials decided to attend despite the alien land law.

One of the most daring and important endeavors undertaken by the education campaign focused on softening the anti-Japanese position of organized labor. In early 1915, when Gulick was in Japan on Federal Council of Churches business, he met separately with Eiichi Shibusawa and Gaimusho officials to propose that an influential figure from the emerging labor movement in Japan be sent to California as a fraternal delegate to attend the convention for the California Federation of Labor. The plan, which received firm backing in Japan, was to capitalize on the international bond between American and Japanese workers as leverage to calm labor's hostility toward Japanese immigration. On his return trip to New York, Gulick stopped in San Francisco and got Paul Scharrenberg, editor of an influential anti-Japanese longshoreman's publication and director of the California Federation of Labor, to welcome Bunji Suzuki and Sadaya Yoshimatsu as fraternal delegates from Japan to the California Federation of Labor's convention, which was held at the same time as the Panama-Pacific Exposition.[39] Before the two Japanese labor organizers arrived in San Francisco, Harvey Guy was downright giddy about their prospects for calming anti-Japanese sentiment. He reported to the Gaimusho, "It seems to me that the severe opposition carried on by the labor [unions] will hardly again be possible."[40]

Guy's optimism, as it turned out, was only partially warranted. The bilingual Suzuki, with the Gaimusho's press bureau in San Francisco writing his speeches in English, charmed representatives of American labor, including Samuel Gompers, by appealing to the promise of labor internationalism. Shibusawa, who accompanied the labor delegates, also drew praise for his support for union organizing in Japan, which on the surface seemed quite different from the hostile relations between unions and industrialists in the United States.[41] To Scharrenberg, strengthening Japan's labor movement could only lead to improved working conditions overseas that would prevent Japanese from immigrating in the first place. But Gulick's attempt to get the labor convention to support his immigration quota plan, which now included a clause to permit the naturalization of Japanese immigrants, was met with deep suspicion and rejected out of hand. Scharrenberg himself was adamant that promoting labor internationalism had no influence on his unwavering support for Japanese exclusion. Due to Gulick's ploy, Scharrenberg was forced to prove his exclusionist credentials when challenged by Phelan and other leaders of the anti-Japanese movement for being soft on the Japanese. Guy reported to the Gaimusho that the fraternal delegates, for all the good cheer they generated in California, did nothing to improve the immigration crisis. Yet Guy would soon become optimistic again about the prospects for racial and international peace.[42]

Crucible of World War

The outbreak of the Great War in Europe in April 1914 at first had little impact on the exclusion debate in California. Wilson declared American neutrality while the education campaign was rolled out and the fraternal delegates did their bit for labor internationalism. Scharrenberg was so enthused by Bunji Suzuki's visit that he invited him to return to the conference the next year, which the labor pioneer did courtesy again of the Gaimusho and Shibusawa. To return the favor, Suzuki invited Scharrenberg and Gompers to tour labor conditions in Japan, but the Americans turned him down fearing that a visit would compromise their exclusionist stance. Nevertheless, Scharrenberg became somewhat friendly to the Japanese in California through his columns in the *Coast Seaman's Journal* and active membership in U.S.-Japan organizations led by Guy and Loomis. At the same time, California's AFL agreed to organize Japanese immigrant workers and not to push anti-Japanese issues in the 1916 state elections. In the next year the education campaign reached a high point as the same federation passed a resolution expressing faith that controversies over the alien land law and naturalization of the Japanese could be resolved peacefully.[43]

By this time, the United States had declared war on Germany and was fighting on the same side as Japan, who had joined the Allies at the start of hostilities. Also, in late 1917 the United States and Japan signed the Lansing-Ishii Agreement that for the time being smoothed over conflicts between the nations regarding the Open Door in China. In this way the apex of good feelings in California reflected the larger context of improved U.S.-Japan relations. On top of this, shortages of foodstuffs during the war proved a boon to Japanese farmers in California, who increased their production and acreage of farmland while agricultural prices skyrocketed. Seeking to prove loyalty to the United States, Japanese immigrants bought a disproportionate share of American war bonds, while a few enlisted in the U.S. Army along with other Asian immigrants. In exchange for enlisting, the federal government promised U.S. citizenship. In this way, America's involvement in World War I proved a golden moment of egalitarianism as Sacramento suspended the push for a stronger alien land law, and hopes remained high that the good feelings would continue.

The situation was not so bright, however, for immigrants whose nations were hostile to or not closely allied with the United States. Worse off were peoples of German descent, who faced strong pressures to prove their loyalty to America and disavow allegiance to a homeland whose military was killing neutral American citizens in the Atlantic Ocean and threatening to ally with Mexico against the United States. The situation darkened when the United States declared war against Germany. One German immigrant was lynched in Illinois for allegedly being disloyal to the United States; meanwhile, the Justice Department sought to identify 480,000 German aliens, more than 4,000 of whom were imprisoned on suspicion for being spies and saboteurs. Even before America joined the war, President Wilson, as well as former president Roosevelt, spoke out harshly against such "hyphenated Americans" who maintained loyalties to their homeland or ethnic group. The hostility shown to German aliens and Americans of German descent revealed the conjuncture of national security and racialized prejudice and discrimination. In this case, the war turned Americans against an old immigrant group that was largely assimilated, most of whom were U.S. citizens, voters with numerical clout, and represented in the ranks and leadership of mainstream labor.[44]

Amid the wave of hypernationalism accompanying U.S. entrance into World War I, Congress in February 1917 passed an immigration act that took a historic step toward closing the gates to Europe as well as Asia. The most controversial part of the legislation was the creation of a literacy test to be required of all arrivals over the age of sixteen. Ever since Henry Cabot Lodge and the Immigration Restriction League came close to enacting this form of restriction in 1897, further attempts to legislate such a test were repeatedly stymied by presidential veto. Whether Republican or Democrat, presidents were unwilling to risk losing votes from eastern and southern European immigrants who made their opposition to restriction via literacy test known through vocal and persistent lobbying. Another problem for the exclusionists was that southern congressmen had shifted to the expansionist side of the immigration debate because they sought to recruit European immigrants to replace the outmigration of whites from the South. Progressive reformers like Senators Lodge and William Dillingham fought back against the egalitarian status quo by establishing a massive, four-year congressional research project to study the problem of immigration. The findings of the Dillingham Commission, published in 1911, recommended continuing Chinese exclusion while also closing the gates to new immigrants from Europe as well as Asian Indians (referred to collectively and inaccurately as "Hindus"). The report deemed single, unskilled male laborers in each of these groups to be uninterested in assimilation and thus unfit for American citizenship. The proposed solution was to check their immigration through the imposition of a literacy test and fixed immigration quotas based on race. But these recommendations languished until the xenophobia induced by the U.S. entrance into World War I stirred up concerns about "hyphenated Americans."[45]

The Immigration Act of 1917 also banned the entrance of laborers from much of Asia and adjacent islands. The exceptions were coastal China (whose laborers had been excluded by previous legislation), American possessions such as the Philippines and Guam, and Japan, for whom the Gentlemen's Agreement and a 1911 commercial treaty remained in place. Given that Korea had become an official Japanese colony in 1910, Korean migration in theory was covered under U.S.-Japan agreements but in fact had already been halted by Korean officials, due to Japanese pressure. This left a relatively small labor migration of Asian Indians as the main group shut out by the Immigration Act. Hearings held by the House Committee on Immigration and Naturalization in early 1914 revealed the rationales for Indian exclusion, which, on the whole, did not differ much from those used against the Chinese and Japanese. Anthony Caminetti, commissioner of immigration in the current Wilson administration, remarked, "I come from the Pacific coast, where we have had two race problems which we have had to fight, and the third one about to be thrown upon us out there." Caminetti made it clear that Indian laborers needed to be excluded because they posed a threat to white workers. Fellow Californian and member of congress Lucas S. Church added that Indians were even worse than the Japanese on this count; given the low wages accepted by the Indian, he said, "a Jap would starve to death where a Hindu will get fat." Church also condemned the religious beliefs of Indians, which compelled them to keep apart from Americans. As a result, "there is certainly no class of people which has ever invaded California who are as clannish as the Hindu." One particular problem, said Church, arose when Indians refused to report crimes within their community, which made it impossible for law enforcement to resolve the cases.[46]

Committee member and Californian John E. Raker maintained that due to their low standard of living and unassimilability, Indians threatened to create permanent cleavages between rich and poor in the United States like what existed in India. Raker's point stemmed from a Jacksonian view of America as a classless society in which pioneers did "honest" work with their hands, close to the soil, and from there climbed the ladder of success. This outlook was evident in his responses to a fellow committee member who saw the base work of Indian immigrants as elevating white workers and to an egalitarian witness who praised the intelligence and cleanliness of the many servants she had while living in India. "I would like to make it possible," Raker said, "that every boy should know how to dig ditches, follow the plow, and work in the mill, and then get up to be one of the best men in this country. I want every girl to know how to cook and sew and run the house, and instead of being drudgery it is good honest work—better than living in idleness and ease. The girl that works in the kitchen and waits on the table should go to the theater and to church with as much pride as the girl who goes to balls every night and rides around in carriages and lives a life of ease. And God forbid the day should come in this country when those who work in our homes shall be of a different class from those for whom they work." Raker's concerns about class polarization corrupting the republican experiment reminds us how the exclusion debate invoked core American values and was not simply a question of hating Asian peoples.[47]

Further testimony touched off fears of political radicalism that were acute during this era of labor warfare. While he could not give "definite information as to whether they [Indian immigrants] teach revolution and anarchy," Church maintained that they did so as "to be in position in the future to rebel against the form of government under which they are at the time living [in India]." But 'T'ishi Bhutia, an educated Indian immigrant representing the Hindustan Association of America, disagreed sharply with Church's view, asserting, "The principles of anarchism are very far from India, because Buddhism prevents the shedding of blood." Rather, he said that Indians as "socialists" sought to overthrow British colonialism through peaceful, "passive resistance."[48]

Beyond the issue of radicalism, the egalitarian defense of Indian immigration resembled the general arguments made by those for the Chinese and Japanese. The Indians, though, had no representation from either British or Indian officials. Instead, they were defended by Bhutia, his colleague Sudhindra Bose, and Mrs. R. F. Patterson, the white American wife of a former U.S. diplomat in India. Patterson especially informed the committee about the greatness of India's civilization, as well as the intelligence, cleanliness, and morality of its peoples. Sudhindra Bose, a college lecturer, emphasized that racially "it is absolutely certain that there is no connection whatever between the Mongolian people and the Aryan blood that runs in our veins." In addition, the assimilability of Indians made them "entirely different from the Chinese and Japanese in regard to clannishness." He sidestepped the thorny issue of miscegenation by saying that like the Jews, Indians could assimilate without marrying across the color line. T'ishi Bhutia, Bose's colleague in the Hindustan Association of America, addressed the miscegenation issue squarely in stating that it was not a problem since both Indians and Americans were Caucasian and that at least 20 percent of Englishmen in India married local women, whose children proved the compatibility between the two peoples. Bhutia gave voice to a rumor—which has not been substantiated—that even the English poet Rudyard Kipling himself was born to an Indian mother. In the end, both Bose and Bhutia agreed that it was all right to exclude laborers from India, but exceptions had to be made for students, agriculturalists, merchants, and others who were not laborers. Bose made it clear that the Gentlemen's Agreement, not the Chinese Exclusion Act, should serve as the model for Indian exclusion: "If you pass an exclusionary law it tends to lower us in the estimation of the civilized world. It renders it almost impossible for us to enter any country where there is no restriction against us. It may bring about international complications. It is very far reaching."[49]

These egalitarian pleas were not answered, as the Immigration Act of 1917 banned Indians, much like earlier legislation did the Chinese. But Congress did go out of its way not to offend India. Senate discussion on the 1917 act paid little attention to Indians per se. Rather, it concentrated on excluding Asians as a race. The catch was to follow State Department directives so that exclusion was done in a way that did not name nations, infringe on existing treaties, or otherwise offend Japan. The solution was to create a geographic zone, based on given coordinates of longitude and latitude, from which immigration was disallowed. This area would become known as the "Asiatic Barred Zone." Some senators wanted to extend the zone to Africa, while others opposed it as an overly blunt instrument that would exclude white people from either Asia or Africa. At the same time, exclusionists like James Phelan, who had been elected to the Senate from California in 1916, pushed hard to abrogate treaties and agreements with Japan, as well as the new Republic of China, to include both of these nations in the barred zone. Others pointed to the apparent hypocrisy of allowing migration from the Philippines but not neighboring islands comprised of the same races or from Chinese who were said to be superior to Filipinos. In the end, America's colonial imperatives and peaceful relations with both China and Japan during World War I prevented the Immigration Act from radically changing the status quo on Asian immigration, with the exception of Indian exclusion.[50]

Besides creating an atmosphere conducive to immigration restriction, the Great War influenced the exclusion debate by starting a transformation in American internationalism that would over time, but not immediately, benefit the egalitarians. This change was evident in 1915, when America began to retreat from its imperial mission in the Philippines. Not long after defeating Filipino independence forces, as well as anti-imperialist protests at home, Roosevelt, Lodge, and other imperialists began to have second thoughts about the "white man's burden." Sure enough, "pacifying" and "uplifting" the Philippines was an expensive, long-term commitment. But, given the archipelago's distance from the core of American naval forces in Hawai'i, it was also one that was almost impossible to safeguard from foreign invasion. Roosevelt and Taft knew this, and despite keeping up the appearance of the imperialist mission, they worried a great deal about it. Wilson did even more to extract the United States from its imperial commitments. In 1916 he and fellow Democrats approved the Philippine Autonomy Act, which declared America's intention to eventually grant Philippine independence. To prepare Filipinos for self-rule, this act (known as the Jones Law for its congressional sponsor William A. Jones) established a new framework for colonial governance that made both houses of the Philippine legislature subject to popular elections.[51]

The Jones Law revealed Wilson's new approach to foreign affairs. Lodge questioned whether he and Secretary of State Bryan even had an approach, criticizing their inability to resolve the alien land law crisis in California that ended up exacerbating U.S.-Japan tension rather than diminishing it, as Roosevelt had done during the segregation crisis. The Massachusetts senator feared that "by sheer feebleness and ignorance they may flounder into [a U.S.-Japan] war." At the same time, Roosevelt, Lodge, and other Republicans disagreed with Wilson's policies regarding the World War, which put a priority on peace at any cost rather than on defeating and punishing Germany for starting the war. But Wilson's Fourteen Points and subsequent peace treaty represented a new vision of internationalism that backed up international treaties of arbitration with the League of Nations, a form of world government that was committed to the theory of preserving the peace through "collective security."[52]

Theodore Roosevelt died in January 1919, just before Wilson began to broker the Paris Peace Conference that ended the Great War and established the foundation of the League of Nations. The combination of Roosevelt's death and the emergence of the league captured a moment of transition symbolizing the emergence of a new form of internationalism based in cooperation rather than on the sort of national competition that led to World War I. In crafting the Versailles Treaty, especially the clause calling for the establishment of a League of Nations, Wilson was hopeful that finally a solution had been found to end all wars. This solution required that the United States come out of its hemisphere to engage with the world on a sustained basis, and not just during times of crisis and war. From Seward's day to Roosevelt's, such international interests usually came with expansionist and egalitarian views on the immigration debate. Here was yet another reason for egalitarians in California, New York, Tokyo, and around the world to be hopeful that the immigration conflict between the United States and Japan that was stilled by the war would recede within a new era of Wilsonian internationalism.

William H. Seward, U.S. senator from New York and U.S. secretary of state, epitomized the nation's ambitions for a commercial empire in the Pacific that underwrote the egalitarian defense for Chinese immigrants against determined exclusionists on the West Coast. A former member of the Whig Party, Seward joined the emergent Republican Party that controlled the federal government during and after the Civil War and helped establish the GOP as the partisan home of international and immigration expansionism. Courtesy of Library of Congress.

The Burlingame Treaty (1868) marked the apex of Republican egalitarianism regarding Chinese immigrants and was ratified at the same moment the GOP was implementing Radical Reconstruction in the South. The photo, taken in the same year the treaty was ratified, shows the first Chinese foreign mission, with Anson Burlingame standing at the center surrounded by Chinese dignitaries and two other foreign agents working for China. Courtesy of Library of Congress.

A TRIO THAT MUST GO.

The exclusion of Chinese laborers in 1882 exemplified the collapse of Republican hegemony and the return of a competitive party system in which western exclusionists found common cause with Democrats, white southerners, and populist-oriented Republicans seeking to overcome the supposed corrupt influence of northeastern big money. The cover image from the satirical magazine *Puck* (September 5, 1883) shows the connection between the decline of the GOP, portrayed as a teary-eyed, emaciated, and wounded elephant, and the exclusion of Chinese laborers. The third figure embodies the simultaneous concern that the ringing of church bells was a public nuisance, which, along with the GOP and Chinese workers, "must go." Courtesy of Library of Congress.

The debate over the exclusion of Chinese laborers continued for more than twenty years after the 1882 act since both exclusionists and egalitarians fought over the interpretation and implementation of the act, as well as over subsequent U.S.-China treaties centered on the immigration issue. A key player in these struggles was the American Federation of Labor, the nation's largest labor organization, which emerged in 1886 amid a nationwide crisis in industrial relations. An influential political force and constant presence on Capitol Hill, the AFL took a hard stand against Chinese immigration. In the photo, its longtime leader Samuel Gompers testifies at a federal commission studying industrial relations in 1915. Courtesy of Library of Congress.

George Frisbee Hoar, U.S. senator from Massachusetts, fought a losing battle to maintain Burlingame egalitarianism in the face of consolidating exclusionism that at the end of the nineteenth century gained strength not only from the AFL but also from northeastern Republicans, who were prompted to shift positions in the exclusion debate amid economic depression and the massive influx of new migrants from Europe and Canada. Even the egalitarian Hoar decried the migration of French Canadians into Massachusetts, although he remained steadfast in defending the Chinese. This 1904 photo was taken in the same year that Congress removed Chinese exclusion from its basis in U.S.-China treaties, thus making it a permanent feature of American law no longer subject to ten-year renewal. Hoar died in this same year. Courtesy of Library of Congress.

While concerns about undocumented Chinese immigrants would persist well into the twentieth century, the crux of the exclusion debate in the new century shifted toward the crisis over Japanese immigration. This photo depicts two leaders who would play a crucial role in this issue. Theodore Roosevelt (*left*) developed an abiding respect for Japan's military prowess and as president defended Japanese immigrants from discrimination and calls for exclusion from the West Coast. At the same time, he joined with California governor and Progressive Party leader Hiram Johnson in declaring Japanese labor migration a menace to white society. The photo of the two men was taken in 1912, when Johnson ran as the vice presidential candidate on Roosevelt's failed attempt to return to the White House, this time as a third-party Progressive. Afterward, Johnson began a long career in the U.S. Senate, in which he remained a bastion of exclusionism and would become known for opposing U.S. overseas expansionism. Courtesy of Library of Congress.

Camp Lewis, Wash. ⟶ Nov. 18, 1918

World War I opened up a new opportunity for Asian immigrants to become U.S. citizens, but the war also fueled the merging of nativism, racism, and national security fears leading to the exclusion of Indian immigration, regardless of class status, through construction in 1917 of the "Asiatic Barred Zone." This zone, which covered most of Asia and the Pacific, marked peoples who were prevented from migrating to the United States, although it exempted prior policies to admit nonlaboring classes from Japan and China. This 1918 photo includes Bhagat Singh Thind (*back row, center, in turban*), an Indian immigrant who was one of hundreds of Asians whose citizenship obtained from military service was revoked after the war. Singh sought legal recourse, but ultimately the U.S. Supreme Court rejected his claim in a 1923 ruling holding that Indians were ineligible for citizenship. Courtesy of David Bhagat Thind.

The debate over Japanese immigration climaxed with an exclusionist victory in 1924
led by the West Coast contingent in Congress, including Albert Johnson (*third from
left*), chair of the House committee that held public hearings on Japanese immigration
in 1920 and subsequently approved legislation to ban it. On the far right is James D.
Phelan, former mayor of San Francisco and U.S. senator, who during the 1920s continued
to battle against egalitarians for Japanese exclusion. Other figures in the photo are
likely members of Johnson's Committee on Immigration and Naturalization. Courtesy of
Bancroft Library, University of California, Berkeley.

When this photo of Chester H. Rowell was taken in 1910, the journalist, publicist, and California Progressive Party leader was squarely in the exclusionist camp on the Japanese question. Yet after the enactment of Japanese exclusion in 1924, he broke with his friend and Progressive ally Hiram Johnson and switched to the egalitarian side. As a member of and publicist for the Institute of Pacific Relations, Rowell sought to end Japanese exclusion by giving to Japan a small immigration quota that would put it on a par with European nations. During World War II, as political editor of the *San Francisco Chronicle*, he was a rare leader of public opinion who vigorously opposed the internment of Japanese Americans. Courtesy of the California History Room, California State Library, Sacramento, California.

Another leading California egalitarian was David Starr Jordan, scientist and president of Stanford University and contemporary of Chester Rowell. Jordan opposed Japanese exclusion mainly because the barring of "aliens ineligible to citizenship" was an overly blunt racial tool that stigmatized the elite and educated classes of Japan. In this photo, probably taken in the 1920s, Jordan poses with four Japanese students at Stanford. During this time, the university became a vital center for the study of East Asia and Asian Americans and hosted the Survey of Race Relations, a major egalitarian research project on racial conflict throughout the West Coast. Ray Lyman Wilbur, Jordan's successor as Stanford president, would lead the IPR. Courtesy of Stanford University Archives.

Second to the West Coast, Hawai'i was the region that played the most important role in the twentieth-century exclusion debate. Annexed by the United States in 1898, the islands were dominated by the sugar and pineapple industries and by a white plantation elite that insulated itself politically, economically, and socially from the large population of Asian immigrants (mostly Japanese and Filipino, but including Chinese and Koreans) Exclusionists portrayed Hawai'i as a dangerous example of unchecked Asian immigration, while egalitarians marveled at its harmonious race relations and the Americanization of its Asian ethnics. Courtesy of Library of Congress.

The U.S. annexed the Philippines in 1898, but unlike Hawai'i, it was not put on a path toward statehood and thus would exist as an American colony until given provisional independence in 1934 (full independence came in 1946). Although prevented from becoming U.S. citizens, Filipinos were able to immigrate to the U.S. metropole, and as Japanese exclusion threatened, they became the preferred source of Asian labor on Hawai'i plantations and West Coast farms. The exclusionist campaign for Filipinos during the late 1920s and early 1930s coincided with efforts for Philippine independence. In lobbying Congress for independence, Philippine political leader Manuel Roxas, pictured in 1923, also challenged the exclusionist depiction of Filipino immigrants as culturally backward and racially incompatible with American institutions. An educated, articulate, and intelligent Filipino with political standing, Roxas boosted the egalitarian cause, even though he was largely indifferent to the experience of Filipino immigrant workers in the United States. Courtesy of Library of Congress

Strikes waged by Filipino agricultural workers in California got the attention of radical civil liberties lawyer Carey McWilliams, who authored a critical history of the state's racialized farm labor in 1939 and in the same year became director of California's Division of Immigration and Housing. McWilliams was a major egalitarian leader advancing causes to end anti-Asian racism and promote interracial relations. During World War II he was the first to publish a study of the internment of Japanese Americans, which was sympathetic to the internees and critical of the racism behind their plight. In this 1945 photo, he is speaking with Dorothy Takechi, who recently had been released from the Manzanar concentration camp and was working with the YWCA to survey Japanese American conditions. Courtesy of Bancroft Library, University of California, Berkeley.

In this 1943 photo, President Franklin D. Roosevelt and First Lady Eleanor Roosevelt accompany May-ling Soong as she goes to present a wreath on behalf of her husband, Chiang Kai-shek, chairman of the Chinese government, at the tomb of George Washington. Her appearance underscored America's alliance with China during World War II, which enabled egalitarians in Congress to repeal Chinese exclusion. The war started the Great Transformation in the exclusion debate during which all anti-Asian laws and policies would be abandoned. The president, however, had a mixed record of egalitarianism because he was ultimately responsible for the internment of Japanese Americans based on unsubstantiated racialized fears of their disloyalty. In contrast, Eleanor expressed faith in the vast majority of Japanese Americans throughout the war. Courtesy of Associated Press.

As the Japanese Americans were interned and Chinese exclusion was being repealed, President Roosevelt in February 1943 authorized the recruitment of an all-nisei army unit that would become the 442nd Regimental Combat Team. About fourteen thousand men served in the 442nd during the war, and it became legendary as the most decorated unit of its size. This March 1943 photo shot outside Hawaiʻi's ʻIolani Palace reveals the heavy participation of nisei troops from the islands, who made up the vast majority of all Asian American GIs during the conflict. Courtesy of Hawaiʻi State Archives, Honolulu, Hawaiʻi.

Another dimension of the Great Transformation was the repeal of Indian and Filipino exclusion in 1946, captured in this photo as President Harry S. Truman signs the Luce-Celler Act. New York representative Emanuel Celler (*directly behind Truman, smiling*) was the bill's major sponsor. Joining Congress in 1923, Celler was a pronounced egalitarian who had vigorously opposed the nation's discriminatory immigration policies. J. J. Singh (*third from right*), president of the India League of America, was a tireless advocate for the equal treatment of Indian immigrants. Other egalitarians pictured include Joseph R. Farrington (*fourth from left*), Hawai'i territorial representative to Congress; Dr. Anup Singh (*second from right*), National Committee for India's Freedom; Leonides S. Virata, (*far right*), representative from the Philippines. Courtesy of Harry S. Truman Library, Independence, Mo.

The last group to benefit from the Great Transformation was Japanese Americans, w after the war continued to face discrimina and hostility on the West Coast where Earl Warren, a leading proponent for the intern as California's attorney general, was now the state's governor. Yet by the late 1940s recognition of the nisei's stellar war recor and the stigmatization of racism resulting war atrocities like the Holocaust lowered t temperature of anti-Japanese antagonism In this undated photo, Governor Warren signs a measure to restore rights to Japane Americans. After becoming chief justice of U.S. Supreme Court, Warren became one o America's best-known egalitarians in hand down the famous desegregation ruling *Bro Board of Education* (1954). Courtesy of Ba Library, University of California, Berkeley.

The start of the Cold War further fueled th Great Transformation by drawing into the egalitarian fold many policy makers who it as a vehicle for anticommunist efforts in East Asia while maintaining the discrimina national origins system. One such policym was Senator Patrick McCarran, sponsor of the McCarran-Walter Act (1952) that ende Japanese exclusion while restricting the migration of Communists and other types radicals. At the same time, McCarran head the Senate committee on internal security that in 1951 subpoenaed Frederick Vande Field to testify about Communist influenc in the IPR. The photo shows Field, who wa in prison on an earlier charge of contempt court, being brought to McCarran's commi accompanied by two federal prison guard While Field was not convicted as part of the government crackdown on the IPR, the organization could not withstand the bad publicity and subsequently folded as one the many victims of postwar anticommun Courtesy of Associated Press.

The significance of Hawai'i to the United States only grew after World War II, as the nation relied on its Pacific Fleet (stationed at Pearl Harbor) for wars in Korea and Vietnam, sought to check now-Communist China, and benefited from the booming U.S.-Japan trade. Thus the way was paved for Hawai'i statehood (1959), which egalitarians celebrated as the ultimate recognition of Asian American loyalty and assimilability. More pragmatically, statehood greatly increased egalitarian political clout through the election of Asian Americans and their allies to Congress. The photo, taken in June 1963 during President John F. Kennedy's visit to the islands, shows him riding with Governor John Burns (*center*), one of the leaders of Hawai'i's "Democratic revolution" that overthrew the planter oligarchy's control. Next to Burns is his protégé Daniel Inouye, a 442nd veteran, who was in the first term of a congressional career that would span nearly forty years in which he would reach the highest echelons of power on Capitol Hill. All of Hawai'i's representatives would contribute to establishing comprehensive immigration reform in 1965 that made it possible for large, sustained (though highly selective) Asian migrations. Courtesy of Hawai'i State Archives, Honolulu, Hawai'i.

Elected to the U.S. House of Representatives from Southern California in 2008, Judy Chu, pictured in 2010, has continued the struggle for fair and nondiscriminatory immigration policies in the face of mounting pressures to exclude and deport the latest wave of feared immigrants. Chu sponsored an approved House resolution in 2012 that expressed regret for past congressional authorization of Chinese exclusion policies. Her rationale for the resolution relied on an understanding of the long exclusion era as an expression of virtually uncontested racism. Ironically, the apology for Chinese exclusion, as in the U.S. government's 1988 redress and apology for Japanese internment, was an egalitarian victory that failed to remember the egalitarian struggles and achievements of the past. Courtesy of Office of Representative Judy Chu.

5   FLOOD CONTROL

NATIONALISM, INTERNATIONALISM, AND

JAPANESE EXCLUSION, 1919–1924

||||||||||||||||||||||||||||||||||||||||||||||||||||||||||||||||||||||||||||||||||||||||||||||||||||||||||||||||||||||||||||||||||||||||

In June 1924, former U.S. senator James D. Phelan wrote a "letter to a Japanese Gentleman" explaining the recent passage of an American immigration act that broke with diplomatic precedent to exclude migrants from Japan. The thrust of Phelan's rationale remained consistent with his turn-of-the-century opposition to Japanese immigration as mayor of San Francisco. In a nod to Herbert Spencer, the Californian argued that Japanese immigrants were genetically incompatible with whites and, as a pariah group—which he conceded was intelligent, hard working, and well organized—threated American workers and farmers, democratic institutions, and the nation's social order. Phelan indicated that the call for Japanese exclusion took on new urgency after World War I, as Japan sought to use the Wilsonian spirit of the newly established League of Nations to tear down race-based exclusion policies around the world. He warned that American and Japanese diplomats had been engaged in a "conspiracy" to grant Japanese immigrants access to U.S. citizenship.[1]

The postwar wave of American isolationism that blocked the United States from joining the League of Nations also resuscitated the long-standing politics of Japanese exclusion that for twenty years had failed to gain much traction in Congress. In the same way that World War I nationalism induced the nativism that made it possible to pass the literacy test and Asiatic Barred Zone, so too did isolationism create the conditions for the further tightening of immigration controls. Isolationist-inspired nativism, not surprisingly, first appeared in California, where exclusionists strengthened the state's alien land law. This time, unlike in 1913, Californians were in step with nativist sentiment across the nation. Though losing his Senate seat in 1920, Phelan continued to lead the exclusion movement as a private citizen. He joined influential state officials and interest groups in fighting a war of public opinion against the egalitarian opposition. Most important, Phelan played a key role in successfully lobbying Congress to pass Japanese exclusion as part of the Immigration Act of 1924. "I [am] repaid for my efforts," he wrote in a private letter; "the Japs are routed."[2]

Phelan's satisfaction reflected the tremendous effort and resources he had expended to achieve exclusion. But the image of a rout grossly simplified the exclusionist victory by leaving unaddressed the strength of the opposition. Alternatives to exclusion—advanced in various guises by the State Department, the Japanese Foreign Ministry, and American friends of Japan like Sidney Gulick—sought to maintain the principle of the Gentlemen's Agreement in which the United States and Japan would mutually agree to stepped-up restrictions so as to save Japan from the embarrassment of being singled out by congressional exclusion. This chapter reveals the significant degree of support in Congress, and even on the West Coast, for the egalitarian alternative. Accounting for this egalitarianism in no way takes away from the hard-won exclusionist victory. Rather, it allows us to better appreciate how difficult it was to achieve.

Isolationist Nationalism and Postwar California

The end of World War I marked a turning point in America's involvement in global affairs. Since the late nineteenth century, the United States had claimed territory and got immersed in issues requiring it to move far beyond its comfort zone in the Western Hemisphere. Peace advocates promoted global arbitration agreements, while Theodore Roosevelt, Hamilton Holt, and others entertained forms of world government to prevent international conflict. Ironically, it was President Wilson, a southerner with little experience or interest in global relations, who brought internationalist dreams to life by insisting that the establishment of a League of Nations be part of the Paris peace treaty concluding World War I. But there was a double irony here; just as Wilson pushed for a huge increase in the nation's international responsibilities, the American public, led by the more globally sensitive Republican Henry Cabot Lodge, refused to follow his lead. The Senate in November 1919 rejected the Treaty of Paris because of its requirement that the United States join the League of Nations. A year later American voters elected a Republican president, Warren G. Harding, who ended any last hope of American membership in the league. At the GOP convention, Lodge summed up the postwar climate of opinion: "We must be now and forever for Americanism and Nationalism, and against Internationalism."[3]

Beyond Wilson's idiosyncrasies and political missteps in selling the league to the American public, four factors explain the misfortune of Wilsonian internationalism. First was the fact that to many Americans, the nation's involvement in the war was mistaken. Always suspicious of big business and government corruption, progressives and radicals blamed U.S. participation in the war on the undue influence of the munitions industry and other "war profiteers." Consequently, many Americans were loath to repeat the same mistake by committing the United States to uphold world peace through the league. Second, the establishment of the Soviet Union and the subsequent failure of international forces, including nearly eight thousand U.S. troops, to overthrow the new Bolshevik regime raised the stakes of fighting communism abroad. Instead, Americans focused attention on shoring up the home front by engaging in the nation's first anticommunist Red Scare. In addition to cracking down on labor unions and radical dissidents, the United States questioned the political ideologies of immigrants, especially Jews from Russia and other parts of eastern Europe, which conventional stereotypes portrayed as highly prone to communism. Third, the sudden reconversion of the U.S. economy from total war produced the first major recession since the 1890s as the labor market struggled to adjust to sudden reductions in government spending and to absorb the returning GIs. The final factor giving Americans pause about joining the league were concerns that in doing so the nation would forfeit the right to close its borders to immigrants. Exclusionists warned that Japan's proposal for the league charter to contain a clause pledging the body's commitment to racial equality was an entering wedge for the elimination of exclusionary immigration policies in the United States and around the world. While President Wilson and the leaders of other white exclusionist nations like Canada, Australia, and South Africa denied Japan's racial equality proposal, there still remained the fear in the United States of massive migration from war-torn Europe.[4]

Harsh economic times combined with fears of a postwar human flood from Europe, immigrant radicalism, and long-standing concerns about the demise of the Anglo-Saxons race to fuel the passage of the Emergency Quota Act in 1921. This was the first measure to cap the number of migrants from all nations, which at 357,000 per year was still too high to exclusionists. The act legislated the Dillingham Commission's recommendation to use immigration quotas to calibrate the nation's ethnic makeup by limiting entries from each country outside the Western Hemisphere to 3 percent of its U.S. population, based on the 1910 census. This emergency measure, after being twice renewed, set the stage for more permanent reductions approved by the Immigration Act of 1924. This measure enacted comprehensive immigration reform that lowered the overall cap to 150,000 while the quotas fell to 2 percent based on the 1890 census, a more restrictive change given that the bulk of new immigrants arrived after this date. What made this great restriction of immigration possible was massive internal migration, stimulated by the war, through which millions of southerners, blacks and whites, moved to the North and West. The southern migration, pushed by prolonged farm crises in the South, continued after the war and came to represent a new source of industrial labor supply that, combined with mechanization and the increased hiring of women, came to replace the reliance on immigrant workers for industrial production.[5]

Thus were the large domestic and international contexts in which Californians revived the push for Japanese exclusion. Similar to the experience of Chinese immigrants in the nineteenth century, the exclusion movement for many years failed to mobilize support in Congress until a dramatic change in political climate and alignments helped the cause. For Chinese exclusion, such an opportunity arose with the reemergence of a competitive party system resulting from the collapse of Yankee Republican control during the Civil War and Reconstruction. For Japanese exclusion, it came with the return of Republicans to power in Washington, D.C., and the proliferation of isolationist nationalism. Here was another irony: Republicans, who more often than not opposed Asian exclusion, now found themselves allied with western nativists and southern racists. Indeed, Senator Lodge, who had helped President Roosevelt write his 1906 address to Congress in which he vociferously defended Japanese immigration, was now the most powerful anti-Japanese voice on Capitol Hill.

That the United States and Japan were allies softened exclusionist demands for the duration of the war. Concerns about the loyalty of German immigrants took the nativist spotlight off the Japanese in California. If discussed at all, issei farmers were celebrated for their patriotic service in buying war bonds and filling shortages of food for the home front. This was a far cry from the alien land law crisis in 1913, when they were vilified as a threat to white land ownership and agricultural jobs. Sidney Gulick sought to capitalize on the good feelings between the United States and Japan forged during the war by launching a major offensive to obtain issei naturalization and thus remove the legal foundation of anti-Japanese policies. The cornerstone of his plan was the immigration quota policy that he had been recommending since he joined the Federal Council of Churches. Like the Dillingham Commission, Gulick sought to use national quotas based on a percentage, between 3 and 10 percent, of an immigrant group's U.S. population. But Gulick's plan was even more restrictionist than the Dillingham Commission's because Gulick's quotas were based only on people who had naturalized and become U.S. citizens. To place Asians on a par with everyone else, Gulick's plan made them eligible to be become citizens.[6]

Through the auspices and huge membership of the Federal Council of Churches, Gulick attracted support from over one thousand prominent Americans in politics, business, and higher education. He also led a vigorous lobbying campaign on Capitol Hill and obtained an audience from the House Committee on Immigration and Naturalization to present his quota plan. But as Gulick was executing his naturalization offensive, U.S.-Japan tension over China resurfaced to end the wartime era of good feelings. At issue was Japan's claim to Shandong, a former German possession in northeastern China seized by Japanese troops during the war. Even friends of Japan were critical of the nation's opportunistic land grab. While Wilson— who did not want to risk Japan rejecting his cherished League of Nations— included Japan's claim to Shandong in the Paris peace treaty, the negative reaction to it in the United States encouraged anti-Japanese forces in California. Within this context, Senator Phelan made Japanese expansionism in China and California the main theme of his reelection campaign and, as ever, benefited from the Hearst press and other prominent newspapers. The senator developed a particularly close connection with the *Sacramento Bee*, whose publisher, V. S. McClatchy, came to play a leading role in the state's anti-Japanese movement.[7]

McClatchy—the chair of California's Board of Land Reclamation who until 1922 shared ownership of the *Bee* with his brother Charles McClatchy— issued a series of long anti-Japanese editorials in the family paper in the spring of 1919. The editorials revolved around three main points through which McClatchy brilliantly repackaged exclusionist rhetoric to engage the nation's postwar isolationism. First, the Californian softened the overtly racist arguments for Japanese exclusion that Gulick warned both offended Japan and the egalitarian spirit of the Treaty of Paris. McClatchy did this by emphasizing that Japanese were racially incompatible but not inferior to whites and that they posed an economic threat, not a racial threat, to American farmers and laborers because their perpetual clannishness and low standard of living gave them unfair advantage. Second, McClatchy tarnished Gulick's stellar reputation in policy-making circles by casting him as a paid agent of Japan. The Americans who supported Gulick's quota plan, McClatchy argued, were unwitting dupes to highly skilled forms of Japanese propaganda that served as a Trojan horse that would over time drastically increase Japanese immigration.[8]

Finally, and most important, McClatchy capitalized on war hatreds as well as on the Shandong controversy to warn Americans that Japan was the "Germany of Asia."[9] He maintained that the Japanese looked to the Germans as their mentors; they not only maintained a secret admiration for the Kaiser but also embraced his militaristic drive for conquest as well as his pragmatic need for "living space" to export excess population. According to McClatchy, Japan's Prussian methods could be seen in its two-faced duplicity in taking Shandong, brutal suppression of independence struggles in Korea, and potential threat to the Philippines should the United States grant its colony independence. To conquer the United States, McClatchy claimed, Japan relied on "peaceful penetration" through immigration. This method had already succeeded in Hawai'i, where the Japanese now made up over half the population (the actual number was 43 percent in 1920). To make matters worse, the nisei, as legal American citizens, would soon control the territory's politics and through their unbending race ties would make Hawai'i a "province of Japan." McClatchy concluded that California promised to be America's last opportunity to repel the peaceful invasion lest it spread to the rest of the nation. The fight on the mainland was to stop the smuggling of picture brides and other immigrants, reduce issei land control, and, of course, spur Congress to override the ineffective Gentleman's Agreement in passing exclusion legislation.[10]

Joining McClatchy and Phelan in the leadership of the postwar anti-Japanese movement was Joseph M. Inman, a California state senator largely responsible for efforts to strengthen the alien land law. In the winter of 1919, Inman and his backers tried but failed to get Governor William Stephens to open a special session of the California legislature so that it could shore up loopholes in the existing land law. Stephens, an Old Guard Republican from Southern California who was not up for reelection in 1920, proved susceptible to Secretary of State Robert Lansing's urging to avoid offending Japan. Not to be denied, Inman took the issue to the public by launching a signature campaign to put a harsh alien land measure on the ballot as a proposition. The effort, after some doubt, proved a success, and the initiative became the most talked-about ballot measure for the November elections. But before the proposition battle took shape, the House Committee on Immigration and Naturalization intervened by holding hearings on Japanese immigration throughout the West Coast. These hearings marked the first major showdown between exclusionists and egalitarians after World War I and thus provided an important window into the postwar exclusion debate.[11]

Hearings and Voices

The congressional hearings, held in seven locations across the West Coast in the summer of 1920, drew over 150 oral testimonies about Japanese immigration from a wide diversity of state and non-state actors. Familiar names for both exclusionists and egalitarians were on the list of testimonies. Phelan, McClatchy, and Chester Rowell testified for exclusion, while Harvey Guy, the missionary secretly connected to the Japanese Foreign Ministry, and George Shima, the issei "potato king" and president of the Japanese Association of America, testified for the opposition. Also on the egalitarian side was John P. Irish, California landowner, former newspaper editor, and political commentator, who would lead the fight against the alien land law initiative. In addition to these major players, the hearings featured a range of everyday people who provided fresh, and at times amusing, insight into the exclusion debate. Two final elements of the hearings were the press, which not just covered but influenced them, and the committee members themselves. By posing questions and making statements during testimony, as well as by offering commentary outside the hearings, the group of congressmen, led by committee chair Albert Johnson, revealed their own complicated thoughts about exclusion.

The congressional hearings provide four important insights into the postwar exclusion debate. First is the fact that egalitarians were well organized and influential. In many ways, the hearings flew in the face of the pronounced anti-Japanese position of California's major newspapers and political campaigns. Over half of those giving oral testimony favored treating Japanese immigrants fairly and opposed singling out Japan for exclusion. In this sense they shared the general spirit of Gulick's quota proposal that would severely limit Japanese immigration as part of an across-the-board reduction for all countries. Nearly two-thirds of the egalitarian testimony came from whites, while Japanese Americans provided the rest. According to a confidential report written for the Japanese Foreign Ministry by the American R. W. Ryder, the Japanese American testimony positively influenced committee members, even Congressman John E. Raker, a dyed-in-the-wool California exclusionist who in 1917 had backed Indian exclusion. When the hearings began, Raker was so brazen in his contempt for Japanese immigrants that Chairman Johnson and Isaac Siegel, a Jewish Republican from New York, warned him to tone down his aggressive questioning and pronouncements for exclusion lest his behavior compromise the fairness of the proceedings. But when the hearings moved north to the state of Washington, Raker's stance moderated. After visiting a Japanese language school in Seattle as part of the committee's investigation, he experienced a change of heart, telling Ryder repeatedly over two days that he could now see such schools as beneficial. As proof of his transformation, Raker issued a public statement at the end of the hearings proclaiming with confidence that Congress would pass a bill that "will satisfy the people of this [West] Coast and at the same time meet the wishes of the Japanese government."

He revealed that "after talking with scores of the leading Nipponese in the United States," he knew firsthand that a mutual trust and understanding had developed between them and the committee.[12]

In addition to Raker, Albert Johnson too expressed a surprisingly moderate view of the Japanese problem that belied his long-standing position as an ardent western exclusionist. Influenced by Phelan's and McClatchy's claims about widespread smuggling of Japanese immigrants, Johnson, a Republican from the state of Washington, came into the hearings suspecting that Japanese Associations, the main vehicle for issei leadership, were involved in the clandestine business of importing "picture brides." During the committee's investigations in Seattle, he in fact discovered evidence of an international ring to smuggle Japanese into the United States. The press pounced on the news, with exclusionist California newspapers implicating the issei organizations as the source behind the illegal migration. This, however, was not consistent with Johnson's findings, which focused on the existence of a smuggling ring but not one working in cooperation with issei organizations. In fact, Ryder "was convinced that Mr. Johnson, as well as the other members of the Committee, became satisfied in mind that the various Japanese Associations were doing a very desirable and necessary work and had no ulterior purposes whatever." At Ryder's urging, Johnson corrected the false and damaging representation of the issei organizations. This incident left Johnson, a former newspaper editor himself, with a bitter taste in his mouth about newspapers in the Golden State. He boasted to Ryder that "those California newspaper-men should come to Washington and get some lessons in honest journalism." As they had done for Raker, the hearings cleared up important myths and fears about the Japanese in Johnson's mind. In the end, the chairman told Ryder that the proceedings assured him that "whatever intention Japan MIGHT once have had to colonize America, I do not believe she holds any such intention or desire now."[13]

The second insight into the exclusion debate provided by the congressional hearings concerns the nature of the egalitarian opposition. During the hearings, the exclusionist V. S. McClatchy accurately characterized it as consisting of religious types who believed in the "fatherhood of God and brotherhood of man," absentee or large landowners who profited from leasing to the Japanese, and internationalists worried that exclusion "may produce friction and international complications."[14] These three groups, each egalitarian stalwarts since the nineteenth-century struggle over Chinese exclusion, were not surprising. But the wealth of testimonies in 1920 offered a more refined picture of the white opposition. Other groups supportive of the Japanese were public school teachers and administrators as well as social workers. These were people, often in close physical contact with Japanese Americans, who shared in the same goals of Americanization and social uplift through education. In this way, they operated much like missionaries and church leaders concerned about both the souls and social habits of their flock. Those with business relations with the Japanese also shared common goals with these immigrants, usually related to profit and the availability of work. They were likely to get to know their business partners, as in the case of John P. Irish, who pronounced his closeness to the Japanese by boasting that he spoke with intelligent and educated members of the group "nearly every day." One of these issei was Jiro Okabe, a young student from Japan who became a schoolboy in Irish's California home. Okabe would master English, study at the University of Chicago, and eventually become a leading Christian intellectual in Japan. When Irish visited Japan to receive an honor from Emperor Taisho in 1922, Okabe, as a member of the National Diet, was there to meet his old friend and former employer.[15]

Another way to understand the relationships between egalitarians and Japanese immigrants is to characterize them as playing a non-zero-sum game in which both sought to win by advancing their common interests. While a zero-sum game is like an election or sporting contest in which there is a definite winner and loser, a non-zero-sum game is like a peace treaty in which both sides can benefit. Thus, in this non-zero-sum situation, teachers won when Japanese American students studied well, as did missionaries when their flock embraced Christian precepts and landholders when tenant farmers harvested a bountiful crop. Internationalists too were seeking common interests with the Japanese through the League of Nations and bilateral diplomacy in which everyone would win by being spared the outbreak of a U.S.-Japan war. On the other hand, exclusionists were playing a zero-sum game in that they saw Japanese immigration as a win-or-lose proposition. They would win by excluding the Japanese because, from their perspective, it prevented them from losing their jobs and land, as well also from losing control of the American social order through the disharmony brought by a seemingly unassimilable element. How one saw Japanese immigrants (from a zero-sum or non-zero-sum perspective) was influenced by occupation, proximity to the Japanese, and the particular labor market needs in a given locality. From a distance like the East Coast, the Japanese problem did not seem to warrant the threat of a U.S.-Japan war. And in western regions in need of farm tenants and labor, Japanese immigrants were seen as a valuable commodity, a win-win proposition that provided economic benefit without disadvantaging any social group.

The testimony of Frank Terrace, a farmer and landholder in Orilla, Washington, who leased to the Japanese and hired them as workers, exemplified the combination of factors that characterized egalitarianism—economic necessity, familiarity with the Japanese, and a non-zero-sum perspective. Terrace left the committee dumbfounded with his recommendation that one million Japanese migrants be brought to the Pacific Northwest to transform cut forests into usable farmland because whites, who flocked to the cities, would not do this kind of work. "In our little town," he said, "there were 17 boys went off farms—went to the war. . . . Not one of them will come back to those farms. This is the condition."[16] When Congressmen John C. Box, Democrat from Texas, insisted that such a large Japanese migration would be akin to recreating the problem of slavery in the Old South, Terrace disagreed, saying that the situation in the Pacific Northwest was totally different in that the Japanese were free laborers and superior to African Americans. When other committee members pressed him about the problems of unassimilable Japanese forming a permanent racial caste, Terrace dismissed their fears, stating that, in fact, he would want them to marry and have children in order to produce more workers. The following exchange captured the dialogue about the problem of racial caste:

> Mr. Raker: Then you are going to bring the Japanese here with his wife, to allow him to raise boys and girls who will become citizens, and deny him the right, and his wife the right, to be citizens; is that right?
>
> Mr. Terrace: Well, I don't know how to answer that question. I sometimes think, probably, they would be valuable citizens as some we have already.[17]

Terrace went on to say that the nisei too would make good citizens and that the Japanese are "the most law-abiding people we have got in this State." Though incredulous regarding his recommendation for one million more Japanese immigrants and his inability to appreciate the problems of racial caste, the committee acknowledged Terrace's "practical" understanding of the "Japanese Question" because he had worked closely with them for the past fifteen years.[18]

The third insight provided by the congressional hearings addresses the contested meaning of race and assimilation. To almost all exclusionists, assimilation for the Japanese required miscegenation with whites, and in this sense they relied on Herbert Spencer's claim that the admixture of Japanese and Europeans would produce a "bad result." Some egalitarians, like Gulick and David Starr Jordan, took on this assumption by highlighting many good Eurasian mixtures. In the same vein, W. R. Lebo, a fertil-izer manufacturer in Tacoma, Washington, testified to knowing "half dozen [Japanese] half-breeds who are very intelligent and whom I can see nothing criminal about." But Lebo and the vast majority of egalitarians shied away from embracing miscegenation between Japanese and Europeans. Instead they distinguished between assimilation by blood and by culture. In the latter case, the Japanese could become good Americans by adopting the na-tion's economic and cultural habits without intermarriage. Mrs. L. S. Wood-ruff, an Americanization teacher in Stockton, California, made this distinc-tion clear when she dismissed Congressman Raker's fears about Japanese marrying whites as a nonissue, given the state's miscegenation laws. "There are always two factors in assimilation," she instructed Raker. "It takes more than [intermarriage] to assimilate, and I believe that the Japanese in their social and cultural life about us—that there will be assimilation." George Warren Hinman, an official for home missionary work headquartered in San Francisco, emphasized the same point as Woodruff in defining assimi-lation for the committee as "the sense of accepting American ideals" and not "simply that of miscegenation."[19]

An exchange between Raker and Thomas Burke, an international law-yer in Seattle, further revealed how different conceptions of assimilation fit within the arguments for both sides of the exclusion debate. In this case the Japanese were compared with European immigrants:

Mr. Raker: What you said about the Japanese people and their high
ideals and their desire to work and be honest, I do not believe
can be questioned, but they have been a race for thousands of
years—separate and distinct. The white people have been the same
way. Now, isn't it your view that it would be unfortunate to try to
assimilate these races physically?
Mr. Burke: Intermarriage, and so on?
Mr. Raker: Yes.
Mr. Burke: Why, of course, it would not be right; it would not be
desirable and the Japanese don't want it. Let me assure you that a
Japanese in the Orient that marries a white woman is looked down
upon.
Mr. Raker: If a Frenchman or Irishman or an Italian goes into any
community and raises a family of boys and girls, and these girls are
going to be married to some of our American boys and these boys
are going to be married to some of our American girls, that breaks
up this group or race division, doesn't it?

Mr. Burke: Yes.

Mr. Raker: And with the Japanese viewpoint, not wanting to physically assimilate our people, it leaves really one of the great questions that confronts us?

Mr. Burke: It leaves the question, if that were to be their aim, like the French, English, and Irish, to come in vast numbers, but a small number of them, in carrying on part of the commerce of the country, and the like of that, would not, it seems to me, present any serious trouble.[20]

Thus Burke accepted Raker's definition of the bad result of Eurasian intermarriage but dismissed it by saying that miscegenation was not wanted by the Japanese in the first place and that a relatively small population of racially clannish Japanese would not hurt American society. John Irish, in an address outside the congressional hearings, posed an alternative view by presenting the lack of miscegenation as a normal part of American experience that Jews and other groups practiced with positive results. Irish argued that "blood assimilation" was not an issue regarding Japanese immigrants because they, like the Jews, preferred to marry their own kind. This lack of biological assimilation was not a problem to Irish because Japanese and Jewish immigrants had shown a remarkable capacity for social, industrial, and financial assimilation in American life. For the Jew in particular, he argued, "we have joined spiritual forces with him and meet him on equal terms of mutual respect, making his rights ours, and all this without blood assimilation." In this way, Irish sidestepped the miscegenation question by arguing that the Japanese benefited the larger society whether or not they contributed to the nation's gene pool.[21]

The final insight provided by the congressional hearings concerns the introduction of new players into the exclusion debate. While representatives from a handful of local unions came out on behalf of exclusion, they were not joined by Paul Scharrenberg or others from the state or national American Federation of Labor. The absence of the AFL from the hearings was punctuated by the testimony of Erwin B. Ault, a radical labor publisher in Seattle who called on workers around the world to reject racial divisions in order to unite against capital. Ault's position was consistent with the philosophy of the Industrial Workers of the World, one of the nation's most radical and violent labor unions during the early twentieth century that sought to unite all workers, be they Asian or white, unskilled or skilled, agricultural or industrial, men or women. The "Wobblies" were at odds with the AFL's conservative craft unionism that divided workers by leaving the vast force of unskilled workers unorganized. Connected to both Socialists and anarchists, Industrial Workers of the World leaders faced hardships during the Red Scare, and union membership subsequently declined precipitously during the 1920s.[22]

But if the conservative craft unionism of the AFL was not a strong presence at the hearings, another band of exclusionists stepped into place. Testimony from members of the American Legion, a new national organization for veterans, highlighted postwar concerns about national security and patriotism. Albert G. Myran, from the American Legion post in Stockton, stated flatly, "We do not believe . . . that they [the Japanese] are patriotic." He cited confidential records from the local draft board showing that Japanese in Stockton evaded the draft. Myran also said the Japanese, as far as he knew, did not contribute money toward the Salvation Army or other public causes. But when it was pointed out that George Shima had purchased $180,000 in war bonds, he dismissed this fact as a savvy economic investment that revealed the insincerity of Shima's apparent patriotism. Thomas W. McManus, chair of the American Legion's National Committee on Oriental Immigration, framed the Japanese issue as a threat to the ability of veterans to recuperate from World War I: "We certainly cannot encourage Americans who served their country in the late war to own farms if they must compete with the Japanese . . . , [and] cannot expect them to live on farms where the surrounding country is owned or controlled by the interests of the Japanese."[23]

Alien Land Law Redux

As soon as the congressional hearings ended in August 1920, attention in California, and around the world, turned to the alien land law ballot measure, known as Proposition 1. While the hearings were a thorough (if not entirely unbiased) investigation into the details and nuances of the Japanese immigration issue, the campaigns for and against the land law measure were an altogether different animal. By definition, this sort of mass politics provoked partisan, polarized, and alarmist rhetoric that painted the issue in broad brushstrokes to provoke an emotional response from voters. If the hearings were run like a criminal investigation, the land law campaigns took the form of a political rally.

Proposition 1 recommended strengthening the state's existing alien land law in four ways. First, it added an outright ban on leasing agricultural land to the existing ban on ownership and, as such, proposed to deny issei the three-year leasing limit under the 1913 law. Second, the new measure would prevent "aliens ineligible to citizenship" from buying stock in companies that engaged in the buying or leasing of agricultural land. Third, it sought to close a major loophole in the alien land law by making it impossible for issei to control land by placing ownership in the names of their minor, American-born children. Finally, Proposition 1 recommended beefing up enforcement of the alien land law and stipulated that violators would be subject to forfeiture of the land in question. Voting "yes" on Proposition 1 meant that one supported strengthening the alien land law in the four ways outlined above, while "no" signaled opposition to one or all these.[24]

In the November 1920 general election, California voters approved Proposition 1 by a wide margin: 668,483 (75 percent) to 222,083 (25 percent). But given the profound influence of the exclusionist Hearst press and the fact that the major candidates for the U.S. Senate and state offices exploited anti-Japanese fears, it was not insignificant that more than 200,000 Californians opposed the measure.[25] In the wake of the election, George Shima accentuated positive aspects of the issei's failed campaign against the measure. In a letter to David Starr Jordan, he contended that, due to "broad-minded Americans" like Jordan, the outcome of the vote was "far more favorable to the Japanese than was universally expected, both by the Americans and the Japanese." The result renewed the issei's faith in America's essential goodness, noting it "clearly shows that the people of California are not willing to be stampeded by the anti-Japanese agitators into an act of unfairness." Shima's confidence in public opinion in the wake of Proposition 1's approval raises an intriguing question: Who else, besides Jordan, voted against the alien land law? By "who," I do not mean only prominent Californians like Jordan but also the social classes or types of voters opposed to anti-Japanese racism. To answer this question, the following analysis focuses on the varying intensity of the opposition to Proposition 1, first across California counties and then in Los Angeles neighborhoods.[26]

Map 5.1, showing California's fifty-eight counties in 1920, reveals the regional basis of the alien land law vote with exclusionist dominance in the north and disproportionate egalitarian strength in the south. Of the ten counties with the strongest exclusionist vote ("yes" on Proposition 1), only a fraction were in the south. On the other hand, Southern California made up 40 percent of the top ten counties with the strongest opposition vote ("no" on Proposition 1). Indeed, save for Santa Barbara County, the twenty-five counties most supportive of restricting Japanese landholding were in the north. Quantitative analysis suggests that among the most exclusionist counties, there was a positive relationship between exclusionism and the degree of Japanese farm ownership. In other words, exclusionism increased

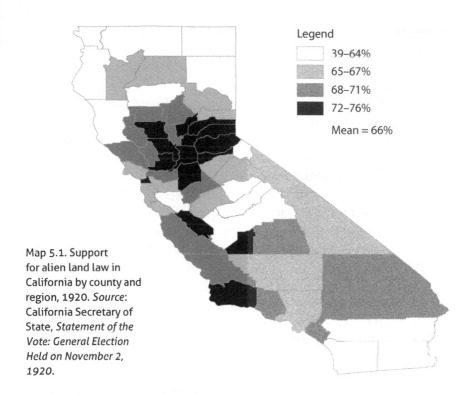

Map 5.1. Support for alien land law in California by county and region, 1920. *Source*: California Secretary of State, *Statement of the Vote: General Election Held on November 2, 1920.*

Legend

☐ 39–64%

◻ 65–67%

▨ 68–71%

■ 72–76%

Mean = 66%

where there was a higher Japanese presence in farm ownership, such as in Sacramento and Placer Counties, where a state high of 20 percent of all farms were owned by Japanese. This finding fits with the exclusionist rhetoric about the Japanese "invasion" of Florin (Sacramento County) and other towns, suggesting that voters in or near such places were the most solid backers of Proposition 1.[27]

There was no significant relationship, however, between Japanese landholding and the vote in counties least supportive of the proposition. The sizable proportion of Japanese-owned farms in Imperial and Los Angeles Counties did not produce a strong exclusionist vote as it did in the Sacramento delta, even though voters in both southern counties approved Proposition 1. This finding fits with regional differences in California. The northern half of the state was the bastion of labor organizing and progressive endeavors at land reclamation that challenged the control of the Southern Pacific Railroad and other large landholders. In both cases, the Japanese were seen as a tool promoting antidemocratic big business. The southern half, in contrast, was the home of business-friendly conservatism. Just as it stood for the open shop, the *Los Angeles Times* opposed Proposition 1 as an unnecessary impediment to the region's economic development. Its owner, Harrison Grey Otis, had a personal interest in opposing the land law as a principal investor in newly irrigated lands in Imperial and San Diego Counties that were being developed by pioneering Japanese and East Indian farmers.[28]

Consistent with the position of Southern California's largest and most influential newspaper, the opposition to Proposition 1 in Los Angeles was stronger than in San Francisco and Sacramento. As the state's largest county, Los Angeles provided nearly 30 percent of all opposition votes. While the above quantitative analysis of California counties provides no clear explanation of the Proposition 1 vote in Southern California, the geography of anti-Japanese exclusionism and egalitarianism is revealed through close study of voting patterns in the city of Los Angeles. Map 5.2 captures the wide variance in the city's opposition to Proposition 1. The percentage of the "no" votes has been recorded for 715 out of the 725 Los Angeles city precincts. The varying shades in map 5.2 correspond to percentage of egalitarianism within a given precinct. White indicates precincts where the opposition vote was weakest, suggesting these were the city's most anti-Japanese areas. The lightest gray connotes a slight rise in opposition but still below the city's 25 percent average. The middle shade of gray represents average to moderately above average opposition, while the darkest gray reflects precincts with relatively strong opposition. Finally, black highlights the city's most tolerant areas, where a majority of voters opposed the alien land law initiative, often overwhelmingly.[29]

If there was a monolithic anti-Japanese consensus in Los Angeles, then map 5.2 would be monochromatically white with flecks of gray and nary a speck of black. This, however, is not the case. While anti-Japanese sentiment was pronounced on the city's south side, northeast, and central areas, egalitarianism existed in the east and especially in the central district and west side. The variance in the Proposition 1 vote testifies to the presence of people who opposed anti-Japanese racism, an important finding in itself given that the existing scholarship virtually ignores the opposition.[30] Yet map 5.2 also supports existing studies of Los Angeles's political and social geography. We know that zoning ordinances located heavy industrial development in the central, southern, and eastern parts of the city while preserving the west side for residential and other low-impact development. Consequently, race and class segregation pervaded the city as white workers settled in areas close to industrial plants on the east and south sides as well as in the city center. Meanwhile, African Americans clustered in the central district along Central Avenue, and affluent whites occupied the city's western regions.[31]

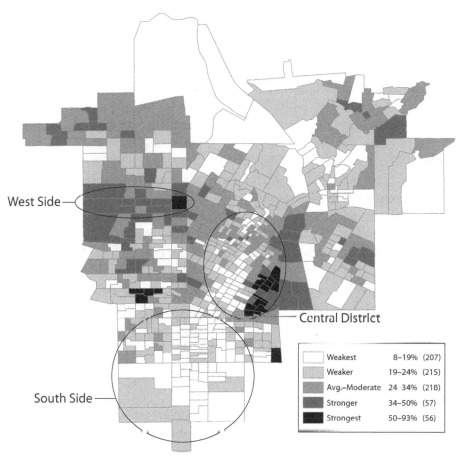

Weakest	8–19%	(207)
Weaker	19–24%	(215)
Avg.–Moderate	24 34%	(218)
Stronger	34–50%	(57)
Strongest	50–93%	(56)

West Side

Central District

South Side

Map 5.2. Opposition to alien land law in Los Angeles, 1920. *Source*: LA-Vote.

A closer look at the west side, south side, and central district confirms the city's race and class segregation while providing a more precise picture of the relationship between geography, demography, and anti-Japanese racism. The west side area circled in map 5.2 reveals the relatively strong opposition to Proposition 1 in one of the city's most affluent areas. The neighborhoods along Wilshire Boulevard, where the egalitarianism clustered, were home to the luxurious Ambassador Hotel and upscale real estate developments including Hancock Park—current site of the Los Angeles mayor's mansion—and Country Club Park, built on land opened up when the city's country club moved to Beverly Hills. Real estate surveys of the area reveal large residential plots becoming more modest in size the farther one moves north or south of Wilshire Boulevard. The relative racial tolerance of affluent Angelenos makes sense given the leading role that much-loathed labor unions played in the anti-Japanese movement. Racial tolerance also fitted the economic interests of the city's elite as they were more likely than workers to engage in business deals with Japanese farmers and to hire issei as domestic servants.

The south side area circled in map 5.2 stands in stark contrast to the racially liberal, though politically conservative, west side. Egalitarianism was at its weakest in this area of small, tightly packed workers' homes surrounding factories such as the Goodyear Tire and Rubber plant in South Park. It is quite likely that the people in this area shared the California labor movement's long-standing antipathy against Asian immigrants. Workers saw Japanese immigrants as a threat to their jobs, standard of living, and the nation's racial purity. That workers became homeowners in Los Angeles added a new element to their racial fears, as they sought to prevent Asian immigrants, as well as blacks and Latinos, from moving into their racially restricted neighborhoods. White hostility, sometimes accompanied by anti-Japanese violence, occurred west of downtown in Pico Heights and Hollywood, east of downtown in Belvedere and Rose Hill, and south of downtown in West Jefferson and South Park. Evidence from the nearby white working-class community of Southgate also reveals a powerful connection between racism and homeownership. One of the main reasons that Southgate residents fought against racially integrated housing was to protect the economic values of their modest homes.[32]

The central district circled in map 5.2 combined both the strongest and weakest opposition to Proposition 1. Here was an area containing working-class whites as well as the city's African American community. White workers inhabited areas with the weakest egalitarianism; blacks lived in those with the strongest. The overwhelming black vote against Proposition 1 resulted from more than a natural alliance between two non-white minorities, even though both groups confronted similar problems related to segregated housing, employment, and public facilities. But as U.S. citizens, African Americans were unaffected by the alien land law. To draw black attention to Proposition 1, officials in the Los Angeles Japanese consulate united with issei leaders during the 1920 campaign to establish the American League of Democracy, an organization designed to promote black-Japanese friendship and political cooperation. The league sponsored dance parties bringing the two racial groups together. More important, it quietly hired African American leaders, including Charlotta Bass, editor of the *California Eagle*, Los Angeles's leading black newspaper, to rally opposition to Proposition 1 in black churches, Negro women's clubs, and other community organizations. Egalitarianism also appeared in editorials and

Table 5.1. Occupational distribution by select Los Angeles precincts, 1920

Occupation (for white male heads of household)	Prop. 1 weakest opposition (exclusionist)	Prop. 1 strongest opposition (egalitarian)
Professional	10	26
Managerial	15	30
Clerical	9	4
Skilled trades	39	18
Low-skilled labor	27	19
Farming	0	3
Total	100 (N = 242)	100 (N = 213)

Source: Census 1920.

advertisements in Bass's paper. In return for the *Eagle*'s support, Bass asked that her counterparts in the local Japanese press report on antilynching campaigns. On Election Day, the American League of Democracy paid poll watchers to monitor voting in African American precincts. A final report of its campaign, submitted to the Japanese Foreign Ministry, estimated that 95 percent of voters within the black community opposed Proposition 1.[33]

If the black vote can be explained by the concerted campaign by African American and issei leaders, then what explains the variance in white opposition to Proposition 1? The Japanese consulate also quietly worked with white Christian ministers, business leaders, and sympathetic labor unions to galvanize opposition against Proposition 1 within the general public. Consulate officers paid agents to organize within labor unions on the basis of fraternal ties between American and Japanese workers; they also brought a follower of Henry George's single-tax movement to a union meeting in which he maintained that the alien land law was a "yellow club" with which the "capitalist politicians" were bashing white workers.[34] But the results fell far short of the success achieved within the black community. Quantitative study of thirty-five precincts distinguished by very high or very low opposition to Proposition 1 sheds light on differences within the white vote.[35] If class status did not matter, then both affluent and working-class areas would vote roughly the same way. Table 5.1 reveals this was not the case. It shows the kinds of occupations prevalent in precincts disproportionately supporting the discriminatory Proposition 1 (or where egalitarianism was weakest) as well as those disproportionately opposed to it (or where egalitarianism was strongest). In focusing on white male heads of household, the analysis controls for race and gender in order to highlight class differences.[36] The findings show that exclusionist precincts where Proposition 1 received its strongest support were working-class neighborhoods in which 66 percent of white males were employed in either skilled trades (39 percent) or low-skilled labor (27 percent). In contrast, egalitarian precincts where the opposition to Proposition 1 was strongest were middle- to upper-class areas where professionals (26 percent) and managers (30 percent) made up the majority.

Thus class was a factor in the Proposition 1 vote in Los Angeles. The working classes were disproportionately inclined to vote for the anti-Japanese alien land initiative, while their bosses and others in the middle and upper classes were more inclined to oppose it. This suggests the success of labor unions in rallying their members to support Proposition 1. In contrast, the data for low-skilled laborers, who at this time remained outside the purview of mainstream labor unions, does not show as significant a difference as that for the skilled workers. It was the union workers who were more virulently anti-Japanese. On the other hand, the higher the status and income of white male breadwinners, the more likely they were to oppose anti-Japanese racism. In this way, occupational status influenced not just where one lived but also how one voted.

To the extent that the opposition vote cannot be explained entirely by geographic and class factors, map 5.3 reveals the intensity of political party affiliation across Los Angeles precincts by using the vote for the U.S. president in the same general election as Proposition 1. The main candidates in 1920 were Warren G. Harding (Republican), James M. Cox (Democrat), and Eugene V. Debs (Socialist). Mapping the level of support for each candidate reveals similar class and geographic patterns to the Proposition 1 vote. The vote for the Republican presidential candidate, shown in map 5.3, reveals the party's dominance in Los Angeles, a long-standing feature of the city's political history and not simply a factor of Harding's landslide victory in California and across the nation. What is important for our purposes was the relative strength of the Republican vote across Los Angeles precincts. The black shaded areas, revealing the strongest support for Harding, were concentrated on the west side, as well as in the African American community in the central district, where the GOP was still very much regarded as the party of Abraham Lincoln. These were the same areas that strongly opposed Proposition 1. Conversely, the Republican vote, while still the majority, diminished significantly in areas in the central district and on the south side that were decidedly anti-Japanese.

The vote for the Democratic Party candidate (not shown) also high-

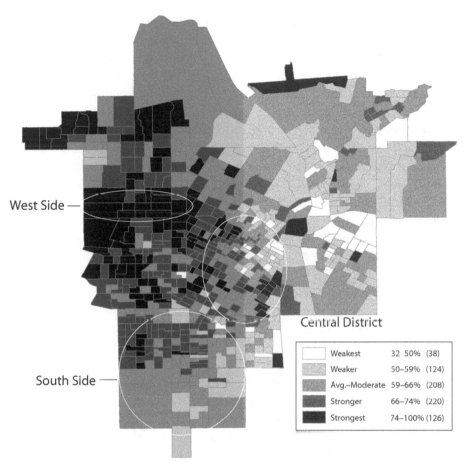

West Side —

Central District

South Side —

	Weakest	32–50% (38)
	Weaker	50–59% (124)
	Avg.–Moderate	59–66% (208)
	Stronger	66–74% (220)
	Strongest	74–100% (126)

Map 5.3. Support for Republican presidential candidate in Los Angeles, 1920.
Source: LA-Vote.

lighted the west side–south side difference, which was evident as well in the central district. The upscale Hancock Park area along Wilshire Boulevard, as well as the African American community along Central Avenue, showed the weakest support for Cox. But the white working-class areas that strongly backed Proposition 1 were much more likely than west side and African American voters to support the Democratic candidate. The same pattern appeared even more starkly in the vote for the Socialist Debs (not shown), who found much more support on the south side than on the west side. The strongest areas of egalitarianism were also the strongest areas to oppose the Socialist Party, while the strongest exclusionism provided strong support for the Socialists.[37]

What emerges from comparing presidential and Proposition 1 voting is a profile of anti-Japanese racism in Los Angeles. The most tolerant areas contained a large proportion of affluent white professionals and high-level managers who were staunch Republicans fearful of efforts by labor unions, Socialists, and other radicals to upset the status quo. At the same time, they opposed the Democratic Party, which symbolized both the white supremacy of the "solid South" and increasing support from northern white, urban workers. The city's other bastion of egalitarianism was the African American community. In contrast, the most exclusionist parts of town contained a higher proportion of white skilled workers influenced by labor unions that, since the nineteenth century, led the charge in California for Asian immigration exclusion. While majority Republican, these areas were more likely than the west side to turn to Democrats and Socialists as alternatives to the typically pro-business GOP. The people in anti-Japanese parts of town feared that big businesses, in seeking corporate profits, were inclined to replace white workers with cheap Asian immigrants who would never unite with them in labor unions. In addition, white workers worried that their home values would collapse if racial minorities were allowed to move into their neighborhoods.

Congress and Exclusion

While James Phelan celebrated the passage of Proposition 1, the California general election in 1920 proved bittersweet for the incumbent senator. Like many Democrats, he fell victim to the Republican presidential landslide that swept Harding into office as an alternative to President Wilson and his internationalist vision. Phelan's Republican challenger, Samuel Shortridge, who also joined the anti-Japanese chorus, defeated the incumbent in riding to victory on Harding's coattails. Yet after leaving the Senate, Phelan continued to play a leading role in the exclusion movement as a private citizen with name recognition, deep pockets, and influence on Capitol Hill. In a highly watched trip to Japan he tried to calm international tensions by explaining that Japanese exclusion was needed in order to forestall conflict between two incongruous races. He also joined with McClatchy, Inman, and California attorney general Ulysses S. Webb to form the Japanese Exclusion League, which (not to be confused with the earlier labor-based Asiatic Exclusion League) was a new organization rooted in a coalition consisting of the American Legion, the California Federation of Labor, the Native Sons of the Golden West, and the California State Grange. While capitalizing on the American Legion's high regard in postwar America, McClatchy, as director of the Japanese Exclusion League, did the yeoman's share of the work conducting research, sending out press releases, and lobbying congressmen and other federal officials. McClatchy remained in close contact with Phelan and exclusionist U.S. senator Hiram Johnson.[38]

The road to exclusion, as McClatchy knew well, was not an easy one. Despite continuing conflict over the Open Door in China and the success of Proposition 1, American hopes for harmonious U.S.-Japan relations were buoyed by the Washington arms limitation treaties, signed in 1922, in which both nations, along with the world's other leading powers, for the first time in modern history agreed to restrict weapons of war, which meant in some cases decommissioning their own battleships and other naval vessels. Soon after, a major earthquake in Tokyo enabled Americans to return the good wishes and humanitarian aid that Japan had shown to the victims of the great earthquake that had struck San Francisco seventeen years before. The two nations in peace and tragedy had many important reasons to resolve the immigration conflict in a way that would benefit both sides, which is what the House Immigration Committee had recommended at the conclusion of its hearings in 1920. To formalize such intentions, U.S. and Japanese diplomats made plans to negotiate a new treaty to replace the Gentlemen's Agreement, which exclusionists criticized as a secret deal that was not being honored by Japan. The new treaty, in theory, would be even more restrictionist by closing the Gentlemen's Agreement's loopholes for family reunification. But at the same time it would prevent discriminatory legislation by removing the urgency for Congress to pass Japanese exclusion. Within this context of transpacific goodwill, McClatchy consciously avoided using explicitly anti-Japanese rhetoric, stressing the economic rather than racial basis for exclusion. By focusing on a "dispassionate consideration of the facts," he sought to woo prominent egalitarians like David Starr Jordan and Harvey Guy to the exclusionist side of the debate. In light of this, McClatchy did his best to play down the name of his organization, the Japanese Exclusion League, so as not to offend potential egalitarian converts.[39]

Despite the fact that President Calvin Coolidge and Secretary of State Charles Evans Hughes were careful about not offending Japan, the exclusionist fight was not entirely uphill. While Japan returned Shandong to China in negotiations at the Washington Conference, its expansionism in Asia and the Pacific remained a major concern to the United States. Here was a moment in which Lothrop Stoddard combined the study of international relations with warnings about what famed eugenicist Madison Grant called the "passing of the great [white] race." Stoddard's widely read *Rising Tide of Color* offered an explicitly racialized internationalism that rejected both the Wilsonian focus on collective security and individual liberties, as well as separate Communist interests in world proletarian revolution. Rather, Stoddard called for white nations to unite by overcoming national conflicts that were disastrously acted out in the "white civil war" of World War I. Such infighting, he bemoaned, allowed the West to overlook the "rising tide of color" led by an expansionist Japan that sought to use immigration and decolonization as a means for world conquest. More than McClatchy's concerns about Japan as the "Germany of Asia," Stoddard's analysis provided an informed theory of contemporary international relations that dovetailed with domestic fears about the yellow peril.[40]

Meanwhile, exclusionists got a lift from the U.S. Supreme Court when it upheld the core of California's alien land law, leaving John Irish's legal campaign against it, like his opposition to Proposition 1, looking for positives in defeat. In this case, he found it in the Court striking down a clause preventing issei from placing land in the name of their American-born children. Even more relevant for the prospects of exclusion were the *Ozawa* (1922) and *Thind* (1923) decisions in which the Court made it clear that Asian immigrants were not "white" and therefore were ineligible for American citizenship. The idea of granting issei U.S. citizenship, which House Immigration Committee chair Albert Johnson had advocated as part of the resolution to the immigration conflict, would now require concerted effort by Congress to eliminate race from the nation's naturalization laws. If Radical Republicans could not do this during the apex of their power in 1870, there was little chance that Congress would do it during the restrictionist era of the "tribal twenties."[41]

By March 1924 the exclusion debate, as had happened so many times before, had reached a political divide, with exclusionists backed by the West Coast and the House, while the egalitarians relied upon the president, the State Department, and the Senate. During the middle of the month, egalitarians maintained the upper hand in more than four days of hearings conducted on Japanese exclusion by the Senate Committee on Immigration. Led by committee chair LeBaron B. Colt, a Republican from Rhode Island, testimony was heard from a handful of leading players on both sides of the exclusion debate, headlined by the exclusionist V. S. McClatchy and egalitarian Sidney Gulick. In pending legislation designed to provide a comprehensive change to the nation's immigration policy, there were three options on the table for how to handle the influx of Japanese immigrants. First, Congress could include Japan in the immigration quota system currently proposed for Europe and all nations whose people were eligible for naturalization; second, Congress could do nothing and let the Gentlemen's Agreement and 1911 U.S.-Japan Commercial Treaty continue to ban laborers while allowing for merchants and other exempt classes; or, third, it could approve a House bill proposed by Albert Johnson that would enact whole-sale exclusion of Japanese and any other immigrants ineligible for citizen-ship with exemptions made for certain classes of "nonimmigrants" such as students, ministers, tourists, and persons engaged in business on a tem-porary basis.[42]

The exclusionists testifying at the hearings strongly backed the John-son bill, the third option. McClatchy, California attorney general Ulysses S. Webb, former senator James Phelan, and current senator Samuel Short-ridge argued that it was necessary to set aside the Gentlemen's Agree-ment because Japan had willingly violated President Roosevelt's original intention, which was to stop the increase of Japanese immigrants in the United States. McClatchy pointed out that while Roosevelt defended Japa-nese immigration at one point in his presidency, during the negotiation of the Gentlemen's Agreement he became convinced that the Japanese made up a race fundamentally incompatible with white Americans and should be totally excluded. This latter view was confirmed, McClatchy revealed, in Roosevelt's autobiography, published in 1913. The dramatic increase in Japanese immigration since 1908, especially the migration of "picture brides," was seen as proof that the Japanese government did not hold up its end of the bargain. This critique of Japan as engaging in underhanded prac-tices reflected the conventional points made by exclusionists about how the growing population of unassimilable Japanese in California imperiled the state's economic and social opportunities for its white residents.[43]

The egalitarians countered by pointing out flaws in the exclusionist posi-tion. David Starr Jordan submitted a letter to the committee claiming that the nefarious image of the Japanese government as violating the Gentle-men's Agreement was dead wrong, for Japan was judiciously abiding by the agreement, and it was a more effective policy than "any arbitrary act could be." Gulick added that the dreaded picture brides were seen by Japan as part of the agreed-upon convention of family reunification for Japanese immigrants already in the United States. Once Japanese officials learned that these brides were unwanted by Americans, they stopped issuing pass-ports to them. The image of a trustworthy Japan epitomized the optimistic ideas that Jordan, Gulick, and a number of supporters with knowledge of Japan confirmed about the assimilability of Japanese people to Western civilization. At the same time, the egalitarians wanted to clear up the popu-lar misunderstanding that they favored unchecked Japanese labor migra-tion, which Jordan made abundantly clear was not the case; both sides, he said, wanted to maintain the exclusion of laboring classes.[44]

While the Senate committee's charge was to listen impartially to both sides of the argument, it was clear from the hearings that its members favored the egalitarian position to restrict Japanese immigrants in a way that would not offend Japan. Chairman Colt reminded exclusionists about the importance of respecting international treaties and agreements and that Congress should set them aside only after diplomatic channels had been exhausted. While he was certain that Congress had the right to abrogate the Gentlemen's Agreement and 1911 Commercial Treaty, he wondered repeatedly whether it was necessary and wise to "build a spite fence" with a friendly nation like Japan. In responding to Senator Shortridge, Colt asked rhetorically: "Suppose you and I have a contract with each other. That is all a treaty is, a contract between nations. You and I have a contract. I have got the power to modify or abrogate it. Do you think it is fair for me, having the power, to do it without first consulting you?" Committee member David A. Reed, Republican from Pennsylvania, was also perplexed by exclusionist insistence for the discriminatory Johnson bill. He asked Shortridge why he was not satisfied with giving Japan a tiny quota of one hundred immigrants per year. That committee members kept asking this question in various guises to different exclusionists testifying suggested they were irritated by their evasive answers. The clearest response came from McClatchy, who stated that even a trickle of immigrants from Japan would be detrimental "because it is an abandonment of the principle that aliens ineligible to citizenship should not be admitted as immigrants." This was a problem, he said, "because if you except Japan and place her in the quota you are at once acceding to her demand that she be placed on the same plane as Europeans, and that conceded, it would only be a question of time when she would demand, as she is demanding now, citizenship and other privileges." In this way, as Chairman Colt put it, the exclusionists feared that a Japan quota would become an "entering wedge" to breaking down the racial barriers to U.S. citizenship.[45]

Both egalitarians and exclusionists were dismayed by their side's chances after the Senate hearings. Even after noting that exclusionists had performed badly at the hearings, Gulick was resigned to defeat. In reporting to Eiichi Shibusawa, he confessed that "the approaching elections, together with the growing demand in the Pacific Coast States for legislation by Congress that will absolutely stop the coming of further Japanese for permanent residence . . . do not present a very hopeful outlook."[46] But Phelan, who was confident that exclusion would pass the House, noted in private that the issue had been "practically lost" in the Senate before he, McClatchy, and Webb began lobbying on Capitol Hill in late March. Phelan blamed Senator Shortridge, the man who had unseated him in 1920, for alienating southern senators in leading the charge for African American rights by pushing both an antilynching bill and the appointment of a black customs official in New Orleans. Southerners, said Phelan, were threatening to buck their own Democratic Party to pay Shortridge back by voting against his beloved Japanese exclusion bill. After Hiram Johnson returned to the capital on April 9, he, along with the California lobbyists, were able to broker a deal with the southerners that ensured their support for exclusion in return for Shortridge's promise to abandon antilynching legislation.[47]

Meanwhile, the exclusionists benefited from a noisy controversy regarding the Japanese ambassador's warning that exclusion would produce "grave consequences" for U.S.-Japan relations. On the eve of the Senate vote on the immigration bill that included the Johnson bill, Henry Cabot Lodge, in one of the last acts of his long political career, mustered up all of the nationalist zeal he had left to condemn Ambassador Masanao Hanihara's warning as a "veiled threat" of war. The response to the majority leader's call to arms was overwhelming as the Senate, in an unrecorded vote, agreed 76-2 to abrogate the Gentlemen's Agreement, which paved the way for Japanese exclusion. Senator Reed said he spoke for the entire Senate Immigration Committee in saying that before Japan's "veiled threat," it had been committed to making an exception of Japanese immigration by combining the U.S.-Japan agreement with a small immigration quota so as not to offend the Japanese people. Reed was one of many senators who voted with deep regret and a "sad heart" to end the framework of the Gentlemen's Agreement.[48]

Interpretations of Japanese exclusion almost always cast it as a political rout in which the potent cocktail of racism, jingoism, and xenophobia made such legislation nearly inevitable. But such a view ignores not only the strength of egalitarianism but also important political contingencies, such as the unlikely southern opposition to exclusion. In contrast, exclusionists like Phelan never underestimated egalitarians; even after the immigration bill safely passed both houses of Congress and after he left Washington and was on board a luxury ocean liner to England, he was still writing letters and telegrams to McClatchy and Johnson warning them about last-ditch efforts to get President Coolidge to veto the legislation. Coolidge, in fact, would have vetoed a Japanese exclusion bill had it not come to him bundled with the comprehensive package of reforms in the Immigration Act of 1924.[49] Another last-minute move in the House was to postpone by eight months the start of Japanese exclusion so that during this time cooler heads could come up with a solution to the problem that would not offend

Japan. This was Coolidge's plan, and it was championed in the House by fellow Republican Albert Johnson, who still sought to have restriction without giving offense to Japan. He tried to calm fears about hordes of Japanese entering the United States by explaining that a quota for Japan would allow only about sixty immigrants each year. A final appeal by House majority leader Nicholas Longworth asked, "Shall we accomplish what we are seeking to accomplish gracefully or ungracefully? Shall we perform what we are about to perform politely or impolitely?" In the end, the attempt to postpone Japanese exclusion failed in two equally close party-line votes won by the exclusionist coalition of Democrats and western Republicans.[50]

The exclusion of Japanese immigrants culminated a quarter-of-a-century-long effort by western exclusionists to overcome opposition from a broad coalition of egalitarians. As in the nineteenth-century movement against the Chinese, the push for Japanese exclusion confronted those seeking to expand transpacific trade and labor migration. But more important in the latter case was the threat of war between the United States and Japan, which compelled presidents, secretaries of state, and congressional leaders to restrict Japanese immigration by means other than humiliating legislation. Moved by Senator Lodge's call to arms against Japan's "veiled threat," Congress ended up offending Japan in approving the Immigration Act of 1924. Lodge, who died five months after exclusion was enacted, would not live to see the grave consequences to U.S.-Japan relations that would follow. But, at the time, nobody in either the United States or Japan could have predicted that these two Pacific powers were headed on the road to war. In fact, the passage of a system of comprehensive immigration restriction, based in national origins quotas, for the first time provided a durable form of security against the human flood of immigration. This allowed exclusionists to soften their views toward Japanese Americans while turning their attention to the continuing influx of another Asian group.

6 SILVER LINING

NEW DEALS FOR ASIAN AMERICANS,

1924–1941

IIIIIIIIIIIIIIIIIIIIIIIIIIIIIIIIIIIIIIIIIIIIIIIIIIIIIIIIIIIIIIIIIIIIIIIIIIIIIIIIIIIIIIIIIIIIIIIIIIIIIIIIIIIIIIIIIIIIIIIIIIIIIIIIIIIIIIIIIIIIIIIIIIIIIII

In 1939, Carey McWilliams became head of California's Division of Immigration and Housing, a position created in 1913 to Americanize foreign-born workers. Unlike his predecessors in office, all of whom were Progressive or Republican, McWilliams was a Democrat. A writer and civil liberties lawyer with Communist sympathies, he was author of *Factories in the Fields*, a Henry George–inspired history of California's farm labor problem that condemned large growers and organized labor alike for the state's "monopolistically owned and controlled system" of agriculture. The critique of land monopolies was taken straight from George, but what was remarkable was McWilliams's utter rejection of his racism. McWilliams paints a sympathetic picture of Asian migrant laborers, emphasizing the importance of working-class solidarity over racial divisions. In this way, he updated George's focus on land distribution by grafting it onto the leftist strategy of interracial labor organizing.[1]

As a public servant in Sacramento, McWilliams represented a surprising change from the California exclusionists who had led successful campaigns for Proposition 1 and Japanese exclusion. In the 1920s it was unthinkable that a radical like him would be appointed to run the Division of Immigration and Housing. Then again, no one could have predicted the Great Depression or President Franklin D. Roosevelt's response. McWilliams was one of many leftist reformers during the New Deal era who undermined the infrastructure of exclusionism in attempting to democratize the nation's industrial relations. This chapter places them squarely within the narrative of the exclusion debate.

In the wake of the exclusionist triumph in shutting out Japanese immigrants, egalitarians launched new efforts to promote racial understanding, including major research projects and campaigns to repeal Japanese exclusion and prevent Filipinos from facing the same fate. Such efforts took advantage of the pervasive spirit for international peace and goodwill generated both by traumatic memories of World War I and by the promise of the League of Nations and international accords like the Washington arms control treaties. The egalitarian cause also benefited from the growing acceptance among the educated elite of new racial theories that disavowed the biological basis of racial discrimination. It was in this context that transformations to organized labor during the Great Depression brought into the egalitarian fold a major national labor federation, the Congress of Industrial Organizations (CIO). The CIO, championed by radicals like McWilliams, challenged the American Federation of Labor's race-based exclusionism, and as such the egalitarians gained their most powerful ally ever within the house of labor. Undergirding this new age of labor organizing were pathbreaking New Deal policies intended to advance economic justice for both whites and nonwhites.

The remarkable reinvigoration of egalitarianism after the enactment of Japanese exclusion provided an important transition to the egalitarian era that would begin during World War II. But before then it had little impact on anti-Asian policies. Conflict over China's sovereignty made it politically impossible to repeal Japanese exclusion while U.S.-Japan relations remained strained for most of the 1930s and into the new decade. During this time, exclusionists also won a struggle to exclude Filipino immigrants. As had happened in the 1870s and again in the 1890s, economic hard times in the 1930s fueled exclusionism—this time directed against Filipinos, who became the final Asian American group to confront racial barriers to immigration. Now with regulations in place to hold back the human flood from all of Asia, and with CIO interracialism gaining force in the labor market, exclusionism became increasingly unmoored from immigration concerns. By the mid-1930s, the dwindling exclusionist coalition turned its attention to national security, as Europe prepared for war and U.S.-Japan relations took a turn for the worse over the island nation's expansionism in China.

Evolving Egalitarianism

After World War I, three American missionaries serving in Japan returned home to join their former colleagues Sidney Gulick and Harvey Guy in the struggle against anti-Japanese racism. One was George Gleason, secretary of the Tokyo YMCA, who revived Francis Loomis's unsuccessful attempt to launch a research project in California to clear up misinformation about Japanese immigrants. Another returnee was Galen Fisher, Gulick's brother-in-law and Gleason's YMCA colleague in Tokyo. After obtaining a master's degree in sociology from Columbia University, Fisher joined the Rockefeller Foundation's newly established Institute for Social and Religious Research, where he steered funds toward Gleason's project that would become known as the Survey of Race Relations. The final returned missionary was John Merle Davis, another administrator in the Japanese YMCA and son of one of the earliest and most famous American missionaries to Japan. Davis became the head administrator of the Survey of Race Relations and relied on Guy to help carry out the project.

The Survey of Race Relations began in 1923 as Congress was considering Japanese exclusion. Given the power of exclusionists at that time, Guy sensed that "it looks like our investigation will be too late, the diagnosis has become an autopsy." Still he joined the survey's executive committee, believing that much could be learned from examining the "corpse." Guy's support for the project stemmed in large part from its new approach to the "Japanese question." The egalitarians behind the survey learned valuable lessons from the failed education campaign in California. They knew well that the Carnegie Endowment had refused to fund Loomis's request for research, fearing that doing so would incur the wrath of anti-Japanese union workers who were already predisposed to see the great industrialist as their enemy. John D. Rockefeller Jr. harbored the same concerns as the Carnegie Endowment, but Fisher and YMCA head John Mott were able to alleviate these by recasting Gleason's original project from a focus exclusively on the Japanese in California into a broadly conceived study of race relations, encompassing many groups throughout the entire West Coast, including British Columbia.[2]

In seeking objective knowledge, the survey brought together exclusionists and egalitarians in search of facts about race relations. In this way, its leaders invited participation from V. S. McClatchy, labor leader Paul Scharrenberg, and other members of the California Joint Immigration Committee (CJIC), formerly the Japanese Exclusion League. McClatchy changed the name of the organization to deflect the charge that its exclusionist politics were damaging U.S.-Japan relations. In order to "mend fences" after exclusion had passed, he accepted invitations to engage in dialogue with egalitarians.[3] In November 1924, he gave a series of joint lectures with George Gleason in Southern California that, McClatchy reported, were bathed in the spirit of friendship and mutual respect. The exclusionist particularly relished the opportunity to address audiences at churches, the Greater Federation of Women's Clubs, and other egalitarian strongholds. McClatchy countered the image of him as a kind of exclusionist Satan by encouraging issei and nisei Americanization and asserting that he was willing to be friends with them. He also supported the survey's effort to move the exclusion debate on to a basis of solid facts. In the end, McClatchy appealed to reason and objectivity rather than to racist fears or invective to explain why America needed race-based immigration exclusion and policies like the alien land law. While the CJIC did not officially support the survey, the project administrator, Merle Davis, deemed it a success that these influential exclusionists were in constructive dialogue with egalitarians and did not object to the survey's preliminary findings.[4]

Another dimension to the survey's objectivity was its focus on rigorous scientific research methods. Gleason thought long and hard about the project's research director, rejecting a number of experts on Asian immigration in favor of Robert Ezra Park, a leading figure in American sociology at the University of Chicago who had little interest in politics or taking sides on the exclusion debate. Yet despite its goal of objectivity, the survey remained an egalitarian cause, as its critics correctly pointed out. Although more interested in laws of human behavior than in crass politics, Park was aligned with egalitarians like Gleason, Davis, and Fisher rather than with exclusionists like McClatchy. Experienced in the study of European immigrants and African Americans, Park embraced the survey as an opportunity to test his theory of the "race relations cycle," which challenged the biologically determined conception of race dominance in the social and physical sciences and earlier had informed Herbert Spencer's view of the "bad result" from race mixing and been used to justify exclusionist politics. Focusing on social adaptation rather than on biological evolution, Park's theory viewed race as a set of ideas (rather than as a fixed physical inheritance) that transformed amid changing experiences confronted by ethnic or racial groups. The changes conformed to a universal process (a "race relations cycle"), moving from the shock of newcomers entering into a society to the ensuing competition for resources between them and existing groups and then to the accommodations that both make to ease competition. In many cases, Park observed, this period of accommodation led to an emotional blending, or assimilation, of old and new groups and was shaped by intermarriage and mixed children. Hence the social theorist came to the race relations survey inclined to reject the exclusionist assumption that the genetic makeup of Asian immigrants precluded their assimilation into American society.[5]

Based at Stanford University, the survey's institutional setting also embodied the spirit of egalitarianism. The school's benefactor, Leland Stanford, had been a partner in the Central Pacific Railroad that hired hundreds of Chinese immigrants, and his widow, Jane Stanford, had ordered the firing of the young sociologist Edward Alsworth Ross in part for inciting protests for Japanese exclusion. Moreover, the man who fired Ross was Stanford president David Starr Jordan, one of Japan's most reliable and powerful friends in the United States. It was during Jordan's tenure that the school established the first chair in Japanese studies on the West Coast from Gaimusho funds secretly channeled through the industrialist Eiichi

Shibusawa. The holder of this chair, Yamato Ichihashi, along with many of his faculty colleagues and Ray Lyman Wilbur, who succeeded Jordan as president, kept the university a bastion of egalitarianism.[6]

The survey's research fit the egalitarian sensibilities of its founders, funders, research director, and institutional context. Its findings obtained nationwide expression in May 1926 when *Survey Graphic*, a publication of the Council of Christian Associations, produced a special issue on race relations, "East by West: Our Windows on the Pacific." The journal contained a description of the survey's goals by Merle Davis and two articles by Robert Park about its findings, including an explanation of how the race relations cycle worked on the West Coast. There also were articles about the economic activities of Japanese and Chinese immigrants, the American-born generation, and U.S. policy regarding the Pacific.

Chester Rowell, the only identifiable exclusionist listed as an author in the *Survey Graphic* issue, further exemplified the Stanford project's egalitarian aims. His contribution contained the spirit of racial tolerance and acceptance that fit well with Park's and Davis's articles. Many of Rowell's points about Asian immigration remained consistent with his earlier exclusionism, which, it might be recalled, took a moderate form that appreciated Japanese civilization and trade, as well as the intelligence and high character of educated immigrants from Japan. But there were noticeable changes in Rowell's racial thinking. Now that blanket Asian exclusion was in place, he became optimistic about the ability of American society to absorb its relatively small Asian American community, maintaining that Asian immigrants adapted so well that their grandchildren "will be, in every spiritual and cultural respect, exactly as American as the descendants of the Mayflower." He was also willing to open the nation's gates to a limited number of new migrants from Asia as long as the overall size of the community remained small. In this way, he stood at odds with McClatchy and other exclusionists who remained steadfast in opposing any Asian immigration, despite their willingness to participate in the race relations survey.[7]

The change in Rowell's position on exclusion owed as much to his thinking about international relations as it did to race relations. While supporting the spirit if not the letter of the original alien land law, he became conspicuously silent about the issue during the subsequent campaign for Proposition 1. During this movement for Japanese exclusion, Rowell broke with his old friend and political ally Hiram Johnson over U.S. membership in the League of Nations, which Rowell supported, while Johnson joined with Henry Cabot Lodge and other Senate "irreconcilables" to defeat it. Rowell's embrace of Wilsonian internationalism led him to support Sidney

Gulick's attempts to prevent Japanese exclusion, which, in turn, incurred McClatchy's suspicions that the California exclusionist was selling out to the egalitarians.[8] At the same time, Rowell also became interested in the Americanization of the second-generation nisei in Hawai'i. A progressive colleague who had moved to the islands sent him reports about the nisei's tremendous social progress, which contradicted the race science of the day that viewed the second generation as fundamentally and forever foreign. Rowell showed great interest in the promise of interracial democracy in Hawai'i despite maintaining doubts based in his strong views about the failure of Reconstruction in the American South.[9]

Rowell's interest in Hawai'i's race relations emerged in the context of concerted efforts to promote nisei Americanization made by Japanese American leaders with the support of Hawai'i planters. Hawai'i, like on the West Coast, experienced a wave of anti-Japanese campaigns in the aftermath of World War I and throughout the 1920s that sounded the alarm about the nisei's "divided loyalty" and the dangers of Japanese language schools as a key source of ethnic indoctrination. In addition, Japanese American workers in 1920 played the leading role in a historic plantation strike in which they combined with Filipino Americans to resist management's old tactic of dividing plantation workers by ethnicity. After the prolonged strike, leaders of the planter oligarchy sought to counter labor organizing with Americanization programs such as recruiting nisei into the U.S. Army to serve the National Guard. In 1931 and again in 1934, the army's Hawaiian Department recommended allowing Japanese Americans to become officers and establishing a specific unit for this ethnic group, but each time officials in Washington, D.C., rejected these requests. One exception occurred in the ROTC program at the University of Hawaii, where a few nisei were commissioned as officers. This was consistent with the egalitarianism of the university's administration and many of its professors, who like David Starr Jordan and others at Stanford supported their Asian students by brushing off exclusionist fears. The final reason for the increase of Americanization activity in the islands had to do with the campaign for Hawai'i statehood, which took on new urgency in 1934 when the Jones-Costigan Act reduced the amount of tariff-free sugar imports permitted from the islands.[10]

Americanization was seen by all parties (planters, workers, Asian American leaders, and also the Japanese government via industrialist Eiichi Shibusawa) as the solution to the islands' tense race and labor relations and national security fears. Since Japanese Americans constituted more than 40 percent of the territorial population, they drew the most attention as both ethnic leaders and the plantation elite sponsored nisei Americanization through local newspapers, public schools, and a series of "New American" conferences that persisted from 1927 until 1941. During this time emerged the Hawaii Japanese Civic Association, which consisted of leading nisei, such as Harvard-trained lawyer Masaji Marumoto, seeking to clear up misunderstandings about Japanese Americans amid persistent fears about their loyalty. Another part of the Americanization campaign involved establishing Japanese studies at the University of Hawai'i as a program with an educational mission to promote understanding between the United States and Japan. The main professor was Tasuku Harada, a Christian convert and Yale graduate who was intimately acquainted with American missionaries like Sidney Gulick and who was embraced by Hawai'i's missionary-cum-plantation elite. Harada came to Hawai'i after conducting research on the Japanese problem in California for Shibusawa's Japan-American Relations Committee in Tokyo.[11]

Hawai'i's Americanization campaign also influenced the establishment of an ambitious international organization that responded to the exclusion of Japanese immigrants in 1924 by seeking to bridge the Pacific through research and interpersonal understanding. The Institute of Pacific Relations (IPR) was begun by the Hawai'i YMCA with the support of Hawai'i planters and major funding from the Carnegie Endowment and Rockefeller Foundation. Its inaugural conference, to be held in Honolulu in the summer of 1925, was designed to ease tensions over Asian immigration by bringing together nongovernmental representatives from every nation that had a stake in promoting peace in the Pacific. The list of persons attending a planning meeting for the conference in New York City read like a who's who of egalitarians, including Survey of Race Relations leaders Merle Davis and Galen Fisher, Stanford University president Ray Lyman Wilbur, Hawai'i planter Frank Atherton, YMCA head John Mott, *New York Times* editor John H. Finely, international relations scholar George Blakeslee, the transforming exclusionist Chester Rowell, and former U.S. ambassador to Japan Roland Morris, who had participated in the failed U.S.-Japan negotiations in the early 1920s to preclude congressional exclusion. Wilbur recommended the conference follow the approach taken by the Survey of Race Relations to promote constructive dialogue by promoting personal relations between exclusionists and egalitarians throughout the Pacific. Rowell agreed, asserting that the coming meeting was a terrific opportunity to lay the groundwork for the survey's expansion to Hawai'i, "the racial laboratory of the world." The IPR's links to the Stanford project were cemented when Wilbur was elected the organization's first president and when Davis left the survey's directorship to serve in the same position for the IPR. Many of the survey's supporters and staff, including Robert Park and California exclusionist Paul Scharrenberg, attended the Honolulu conference, becoming IPR charter members. Park himself explicitly compared the IPR to the survey in saying that both focused on promoting a friendly international atmosphere that would enable different peoples (Japanese and Americans, in particular) to develop a personal understanding of each other.[12]

As the Stanford project wound down, the IPR replaced it as the center for research-based egalitarianism. While the international organization lacked the survey's concentrated study of the West Coast, it more than made up for it with its vastly expanded scope (reaching around the world), resources, and number of experts. Each participating nation organized its own research committee, and in this way the IRP's biannual conferences and publications represented a broad array of perspectives and findings.[13] As exhibited at its inaugural conference in Honolulu, the IPR paid close attention to the exclusion of Asian migrants by the United States, Canada, Australia, and New Zealand. Its American committee was sympathetic to repeated pressure from the IPR's Japanese members to resolve the humiliation of exclusion. To this end, the Kyoto conference in 1929 was the site where Hawai'i planter and San Francisco business leader Wallace Alexander struck a silent bargain with Paul Scharrenberg, who as an exclusionist had shown in 1915 surprising sympathy for Japan in hosting the Japanese fraternal delegates for a labor conference in California. The deal was for Scharrenberg to get the California Federation of Labor to permit a policy allowing for the immigration of a small number of Japanese migrants. In return, Scharrenberg insisted that his collaboration must remain secret and that overt agitation for the quota by noisy egalitarians like Gulick be prevented. Alexander, in turn, worked with the president of the IPR's American committee to keep Gulick and other missionaries from ramping up efforts against Japanese exclusion.[14]

Thus was reflected what has been called the "business initiative" to end Japanese exclusion by securing an immigration quota for Japan. Businessmen like Wallace Alexander played a leading role in this quota cause. A veteran of the California education campaign and leader of Alexander & Baldwin (one of the "Big Five" Hawai'i sugar companies), Alexander worked to bring together U.S. and Japanese officials to negotiate a new treaty that would allow a token number of Japanese immigrants to get around exclusion.[15] But that effort failed when Gulick broke his silence and, as a result, Scharrenberg's support for the quota wavered. As it turned out, business leaders from the Northwest proved more effective in gaining influential support for the quota campaign. Prompted by a new crippling tariff on wood products passed by the Japanese Diet, lumber producers in Washington, who were already suffering from the effects of the Great Depression, tried to curry favor for tariff relief in Tokyo by seeking to end the humiliation of exclusion. Led by business owner J. J. Donovan and A. E. Holden of Seattle's Japan Society, the Northwest campaign obtained endorsements from the National Trades Council and U.S. Chamber of Commerce, the first national organizations to support the quota cause. The Northwest movement also made inroads to securing support from the Washington branch of the American Legion. More important, Donovan and Holden pressured House Immigration Committee chair Albert Johnson, a representative from Washington State, to support quota legislation. Johnson, a noted exclusionist who had supported modest Japanese immigration, stunned both sides of the debate in backing the idea of a quota for Japan. McClatchy cursed him for being "wobbly." But, in the end, it was Donovan, Holden, and Alexander who were disappointed. The quota that Johnson advocated was to give slots to Japan for only non-Asian immigrants (or those eligible for naturalization).[16]

While egalitarians remained hopeful that the time was right for a Japanese quota, American public opinion soured on Japan after September 1931, when officers of the nation's military in Manchuria seized the region from China. The United States refused to recognize Japanese sovereignty over the newly named puppet state, "Manchukuo," and in 1933 Japan pulled out of the League of Nations as a result of the international body's condemnation of its expansionism. A testament to the persistent strength of egalitarianism, the quota cause was picked up by subsequent advocates even as its chances diminished with the difficult turn in U.S.-Japan relations.[17]

Filipinos and the Exclusion Debate

While it goes too far to assert that exclusionists' attempts to mend fences with Japan were duplicitous and insincere, their involvement with the Survey of Race Relations, the IPR, and the quota cause had no impact on their steadfast resolve to defend Asian exclusion. In many ways, they were practicing good sportsmanship after a hard-won victory over the egalitarian friends of Japan; because the gates were securely closed to the Japanese, exclusionists could become diplomatic, even magnanimous. But this was not the case regarding Mexicans and Filipinos, whose migration to the United States remained largely unchecked by the restrictionist reforms of the 1924 Immigration Act. Although exclusionists were more concerned about Mexico given its close proximity to the United States, their chances for obtaining exclusion legislation were better regarding Filipinos. After the nation had been secured from mass migrations of Chinese and Japanese (not to mention peoples from India), the exclusion debate centered largely on this "third Asiatic invasion."[18]

Filipino immigration followed a similar pattern to earlier Asian migrations. By 1909, laborers drawn to Hawai'i's sugar plantations replaced the early wave of elite students (pensionados) as the largest migrant stream from the Philippines. Filipino workers were recruited to replace the Japanese, much like the Japanese had been recruited to replace the Chinese before them. The Filipinos came amid a general strike by Japanese plantation workers, as the Hawai'i planters sought to diversify the labor force in order to prevent future unrest. The combination of another Japanese-led strike in 1920 and the possibility of Congress excluding Japanese immigrants increased the demand for Filipino migration to the islands. As colonial subjects, Filipinos enjoyed the free right of entry to the United States and its territories. Even before 1924, West Coast agricultural, fishing, and canning businesses recruited Filipino workers from Hawai'i as well as directly from the Philippines. By 1930, the U.S. Census counted 63,052 Filipinos in Hawai'i, 30,470 in California, and 3,480 in the state of Washington. In addition, nearly 2,000 seamen were based in New York while serving as stewards on international shipping lines.[19]

The sudden increase in Filipino laborers in California put them in the crosshairs of the state's well-organized exclusionists. By 1928, V. S. McClatchy and the CJIC got California representative Richard Welch to sponsor a Filipino exclusion bill that relied on many of the same rationales behind Japanese exclusion. Yet exclusionists faced stiff opposition in Congress despite enjoying the support of Albert Johnson, still chair of the House Committee on Immigration and Naturalization. The challenges to Filipino exclusion were apparent in congressional hearings on the Welch bill in April 1930. The exclusionists, with Johnson presiding, began the hearings in firm control of the discourse. Welch opened by blaming Mexican and Filipino immigration for exacerbating and prolonging the calamitous depression sparked by the crash of the New York stock market nearly six months earlier: "We know that every peon Mexican that comes into this country, as we know that every Filipino laborer who comes into this country, means adding one to the great army of the unemployed." To Welch, Mexican and Filipino "cheap labor" was a problem because it brought out the dark side of Americans. He feared that "when those American men are turned out upon the streets, replaced by Filipinos or the peon Mexicans, they are driven to desperation and in many cases actual crime."[20]

The focus on unemployment and social disorder was an obvious attempt to connect immigration issues with Depression-era fears. But it also enabled exclusionists—at least in their own minds—to play down the idea of racial superiority by pinning the blame on Filipino laborers in a way that insulated elite Filipinos from culpability. Here was a lesson learned in the earlier struggle against Japanese immigration when the opposition repeatedly chastised exclusionists for being racist and discounting the significance of Japanese civilization. McClatchy made class differences among Filipinos clear in his testimony: "I distinguish between the capable and ambitious and creditable young Filipinos, over here for an education, and the discreditable ones who would be repudiated by the Filipinos themselves as being an injury to them." McClatchy took the class distinction one step further by arguing that elite Filipinos agreed with his characterization that "riffraff" from the islands were unworthy immigrants who damaged U.S.-Philippine relations. Here he was playing on the existing division between students and laborers in the United States to which Filipino witnesses themselves would attest, even though they disagreed sharply with McClatchy's exclusionist position. Manuel Roxas, Speaker of the Philippine legislature, was part of a select commission of leading legislators from the islands who came to Washington, D.C., to testify for Philippine independence and against race-based exclusion. While deploring McClatchy's alarmist and racialized view of Filipino immigrants, he too distinguished between worthy students and unworthy laborers and thus allowed for banning the secondary migration of Filipino workers to the U.S. mainland from Hawai'i plantations.[21]

Another way exclusionists softened the notion of race superiority was by invoking the theory of racial incompatibility. California attorney general Ulysses S. Webb, following in the footsteps of Chester Rowell's moderate exclusionism, emphasized that the problem with Filipino immigrants was one of "race incompatibility, the natural antagonisms of racial characteristics that prevent the amalgamation of the people, that prevents their coming together, [and] that causes conflicts in acts and conduct." In this way, he viewed both whites and Filipinos, through no fault of their own, as chemically bound to a relationship fraught with tension and social disorder. McClatchy, too, placed stock in the theory of racial incompatibility as a diplomatic means to soften the blunt force of exclusion. Consider his disclaimer regarding the call to ban Filipino immigration: "There is no question in our minds, and no pretense of racial superiority in this matter. In the face of the distinguished Filipinos attending this hearing no intelligent man would offer such a suggestion. But it is racial prejudice on both sides which makes it practically impossible for the white race and colored races to get on in the same environment, in large numbers, under the same political and social conditions. The idealist will say that is an unfair prejudice, and it should be obliterated. I say that is nature's safeguard against *miscegenation*."[22]

Exclusionists were convinced that Filipinos, like all "colored races," were unassimilable in American society because they could not marry white women without provoking primordial resentments in both peoples that often led to disorder and violence. In this way, the "sex problem" loomed large in the hearings regarding Filipino exclusion, although it would be an overstatement to say that it served as a kind of Freudian subtext behind every exclusionist claim. McClatchy noted that the sexuality of Filipino immigrants made up the "most serious phase of the question." In comparing the Filipino problem with southern race relations, Webb, again like Rowell, bemoaned the fact that Americans "have struggled with the nonassimilable, the incompatible, the unavoidable lack of harmony resulting between the whites and the blacks on this continent since the induction of blacks here."[23]

Preoccupation with the sex problem stemmed in large part from recent race riots (January 1930) in Watsonville, California, that had garnered international attention. The conflict featured the killing of a Filipino farmworker as part of a dispute over "cheap labor" exacerbated by fears regarding sexual relations between Filipinos and white working-class women. While Watsonville's mayor sent written testimony alerting the committee that the nation had a warped view of what happened and that he still welcomed Filipino workers to his agricultural region, exclusionists focused on the sexual component of the riots. McClatchy relied on the expertise of David Barrows, an anthropologist, former president of the University of California, Berkeley, and self-described friend of Filipinos who served in the early days of the American colonial government in the Philippines. In a recent article published in the bulletin of the Commonwealth Club, California's prestigious policy forum, Barrows contended that Filipino "vices are almost entirely based on sexual passion" and that the utter lack of sexual restraint led "all types of Filipinos" to engage in conduct that would create social problems in American life.[24]

The egalitarian opposition to the Welch bill sidestepped the importance of Filipino sexuality. Manuel Roxas dismissed accusations of the purported sex problem by reminding the committee that it stemmed from a single instance of conflict in Watsonville. Manuel Briones, the majority leader of the Philippine legislature, blamed the conflict on difficult conditions in California—an imbalanced sex ratio between Filipino immigrants and antimiscegenation laws—which prevented Filipinos from having a normal marriage life.[25] Other opponents to the Welch bill ignored the sex problem in order to tackle less charged exclusionist arguments. Samuel Dickstein, a New York City Democrat on the House Committee on Immigration and Naturalization, was skeptical of exclusionist claims that Filipinos were displacing white labor. He asked Welch if it was not a fact that "the labor that these Filipinos do . . . is labor that white men will not perform?" Dickstein came to the question of Filipino exclusion as an ally who deeply resented the Anglo-Saxon preferences of the nation's national origins system. A Jewish American serving as a minority member on the Immigration Committee since he entered the House in 1923, he harshly questioned representatives of "so-called patriotic societies," such as John Trevor of the exclusionist American Coalition, a well-known backer of national origins quotas. The New Yorker tried to tarnish their testimony against Filipino immigrants by casting them, and a scholar supporting their claims, as hired guns paid by exclusionist organizations.[26]

Representatives of Hawaiian sugar interests, too, emphasized the much-needed labor of Filipino workers. Unlike Dickstein, the lawyer for the Hawaiian Sugar Planters' Association supported the national origins system but made an exception for "our outlying possessions that are far different from those in our mainland." The planters, he recounted, had hired Portuguese, Spanish, Russians, and Puerto Ricans, but none of these "white" groups worked out as well as Asians. Given that Chinese and Japanese immigrants were excluded and that no others besides Filipinos were available, the planters were not shy about stating that their opposition to the Welch bill was "based upon . . . primarily . . . our individual interests . . . [because we] need the labor there."[27]

Opponents also took exception to the exclusionist representation of Filipinos as un-American or anti-American. Hawaiian Sugar Planters' Association vice president Royal Mead responded to Webb's statement that Filipinos would not fight for the United States during a time of war by highlighting those in Hawai'i who during World War I "enlisted by the thousands and went into our Army and manned our Army posts from Schofield Barracks to Fort Ruger." No one testified to Filipino loyalty with more authority than Brigadier General Francis Lejeune Parker, chief of the War Department's Bureau of Insular Affairs. Parker shifted the issue under discussion from the exclusion of foreigners to the dishonoring of twenty-five thousand veterans from the Philippines who had served the United States faithfully during World War I. Filipinos, he stated, were not aliens but "people who owe allegiance to our government, who are entitled to the protection of that government, and who evidenced their whole-hearted loyalty and patriotism to the United States in the great war." Parker's emphasis on Filipino patriotism signified his broader characterization of the Welch bill as "a very sudden reversal" to America's thirty-year drive to democratize and uplift the Philippines. A crucial part of this colonial education, he reminded the committee, was to encourage Filipinos to come to the United States in order to "take advantage of the exceptional opportunities offered by our educational institutions . . . and to study our political institutions, to fit themselves to enter more promptly and fully into their own affairs at home."[28]

The most coordinated opponents to the Welch bill were political actors from the Philippines, including Manuel Roxas and the Philippine legislature's majority and minority leaders. While Dickstein, Parker, and others raised the crucial issue that the colonial status of Filipinos prohibited their exclusion, the testimony of these elite Filipinos provided the most damning opposition to exclusionist claims. Roxas offered the longest and most powerful testimony against the Welch bill. Like Parker, he stated categorically that Filipinos were not legally aliens, and therefore the attempt to place them on the same level as Chinese or Japanese immigrants was fundamentally misguided. He invoked the fraught history of the U.S.-Philippine War to underscore the fact that Filipinos had had U.S. sovereignty imposed on them; they assumed duties and responsibilities to the United States but in return gained certain privileges and rights, such as U.S. passports and free entry to the metropole. Further, Roxas strongly disagreed with Webb and McClatchy's assertion that the Welch bill followed a precedent set by British dominions in excluding colonial subjects from other crown colonies. Roxas replied forcefully, "I say unhesitatingly that the action contemplated in this bill has no precedent in the annals of colonization since the birth of time." He added that even under Spanish rule, Filipinos maintained the right to enter the metropole.[29]

A central concern for the Filipino legislators was maintaining reciprocal U.S.-Philippine relations. Roxas used the example of free trade to show the harmony between the two peoples; Americans, he said, do not charge a tariff on Philippine imports, nor do Filipinos charge a tariff on U.S. imports. Excluding Filipino immigrants would upset this balance because the Philippines would be given no chance under the colonial relationship to exclude Americans from coming to the islands. The only way reciprocity could be preserved, Roxas argued, was to grant the Philippines independence so that Filipinos would be able to mirror U.S. immigration policies by erecting its own wall against Americans. Here was the crux of the matter for the Filipinos at the hearings, each one a pronounced nationalist. They had come to Capitol Hill to urge Congress to make good on its 1916 promise in the Philippine Autonomy Act to grant independence to the colony, if possible immediately. Dr. Hilario Moncado, an influential Filipino immigrant leader, even assured exclusionists that independence would solve the problems regarding Filipino laborers. "I assure you," read his written testimony, "that if Congress will pass a law definitely granting our independence at some early date, that a very, very large proportion of the Filipinos now in this country will make it their objective to be back in their beloved homeland in time to greet the raising of the flag that means vastly more to them than anything that the United States may offer to keep them here."[30]

The nationalist call for Philippine independence featured an overt rejection of colonial assumptions of Filipino backwardness and racial inferiority that initially had pushed Americans to assume the "white man's burden." Roxas explicitly called out Webb, McClatchy, and other exclusionists for the prejudice that lurked beneath their strategic disavowals of American race superiority. He dismissed their economic arguments for Filipino exclusion by asking why they focused on such a small group of laborers, when the much larger numbers of Mexicans, Canadians, and Puerto Ricans—and Europeans under quotas—were also taking American jobs and thus stirring up social unrest. Roxas took particular offense at McClatchy's alarmist call for exclusion that noted that any "head-hunter who has the price is perfectly free to come over [to the United States]." Roxas flagged this comment as displaying utter ignorance of the Philippines, since any instance of "head-hunting" would be prosecuted as a crime. Such a statement, he said, was akin to forming an opinion about America based on the fact that its localities experience more crime than their counterparts in the Philippines. "However, we are not judging the American people by what criminals do," he pointed out, "but rather by your efforts to punish them."[31]

Hawai'i's delegate to Congress Victor Houston added to the critique of exclusionist views by taking on the theory of racial incompatibility. In responding to McClatchy's assertion that "Hawaii offers herself as a terrible example of the penetration of colored races" because it "is hopelessly lost to the white race," Houston stressed the fact that Hawai'i's economy was run by corporations "practically all of which were controlled by Caucasians." Houston made it clear that the melting pot in Hawai'i was not a delusion: "We in Hawaii have . . . rather prided ourselves that because of lack of racial prejudice in the islands . . . we have always felt that there is a real melting-pot there and that it is working and may possibly serve as an example to the rest of the world." In criticizing the exclusionist witnesses, Houston found common cause with Dickstein in denouncing the specter of racism, including anti-Semitism. Houston likened the animosity toward Filipino immigration to recent opposition to eastern European immigrants, especially Jews, in South Africa. "That is the sort of racial prejudice," he concluded, "that has ruined the world." He then concurred with Dickstein's rhetorical question that asked "Has it not been so to a certain extent right here in the United States also?" The connection between Dickstein and Houston symbolized the new kind of political alliance made possible by the Immigration Act of 1924. Before this time the legal standing of European new immigrants, as well as the retention of open borders to Europe before the 1920s, prevented them from forging close political alliances with Asian immigrants. But the discriminatory national origins quotas marginalized both groups from Anglo-Saxon standards for entry.[32]

In the end, the Welch bill died in committee as it became obvious to everyone at the hearings that legal structures of U.S. colonialism in the Philippines, along with a pronounced opposition that would hold the federal government responsible for its colonial wards, trumped the rationale for exclusion. A simultaneous push in the U.S. Senate led by California exclusionist Samuel Shortridge also met defeat. The Senate debate took place on the Senate floor ten days after the House hearings had concluded. Senate rules prohibited participation by the Filipino legislators, and even the official U.S. delegates (resident commissioners) from the Philippines, who had a voice in the House debate, remained outside the proceedings. Shortridge reprised the arguments of Welch, McClatchy, and Webb in pushing for Filipino exclusion. Opposing him was Hiram Bingham, a Connecticut Republican who was born in Hawai'i and descended from two generations of American missionaries in the islands. Shortridge's proposal, which came as an amendment to a bill targeting limitations on Mexican immigration, was voted down 23–41 with 32 senators not voting.[33]

The defeats of the Welch bill and Shortridge amendment made it clear that exclusionists lacked the ability to pass a stand-alone exclusion act. Their only chance was to attach it to the issue of Philippine independence that was gaining momentum in Washington, D.C. In this way exclusionists joined sides with tariff protectionists and Filipino nationalists at the expense of Filipino immigrants. The issue of exclusion was entrusted to the House and Senate Committees on Territories and Insular Affairs, which held joint hearings to discuss three different independence bills submitted by Senators Henry B. Hawes (a Democrat from Missouri), Bronson M. Cutting (a Republican from New Mexico), and Butler B. Hare (a Democrat from South Carolina). None of these bills addressed immigration issues out of fear that the Philippine legislature would reject them. But during the 1932 hearings on these measures, Roxas and other Filipino legislators made it clear that their colleagues would accept exclusion as part of the price of freedom. Congress, in turn, passed the Hawes-Cutting-Hare Act in 1933 over President Herbert Hoover's veto. Internal politics in the Philippines delayed approval of this act until the next year, when a new U.S. Congress and president sent the same proposition back across the Pacific—this time featuring the names of the new chairs of the Committees on Territories and Insular Affairs.[34]

The Tydings-McDuffie Act, more popularly known as the Philippine Independence Act, created a ten-year countdown to freedom during which Filipinos would establish a commonwealth that continued the colonial relationship virtually unchanged while the islands prepared for self-rule. The main exception concerned immigration. Citizens of the Philippines now would be counted as aliens and not as nationals. This new status, unlike the rest of the Independence Act, went into effect with its enactment in March 1934. Consequently, Filipinos, save for a few from exempt classes, were now banned as "aliens ineligible to citizenship." The Philippines received a symbolic quota of fifty (to be used only by non-Asians), which was half the total of eligible migrants from China or Japan. In this way, Filipino exclusion continued the long-standing pattern of legislation that stigmatized Asian immigrants while preventing entry to the United States of all but a handful of elites from the exempt classes. Scholars have noted that although the Independence Act brought together the strange bedfellows of tariff protectionists and Philippine nationalists, it was made possible largely due to the climate of opinion and fear regarding unchecked Filipino immigration. One portrays Filipino nationalists as being forced to strike a "Faustian bargain" for independence by accepting exclusion.[35] Another makes it clear that Philippine independence was not an early expression of decolonization; rather than emerging during the era of Wilsonian internationalism, it was a product of what John Higham has called the "tribal twenties," an anti-immigration period marked by Japanese exclusion and the national origins system.[36]

Highlighting the continuities between Filipino exclusion and earlier forms of anti-Asian racism is not wrong. But doing so in a way that downplays the significant changes in the conditions for the exclusion debate misrecognizes three crucial themes during the period of late exclusionism. First was the continuing importance of the opposition to anti-Asian racism. Whether they knew it or not, opponents to Filipino exclusion were in step with the egalitarianism of the Survey of Race Relations and the IPR, with the latter organization publishing the first book-length analysis of Filipino immigration while Congress was considering exclusion. Bruno Lasker, author of the IPR study, examined both sides of the congressional debate and ended his book with a question that revealed an egalitarian proclivity: "Can the movement of Filipinos to the mainland of the United States be stopped in the immediate future without injury to American foreign relations in the Far East, without precipitating an unwise and dangerous change in our political relations with the Philippine Islands, without upsetting the labor situation in Hawaii, without prejudice to the legitimate ambitions of the Filipino people themselves?"[37] Moreover, Samuel Dickstein's criticism of exclusionary racism signaled the convergence of political interests between advocates for Asian immigrants and the more politically powerful champions of immigrants from southern and eastern Europe.

The second change evident in the debate over Filipino exclusion was the discrediting of the overt language of racial prejudice. Gone were the days when exclusionists could make racist claims about Asian immigrants with impunity. Thus McClatchy's strategic disavowal of Asian racial inferiority revealed his acute awareness of the liberalizing climate of opinion about race. In a virtual apology to Roxas during the Welch bill hearings, Chairman Johnson cast exclusion as a necessary evil, not an unambiguous social good: "It is like an amputation. It is painful, but sometimes it has to be done."[38] Roxas, and the other Filipino leaders, revealed the final and most important change in the exclusion debate. Asian representatives, who because of their legal standing within the U.S. political system, became effective lobbyists on Capitol Hill. When Ambassador Masanao Hanihara opposed the push for Japanese exclusion in a private letter to the U.S. secretary of state, his attempt at lobbying was exposed as an outlandish foreign challenge to American sovereignty. As wards of the United States, Roxas and the other Philippines legislators avoided Hanihara's dilemma. This was especially true of the official Philippine delegates who served as nonvoting members of the House of Representatives. In this way, Filipinos introduced a new and increasingly important element into the exclusion debate: empowered Asian voices of opposition with legal, cultural, and patriotic standing. The role played by these agents was crucial to the defeat of the Welch bill and to framing the Independence Act as a liberal recognition of Filipinos' capacity for self-government rather than as a harsh statement against the racial character of Filipino immigrants. To be sure, Filipinos suffered the same fate of exclusion as all other Asian groups, but the process in which this occurred testified to the beginning of the end to the perfect storm of exclusion. The lack of legal standing that prevented them from becoming eligible to citizenship was one of the four Asian American vulnerabilities that would continue to erode as the full force of the "Roosevelt Revolution" emerged.

Challenging Exclusionism

The most debilitating Asian vulnerability in the exclusion debate was the lack of legal standing that prevented them from becoming American citizens. While the barrier to naturalization subjected them to exclusion, alien land laws, and other forms of discrimination, it also diminished the political clout that they could potentially have wielded as voters and concerned parties. Unlike the Filipinos who served the U.S. military and the nation's colonial endeavors, the vast majority of Chinese, Japanese, Indian, and Korean immigrants were barred from claiming these sorts of ties to their adopted homeland. But a small minority of them could make such claims because they had enlisted in the U.S. military when the nation was eager for recruits during World War I. The Act of May 9, 1918, enabled even "aliens ineligible to citizenship" to obtain the right of naturalization upon successful completion of military service. During the postwar campaign for Japanese exclusion, McClatchy, James D. Phelan, and other Californians organized to prevent the federal government from fulfilling its obligation to these veterans. In May 1925 the Supreme Court handed the exclusionists their victory in *Toyota v. United States*, which declared the Act of May 9 invalid with respect to granting citizenship to Asian immigrant veterans, although a clear exception was made for Filipinos who served in the U.S. Navy or Marines. Save for these Filipinos, the *Toyota* decision stripped away U.S. citizenship from those veterans who already had taken advantage of the naturalization benefit.[39]

But as in the cases of the Survey of Race Relations, the IPR, the campaign for a Japanese immigration quota, and Philippine independence, the drive to restore naturalization rights to Asian immigrant veterans witnessed unexpected goodwill and cooperation from even the most ardent exclusionists. By March 1935, the American Legion, the Veterans of Foreign Wars, and McClatchy's CJIC all supported the Nye-Lea Act, which was passed that year, rendering the *Toyota* decision moot by allowing all qualified veterans to become U.S. citizens. While remaining resolute on protecting the nation's borders against Asian immigration, exclusionists softened their position regarding those already in the country, as well as the American-born generations. Nowhere was this more apparent than in a CJIC statement released while Congress was working on the Nye-Lea Act. The organization condemned in the strongest terms a recent claim made to a congressional committee that there were five hundred thousand armed Japanese in the United States. McClatchy and CJIC chairman John Fisk warned that such a "fantastic dream" threatened to "disturb friendly relations and mutual appreciation now existing between Japanese and Caucasians in California, which had developed since settlement of the immigration question in 1924." They pointed to the organization's support for legislation to grant citizenship to Asian veterans as an important expression of the post-1924 era of good feelings.[40]

As befitting McClatchy's meticulous political style, the CJIC statement sought to remove any obstacle that might prevent the successful passage of the Nye-Lea measure. The text assured that while some issei were violating the alien land law and others were engaged in smuggling of illegal immigrants, "these matters can be corrected by law and by law enforcement, and they do not reflect upon the great body of the Japanese population in California." Moreover, the CJIC expressed its confidence in the patriotism of the Japanese American Citizens League, a nisei organization established in 1929 that was the mainland equivalent of the Hawaiʻi Japanese Civic Association in seeking to calm anti-Japanese fears and advance Americanization and ethnic group interests. "It is fairly certain," the statement proclaimed, "that the Japanese-American Citizens League, in which most of the grown Japanese of American birth seek to perfect themselves in American citizenship, would discourage and expose, if it could not prevent, a movement which would inevitably wreck the future careers of its members."[41]

The House hearings on Californian Clarence Lea's bill followed the CJIC script regarding the patriotism of Asian Americans. The star witness was Tokutaro ("Tokie") Slocum, a veteran born in Japan who had served in the U.S. Army during World War I. Slocum was not just a Japanese American Citizens League leader but also an active member of the American Legion and Veterans of Foreign Wars, and he worked tirelessly for many years to obtain support from nearly every state organization of these veterans groups. He also received financial backing from the IPR's Wallace Alexander, although both parties kept this quiet because Alexander was at odds with exclusionists regarding the cause to obtain an immigration quota for Japan. In testifying for what became the Nye-Lea bill, Slocum emphasized his war record and roots in the nation's heartland (North Dakota). A letter from his commanding officer during the war read, "My friend, Slocum, is as good an American as I am, and has offered to prove it with his own blood—and I know of no other final proof." The House committee, in turn, was impressed with the veteran's all-Americanism, eloquent command of English, and patriotic spirit.[42]

The Nye-Lea measure, which was approved in 1935, came through the House Committee on Immigration and Naturalization, now chaired by Samuel Dickstein. The election of Franklin D. Roosevelt as president in 1932 put the Democrats in control of the legislative and executive branches for the first time in sixteen years. Dickstein and other liberals no longer had to contend with Albert Johnson, who lost not only his chairmanship but also his seat in Congress. He returned to journalism in his native state of Washington, where died in 1934. In that same year, McClatchy warned CJIC members of the Roosevelt administration's "determined effort to loosen immigration restriction laws to make it easier for undesirables to enter and easier for them to remain after illegal entry." McClatchy paid particular attention to Dickstein, "a Tammany New Yorker" and "ardent antirestrictionist, who has the record for many years of introducing more bills to make holes in the restriction dyke than any ten men in Congress." That the Democrats were in charge did not mean that exclusionism was dead, for the Immigration Act of 1924 and its national origins system stood as monuments to the work of Johnson, McClatchy, and the rest of their peers. While the Democrats could not dismantle exclusionism, they sought to humanize it by emphasizing the importance of racial egalitarianism in the nation's immigration and naturalization laws.[43]

In addition to the Nye-Lea Act, the new egalitarian ethos was evident in legislation designed to have the federal government return unemployed Filipino immigrants to the Philippines free of charge. Scholars portray this repatriation plan as the follow-up to Filipino exclusion; in addition to stopping the incoming migrations, the goal was also to expunge all trace of this unwanted Asian group from the United States.[44] Consequently the New Deal framework in which congressmen discussed repatriation (to help the poor and unemployed) is now seen as a smokescreen for their real exclusionist motives. This was no doubt true for members of Congress like Richard Welch or for AFL representative William Hushing, both of whom testified before Dickstein's committee with exclusionist designs couched in humanitarian concern. But the vast majority of witnesses and committee members at the hearing revealed a degree of sincerity for the distressed Filipinos that, while not purely selfless, was in stark contrast to the exclusionists' crocodile tears. Illinois congressman Adolf Sabath, for example, threw his support behind repatriation at the urging of the Filipino Cultural Center in Chicago, from whom he learned about the "sad plight" of about

5,500 Filipinos in the city "who, due to existing conditions, are out of employment, have no place to live and are unable to provide for themselves." Sabath, like Samuel Dickstein, was a long-standing House egalitarian who had staunchly opposed national origins quotas as discriminatory to southeastern Europeans. Though sympathetic to the Filipino unemployed, Sabath also feared that the Filipinos "might be tempted or forced to do something which they would dislike to do and which would be detrimental not only to them but even to all of their people."[45]

In sponsoring the repatriation measure, Dickstein also displayed a combination of selfish and selfless motives, although the balance of his public remarks clearly tipped to the latter. This was consistent with his pronounced opposition to the features of exclusionism that discriminated against southern and eastern Europeans. Amid a conflict between exclusionists and egalitarians during a committee hearing in 1935, Dickstein assured both sides that "[we] are simply trying to relieve this country of the burden of caring for public charges, and we do not mean any [bad] reflection on any people." Dickstein's humanitarianism was on full display at an earlier hearing in 1933 when he fully supported the testimony of Philippine resident commissioner Camilo Osias, who strongly backed the repatriation measure. Dickstein, in speaking for the entire committee, said, "We do feel that there is an unusual condition existing at this time and that the Filipinos seem to have more difficulty than any other group . . . , and in view of the fact that the Filipinos want to get their independence and everything that goes with it, we thought it would be an act of kindness to alleviate their condition by giving them an opportunity to go back to their home land and at the same time they are removed from the need of charity and the dangers that go with their present situation."[46]

Labor Secretary William Doak was more concerned than Dickstein about being fair, rather than kind, to Filipinos. Since being appointed by President Hoover in 1931, Doak sought to reduce unemployment by removing workers from the country through a little-known clause in the Immigration Act of 1917 that permitted financially distraught aliens, who had arrived within three years, to petition the federal government to return them free of charge to their homelands. Doak's main targets were Mexicans in Southern California, who in cooperation with the Mexican consulate were repatriated to their hometowns across the border. The labor secretary now had his sights on Filipinos and thus was in full support of the Dickstein measure because "it is very important to give the Filipinos the opportunity to take advantage of a repatriation provision, the same as any other national."[47]

The clearest evidence that exclusionism was not behind Philippine repatriation was the fact that it never would have been possible if not for co-operation from both elite and working-class Filipinos. Resident Commissioner Pedro Guevara, in the 1935 hearings, argued at length with some members of the committee who treated repatriation more like a form of forced deportation and permanent exclusion. While these members wanted to add a clause to the measure that would foreclose the possibility that the repatriates would return to the United States, Guevara insisted this was unnecessary because the Independence Act had recently enacted exclusionary measures against Filipinos. He warned that adding another restriction on top of this preexisting exclusion would insult the people of the Philippines and harm international relations. As a result, the repatriation program said nothing about restricting the return of its participants, save for the fact that they would need to satisfy the racial bar to immigration and be limited to the quota of fifty admissible persons per year.[48]

Resident commissioners also assured American lawmakers that repatriation would attract a considerable number of Filipino immigrants, a pragmatic point that most likely sold Congress on the program. Camilo Osias vouched that even though the Philippines was not as wealthy as the United States, Filipino immigrants would be better off there because they preferred its climate and social customs. Guevara maintained they were also better off because there was no unemployment in the Philippines and plenty of work on the farms. Many of the immigrants, he said, "belong to well-to-do families having their own farms and they do not need to undergo hardships they are experiencing in the United States." Even more convincing than the arguments by resident commissioners was a report authorized by Labor Secretary Doak that relied upon the perspectives of Filipinos in the Legionarios Club of Los Angeles. This organization stemmed from the Legionarios del Trabajo, a mutual aid society in the Philippines that followed Filipino migrants to California. The Legionarios told Doak's researcher Murray Grasson that 90 percent of the Filipinos in Los Angeles were suffering from unemployment and thus a large number of them (fifteen thousand) would likely avail themselves of a free trip back to their homeland sponsored by the federal government. In his testimony during the 1933 hearings, Grasson confused the Legionarios as being a branch of the American Legion, which gave patriotically inclined committee members even more confidence in their claims.[49]

As it turned out, the repatriation program that began in 1935 and was repeatedly extended until 1941 attracted only 2,190 participants. This was fraction of the Filipino immigrants who reportedly had expressed interest in it. A number of reasons can explain the failure, such as the stigma of receiving public assistance and the growing fear among Filipinos that repatriation was, as Carey McWilliams put it, "deportation in disguise." The timing of the program was also key. Before the Independence Act, the virtual open door to colonial migration left the U.S. labor market accessible to families in the Philippines; even if repatriates could not return, a son, sibling, uncle, or cousin could still benefit the family by venturing to America. Independence raised the family stakes considerably, while exclusion removed the chance that it could ever again have a lifeline to the United States. Here was a Faustian bargain that few Filipinos were willing to accept. A final reason for the failure of the repatriation program had to do with the promise of Roosevelt's "Second New Deal." In the same summer that FDR signed the Repatriation Act, he also approved the Wagner Act and the Social Security Act, two forms of legislation that would revolutionize labor relations and welfare programs in the United States, respectively. Even though these reforms did not end the Depression, and even though they privileged U.S. citizens and often discriminated in other ways against racial minorities and the poor, they were based on an inclusive spirit of industrial democracy and comprehensive caretaking that offered hope for a better future to millions of residents who had yet to benefit fully from the Roosevelt Revolution.[50]

Signs of hope for Asian Americans also emerged from transformations in the nature of organized labor. The Wagner Act, labor's "Magna Carta," awarded precious legal standing through the federal government's guaranteeing their right to organize, to engage in collective bargaining, and to seek redress of grievances through the newly created National Labor Relations Board. But it did not necessarily undermine the AFL's split labor market framework that safeguarded the "aristocracy of labor" from Asian immigrants and other unorganized workers. The challenge to the AFL, instead, came from the broad movement for industrial unionism emerging with great force during the Depression through a wave of labor strikes and renewed interests among American workers in the Communist Party. Industrial unionists eschewed the idea of splitting the labor market between organized and unorganized sectors in favor of creating one big union to present a united front against management. Essential to this strategy, as tried in earlier efforts by the long defunct Industrial Workers of the World, was organizing Asian Americans and other workers whom the AFL largely had ignored. The resurgence of industrial unionism reached a milestone in 1935 when John L. Lewis led the United Mine Workers out of the AFL to form the Congress of Industrial Organizations (CIO). Within two years, CIO membership swelled to four million workers, with an especially strong foothold in the crucial and previously unorganized steel and automobile industries. While the AFL remained a major player in industrial relations (as will be shown in the exclusion debate), the CIO became a powerful counterweight to its craft unionism and influential brand of exclusionism.[51]

The institutionalization of industrial unionism influenced the exclusion debate by providing union recognition for Asian Americans. The organization of Asian American workers actually began in 1933 with the AFL chartering a union comprising mainly Filipino cannery and farmworkers in the Pacific Northwest. Persistent racial problems with the AFL, however, caused this union in 1938 to disaffiliate with that federation and to join the CIO, becoming part of the United Cannery, Agricultural, Packinghouse and Allied Workers of America (UCAPAWA). Meanwhile, Harry Bridges, a sailor and Communist from Australia, was organizing laborers on the waterfronts of San Francisco and through the West Coast. In forging the International Longshoremen's Association, Bridges clashed directly with Paul Scharrenberg's AFL-affiliated Seamen's Union. In 1937 Bridges left the Longshoremen's Association to form the new, more radical International Longshoremen's and Warehousemen's Union (ILWU), which was quickly affiliated with the CIO, while Bridges became the federation's point man on the West Coast. From there the ILWU expanded to Hawai'i and organized dockworkers on the Big Island at the request of local labor organizer and Communist Jack Kawano. In criticizing the violent suppression of ILWU strikers by Hilo police, a National Labor Relations Board report portrayed Hawai'i as "the picture of fascism" and its workers as "more slaves than free." True to their Communist sensibilities, Bridges and Kawano rejected all forms of racism and in doing so embraced Asian Americans within the house of labor. Thus, while most Asian Americans were small farmers and business owners who did not join labor unions, and in some cases actively opposed them, the new unions gave more Asian Americans access to economic benefits of unionism. More important for the exclusion debate, the CIO provided a new level of political clout from an American labor federation with four million members.[52]

The new unionism provided the backdrop in which Carey McWilliams became involved in California labor relations and, by extension, the exclusion debate. Intense strikes waged in part by Filipino agricultural workers in the early 1930s caught McWilliams's attention while he was transitioning from an interest in literary critique and legal practice to a lifelong engagement with progressive social issues. The strikes were consistent with the Communist Party's larger attempt to organize farmworkers, a labor supply long overlooked by American unions and therefore ripe for industrial unionism. In *Factories in the Field*, McWilliams applauded the Filipino as a "real fighter" whose "strikes have been dangerous" to farm owners.[53]

Congressional hearings on a measure to make Filipinos eligible for citizenship revealed the direct challenge that new unionism posed to exclusionism. Sponsored by New York representative Vito Marcantonio, this legislation in the spring of 1940 appeared before Dickstein's House committee. Marcantonio, reputedly one of the most radical members of Congress and the only one representing the American Labor Party, condemned the inability of Filipinos to become citizens as "purely discriminatory." Because there were no Filipinos in his largely Italian and Puerto Rican district in East Harlem, he emphasized the bill's pure motive to stand up for the principle enshrined in the Declaration of Independence that "all men are created equal." Aware of the firewall of immigration exclusion, Marcantonio made it clear that by giving Filipinos the right of naturalization, his bill did not even suggest opening the door to new immigration. Marcantonio drew upon support for his measure from the national CIO, UCAPAWA, and Carey McWilliams. A CIO resolution praised Filipino workers for demonstrating "their allegiance to the United States in their determination to fight along with the rest of the American people for the preservation of democratic institutions." In introducing McWilliams's letter of support for Filipino naturalization, Marcantonio portrayed him as a "very highly respected person throughout the United States because of his knowledge on questions relating to immigration and housing."[54]

Exclusionists rallied to oppose the Marcantonio bill. Paul Scharrenberg, now chief Washington, D.C., lobbyist for the AFL, tagged the bill as a radical CIO scheme supported by the organization's agricultural workers and by McWilliams, who he said was its former attorney in California. Scharrenberg discredited McWilliams's credentials, contending that "I doubt very much until he was appointed on the Commission of Immigration and Housing whether he knew anything about immigration." At the same time, the AFL representative touted his own vast experience with the "Oriental problem" gleaned in part from having served earlier on the same California commission that McWilliams was now running. The old exclusionist implied that Marcantonio was being used by CIO radicals and that he was naive to think that naturalization rights for Filipinos would have no impact on immigration laws because Asian exclusion was predicated on keeping out "aliens ineligible to citizenship." Marcantonio did not take Scharrenberg's rebuke sitting down. He defended McWilliams as an "outstanding citizen of the State of California" and turned the tables on the AFL representative by accusing his organization of wanting to "tear down standards of living of American workers" by keeping Filipinos as a permanent source of cheap labor that land owners could use to undercut wages for everyone. Faced with stiff exclusionist opposition, Marcantonio referred to his bill as one of the "lost causes" that he was advocating. In doing so, he played down the support his measure received from the State Department, which was on board with its intention but had cautioned Congress to wait until the Philippines was fully independent in order to eliminate the legal complexities attending to the category of colonial nationals. Dickstein, in attempting to cheer up Marcantonio, noted that the State Department "has given you and your group some hope."[55]

The bills seeking naturalization for Indian immigrants in the United States, while receiving support from key players on Capitol Hill, had as little chance of approval as those for Filipinos. Hearings were held in 1939 on a measure to provide naturalization rights to some three thousand persons from India who had migrated to the United States before the 1923 *Thind* decision foreclosed their ability to become U.S. citizens and in some cases stripped them of citizenship. Attempting to calm exclusionist fears about reopening the possibility of a human flood from Asia, Indian immigrant and academic Hardias T. Muzumdar assured Dickstein's committee that the bill made no "radical changes in your immigration laws." It simply allowed a limited and finite number of immigrants—many of whom were married to American citizens—to move from the "periphery of American life" by being able to "participate in the civil, political, and social affairs of this country." As in hearings on Indian exclusion that resulted in the Immigration Act of 1917, the egalitarian opposition included testimony that the peoples of India were considered Caucasian and thus were scientifically proven to meet the whiteness standard for citizenship. But, again, Scharrenberg in his capacity as AFL representative made it clear that skin color had nothing to do with his organization's opposition in this case: "I have been in the Orient a number of times and I have seen both Chinese and Japanese as white as anyone in this room." He saw the bill as an opening wedge to undermine the legal edifice of Asian exclusion that began with such seemingly harmless measures like servicing justice to three thousand Indians but would then give way to claims by Chinese and Japanese immigrants. "Then," he said, "they will find some other means of breaking some other little hole in the immigration law." At separate hearings in 1940, a representative from the American Legion echoed Scharrenberg's remark in asserting that his organization opposed "legislation of this kind that will poke a hole in the dike" and set a precedent "for undermining and weakening [immigration] legislation that we hope will be strengthened." Nothing came of the effort for Indian naturalization, as exclusionists remained in firm control of Congress.[56]

Textbook Security Fears

A major part of the IPR's "experiment in understanding" centered on challenging the distorted image Americans had about Asian peoples. This was true even in the "racial paradise" of Hawai'i, where the fears of Japanese American disloyalty rekindled as U.S.-Japan conflict grew after Japan's invasion of Manchuria in 1931. Consistent with the educational mission of Japanese studies at the University of Hawai'i, the IPR, in the fall of 1934, sought to bridge understanding across the Pacific by developing a new textbook about the culture, civilization, and history of Japan. The draft, which consisted of three hundred mimeographed pages, was tested at four Honolulu-area high schools (Punahou, Kamehameha, McKinley, and Roosevelt).[57]

The textbook was sponsored by the Honolulu branch of the IPR, with the blessing and support from the Territory of Hawai'i's superintendent of schools, to create more "authentic" curriculum materials on East Asia at a time when little, if anything, about the region and its peoples was taught at any level of American education. In the late 1920s, Yale historian Kenneth Latourette reported to the IPR that the "great majority" of college and university students were "blissfully ignorant of the existence of the Far East." In sponsoring the creation of new curricula, the IPR sought to calm America's hostility and mistrust of Japan that reemerged with each U.S.-Japan crisis. Locally, the IPR was catering to the demand for such a textbook from Honolulu's large Japanese American population, which saw it as useful for the increasing number of high school graduates seeking schooling and jobs in Japan.[58]

Seven months into the textbook's trial period, the McClatchy press learned of it and used mainland papers (including the *Sacramento Bee*) to sound the alarm about a foreign intrusion into the minds of innocent American students. The press maintained that the textbook was part of a nefarious plot hatched in Tokyo for the "purpose of maneuvering the United States into a position of inferiority [vis-à-vis Japan]." The main concern was that the textbook presented recent U.S.-Japan relations from Tokyo's perspective by misrepresenting the process and necessity of Japanese immigrant exclusion. The newspapers based their claims almost entirely on press releases from McClatchy's CJIC. In the fight against the IPR textbook, the exclusionist found common cause with Kilsoo Haan, a Korean immigrant in the Hawai'i Territorial Senate who already had been condemning the textbook as Japanese propaganda. A Korean nationalist with expertise in the Japanese language, Haan represented a seemingly one-man organization called the Sino-Korean Peoples League that both the IPR and U.S. intelligence officials warned was not to be trusted.[59]

The story about the IPR textbook quickly spread beyond McClatchy newspapers to the Hearst press (including the *San Francisco Examiner*) and even to the respected and independent *Christian Science Monitor*. The *Monitor* quoted Haan at length, who said that he had been threatened with deportation unless he retracted his criticism of the textbook. But it was McClatchy's statements that received the bulk of the mainland attention, as the contents of his numerous press releases repeatedly found their way into the *Monitor* and many other newspapers. In this way, Americans learned the names of Japanese individuals and organizations involved in the "textbook plot." In addition, the nation learned to be suspicious of the Japanese "collaborators," such as the textbook's author, Helen Gay Pratt.[60]

The IPR refused to engage McClatchy directly, hoping the controversy would blow over. In a private letter, the leader of the Honolulu IPR, Charles Loomis, asserted, "There is nothing that McClatchy likes better than a fight. . . . Let's disappoint him." Helen Pratt concurred in telling Loomis that it was useless to reason with "fanatics" like McClatchy. The IPR, however, was not passive. Its officials and members waged a vigorous behind-the-scenes battle to counteract criticism of the textbook. Hawai'i's superintendent of schools, Oren E. Long, a New Dealer and former schoolteacher sympathetic to the underdog, wrote a letter to his counterpart in California thoroughly discrediting claims made by Kilsoo Haan and assuring that the textbook was produced by loyal American citizens and not by Japanese government officials. He added that Americans would be "pretty dumb if they permit Japan or any other foreign country to determine what is going into textbooks used by American school children." Another staunch opponent of McClatchy was Wallace Alexander, leader of the failed campaign for a Japanese immigration quota. Alexander opposed McClatchy's "Japanese Bugaboo" in the *San Francisco News*, proclaiming that the IPR textbook was the "Lord's own work" because "we need to know all other peoples better, and particularly those who are separated from us by radically different backgrounds of color, religion and language."[61]

At the same time, IPR officials in California and New York managed to thwart McClatchy's attempts to get the *San Francisco Chronicle* and *New York Times* to run his press releases. The *Times* went a step further in July 1935 by addressing the textbook controversy from the perspective of the book's author. In the article, Pratt denied that her book was either "pro-

Japan" or "anti-American"; rather, it represented a sincere attempt to be objective.[62] The *Honolulu Star-Bulletin* also proved no friend of McClatchy, Haan, or the anti-Japanese rhetoric surrounding the textbook. This was not surprising given that the paper had been owned by IPR founder Frank Atherton and was now controlled by Wallace Farrington, who as territorial governor would lead the campaign for Hawaiian statehood. The paper's editor, Riley Allen, also had a long history of befriending Japanese Americans. He responded to the textbook controversy by stating that while an "estimable and likable gentleman," McClatchy had long "made up his mind that the entire United States was threatened by the 'invasion' of Japanese and he has been seeing ghosts ever since."[63]

To resolve the controversy, the IPR invited feedback from McClatchy regarding the textbook. In this way, Pratt, Loomis, Allen, and IPR executive secretary Fredrick Vanderbilt Field thanked him for pointing out crucial errors in the text. In private, though, they admitted that his protests required that Pratt rewrite the entire book in a way that not only corrected the mistakes that McClatchy singled out but also played down the immigration issue and excluded personal judgments about it. While agreeing to strip out long excerpts of Japanese literature and to not send the revised draft for review to Japanese nationals, the textbook team refused to engage McClatchy's substantive points.[64]

The proposed revisions, of course, did not assuage the inveterate exclusionist. On the contrary, McClatchy took his case directly to IPR members by circulating a statement seeking to turn them against the textbook. This provoked Field, leftist activist and descendant of the railroad magnate Cornelius "Commodore" Vanderbilt, to engage in direct correspondence with McClatchy. Field, a known Communist, came to the IPR in 1929 through his interest in China and found work as a research assistant for Bruno Lasker's study of Filipino immigration. By 1937, Field was the American IPR's head staff member and in this capacity engaged McClatchy's criticisms of the IPR's Japanese history textbook. Field was cordial at first, apologizing for the textbook's errors of fact. But when McClatchy continued to send critical letters to the IPR membership, the IPR secretary became frustrated, challenging the idea that the textbook worked against America's best interests. "It would seem to me," wrote Field, "that few things were more un-American than preventing American students from obtaining knowledge of other peoples and other countries with whom, as citizens of the United States, they would have to have intimate and important relations." In another letter, Field accused McClatchy's CJIC of having "absolutely no interest in accuracy" but being, "on the contrary, devoted to a type of malicious slander designed to discredit reputable organizations and to do what harm you can to international relations."[65]

By the publication of Pratt's textbook in the fall of 1937, the controversy was over. McClatchy, although admitting that Pratt had made important corrections, remained unhappy with the book's presentation of the immigration issue. He continued his guard against the yellow peril for a few more months until he died in 1938. This was a blessing of sorts for Pratt, who wrote to Field that she had no doubt about where McClatchy would spend his afterlife. But, as the next chapter will discuss, the suspicions about the loyalty of Japanese Americans did not die with McClatchy.

It is tempting to see the textbook controversy as a sign of the continuation of the anti-Japanese movement from the 1924 exclusion to World War II. From this perspective, the racism that fueled Japanese exclusion remained as strong as ever throughout the 1930s, only to increase in magnitude after Pearl Harbor. Thus McClatchy's involvement in the textbook controversy represented another link in the chain of events culminating in internment. This would be the conventional way to understand the textbook controversy. But the controversy itself is not easily fitted into the conventional mold. True, McClatchy was able to advance his views through the media and influence with California state officials. But he (not to mention Kilsoo Haan) also faced stiff opposition from influential newspapers like the *New York Times* and the *Honolulu Star-Bulletin*, as well as from the IPR leadership and the organization's members and allies. Indeed, the emergence of the IPR's thriving international network and influence established a new and formidable opposition to the anti-Japanese movement. By the late 1930s, it was no coincidence that McClatchy operated as largely a one-man crusade, which befitted the concomitant decline in scientific racism, the New Deal's atmosphere of antiracism, and the CIO's opposition to exclusion. During this period of late exclusionism, egalitarians had recovered much of the political momentum lost with Japanese exclusion. In this way, the fateful destruction of Pearl Harbor by the Japanese navy would catch both egalitarians and exclusionists off guard and place Japanese Americans in Hawai'i and on the West Coast under an intense spotlight of suspicion.

7 WINDS OF WAR

INTERNMENT AND THE GREAT TRANSFORMATION,
1941–1952

On February 19, 1942, President Franklin D. Roosevelt issued Executive Order 9066, which empowered the War Department to take measures to secure West Coast defenses in light of Japan's attack on Pearl Harbor nearly eleven weeks before. America was at war with Japan, and although his order did not name any groups, FDR was aware that it would justify the evacuation and internment of 112,000 Japanese Americans. While the president, following his fifth cousin Theodore Roosevelt, held Japanese civilization in great esteem and made friends with select gentlemen from Japan, he also shared the earlier Roosevelt's growing conviction that the Japanese were unassimilable with whites. It was no coincidence that the implementation of EO 9066 would embody FDR's persistent assumption that the Japanese could never truly become American. Yet during the war, the president also took egalitarian positions that contradicted his internment order. He welcomed nisei into the U.S. Army and quashed fears about German and Italian enemy aliens in the United States, who, unlike their Japanese counterparts, would escape mass evacuation. Moreover, FDR supported the repeal of Chinese exclusion, and although he died before Congress lifted the ban on Filipinos and Indians, it seems likely he would have favored this too. The repeal measures marked the beginning of the end to the exclusion era by removing not only the ban on immigration but also the long-standing legal handicap of ineligibility for citizenship.

This chapter examines Japanese American internment and the Great Transformation in the exclusion debate within the context of World War II and the dawning of the Cold War. The outbreak of hostilities elevated national security concerns to a paramount position in the exclusion debate, displacing worries about the human flood, standards of living, and trade and diplomatic relations. In so doing, the war transformed political discussions about Asian subjects in two contrasting ways. On the one hand, it handed exclusionists their greatest triumph, for the removal of the West Coast Japanese Americans could never have been achieved outside of the war emergency. Major U.S. defeats abroad and vulnerabilities at home, combined with deep suspicions of Japanese espionage and sabotage in Hawai'i and on the West Coast, pushed exclusionists in the U.S. Army and War Department to engage in mass evacuation of Japanese Americans rather than to follow a more racially egalitarian and constitutionally sound process of removal insisted on by the U.S. attorney general and authorities within the Justice Department.

On the other hand, World War II provided a golden opportunity for egalitarians to dismantle U.S. policies discriminating against migrants from America's Asian allies—China, India, and the Philippines. In one fell swoop, the war transformed the exclusion debate by creating the conditions for Congress to repeal restrictions against Filipinos, Indians, and Chinese. In addition, FDR and military officials sought to overcome the racism behind the internment, which, like the discrimination against Asian allies, proved a handicap to the war effort. In this way, the director of the War Relocation Authority, the civilian agency in charge of the concentration camps for Japanese Americans, sought to transform the tragedy of the internment into a teachable moment to those Americans—including the president himself—who wrongly believed that blood equaled loyalty. After the war, nisei veterans became powerful new egalitarians on Capitol Hill who spearheaded the repeal of Japanese exclusion, which all but ended the perfect storm of exclusion. Recognized for their patriotic service, such ethnic egalitarians became known not just as champions for Asian American rights but also as global symbols of anticommunism.

Military Necessity and the Triumph of Exclusionism

The Pearl Harbor attack on December 7, 1941, followed by the U.S. declaration of war against Japan, set in motion the immediate FBI roundup of 1,291 Japanese (367 in Hawai'i, 924 on the mainland) as well as 857 Germans and 147 Italians. For the Japanese, FBI and naval intelligence officers, well before Pearl Harbor, had identified the detained subjects as potential subversives because they had served as ethnic leaders or otherwise maintained close ties to Japan. Their detention was a precautionary measure that did not reflect the Justice Department's blanket suspicions about the 112,000 Japanese Americans on the West Coast or the nearly 158,000 in Hawai'i. In fact, Attorney General Francis Biddle, as well as FBI director J. Edgar Hoover, adamantly resisted calls for mass evacuation of Japanese Americans—let alone Germans, Italians, or other enemy aliens. Despite an inflammatory statement by the secretary of the navy blaming Pearl Harbor on fifth column activity by Japanese Americans, and despite subsequent press reports that gave credence to unfounded rumors of disloyalty in Hawai'i, there was no great call for the internment for nearly one month after the initial attack. While Congressman Leland Ford excoriated Japanese American disloyalty, others from California testified to the group's trustworthiness, such as Representatives John Coffee and Martin Voorhis, as well as Senator Sheridan Downey. A public opinion poll, conducted during the last week of January and based on the views of 192 residents in four California localities, found the majority of pollees satisfied with the current, limited measures being taken regarding enemy aliens, while only a third of them wanted more severe action to safeguard the West Coast. The poll also showed that roughly an equal number of Californians viewed the Japanese population as "virtually all loyal" as opposed to "virtually all disloyal." Yet many of those who saw them as loyal admitted that they remained suspicious of Japanese Americans because it was difficult to tell the loyal from the disloyal.[1]

Within this context, Chester Rowell, now political editor of the *San Francisco Chronicle*, threw his considerable weight as California's leading journalist against race prejudice and war hysteria. In October 1941, as U.S.-Japan relations were spiraling toward war, Rowell joined the Institute of Pacific Relations egalitarians such as Galen Fisher, Ray Lyman Wilbur, and Wallace Alexander to defend the civil liberties of Japanese Americans by establishing what would become the Committee on National Security and Fair Play. California governor Culbert Olson served as the committee's honorary chairman. Because the internment question turned on racial traits and potentialities, not on miscegenation, Rowell was able to support Japanese Americans without reservation. After all, he had argued repeatedly that Japanese immigrants and especially their children were more capable of adapting to American culture than most migrants from Europe and therefore posed no threat as long as their numbers remained small. Rowell wrote at least eight columns in the months following Pearl Harbor arguing that race should not be a factor in any policy to protect the West Coast. "The way to distinguish fifth columnists, spies and saboteurs," he said, "is to watch, not their complexions or their names, but their conduct." Rowell took aim at certain opportunistic "demagogues" for exciting the masses on the Japanese question. He also blamed the U.S. Navy for the failure at Pearl Harbor and did not mention popular rumors of Japanese American complicity in Hawai'i. While in no way denying the danger of espionage and sabotage, he urged Californians to "keep our heads against hysteria and small politics, and against the vigilantism they breed." The consequence, he cautioned, of discriminating against Japanese Americans not only would be racial, moral, and constitutional injustice but also would set back the war effort by playing into the hands of Japanese propaganda that portrayed the United States, and its European allies, as white racist and imperialist bullies.[2]

Rowell's calls for calm fell on increasingly deaf ears as the campaign for evacuating Japanese Americans ramped up in late January 1942. The release of findings from the presidential commission studying Pearl Harbor proved a game changer. Headed by Supreme Court justice Owen Roberts, the commission confirmed the existence of Japanese spy rings in Hawai'i that included members of the local population who were not attached to Japan's diplomatic corps. The fact of Japanese espionage should not have surprised Americans, given the widely reported news in June 1941 of the FBI's arrest of two suspected spies in Los Angeles, one the valet of film star Charlie Chaplin and the other a student at the University of Southern California. But after Pearl Harbor, the idea of Japanese spying took on an urgent and sinister cast. The Roberts report pushed Governor Olson to abandon his egalitarianism by demanding the mass evacuation of Japanese Americans. Nearly a week before EO 9006 was issued, Walter Lippmann, one of the nation's most respected newspaper columnists, warned of the "imminent danger" of a "Japanese raid accompanied by enemy action inside American territory." Lippmann sought to provide a "sober statement of the situation . . . based not on speculation but on what is known to have taken place and to be taking place." He listed three so-called facts: the Japanese navy long had been engaged in spying on West Coast defenses; communication was taking place between enemies at sea and on land; and the absence of any major acts of sabotage by Japanese Americans was an ominous portent of things to come. On this last point, he noted that from "what we know about Hawaii and about the fifth column in Europe, this [the absence of sabotage] is not . . . a sign that there is nothing to be feared. It is a sign that the blow is well organized and that it is held back until it can be struck with maximum effect."[3]

At the same time as Lippmann was alerting the nation to the threat of fifth column activity, the West Coast delegation in Congress, led by the old exclusionist Hiram Johnson, met with the president to demand that he and the Justice Department do much more to protect their constituents. The delegation issued stern recommendations for the mass evacuation of Japanese Americans. Support for the group that once existed in Congress withered in the face of the incited and unified western delegation. In this context, Clarence Lea ignored the faith he had placed in issei veterans in sponsoring the Nye-Lea Act in 1935. Southerners like Martin Dies (Texas), Senator Tom Stewart (Tennessee), and John Rankin (Mississippi) joined the western crusade. Befitting the long-standing racial alliance between the South and West, Rankin was particularly forceful in shouting on the House floor, "Once a Jap, always a Jap!" He explained, "You cannot regenerate a Japanese, convert him, change him, and make him the same as a white man any more than you can reverse the laws of nature." The boisterous backing on Capitol Hill for mass evacuation squared with public opinion polls showing growing distrust on the West Coast of Japanese Americans and dissatisfaction with the Justice Department handling of enemy aliens.[4]

Yet no matter how much congressional leaders roared, mass evacuation during wartime was not subject to legislation or voting. The ultimate authority rested with President Roosevelt, whose lack of empathy for Japanese Americans, one FDR expert concludes, enabled him to relinquish command to the War Department "without making any effort to determine whether any [military] necessity existed [for internment] or if a less extreme policy could be designed." Secretary of War Henry L. Stimson, in turn, left the fate of Japanese Americans in the hands of the commander of West Coast defenses, Lieutenant General John L. DeWitt. There has been much written about the decision to intern Japanese Americans that details the fractious negotiations between officials in the War and Justice Departments and finds fault especially with DeWitt as well as with the army's top lawyer, Provost Marshal General Allen W. Gullion, and his assistant Karl R. Bendetsen. The evidence is clear that Gullion and Bendetsen shared the racial beliefs and fears of the most hardcore exclusionists, which was not the case for Stimson or Assistant Secretary of War John J. McCloy, who were reluctant to intern U.S. citizens. Justice Department officials, including Attorney General Biddle, Assistant Attorney General James H. Rowe, and head of the Alien Control Unit Edward J. Ennis, remained as egalitarian as possible, although they reluctantly bowed to FDR's support for the internment and even before this discriminated against the Japanese more than against other enemy aliens.[5]

The evidence on DeWitt is more complicated. Most critics have focused on his final recommendation for the internment (which one historian claims was written by Bendetsen): "In the war in which we are now engaged racial affinities are not severed by migration. The Japanese race is an enemy race and while many second and third generation Japanese born on United States soil, possessed of United States citizenship, have become 'Americanized,' the racial strains are undiluted." As a result, the final recommendation concluded that "along the vital Pacific Coast over 112,000 potential enemies, of Japanese extraction, are at large today." This rationale for the internment made DeWitt appear like Congressman Rankin, an inveterate white supremacist who thought first and foremost about race. But, in fact, DeWitt did not think that blood *always* equaled loyalty because he admitted that the majority of Japanese Americans were not a problem. The real difficulty for him was being able to distinguish the loyal from the disloyal, which would prove a major problem in the event of a likely Japanese commando raid on the woefully unprotected West Coast. In this sense, he was no different from the egalitarian Edward Ennis, who explained the difficulties of defending the coast to a congressional committee overseeing the budget for his Alien Control Unit. In March 1942 he said, "We are moving the entire Japanese population on the West Coast, but we are convinced that the dangerous persons among them constitute no more than a very small percent of the whole population, but we cannot tell who the dangerous ones are. The loyal Japanese themselves will tell you that they cannot tell who are the dangerous ones. As a preventive measure, we will undoubtedly intern a large number of people that we do not have enough against to punish them. This is a matter of prevention and not of punishment."[6]

Furthermore, DeWitt changed his mind about internment from initially opposing it to then calling for the mass evacuation of *all* enemy aliens on the West Coast. Only after he was dissuaded from interning Germans and Italian enemy aliens did he focus entirely on the Japanese. Ennis recalled that DeWitt came to realize that German and Italians were "strongly politically integrated on the West Coast" and, unlike the Japanese, could not be removed easily. Because of their inability to become citizens and voters, the Japanese carried much less political weight and thus made it more possible for the War Department to carry out an abundance of caution by removing them. A final complication regarding DeWitt's internment decision concerned his understanding of the broader context of the war in the Pacific, especially in the Philippines, where he had served four tours of duty. As one historian points out, DeWitt paid close attention to internment of American citizens in the Philippines, as well as in Japan. An important benefit of the mass evacuation and confinement of Japanese Americans was to generate a sizable pool of hostages to exchange for Americans seized by Japanese forces. The complexities of DeWitt's motivations for the internment in no way detracted from the gift he gave to exclusionists, who in their wildest dreams never could have imagined that the entire Japanese population would be removed from the West Coast.[7]

Hawai'i, however, was a different story, as egalitarians gained the upper hand and prevented the mass evacuation or confinement of Japanese Americans in the islands. After the Pearl Harbor attack and amid the flurry of rumors about the loyalty of Japanese Americans, the Hawaii Department of the U.S. Army remained undecided about what to do concerning the local ethnic population. Over one hundred nisei reservists, called to duty after December 7, stood guard along with fourteen hundred nisei draftees throughout the islands, protecting them from additional attack. But on January 19, 1942, the reservists (not the draftees) were dismissed from the Hawaii Territorial Guard per the orders of the islands' new military governor, Delos Emmons, who replaced General Walter C. Short after the general took the fall for Pearl Harbor. Coming from the mainland, Emmons was not familiar with the local Japanese American population, and furthermore, he was being pressured by President Roosevelt to place national security before labor needs by enacting mass internment.[8]

But Emmons proved a quick study regarding the nisei, and on the advice of many local egalitarians, including Cecil Coggins of the Office of Naval Affairs, he resisted the presidential pressure in becoming what one historian calls the "shield of Hawai'i's nisei." Emmons sent slightly more than 1 percent of Japanese Americans (fewer than two thousand) to internment camps either on the mainland or in the islands. In addition, he, along with Admiral Chester Nimitz, head of the Pacific Fleet, successfully campaigned Washington to create the all-Japanese 100th Battalion out of the nisei draftees in Hawai'i and send them to battle. Later on this unit would be joined by the 442nd Regimental Combat Team, which consisted of newly recruited Japanese Americans, the vast majority from the islands. Part of the rationale for drafting a new wave of nisei came from the dismissed guardsmen, who grouped as a volunteer service battalion and in so doing gained the respect of Assistant Secretary of War John J. McCloy and First Lady Eleanor Roosevelt. FDR announced the acceptance of nisei volunteers to the U.S. Army by saying, "No loyal citizen of the United States should be denied the democratic right to exercise the responsibilities of his citizenship, regardless of ancestry." Meanwhile other egalitarians in Hawai'i, such as head of the FBI Robert Shivers, Honolulu police officer John Burns, the YMCA's Hung Wai Ching, and IPR leader Charles Loomis, organized Japanese Americans into counterespionage groups to report on disloyalty within their ethnic group. One of the key players here was the Emergency Services Committee (ESC), chaired by nisei Masaji Marumoto, who was a founding member of the Hawaii Japanese Civic Association. Marumoto represented a direct linkage between the Americanization programs of the 1920s and 1930s and the counterespionage work during the war.[9]

Even on the mainland with EO 9066 being implemented, the exclusionist victory was compromised, as egalitarians, though supporting the internment order, struggled to give it the most liberal interpretation possible.

The tug-of-war between both sides of the exclusion debate was evident in congressional hearings held to investigate the problem of enemy aliens on the West Coast. Fearful of witch hunts against Japanese Americans, Carey McWilliams called on Congress in late January 1942 to investigate the situation. The response was positive, and in just over a month California representative John Tolan chaired public hearings in San Francisco, Los Angeles, Portland, and Seattle. The Tolan Committee investigation began just after FDR issued EO 9066, and while the hearings were underway DeWitt announced on March 2 the creation of a military zone along the West Coast from which all Japanese Americans were to be removed. Surprisingly, about equal numbers of egalitarians and exclusionists testified at the hearings. While egalitarians — religious leaders, scholars, educators, the CIO, and the Japanese American Citizens League (JACL) — opposed mass evacuation, the overall tenor of the hearings supported DeWitt's proclamation. Public officials were nearly unanimous in support of mass evacuation. Three from California, the state containing more than 80 percent of West Coast Japanese Americans, provided some of the most important testimony at the Tolan hearings. Two of them (the state's governor and mayor of its largest city) had no connection to the legacy of exclusionism, while another (the state's attorney general) reached out to exclusionists and shared their conception of the Japanese menace.[10]

The first official was Los Angeles mayor Fletcher Bowron, who before Pearl Harbor saw himself as having a "very satisfactory" relationship with the local Japanese community. The mayor made it clear to the Tolan Committee that his support for mass evacuation was "not by reason of any racial or other prejudice." He praised Japanese Americans as being "law abiding, industrious, and cooperative" and asserted that until the attack on Hawai'i he was convinced that "their avowed patriotism was sincere." Bowron had declared his faith in August 1941 to a large gathering in Little Tokyo celebrating a popular Japanese festival, while Japanese Americans themselves returned his trust by supporting his administration. But after Pearl Harbor his opinion soured. Because of the overriding impression of fifth columnists in Hawai'i, the mayor became convinced that many within Little Tokyo knew about the attack and were lying low to launch something similar in Los Angeles. His testimony revealed a deep sense of betrayal from a community he once trusted. He now questioned the sincerity of Japanese American patriotism(was it a ploy to create a false sense of security?) and wondered about the interest on the part of some Japanese to study the city's water system (was it to plan acts of sabotage)? In the end, Bowron supported mass evacuation because he knew of "no way to separate those who are patriotic and are, in fact, loyal at heart, and those who say they are patriotic and, in fact, are loyal to Japan." Because the United States was now engaged in a "total war" in which fifth columnists played a vital role, he concluded that "the only wise thing to do is take precautions for the defense of the country." This meant placing trust in General DeWitt's description of the Japanese threat and his plans to resolve it.[11]

The second official was Governor Culbert Olson, the liberal New Deal Democrat who had attracted Carey McWilliams to his administration. In the fall of 1941, the governor had stood up for Japanese American loyalty. "If the friction aroused by relations with Japan should generate much heat," he announced, "in dealing with them I shall rely upon the fact that recognition and protection of the rights and safety of minorities has always been the basic tenet of the American Government and the American sense and practice of fair play." After Pearl Harbor, Olson declared a state of emergency in California. He worked closely and cooperatively with General DeWitt to shore up the state's defenses, save for his opposition to the general's plans for mass relocation due to Olson's concerns about the negative impact that removing Japanese farmers would have on the state's food supply. But by the Tolan hearings, the governor came to support mass evacuation, although he still believed that "a large part" of the ethnic community was "so completely divorced of any natural feeling of loyalty or sympathy to the militarists of Japan, and its brutal aggressive methods, as to be wholly horrified at the way their racial nation has gone." Because the danger of the internal threat was supposedly imminent, and because California was on the "front line of defense fighting the Japanese," Olson was at pains to recommend removal of all Japanese Americans so as not to take any chances. He called on those who were loyal to put up with the "inconveniences" of evacuation until the federal government had the time to figure out who among them were disloyal. At the same time he sought to uphold the evacuees' property rights by cracking down on "chislers" who would exploit them in a time of confusion and crisis.[12]

In the end, the governor's support for mass evacuation rested not on the legacy of anti-Japanese racism but on the great fear and uncertainty of the moment. Americans, he said, "would be naive indeed if we did not recognize that there is a large part—we don't know how large, nobody can say, but we get it from our Japanese American citizens themselves—there is a considerable part of the Japanese population who are distinctly in sympathy with Japan and who do constitute an element that would engage in military assistance, or any kind of assistance in fifth column opportunities." Like DeWitt, Bowron, and many others including FDR, Olson bowed to racial convention in agreeing that it was more difficult to spot disloyalty among the Japanese than among Germans or Italians.[13]

The final California public official providing testimony at the Tolan hearings was state attorney general Earl Warren, whose call for mass evacuation proved the most influential of the three. Warren took over in Sacramento from the exclusionist Ulysses S. Webb, who over nine terms in office had done as much as anyone in the state to enact and enforce anti-Asian policies. A Republican with a vision for social planning, Warren looked up to progressives like Webb and especially Hiram Johnson. He was also a favorite of V. S. McClatchy. After Pearl Harbor, Warren worked with the California Joint Immigration Committee, which now included McClatchy's son, to pressure DeWitt to intern the state's Japanese population. Warren, however, was not a dyed-in-the-wool exclusionist. He upheld the rights of Japanese American state employees who had been released in the wake of the Hawai'i disaster. And unlike the CJIC witness at the Tolan hearings, he made no mention of California's legacy of exclusionism. Warren's testimony focused on the facts of the Japanese threat in California as they were known at the time. If there was a subtext to the strong case he made for mass evacuation, it had less to do with the backstory of exclusionism than with his well-known gubernatorial ambitions, which compelled him to get in front of Governor Olson to protect the state from the Japanese threat. Warren would declare his candidacy for the governor's race in April 1942 and win the November election. Ever since Warren and Olson came to Sacramento in 1939, the two men were partisan rivals, and just after Pearl Harbor whatever relationship they had took a turn for the worse over the governor's handling of the war emergency. In the Tolan hearings, Warren appeared as a confident law-and-order conservative who emphasized the importance of paying attention to the needs of local law enforcement. This position appeared in stark contrast to Olson's image as a softhearted New Deal liberal who reluctantly and belatedly supported mass evacuation.[14]

Attorney General Warren made four points about Japanese Americans to the Tolan Committee. First, like Walter Lippmann and others, he warned against Californians being lulled into a false sense of security—a "fools paradise"—because the group so far had shown no sign of disloyalty. To prove that state law enforcement had not fallen down on its watch, he shared the findings of a poll of chiefs of police, district attorneys, and sheriffs of all larger cities. The results showed an almost "universal conviction that . . . there is grave and immediate danger of sabotage and fifth column activity from the Japanese population, and that their removal at once from the vicinity of vital establishments and areas is imperative in order to eliminate such danger." Second, Warren provided maps showing Japanese residences in close proximity to every "vital establishment" in the state. Aware that such a pattern of residence was mostly the result of "mere coincidence," he made it clear that he rejected an alarmist interpretation that would view the pattern as resulting from "some vast conspiracy." Rather than cast blanket suspicion, Warren focused on particular locations, such as Santa Barbara County in which the Japanese lived close to oil storage facilities that just two weeks before were fired upon by a Japanese submarine, an alarming attack that seemed to confirm the imminent Japanese attack on the West Coast. Rumors of ship-to-shore communication during what turned out to be an isolated and minor incident were rife during the Tolan hearings.[15]

Warren's final two points addressed the dearth of information about the Japanese threat. He complained that the state's law enforcement lacked basic knowledge of the names and addresses of local Japanese populations because this information was reserved for federal officials. As a result, he said, "it is like fighting with a blindfold on." Another way in which the state was blinded to the enemy threat, said Warren, was Japanese residents' refusal to inform on subversive activities within their community to the extent that German and Italian Americans did. His opinion was confirmed by testimony from a special FBI agent in charge of the Los Angeles district, although one nisei witness strongly disagreed. Thus, in the moment of great fear and uncertainty, Warren was convinced that a Japanese fifth column existed in California and that the state was nearly helpless to stamp it out. He opted to remove all Japanese from the state to make it easier to protect Californians from attack. Mass evacuation, he added, would remove the burden of having to preserve the peace in the likely event that an enemy attack would trigger anti-Japanese riots.[16]

In the end, Warren brilliantly carried on the tradition of California exclusionism as DeWitt and other federal authorities relied upon his maps and other evidence documenting the Japanese threat. But public officials, military leaders, exclusionists, President Roosevelt, the yellow press, and California law enforcement were not the only ones who made bad judgments about the supposed fifth column threat on the West Coast. So too did egalitarians, although they did not necessarily support mass evacuation. George Gleason, formerly of the Survey of Race Relations, submitted written testimony on behalf of a long list of religious and community leaders in Southern California recognizing the "abundant proof among alien residents on the Pacific coast [that] there are some who, if uncontrolled[,] might at the time of crisis contribute directly to the success of an enemy attack." Testifying in person, Gleason confirmed the dominant assumption that the Japanese posed the main threat on the West Coast, although he added that this had to do with the geographic proximity of Japan rather than with racial allegiance. He saw German and Italian aliens as the major threat on the East Coast. In the end, the old missionary stressed that evacuation should be based on military protection and not on race hatred, prejudice, or selfish economic interests. He called on the army to distinguish between loyal and disloyal Japanese while suggesting it should err on the side of caution by agreeing with Chairman Tolan's statement that "one person could do a lot of damage."[17]

Gleason's longtime colleague Galen Fisher also pushed for selective evacuation that would remove the issei but allow the nisei to remain on the West Coast. An IPR adviser, Fisher submitted to the Tolan Committee a written statement as the executive secretary of the Committee on National Security and Fair Play. The statement listed ten reasons to support selective evacuation, some of which addressed the impracticality of removing the entire ethnic community and the federal government's lack of concrete plans for the evacuated people. Owing to his missionary experience and connection to the IPR, he also argued that mass evacuation of Japanese and not Germans or Italians would inadvertently "give the military rulers of Japan the finest sort of propaganda to support their claim to be 'the protectors and deliverers of the colored races of Asia from the arrogant and race-biased white nations.'" Here was Sidney Gulick's old notion of the "white peril" to international relations in the Far East updated for the circumstances of World War II, for experts on Japan had long known how deep was the resentment in East Asia against the notion of white racial supremacy. Yet in opposing mass evacuation, Fisher focused less on the wounded pride of the Japanese overseas than on the patriotism of Japanese Americans on the West Coast. "Like many other Americans who have long known hundreds of Japanese," he maintained, "I would testify that among their most marked traits are loyalty and gratitude. I strongly believe that the Nisei citizens will, with few exceptions, be as loyal to the United States as any other group of citizens." The "exceptions" he pointed to were so-called kibei, who were American-born citizens raised and socialized significantly in Japan. While Fisher had no trouble distinguishing between loyal nisei and disloyal kibei, Warren, DeWitt, and other supporters of mass evacuation held up the confusion between the two as justification for removing American-born Japanese. After the hearings, Fisher identified the issei as the real threat within the ethnic community: "That there were potential fifth columnists among them is hardly open to doubt, as the arrest of over 2,000 by the FBI attests, although no wide-spread plot has been uncovered." While he continued to insist on the loyalty of the nisei, he admitted that mass evacuation was possibly "unescapable under war conditions."[18]

Like Fisher and Gleason, other egalitarians backed selective evacuation, but they too could not guarantee that no one in the remaining loyal population would engage in acts of sabotage. This was the impossible margin of error required during a moment of great fear and uncertainty. Louis Goldblatt, from the California CIO, offered perhaps the strongest criticism at the Tolan hearings of the irrational "wolfpack" hunting Japanese Americans. But even he conceded (wrongly, as it turned out) that local Japanese may have been involved in the Pearl Harbor attack.[19] Carey McWilliams qualified his confidence "that large numbers of citizens of Japanese descent are loyal to the United States" by admitting that "it might be difficult and perhaps even impossible to differentiate between the loyal and disloyal" among them. Consequently, McWilliams argued for selective evacuation, not because all Japanese Americans were loyal, but because their farms were vital to the state's food supply. He, like nearly everyone at the Tolan hearings, was certain about the loyalty of the "vast majority of aliens of Italian and German nationality."[20]

Finally, Japanese Americans themselves testified to the threat of disloyalty within their community. When asked whether "your people" remained loyal at Pearl Harbor, JACL leader Mike Masaoka said the evidence was mixed: Secretary William Franklin Knox himself admitted that some Japanese "turned guns on the invaders," but the "reports would seem to indicate another thing—sabotage." Fellow JACL member Dave Tatsuno addressed this question by making a sharp distinction between Japanese Americans and government agents for Japan. While he was certain that disguised agents committed much of the "treacherous act" in Hawai'i and were probably operating in California, he assured Chairman Tolan they had no connection to Japanese Americans. Yet Tokutaro Slocum, the Japanese immigrant who secured citizenship for himself and other Asian World War I veterans through extensive lobbying for the Nye-Lea Act, made no distinction between Japanese spies and long-standing Japanese immigrants. He replied to Earl Warren's complaint about the lack of informants within the ethnic community by boasting that in the wake of Pearl Harbor, he went "over the top" to root out disloyal immigrant aliens in Little Tokyo.[21]

Like their white egalitarian allies, the nisei advocated for selective evacuation to allow loyal Japanese Americans to remain on the West Coast. But if the federal government deemed it necessary for the whole community to leave, they swore to make this sacrifice willingly for their beloved nation. Masaoka put his faith in the fairness of "military and Federal authorities" while distrusting the selfish motives of "political or other pressure groups" on the West Coast. If the former called for mass evacuation, "we will have no hesitation in complying with the necessities implicit in that judgment." But if it resulted from the latter's self-interests, then "we feel that we have every right to protest and to demand equitable judgment on our merits as American citizens." Masaoka's strategy of cooperation, which was consistent with the JACL's overall position, revealed an astute understanding of the past in which Asian Americans could usually expect much fairer treatment from federal authorities than from local and state officials on the West Coast. Such a strategy also emerged from the utter lack of viable options. The moment of great fear and uncertainty left Japanese Americans few choices other than to throw themselves at the mercy of federal officials. The results, as will be shown in the next section, were mixed. DeWitt, Stimson, and FDR backed mass evacuation and internment and thus proved no more receptive than West Coast officials to the selective evacuation of Japanese Americans. Yet the civilian agency established to oversee and manage the internment proved surprisingly egalitarian.[22]

Internment Egalitarianism

The story of the removal and confinement of Japanese Americans has been well told. DeWitt's establishment of a military zone along the West Coast started the process through which the army speedily evacuated them to horse racetracks, county fairgrounds, and other temporary holding centers where they were confined until the federal government figured out what to do with them. Meanwhile, FDR established the War Relocation Authority (WRA), a civilian agency housed in the Department of Interior that inherited the evacuated people from the military. The president appointed New Deal administrator Milton Eisenhower, brother of General Dwight D. Eisenhower, to head the WRA. Convinced that the vast majority of Japanese Americans were loyal, Eisenhower sought a quick transition so they could resume normal lives as best they could outside the military zone. His plans, however, were foiled when ten western governors (excluding Olson) insisted that the Japanese Americans relocated to their states be confined in concentration camps—a logical position given the army's patent distrust of them. Thus began the erection of WRA camps, scattered throughout the rural West as far east as Arkansas, that would house and confine the vast majority of the evacuated population throughout the war.[23]

Historians have portrayed the camps as representing one of the bleakest chapters in the history of American civil liberties. These were isolated, dusty, crowded, intemperate, and overall uncomfortable places where innocent people struggled to reconstruct their shattered lives with few amenities, resources, and, most important, freedoms. Armed sentries, watchtowers, and barbed-wire fences guarded the camps. On top of all this, WRA administrators, despite good intentions, made crucial mistakes that elicited mistrust between internees and the WRA staff and in some camps provoked riots, beatings, protests, and arrests that to the broader public confirmed the disloyalty of Japanese Americans. The camps were powder kegs of misunderstanding, unintended consequences, and repressed rage. Nowhere was this more evident than at Tule Lake, where "troublemaking" internees were sent in order to preserve order in the nine other WRA camps.[24]

The disturbing image of the camps often causes us to forget or play down the fact that the WRA was a bastion of egalitarianism. Under Eisenhower and especially his successor, Dillon Myer, the agency's general inclination was to be sympathetic toward Japanese Americans. Myer replaced Eisenhower after the latter served for only four months. The new director consistently opposed the military's assumption of Japanese American disloyalty. He addressed this point forcefully in his "inside story" of the internment where he documented the WRA's "continuing battle of the racists" that pitted him against the WRA's persistent and powerful critics such as western congressmen, the American Legion, and the yellow press who opposed the "coddling" of internees. In the end, Myer contended that the WRA struggle paid off because the American people showed the world that "we can rise above sordid hate and bitterness of racial antipathy and the discriminatory practices stemming therefrom."[25] Here we find Myer patting himself on the back as an American savior, while a more critical interpretation would dismiss this portrayal as self-serving propaganda. The truth, as one historian of the internment, Alice Yang Murray, deftly reveals, is somewhere in between the view of him as savior or hypocrite. According to her, Myer changed his view of internee loyalty depending on the circumstances and audience. While defending them against the "racists," he also agreed with the military that they were a danger to national security. The reality was that Myer, like other liberal public figures in the 1940s, was a pragmatist whose sympathy for the internees was tied up with changing political and international circumstances during World War II.[26]

The WRA's upper-level administrators shared Myer's pragmatic sympathy for the internees. In a public address in October 1945, Robert Cozzens, the agency's assistant director, identified the challenges faced by antiracists in America seeking to help the internees. "Those of us," he said, "who recognize the constitutional demands for political and economic equality of all men must also recognize that there are elements among us who adhere to a long-rejected doctrine that this is a white-man's country." Other WRA administrators—including Wade Head and John Collier at Poston and Solomon Kimball and E. R. Fryer at Manzanar—were even more committed to nondiscrimination than either Myer or Cozzens. Yet the most consistently progressive and sympathetic advocates for the internees were the white social scientists the WRA hired, or allowed to operate within the camps as neutral observers, to help the agency create policies reflecting internee points of view. Many of these social scientists were influenced by Robert Park's race relations cycle and other now well-established theories that rejected the notion that blood, or biology in general, influenced one's loyalty or character. The largest scholarly project taking place within the camps—the Japanese American Evacuation and Resettlement Study—was led by the wife of one of Robert Park's close scholarly friends. It received major funding from the egalitarian Rockefeller Foundation.[27]

Carey McWilliams was also friendly with the WRA and later on referred to Dillon Myer as a "humane and decent man." Like the social scientists in the camps, McWilliams worked in cooperation with the WRA to conduct research for what would become in 1944 the first published study of the internment experience. The author's egalitarianism was evident in the book's title: *Prejudice: Japanese-Americans, Symbol of Racial Intolerance*. Prepared for the IPR, this study combined the organization's interest in international perspectives on Japanese exclusion with McWilliams's own knowledge about racism in California and the American West. The goal was to "indicate how racial ideologies come into existence." Moving away from the focus on systems of labor and land distribution found in his first book, *Factories in the Field*, McWilliams maintained that the anti-Japanese racism behind the internment derived from a transpacific tragedy in which the long-term plan by the "military cliques in Japan" to go to war against the United States was made possible by the migration of numbers of Japanese. The migration, in turn, triggered in California forms of racism inherited from the unresolved racial conflict in the American South. McWilliams relied in large part on the theories of Robert Park and other social scientists who studied Japanese Americans within the context of race relations and globalization. He focused on the relationship between the internment and Japanese war propaganda, as well as on its implications for future U.S. relations with Japan and other Asian nations. The book's major policy recommendations were for Congress to pass a joint resolution declaring an end to discrimination based on color, creed, or national origin; to eliminate the poll tax and pass antilynching legislation; to expunge racism from immigration and naturalization codes; and to back up all of the above by creating a federal sanctioning body to investigate claims of misdeeds and, if need be, hand down punishment.[28]

One of the most important expressions of WRA egalitarianism was support for nisei soldiers and soldiering. While military and civilian officials in Hawai'i, as well as local Japanese Americans and Eleanor Roosevelt, deserve credit for the establishment of the all-nisei 442nd Regimental Combat Team, so too do WRA leaders. While General DeWitt sought to place heavy restrictions on nisei enlistees, Dillon Myer's representative to the War Board, Thomas Holland, lobbied to have the army use them to the fullest extent possible. Save for a small minority of internees, Holland found them to be good Americans seeking "an opportunity to enter combat service and prove their loyalty by actual duty." While FDR noted the right of nisei to defend their country in war, he and the War Department sided with the WRA largely because of the pragmatic benefit that nisei soldiers would have for U.S. attempts to undermine Japanese war propaganda that denounced America as the enemy of nonwhite peoples. The Office of War Information, which included fulsome support from Milton Eisenhower upon his reassignment from the WRA, impressed the War Board with the importance of using nisei soldiers for the propaganda war.[29]

Another important part of WRA egalitarianism was its resettlement programs. While many scholars fault the agency for its assimilationist goals and constant monitoring of "freed" internees, some applaud its crucial efforts on behalf of the former internees to secure jobs, housing, and college enrollment outside the West Coast. In light of such programs, one historian of postwar race relations in Los Angeles has claimed that "not since the Freedmen's Bureau had a federal agency worked so diligently to improve race relations."[30] WRA field offices in Los Angeles, Chicago, and many other cities acted as government-sponsored civil rights agents for relocating Japanese Americans. When a nisei veteran faced housing segregation in Southern California, it was WRA field workers who arranged for top U.S. military leaders to speak out against the racist treatment. In this capacity, Roger W. Smith, commander of the famed 442nd all-nisei battalion, defended one of his former men against white residents in Orange County, California. "We thought we closed the deal when we finished the war on both fronts," Smith said, "but this is rather debatable when some of the things for which we fought are being attacked here at home."[31]

Local nongovernment groups worked closely with the WRA to assist in internee resettlement. A good example was the Pacific Coast Committee on American Principles and Fair Play (or Fair Play Committee), which was headquartered in Berkeley, California. An offshoot of Galen Fisher's national organization in support of Japanese Americans, the Fair Play Committee promoted the achievements of nisei soldiers and generally served as what its leader, Ruth W. Kingman, called "an unofficial public relations representative" for the WRA and many other bodies of the federal government.[32] The Fair Play Committee was initially based at the Berkeley YMCA, where Kingman's husband, Harry Kingman, served as executive secretary. The couple spent much of the 1920s in China working for the YMCA's program for international students and where Harry had been born in 1893 as the son and grandson of missionaries. When the army rescinded the evacuation order on December 18, 1944, and the WRA immediately followed by announcing the closing of its camps within one year, Kingman kicked her organization into gear to prepare the West Coast for the return of Japanese Americans. In mid-January 1945 the group organized a conference on "interracial cooperation" at the Palace Hotel in San Francisco that brought together federal, state, and local government officials from the WRA, federal Social Security agency, War Manpower Commission, Federal Public Housing Administration, and many other agencies to address problems related to the resettlement of the Japanese population. The gathering also drew an even longer list of nongovernment organizations, including the NAACP, the CIO, and the JACL. In following up on the conference, Kingman reported that workers from the YMCA, the YWCA, the Federal Council of Churches, and other egalitarian organizations disbursed throughout California to mobilize "fair-minded" people to support the returning evacuees, especially those who had confronted violent resistance.[33]

Kingman also addressed employment discrimination and the protection of civil liberties. She praised the International Longshoremen's and Warehousemen's Union for expelling two of its members who discriminated against a fellow nisei worker. In this incident, Louis Goldblatt, the California CIO leader and ILWU founder, lived up to his support for Japanese Americans at the Tolan hearings by opposing the anti-Japanese hostility of the ILWU local in Stockton, California, in order to secure jobs for resettled nisei, a crucial part of the larger strategy of interracial organizing. Surprisingly, a few months before, the AFL's national organization joined labor egalitarians by openly opposing the persecution of Japanese Americans. This action compelled the exclusionist Paul Scharrenberg to complain to AFL president William Green that such a proclamation would give the false impression that the evacuees were welcome in the Golden State.[34] In 1943 Scharrenberg himself had returned to California to become director of the Department of Industrial Relations in Governor Earl Warren's administration. The two men, as well as the new state's attorney general Robert Kenny, shared bonds of progressivism and exclusionism. To discourage Japanese from returning to California after the war, the governor had Kenny step up prosecution of alien land law violations. Warren also signed legislation preventing them from obtaining commercial fishing licenses.[35]

But as he showed before the evacuation, Warren's exclusionism had important limits. When the military rescinded the evacuation order on December 18, 1944, the governor urged all Americans to "join in protecting constitutional rights of the individuals involved" and to "maintain an attitude that will discourage friction and prevent civil disorder." Attorney General Kenny fell in step. To address the more than eighty reports of arson and threats perpetrated against the returnees during the first half of 1945, the Fair Play Committee organized a second conference in Sacramento to, as Kingman noted, "call attention to the determination of both the Governor and Attorney General to maintain law and order." At the conference, Kenny began the session on "racial tensions and the law" by reading a statement issued by the American Civil Liberties Union (ACLU) in which the organization offered a $1,000 reward for "information leading to the arrest and conviction on a felony charge of persons who molest the returning Japanese Americans." Meanwhile in Los Angeles, Mayor Fletcher Bowron, who had expressed grave suspicions about Japanese American disloyalty during the Tolan hearings, changed his mind and was welcoming home nisei with the assurance that "everything which local government can do to make your relocation smooth and pleasant is being done." Bowron stressed that our "democracy recognizes no distinctions of race, color or creed," and that "our citizens, whatever their origin, are Americans working together in the great common effort" to win the war.[36]

Military Necessity and the Repeal of Exclusion

That Bowron and Warren exhibited both exclusionism and egalitarianism at the same time testified to the complex racial nature of World War II. While Hitler was conquering nations and slaughtering millions in the name of the "master" Aryan race, the United States and Japan were engaged in what one historian calls a "war without mercy" in which racism on both sides shaped military strategy, mobilized societies, and elevated the will to kill. While the Pacific War opened in the United States with the great fear and uncertainty of fifth columnists that justified the internment, federal officials soon realized that winning the war required avoiding the "white peril." As egalitarians had long warned, the racism against Japanese Americans played into the hands of Japan's attempts to unite Asians against the racist and imperialist white Allies. Humanizing and moderating the internment and establishing the all-nisei 442nd Regimental Combat Team were part of U.S. efforts to change the narrative about American racism. But for the nation's allies in Asia, even more important was the repeal of immigration exclusion and granting of naturalization rights. This prompted congressional involvement in the propaganda war against Japan.

Not long after America entered the Pacific War, Chinese diplomats made it known to their U.S. counterparts that the alliance between the two nations should live up to the humanitarian ideals for which the Allies were fighting. The State Department responded by working with Great Britain to create a treaty in January 1943 in which both these imperialist nations renounced unequal treaties with China that for over a century had granted their overseas citizens rights to markets, property, and extraterritoriality. China finally stood on equal legal terms with the West. The Chinese also wanted the U.S. and British dominions and colonies to repeal immigration exclusion but were discouraged from this request by Secretary of State Cordell Hull, who worried that it might jeopardize the treaty's chances for ratification. Dean Acheson, an assistant in the State Department's Division of Far Eastern Affairs, explained to the minister counselor of China's embassy in Washington, D.C., that "we had hoped in the brief treaty to take care of extraterritoriality and immediately related matters and to avoid going into extraneous questions or wandering afield in any way that might cause delay."[37]

The ratification of the Treaty for the Renunciation of Extraterritoriality in China opened the door for Congress to take up the issue of repealing Chinese exclusion. In December 1943, with strong support from FDR and the State Department, Congress repealed Chinese exclusion in an overwhelmingly egalitarian vote. The president said the act would "correct a historic mistake and silence the distorted Japanese propaganda."[38] But it did not turn the clock back to the pre-1882 days of free Chinese migration, for that opportunity was seemingly lost forever under the national origins regime. Rather, the inclusion of China in the national origins system meant it received a quota of 105 Chinese (not white) migrants per year. In addition, the repeal of exclusion granted the right of naturalization to Chinese aliens who now were no longer "ineligible to citizenship." The debate regarding this act was expressed in hearings called by Samuel Dickstein's House Committee on Immigration and Naturalization in May and June 1943. Since this was the first time that Congress engaged in serious discussion to repeal Chinese exclusion, these hearings provided an important index to the wartime development of the immigration debate.[39]

The hearings attracted many of the usual parties. Representatives from the AFL, patriotic societies, the VFW, and the American Legion made up the core of the exclusionist camp; the egalitarian side received support from missionaries, the Federal Council of Churches, the CIO, and other radicals. Southerners on the House Immigration Committee, as was common, infused the Chinese question with concerns about black-white relations. And Dickstein, as chair of the proceedings, continued to interject into the debate his brand of liberal, New York Democratic politics. But the major difference in the immigration debate during wartime was that exclusionists were outnumbered and outmatched. More than ever, Dickstein's egalitarianism influenced the tenor of the hearings as he became an unabashed partisan for repeal. He challenged John Trevor of the exclusionist American Coalition, who fought repeal by arguing that the smuggling of Chinese would increase if China was given a quota. Dickstein pointedly cautioned Trevor not to "throw the whole dirt on the Chinese" since he knew British people who had been smuggled into the country despite their very generous immigration quota. When the representative from the American Legion opposed the repeal bills because they would become an "opening wedge" for a flood of Asians into the United States, the chairman was flabbergasted at how the legion could come to that conclusion. "Let me state here," he declared, "that the problem of coolie labor or any other labor, is not involved here at all." Since China's quota was only a little over one hundred persons per year, he failed "to see how this small number can in any way endanger our economy." Dickstein was also "rather disappointed" that the VFW, an organization in which he held membership, refused to back the repeal bills. The chairman's handling of the only witness at the hearings who showed an open racial hostility toward Chinese, blacks, and Jews spoke volumes about how far Congress had come since the initial enactment of Chinese exclusion, when such racism was commonplace and legitimate. Dickstein dismissed as un-American this witness's "bigoted point of view," which was "more in accord with Nazi and Fascist ideologies." The committee moved to strike her testimony from the record, although in the end the motion was withdrawn. The one concession that Dickstein made to the exclusionists was to address their fear that by repealing exclusion, thousands of Chinese from Hong Kong or the Caribbean would enter the nation under the British quota or exceptions made for the Western Hemisphere, respectively. This explains why the final law carried on a racialist element by counting Chinese who lived anywhere in the world against China's tiny national quota.[40]

Powerful testimony provided convincing proof that repealing exclusion was necessary to counter Japanese war propaganda. One was by Kilsoo Haan, the Korean nationalist who had supported McClatchy in the IPR textbook controversy. Haan had the distinction of warning the same House committee before the war about Japanese espionage and fifth column activity directed at the United States. Now respected as the "man who tipped us off on Pearl Harbor," he announced that Japan was planning to forge a separate peace with China that would allow them to dominate Asia and the Pacific by cutting out Americans and the West from that part of the world. In this case, the "Atlantic Charter will become a meaningless gesture of Anglo-American declaration of policy unless more positive action is adopted proving that Anglo-Americans mean what they say." Haan maintained that repealing Chinese exclusion in addition to renouncing extraterritoriality in China were "timely and psychological moves to win over millions of doubting Chinese and other Orientals toward America." Richard Walsh, book publisher and editor of the liberal transpacific magazine *Asia and the Americas*, provided more concrete evidence of Japanese propaganda in the form of translated radio broadcasts beamed to China. One March 17, 1943, one such broadcast reported that "while white people are free to live in China, the Chinese cannot enter the United States." Another noted that the provisional Chinese government in Chungking

> must know . . . that throughout the greatest part of the western States of America the Chinese are rigidly prohibited through crafty legal racial restrictions from residing anywhere except in the most undesirable neighborhoods. The Chungking authorities must also know that the Chinese are rigidly excluded from attaining American citizenship, by naturalization, a right which is accorded to the lowliest immigrant from Europe. The Chungking authorities must know the social customs in America force the Chinese to remain in the most menial occupations, dispised [sic] and mistreated and, at best, patronizingly tolerated with contemptuous humor.[41]

The main problem with Japanese propaganda, said Walsh, was the "unhappy fact" that it was all true. Thus it was a "matter of downright military necessity that before great numbers of American soldiers go into China to fight besides Chinese soldiers, living among Chinese people, using Chinese resources and Chinese soil as our base against Japan, we should recognize and establish the equality of China as our ally, by repealing the exclusion laws."[42]

In addition to seemingly factual accounts of Japanese propaganda, two China experts compelled a great deal of respect. One was Pearl S. Buck, the famed American Nobel laureate for literature and former missionary in China. Buck, who was now married to John Walsh, confirmed that all Chinese, not just the nation's diplomatic corps, felt the sting of exclusion, and so they would appreciate the repeal of this persistent national humiliation. The second expert was Walter Judd, a former medical missionary in China and newly elected Republican member of Congress from Minnesota. Judd knew that the disgrace of exclusion was not limited to the Chinese but spread throughout Asia and that the "single, most important cause for our being at war with Japan is the Exclusion Act of 1924." Buck explained that this act caused the "death blow of liberalism" in Japan and thus paved the way for militarists who, unlike Japanese liberals, spurned cooperation with the United States. Judd had originally wanted to sponsor a bill that would repeal exclusion for all Asian groups, including the Japanese, but he was convinced by senior colleagues that given the anti-Japanese consensus in Congress and throughout the United States, it was better to save this until after the war. Nevertheless, Judd made it clear that he believed the internment was a "bad mistake" and that "Japanese born and educated in America and treated fairly are just as loyal to America on the whole . . . as are the sons of Englishmen or Germans."[43]

The testimony of Lewis Hines, who replaced Scharrenberg as the AFL Washington lobbyist, showed how concerns about winning the war trumped the old argument for protection from "hordes of these people." At this time, the federation was still two years away from switching to the egalitarian side, much to Scharrenberg's chagrin, in supporting the return of Japanese Americans to California. In addressing Chinese immigration, Hines was aware of the pronounced war sympathy for the Chinese in the United States. He thus disavowed being motivated by racial prejudice by singing the praises of Chinese soldiers, citizens, and especially workers. He argued that Congress should postpone repealing exclusion until after the war, not just because of the potential damage this action would have on American laborers but also because their Chinese brethren were unconcerned about such matters of symbolic diplomacy. Committee member Noah Mason, a conservative Republican from Illinois, criticized Hines's statements as "largely based on misinformation, and, therefore, fall on their own weight." Mason was convinced by China experts such as Buck and Judd that "this was a very important emergency war measure and cannot wait until after the war, in order to offset present day Japanese propaganda which is undermining the morale of China." He added that the State Department, by rescinding extraterritoriality, had already taken away "one of the legs of . . . Japanese propaganda," and now Congress had the opportunity "to take away the other leg upon which . . . [it] is based."[44]

Congressman Mason articulated another pragmatic reason for supporting repeal: the mythic China market. In arguing against the American Legion's opposition to repeal, he explained that after the war, exports would be crucial for the health of the machine-tool industry in his district. "China," he stated, "has the greatest need for machine tools of any country in the world," and it "is the only market where we can dispose of these surplus machine tools." Congressman Warren Magnuson, one of the sponsors of the repeal legislation, echoed Mason's remark while adding an internationalist spin that sounded like it was straight from an IPR conference: "We are gradually working toward a postwar era wherein the greatest development will be in the Pacific. . . . I think every man in this room is going to see the day when you can get in your automobile in Washington, D.C., and drive to China; and that is not too far-fetched. It is only a few short miles across the Bering Strait. Our air lines are branching off to China. . . . We are going to be able to step into an air-line office here and be in China the next day. . . . All these things are factors that enter into this [legislation]."[45]

In the shrinking Pacific World in which the United States was also allied with the peoples of the Phillippines and India, the arguments used to repeal Chinese exclusion were applied almost verbatim to calls to repeal exclusion against these other groups. By July 1946 President Harry S. Truman signed the Luce-Celler Act, which ended Indian and Filipino exclusion and granted each group the right to naturalization. This removed them from laws discriminating against "aliens ineligible to citizenship" and permitted 105 persons from each country to enter the United States under the national origins system. Separate hearings on naturalization bills for each group held during the war were replete with egalitarian arguments based on racial justice for loyal and industrious resident aliens, as well as with pragmatic military rationales and the promise of postwar internationalism and markets. The only signs of exclusionism in these hearings were the VFW's call to limit Filipino naturalization to war veterans and AFL opposition to Indian naturalization as a threat to American workers, a point, not surprisingly, that the CIO representative quickly countered. The hearings on Indian immigration broadened beyond the naturalization rights for 3,000 older migrants to push for the equal treatment of all Indians in the United States, a more liberal position that was associated with the independence of India, achieved one month after President Truman signed the Luce-Celler Act. Filipinos, whose homeland had already achieved independence by this time, continued to draw support from radicals such as Congressman Vito Marcantonio and now the Communist-led Committee for the Protection of Foreign Born.[46]

The impact of the war was so powerful that the hearings on Filipino naturalization showed no evidence of the pronounced fear that migrants from the Philippines posed a sexual threat to white women. What opposition there was to the naturalization bills made no mention of the "sex problem" that had been so evident in the earlier debate over Filipino exclusion. Moreover, Filipino witnesses turned this problem on its head by claiming that miscegenation with white American women and the birth of interracial U.S. citizens were positive signs of the group's assimilation. Leo Fernandez, a World War I veteran and chair of the Filipino-American National Council, pointed to a community in Louisiana in which Filipinos had intermarried with whites and produced mixed American citizens for over a century. That community, said Fernandez, symbolized the degree of intermarriage that existed in Filipino America. In this way, "marrying here with [white] Americans, our children are going to be American citizens by right of birth, and in twenty years . . . the Filipinos will hardly be recognized." Dr. Diosadado Yap, who represented Filipino organizations in the United States and Hawai'i, called the committee's attention to the problems that Filipino residents and even their American wives had in finding employment due to discrimination against "aliens ineligible to citizenship." He pleaded with the committee to consider their dilemma: "How can these loving parents bring up a respectable American family when subjected to such anomalous, un-Christian and un-American conditions?"[47]

Internationalization and the Cold War

World War II ended the era of American isolationism that from its beginning in 1919 had weighed against egalitarianism. Remaining within their own hemisphere, where U.S. hegemony ruled, lessened the need for Americans to experiment with new forms of international community. The internationalists of the IPR and Survey of Race Relations, on the contrary, were far more likely to favor egalitarian views of Asian immigrants. Such internationalism reigned supreme in the postwar era. As such, it was fitting that Chester Rowell lived just long enough to witness the birth of America's internationalist age, cemented by the country's leading role in establishing the United Nations in 1945, three years before his death. Likewise, it made sense that the old isolationist and exclusionist Hiram Johnson (Rowell's former Progressive Party ally) died before the new internationalist context influenced the total dismantling of the anti-Asian policies that he had been so instrumental in establishing. Johnson's replacement, Senator William F. Knowland (appointed by Governor Earl Warren upon Johnson's death in office), revealed the sudden change in fortunes for exclusionism. Knowland favored the ending of Asian exclusion and not coincidentally became a leading proponent on Capitol Hill for U.S. foreign aid and intervention in Asia. Another sign of the times occurred in 1953 when Henry Cabot Lodge Jr., grandson of the irreconcilable senator who opposed the League of Nations as well as Japanese immigration, served as U.S. ambassador to the United Nations.

In California, the repeal of Chinese, Indian, and Filipino exclusions left the Japanese as the main victim of discriminatory state and local public policies. As noted, Governor Warren expressed ambivalence toward Japanese Americans by upholding their civil liberties while at the same time subjecting them to increased prosecutions under the alien land law. Such a mixed message underscored the continuing strength of the anti-Japanese consensus even after the great fear and uncertainty had subsided. A new president offered a hopeful sign of change. Unlike FDR, who died during his fourth term in April 1945, Harry Truman took an active interest in defending Japanese American civil liberties. He was particularly upset by the wave of vigilantes seeking to discourage their return to the West Coast. While stymied by states' rights to stop such acts of terror, Truman channeled his outrage in a positive direction by honoring the all-nisei 442nd Regimental Combat Team upon its return from Europe. In a ceremony at the White House in July 1946, the president commended the heroic soldiers: "You fought not only the enemy," he declared, "but you fought prejudice—and you have won."[48]

The victory achieved by nisei soldiers abroad was not necessarily a "double victory" against racism on the West Coast. In October 1946 the California Supreme Court upheld the legality of the alien land law in a test case prompted by Warren and Kenny's stepped-up prosecutions of those who had sought to violate it. The court upheld a lower ruling that allowed the state to take over land controlled by Kanjiro Oyama, who had put it in the name of his six-year-old son, Fred. As the high court was deciding on the Oyama case, exclusionists established a state proposition to make it nearly impossible to repeal the alien land law by embedding it into the state constitution. Yet the campaign for Proposition 15 disappointed exclusionists as almost 60 percent of voters rejected it. Moreover, Californians as a whole seemed to be obsessed no more with Japanese threats as only 41 percent of those who went to the polls in November 1946 bothered to vote on Proposition 15 (the figure for Proposition 1 in 1920 was 87 percent). As map 7.1 reveals, key northern counties like San Francisco were strongly egalitarian ("no" vote) on the alien land measure, although Sacramento and others within the Sacramento Valley remained bastions of anti-Japanese voting.

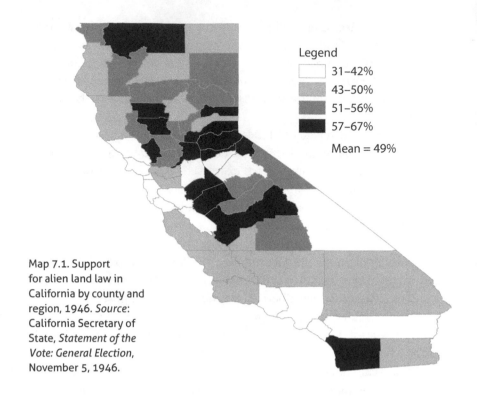

Map 7.1. Support for alien land law in California by county and region, 1946. *Source*: California Secretary of State, *Statement of the Vote: General Election*, November 5, 1946.

Legend
31–42%
43–50%
51–56%
57–67%

Mean = 49%

Southern California, with the exception of San Diego, remained an egalitarian stronghold. Here was the first clear sign that the hostility against the returning Japanese was more bark than bite. Joe Grant Masaoka, brother of Mike Masaoka, led the JACL's successful opposition, noting that the measure would "seize lands and homes of American GIS of Japanese ancestry" who had "earned the right to fair play and decent treatment for themselves and their families."[49]

The victory over Proposition 15 gave hope to continuing legal challenges to the alien land law, even though it did nothing to remove the law itself or stop the state from prosecuting Japanese American land owners. Former State Department official Dean Acheson offered pro bono services to Kanjiro and Fred Oyama as they asked the U.S. Supreme Court to overturn the California high court ruling. Acheson, the future secretary of state who had been involved with rescinding U.S. and British extraterritoriality, added important weight and experience to Oyama's ACLU and JACL lawyers. In January 1948 the Supreme Court in an 8–1 verdict prevented the Oyamas' land from escheating to the state of California by finding that the alien land law violated Fred's constitutional rights. In a second case following on the heels of the Oyama decision, the Court protected the rights of the issei as well as the nisei. It ruled in *Takahashi v. California Fish and Game* that laws barring aliens ineligible for citizenship discriminated against the equal treatment of Japanese, in this case to purchase a commercial fishing license. The confirming blow came in 1952 when the California high court, based on the *Oyama* and *Takahashi* decisions, and in response to test cases launched by the Masaoka brothers and issei newspaper publicist Sei Fujii, ruled the alien land law invalid under the Fourteenth Amendment's equal protection clause. The significance of postwar internationalism was evident in the *Fujii* decision, when a state appellate judge found the alien land law at odds with the United Nations charter and Declaration of Human Rights, which, unlike the League of Nations, upheld racial equality as a fundamental human right. The final end came in 1956 when nearly 70 percent of California voters approve repealing the alien land law.[50]

The writing was on the wall for exclusionist policies in California. After the *Oyama* and *Takahashi* decisions in 1948, Governor Warren removed the allocation for escheat cases from the attorney general's budget. In that same year, the JACL's news organ, the *Pacific Citizen*, could state with confidence that the seemingly powerful California exclusionists had been routed, save for "a few assorted crackpots [on] the lunatic fringe of racism."[51] At the same time, Mike Masaoka lobbied on Capitol Hill for legislation to compensate internees for property losses incurred because of the mass evacuation. Testimony on the measure in May 1948 before a subcommittee of the Senate Judiciary Committee revealed the emergence of a new consensus of opinion about EO 9066, how the internment was seen as a terrible mistake. Those testifying included John J. McCloy (former assistant secretary of war), Francis Biddle (former U.S. attorney general), Edward Ennis (former head of the Justice Department unit handling the internment), Dillon Myer, Galen Fisher, and Mike Masaoka. Each gave strong support to have the federal government pay "evacuation claims." This was consistent with backing from Secretary of War Henry Stimson, the Department of Interior, and the entire West Coast delegation in Congress. In fact, Masaoka reported that not one member of Congress voiced opposition to the measure, which was signed into law later that year.

The regret expressed at the hearings derived from two proven facts regarding Japanese American loyalty. First was that no known acts of disloyalty had been attributed to Japanese Americans at Pearl Harbor or any time during the war. Dillon Myer confirmed that the WRA "traced down every case that was reported in the way of rumor, and I know of no instance, and I think the record will show that no one else knows of any instance, of any case of sabotage or espionage on the part of the Japanese or people of Japanese ancestry in this country."[52] The second fact that was established during the hearings addressed the significance of nisei soldiers. To McCloy, their war record "was so brilliant and . . . so eloquent of the loyalty of this portion of our population that I think it is one of the brightest pages in the annals of our military history as well as of our national history." The utter fact of Japanese American loyalty enabled the hearings to sidestep "troublemakers" in the WRA camps who had previously been seen as proof of the group's disloyalty. Further, it allowed Edward Ennis to lament the internment as "one of those [morally wrong] incidents of war which cannot always be avoided," as stated by his former boss Francis Biddle. Ennis, who was then serving on the ACLU board, laid much of the blame for the mistake on the shoulders of General DeWitt and the pressures placed on him for mass evacuation from West Coast officials like Earl Warren, Culbert Olson, and Fletcher Bowron. To be fair, said Ennis, the factors leading to the internment decision were "too complex for a simple answer." DeWitt faced the very real problems of vulnerable West Coast defenses and no knowledge of Japanese attack plans. Initially, too, the general did not think mass evacuation was necessary. But in the end, Ennis testified, EO 9066 came down to DeWitt's inability to see beyond race in finding it impossible to distinguish between loyal and disloyal Japanese Americans. Given that both FDR and Stimson entrusted the general with making the decision, Ennis, in what to former internees must have been a painful understatement, noted that "perhaps it might have been better if the decision were in the hands of a person with a broader understanding of racial relations." The Evacuation Claims Act would prove an inadequate compensation for the internees' loss of property, to say nothing of their rights and dignity. But at the time it was heralded as removing yet another crucial piece of the stigma of disloyalty that haunted Japanese Americans.[53]

The last major policy discriminating against Japanese Americans was immigration exclusion and ineligibility for citizenship, and so it was that Mike Masaoka joined forces with Walter Judd and other egalitarians who had led the campaign repealing Chinese, Filipino, and Indian exclusion. In 1948, the same year Congress passed the Evacuation Claims Act and the U.S. Supreme Court vitiated the alien land law, Dickstein's House committee held hearings on the Judd bill, which proposed to end exclusion and provide naturalization rights for all Asian groups. Judd's purpose was clear: the bill "will work to remove the stigma that at present attaches to complete prohibition of immigration of certain races, and yet will make sure there will not be any flooding of America with people of lower economic standards or other cultural patterns." This was the bill that Judd had wanted to sponsor during the war but, due to the hostility against the Japanese, post-poned in favor of legislation focusing narrowly on the Chinese. The Judd bill proposed that all nations within a large geographical region designated as the "Asia-Pacific triangle" (including Japan, China, India, and the Phil-ippines) would receive a minimum quota of 100 per annum (Japan's was 185) along with naturalization rights. As in the act repealing Chinese exclu-sion, the Judd bill also sought to eliminate a "back door" into the United States by counting diasporic Asians from anywhere in the world against the quota for their ancestral homeland—this included persons from the West-ern Hemisphere who descended from at least one Asian parent.[54]

Walter Judd served as another important sign of the times, but in this case revealing the transformation not from exclusionism to egalitarian-ism but within the egalitarian side. A former medical missionary to China, Judd was motivated by religious, personal, and geopolitical reasons to end anti-Asian racism in the United States. The Chinese Communist Revolu-tion in October 1949 presented him, and all Americans, with perhaps the most compelling reason yet to discard exclusionist policies: to win the Cold War. While anticommunist fears had contributed to ending the alien land law and passing the Evacuation Claims Act, they came to drive egalitari-anism after the Chinese revolution and the subsequent outbreak of war in Korea that pitted U.S. troops against Communist troops from both North Korea and the recently established People's Republic of China. Republicans sought to pin the "loss of China" on Truman's Democratic administration and the inefficiencies of the bloated New Deal state. Yet anticommunist politics was a bipartisan affair as Republicans Walter Judd and Senator William Knowland joined with conservative Democrats like Senator Patrick McCarran to form an "Asia-first" bloc in Congress that vociferously lobbied for aid to Chiang Kai-Shek's Nationalist regime in Taiwan (known then as Formosa) and for actions discrediting the People's Republic of China within the global community, which included blocking its attempt to be seated in place of Taiwan in the United Nations. During and after the Korean War, "Asia-firsters" supported the vigorously anticommunist regime of Syngman Rhee, first president of South Korea (established in 1948). Rhee, and other Korean immigrants like Kilsoo Haan, had long lobbied U.S. officials to sup-port Korean independence from Japan. In a similar way, Manuel Roxas, first president of an independent Philippines (established in 1946), was a famil-iar face on Capitol Hill, having lobbied before the war to free his country from colonialism and against Filipino exclusion. Roxas proved every bit the anticommunist as Chiang Kai Shek or Syngman Rhee in suppressing the peasant-based radical Hukbalahap movement in his country.[55]

The Asia-firsters also led and supported congressional investigations of the IPR, including the infamous Wisconsin senator Joseph McCarthy's accusations that key IPR leaders were Communists and had influenced the State Department's "loss of China." One of the victims of the anticommunist purges was Frederick Vanderbilt Field, the leftist IPR staffer who in the late 1930s had defended the organization's new textbook on Japanese history against criticisms waged by V. S. McClatchy. Field, who had been active in the Communist Party during the 1930s and 1940s, was sentenced to three months in a federal prison for contempt of court when he refused to name Communist friends and associates.[56]

The Cold War climate proved optimal for Judd's bill and others designed to end Japanese exclusion. Like campaigns against the alien land law and for compensation for internee property losses, egalitarians benefited from the celebration of nisei war heroism and regret for the internment. McCloy and General Mark Clark, commander of the 442nd Regimental Combat Team, supported the bill by offering the highest platitudes to the nisei soldiers.[57] As was common in hearings to repeal Chinese, Indian, and Filipino exclusion, the egalitarian testimony focused heavily on the impact that U.S. immigration and naturalization policies had on international relations. Many witnesses criticized the exclusion of Japanese in the first place for causing Japan to attack the United States. While Judd had raised this point at the earlier hearings for repealing Chinese exclusion, it now took on the air of an established fact, much like the consensus of opinion that the internment was a mistake. Two pre-war U.S. ambassadors to Japan spoke to the grief that Japanese exclusion had caused them during their terms in Tokyo. One, Joseph Grew, explained at length how the embarrassment of exclusion forced the liberals from power, which sent Japan down the road toward militarism and war. Dillon Myer and an official in the occupation forces of Japan echoed the barrage of scorn placed on Japanese exclusion. But even more important was testimony focused on the contemporary problems that exclusion posed for the current international crisis. Judd explained that the United States was in a fierce competition with the Soviet Union to win the hearts and minds of a billion Asians. "Which way will they go?" he wondered. "With the democracies as they wish? Or, in despair and hopelessness, with the totalitarians? This bill is a powerful weapon in that struggle." In Senate hearings, Dean Rusk, deputy undersecretary of state, supported repeal legislation as benefiting U.S. foreign policy: "Almost all of Asia has recently attained or is in the process of attaining self-government. The Asian governments, reflecting the deep seated sentiments of their peoples, regard the existence of the racial bar in our immigration and naturalization laws an impediment to the fuller development of friendly and co-operative relationships between themselves and the United States."[58]

The Cold War in Asia also pushed longtime exclusionists to abandon their racist positions. While John Trevor of the American Coalition continued to oppose repeal as an "opening wedge" to free migration from Asia, the American Legion and the AFL relented in the face of the overwhelming support of egalitarianism, although the veterans opposed the returning of U.S. citizenship to the so-called disloyal internees who had renounced it during the internment. At joint congressional hearings in 1951, Walter Mason put the labor federation on record as having "no desire to see arbitrary, discriminatory, or unfair barriers in order to restrict immigration." Moreover, the AFL representative criticized the Asian-Pacific triangle component of the proposed legislation for subjecting the peoples in this vast area to policies (counting diasporic peoples against their ancestral homelands) that did not affect those living outside the triangle. He worried that "this form of discrimination may still be a serious impediment to good diplomatic relations with Asiatic countries and could be used by the Communists to great advantage to hurt our position in Asia." The AFL's support for the repeal of Japanese exclusion was likely the first time in its sixty-five-year history that its representative criticized an immigration policy for discriminating against Asians. This historic turnabout was part of the transformation of organized labor occurring during the Cold War in which the open shop came under attack, leftists were purged, and goals were narrowed to workplace issues; and in 1955 the nation's two leading labor federations merged to form the AFL-CIO.[59]

Thus with the AFL's blessing, what was essentially the Judd bill gained approval from the appropriate Senate and House committees. In 1952 it became incorporated into the omnibus McCarran-Walter Act that the Democratic Congress approved over President Truman's veto. Despite ending Asian exclusion once and for all, this immigration act was a conservative document. It reflected the Cold War fears of the day by making it lawful to exclude and deport Communists and their "fellow travelers." Truman opposed the measure because it offended potential eastern European allies by maintaining the national origins quota system favoring the admission of "Anglo-Saxon Protestants." Little noticed at the time, the McCarran-Walter Act defined three types of immigrants: regular ones, who counted against national origins quotas (up to 270,000 per year from the Eastern Hemisphere); those with special skills or relatives of U.S. citizens who were exempt from quotas; and refugees from Communist countries, who also entered outside the national origins system. While the tiny quotas severely limited the number of Asian migrants entering through the "front door," the second and third categories of immigrants offered additional opportunities to gain admission to the United States. Until the national origins system was abandoned in 1965, Asians were much more likely than other immigrants to pass through these two "side doors." So it was that the end of the perfect storm of exclusion paved the way for the return of significant, though selective, streams of Asian immigration.

8 AFTER THE STORM

DEBATING ASIAN AMERICANS

IN THE EGALITARIAN ERA

||||||||||||||||||||||||||||||||||||||||||||||||||||||||||||||||||||||||||||||||||||||||||||||||||||||||||||||||||||||||||||||||||||||||||

During the 1960s, Ronald Takaki "was born intellectually and politically" as a graduate student amid the heyday of campus protests at the University of California, Berkeley. Grandson of Japanese plantation workers in Hawaiʻi, Takaki wrote a Ph.D. dissertation on race relations in the American South, another region indelibly marked by the subordination of nonwhite plantation labor. In 1972 he returned to the Berkeley campus as a professor of ethnic studies and over the next thirty years pioneered the field of multicultural history, which expanded his expertise on black-white relations to include analysis of Asians, Latinos, white ethnics, and Native Americans. Given his personal background, which included a Chinese American stepfather, Takaki devoted special attention to the history of Asian Americans. One of his most widely read books highlighted the lasting legacy of anti-Asian racism and the historical agency of Asian subjects in a way that popularized Asian American history within and beyond the academic community.[1]

Takaki's education and career trajectory embodied the bitter end to the exclusion debate and the emergence of different kinds of controversies regarding Asian Americans. While he was an undergraduate, his home territory of Hawaiʻi became the nation's fiftieth state, which, given the islands' demographics, meant the election of the largest-ever influx of Asian Americans to the U.S. Congress. Here was a perfect example of the kind of electoral and legislative power that European ethnic groups had enjoyed and that Asian Americans until now had lacked. In 1965, while Takaki was in graduate school, Congress, with the support of Senate and House members from Hawaiʻi, eliminated the last major piece of exclusionary immigration policy, the national origins system. While the McCarran-Walter Act of 1952 had removed bans on Japanese immigration and citizenship rights, it left intact discriminatory quotas that reserved all but a tiny fraction of immigration slots for Europe. As such, the final end to the exclusion era came in 1965 when President Lyndon Johnson initiated legislation that provided Asian (and other non-Anglo) immigrants with much greater opportunities to enter the United States. This action fell in line with the administration's Cold War strategies and landmark civil rights legislation to produce a major transformation in American race relations that for the first time since Reconstruction put the full force of the U.S. government behind the dream of racial equality. Comprehensive immigration reform marked the ultimate egalitarian victory. Gone were the days when national and local politics were driven by overt fears of Asian unassimilability, untrustworthiness, and incompatibility with American institutions; gone was the formal imperial subordination of Asian nations and their immigrants; and gone too were politically and legally disempowered Asian Americans who had to rely on the good graces of white policy makers and home-country representatives to promote group interests.

Yet the triumph of egalitarianism did not remove Asian Americans from political controversy. Although no longer headline news as a mass threat, they continued to be the subject of nationwide debates about institutional racism, equality of opportunity, and abuses of state power. These conflicts pitted two types of egalitarians against each other. Progressives like Takaki saw Asian Americans as victimized minorities whose past and present experience justified expansive state action against all forms of racism in not just the law but also every facet of American society and culture. Neoconservatives, on the other hand, opposed the expansion of state authority beyond guaranteeing a bare-bones interpretation of civil rights (nondiscrimination and equal opportunity before the law). To this end, they lionized Asian Americans as "model minorities" who overcame racism without needing much, if any, government assistance.

Both progressives and neoconservatives were "egalitarian" in that they opposed white supremacy and overt racial discrimination. But within the context of the civil rights revolution and its backlash, the meaning of "egalitarianism" changed to align with multicultural progressivism, which Takaki epitomized. Meanwhile, neoconservatives assumed the "exclusionist" side of the debate, which opposed expansive racial reforms and could be consistent with the backlash against civil rights reforms. This chapter explores both the triumph of egalitarianism, through Hawai'i statehood and comprehensive immigration reform, and the fracturing of it, through new debates during the civil rights era about Asian Americans as model minorities and about reparations for Japanese American internment. Both of these latter issues fostered the memory of past anti-Asian racism while forgetting the exclusion debate and in this way produced an intriguing historical amnesia.

Hawai'i and the Cold War

Second to the West Coast, Hawai'i was central to the development of the exclusion debate. In fact, both of these regions were interrelated and influenced by the same factors of trade, imperialism, and immigration, as well as by national security and labor relations. In this way, it might be best to see Hawai'i and the West Coast as different nodes in the formation of America's larger transpacific world system that included William H. Seward's vision of a transportation network linking the nation's East Coast to China that would carry peoples and goods back and forth across the Pacific. But Hawai'i and the West Coast contributed in different—and in many respects, antagonistic—ways to the exclusion debate. While the plantation oligarchy's paternalism toward Asian Americans sanctioned white supremacy and racial segregation, it was based on a circumscribed labor market almost exclusively dependent on Asian workers. This created a population in the islands that by the early twentieth century was majority Asian American, which in turn resulted in intimate and daily inter-ethnic interactions that broke down social barriers and reinforced the "aloha discourse" portraying Hawai'i as a racial paradise, which, as chapter 7 revealed, even operated under martial law during World War II. In contrast, Asian Americans on the West Coast remained a small fraction of the population, largely ostracized by law, work, residence, and custom from the white mainstream. Before the 1960s, West Coast egalitarian discourse promoting Asian American civil rights advanced by Chester Rowell, Carey McWilliams, and many others remained exclusive to a minority of internationalists, leftists, and Christian humanitarians. Yet it was during the Cold War that the aloha discourse merged with the nascent conception of West Coast multiculturalism to establish Asian Americans as major players in the nation's racial politics.

The collapse of the plantation oligarchy set the stage for the democratization of Hawai'i in which the majority population of Asian Americans for the first time would exert political power commensurate with their numbers. A good part of the change stemmed from organized labor and the Communist Party. Although obeying a no-strike pledge during World War II, Jack Kawano got Harry Bridges, leader of the International Longshoremen's and Warehousemen's Union, to let the union move from organizing Hawai'i's docks to organizing its sugar and pineapple plantations. By controlling workers on the plantations, as well as dockworkers in Hawai'i and on the entire West Coast, the ILWU was in a good position to counter the power of the planter oligarchy. In two short years, from 1944 to 1946, the union's membership skyrocketed from fewer than a thousand to thirty thousand due in part to the organizing skills of the ILWU's Jack Hall, who deployed the CIO goal of one big industrial union that made obsolete the tradition of ethnic-based organizing. After the war, the ILWU waged a series of devastating strikes on sugar and then pineapple plantations, which was followed by the shutting down of Hawai'i's docks. The planter oligarchy responded by getting Congress to investigate the labor situation in Hawai'i, which resulted in a series of anticommunist purges that caused great personal and organizational strife but, in the end, did not seriously compromise the ILWU's newfound power vis-à-vis the planter elite.[2]

Another part of the union's muscle was political. During the war, the ILWU's Jack Kawano had engaged in counterespionage activities with other nisei through the Emergency Services Committee and in this capacity became a trusted member of John Burns's plans to overhaul Hawai'i's Democratic Party in order to defeat the planters' Republican rule in the territorial legislature. A white man raised on Oahu and intimately familiar with native Hawaiians, Burns got to know and trust Japanese Americans as a police officer involved in counterespionage work during the war. A populist with sympathy for Communists and organized labor, Burns got along easily with Kawano and his ILWU companion Jack Hall, but given the anticommunist climate, he also relied upon the large body of Japanese American voters to further his political ambitions. After the war he became an honorary member of the 442nd Regimental Combat Team and 100th Battalion and cultivated a cohort of nisei veterans such as Daniel Inouye to run for political office as Democrats. By 1948 Burns's group controlled the Democratic Party, and after the fateful territorial election of 1954, Democrats, for the first time, controlled the territorial legislature, a change known as the "Democratic Revolution." The twenty-two party members (sixteen of whom were Japanese Americans) enjoyed a wide margin over the eight Republicans. Two years later Burns himself was elected Hawai'i's representative to Congress, where he would continue the planters' long-standing campaign for Hawai'i statehood while claiming it as a Democratic initiative.[3]

Hawai'i's path to statehood was more carefully studied in Congress than were the paths of the thirty-six earlier territories that had gone through the same process. Since 1935, House and Senate Interior and Insular Affairs committees had conducted twenty-two hearings about the matter in which over 850 witnesses had testified. The sticking points included the physical separation of the islands from the U.S. mainland and the presence of communism as exhibited through the rise of the ILWU. But underneath both of these issues were grave concerns about the loyalty and assimilability of the islands' overwhelming Asian American population.[4] Indeed, according the historian of Hawai'i statehood politics, the main obstacle came from a bloc of southern Democrats in Congress who guardedly opposed civil rights legislation. In this way, statehood for the "racial paradise" of Hawai'i threatened to undermine their segregationist position and would add two more senators and one representative likely to vote against them. Statistical analysis of House roll-call voting in two different Congresses (80th and 85th) that took up Hawai'i statehood supports the notion that the issue was linked to votes on civil rights bills.[5] And so it was that Representative Burns achieved a deal on statehood by arranging to pair Hawai'i's entrance into the nation with that of Alaska, a more conservative territory whose congressional delegation would likely support the southern bloc on civil rights. Burns was also able to win enough moderate southerners to his side, most notably House and Senate majority leaders Sam Rayburn and Lyndon Johnson, both from Texas. Hawai'i was admitted as America's fiftieth state in August 1959 and soon thereafter elected two Asian Americans to Congress, Hiram Fong (Senate) and Daniel Inouye (House). The other senator was Oren E. Long, the superintendent of Honolulu public schools who in the late 1930s had defended the Institute of Pacific Relations' Japanese history textbook against V. S. McClatchy's attack.

Support for statehood came from familiar egalitarian sources, including the planter elite, Mike Masaoka and the Japanese American Citizens League, nisei veterans, the AFL-CIO, civil right advocates, and a wide range of internationalists such as the Asia-first lobby. At Senate hearings in 1950, California senator William Knowland made it clear that Hawai'i statehood was essential to winning support for the United States from the peoples of Asia during a crucial moment of Cold War crisis. He brushed aside fears that Communists had infiltrated the islands and accepted the fundamental loyalty of Asian Americans in asserting, "The people of Hawaii have much to offer in helping to interpret the spirit of America to the Far East, containing more than half the world's population. They can do equally as much in helping the United States to understand the complex problems of that vast area of the world. Never before was it more important to the peace of the world and the very security of this Nation that such mutual understanding be achieved."[6]

Another Californian proved instrumental for Hawai'i statehood. This was House representative Richard Welch, who had joined with McClatchy and other California exclusionists in leading the congressional campaign for Filipino exclusion and who as late as 1940 had opposed Filipino naturalization. In March 1947, as chair of the House Committee on Public Lands, Welch held hearings on Hawai'i statehood in which he heard testimony from Walter Judd, Admiral Chester Nimitz, former Hawai'i FBI head Robert Shivers, the ILWU's Jack Hall, and many other supporters of Hawai'i statehood who upheld the territory's Asian American population as a benefit to American ideals, institutions, and international relations. A month later Welch himself gave testimony reporting that his committee was unanimously in support of legislation to "enable the people of Hawaii to create a constitution and state government and to be admitted to the Union on an equal footing with the original states." Nowhere in his testimony or the hearings he conducted did Welch reveal his feelings about Asian Americans. Yet his silence, as well as support for statehood, spoke volumes about how much the exclusion debate had turned away from the racism of his past. At the end of a twenty-three-year career in Congress, Welch found himself on the egalitarian side of the exclusion debate.[7]

Equalizing Immigration Quotas

In January 1965 former Senate majority leader and now president Lyndon Johnson returned to Capitol Hill to urge Congress to eliminate the discriminatory national origins system, which was based on the assumption that "men and women from some countries are, just because of where they come from, more desirable citizens than others." In praising Walt Whitman's pluralistic view of America as a "nation of nations," the president criticized its immigration law as "incompatible with our basic American tradition" and harmful to the "success of our foreign policy." His proposal for comprehensive immigration reform was similar to efforts by earlier Democrats Harry S. Truman and John F. Kennedy but had a different result. Ten months after his special address to Congress, Johnson signed the Immigration and Nationality Act (also known as the Hart-Celler Act), which gave every nation outside the Western Hemisphere an equal (and much increased) quota of 20,000 immigrants per year, up to a ceiling of 170,000. The new law also scrapped the Asia-Pacific triangle, a compromise measure in the McCarran-Walter Act that lowered already minuscule immigration quotas for Asian and Pacific nations by counting Asians from any country in the world against the quota for their ancestral homeland. The equalization of national quotas meant that immigration quotas no longer considered race. At the same time, the new law continued the McCarran-Walter Act's immigration preferences that focused on family reunification, followed by job skills and then refugees from Communist countries. In this way, Hart-Celler codified a series of ad hoc measures that since World War II bypassed the tiny Asian quotas by allowing entry to war brides, refugees, orphans, and others. The front door was now open to 20,000 people per year from each Asian country, while side doors via student visas and special legislation for refugees would provide other means of entry. Hart-Celler proved a bonanza for Asian immigration, and because of its quotas and overall regulation it obviated fears of an uncontrollable flood from abroad because the numbers could always be decreased.[8]

Congressional hearings on immigration reform revealed less conflict than was evident in the formation of the McCarran-Walter Act (vetoed by Truman) or even the national origins system in 1924 (opposed by egalitarians). The American Legion, whose support for repealing Japanese exclusion in 1952 had altered its long-standing exclusionism, returned to its exclusionist roots in 1965 by defending the national origins quotas, which its representative Clarence Olson said were not discriminatory because immigrants from all nations had access to the United States. Olson, however, said nothing about the grossly uneven distribution of the quotas around the world, nor did he raise concerns about Asian immigration. By 1965 the American Legion was no longer in the business of generating fear about Asian immigration or defending anti-Asian policies, a conspicuous silence testifying to the ultimate egalitarian victory. The few dyed-in-the-wool exclusionists who raised the specter of the yellow peril were drowned out by the overwhelming support for the proposed reforms led by now-familiar egalitarians—the State Department, advocates for civil liberties, progressive labor unions, urban Democrats, Asia-first conservative internationalists, and now nearly the entire West Coast congressional delegation.[9] Secretary of State Dean Rusk emphasized how the legacy of anti-Asian elements in the nation's immigration policy hurt its foreign relations in Asia, while the ACLU's David Carliner raised the old claim that Japanese exclusion had contributed to the decision to bomb Pearl Harbor. The AFL-CIO's representative addressed Cold War concerns by asking rhetorically, "Why should we limit Japan, our democratic partner, to a quota of 185 immigrations a year while assigning to our enemy, Soviet Russia, a total of 2,697?"[10]

The JACL, another familiar advocate for Asian American interests, also backed comprehensive immigration reform. The organization's well-respected lobbyist Mike Masaoka testified at Senate hearings while submitting an extensive written statement detailing anti-Asian features of current immigration law and how Johnson's plan corrected them. Masaoka had been a powerful voice in favor of the McCarran-Walter Act because it granted naturalization to issei and "voided more than 500 Federal, State, and local discriminatory acts against people who by race were ineligible to citizenship." But thirteen years later he opposed the McCarran-Walter Act as a flawed measure, maintaining that Asian Americans were no longer satisfied with its "token" immigration quotas for Asian and Pacific nations. While these nations constituted over 50 percent of the world's population, they received only 1.5 percent of America's immigration quotas. Contributing to the tiny quota size, Masaoka pointed out, was the fact that the national origins system did not take into account Hawai'i (admitted to statehood after the McCarran-Walter Act), whose large Asian population would have increased the Asian quotas slightly. And making matters worse, he concluded, was the discriminatory Asia-Pacific triangle formulation.[11]

What changed in the years between 1952 and 1965 that caused the JACL and other Asian American advocates to oppose the McCarran-Walter regime? The answer comes in two parts. First, the costs for discriminating against Asians grew as the United States became increasingly invested in the Asia-Pacific region. Masaoka noted the rapid increase in U.S.-Japan trade, something he knew firsthand as a lobbyist for Japanese trading companies. But the main investment was military and political as the United States fought the Korean War (1950–53) and since 1964 was sending troops to Vietnam. U.S. officials also worked to offset Communist influence from China and the Soviet Union by vigilantly fostering cooperation with Asian nations, especially Japan—deemed the linchpin of their anticommunist efforts.[12]

The dramatic increase in newly independent nations also raised the stakes for discriminating against Asian immigration. In the time since McCarran-Walter passed, the number of United Nations member nations almost doubled, from 60 in 1952 to 117 in 1965. While Africa provided the vast majority of new members, it was Asian nations such as China and Indonesia that galvanized the movement to advance the collective interests of these new nations by keeping them out of the orbits of either the United States or the Soviet Union. U.S. officials felt threatened by this nonalignment movement and thus faced added pressure to promote civil rights at home so as to attract Asian and African nations to the U.S. side of the Cold War. Masaoka pointed out that America's woefully imbalanced immigration quotas—allocating 1.5 percent to the Asia-Pacific region, .47 percent to Africa, and 98 percent to Europe—posed a problem for U.S. interests in the Third World. Equalizing quotas for the three continents, he implied, would send a clear message of cooperation to the country's Asian allies: "Now imagine if you were Vietnam and you had the same quota as [tiny] Liechtenstein, if you were . . . [South Korea] helping to defend America's rights, what would you think if the quota for your country . . . was equal to . . . a country like Monaco? The Philippines, once a territorial possession of the United States, has a quota equivalent to the Free City of Danzig. . . .

Hungary, which is only one-tenth of the population of Japan, has more than five times the annual quota of Japan."[13]

In addition to the increased stakes of U.S. interests in Asia, the second great change that occurred between 1952 and 1965 was a dramatic rise in expectations for racial equality. While the civil rights movement encouraged Asian Americans to imagine a nation without racial barriers, the great change in expectations also derived from their own political successes. The most dramatic of these was Hawai'i statehood, which resulted in a tremendous boon to Asian American interests on Capitol Hill. By 1965 all four of Hawai'i's delegates to Congress were Asian American, as Hiram Fong was joined in the Senate by Daniel Inouye, while Spark Matsunaga, a 442nd veteran like Inouye, and Patsy (Takemoto) Mink were in the House. All of a sudden there was a group of Asian Americans in Congress motivated to remove anti-Asian discrimination from federal statutes.[14]

Of Hawai'i's two senators, Hiram Fong played the more visible role in supporting comprehensive immigration reform. A member of the Senate Immigration and Naturalization Committee, Fong took a keen interest in moving beyond repealing Asian exclusion to traveling the "last mile . . . to eliminate all vestiges of discrimination in our land." In a speech on the Senate floor he framed the immigration reform in light of proposed civil rights measures: "For as we move to erase racial discrimination against our citizens, we should also move to erase racial barriers against citizens of other lands in our immigration laws." The question, according to Fong, cut to the heart of the nation's democratic heritage, for "our present immigration laws . . . directly contradict the spirit and principles of the Declaration of Independence, the Constitution of the United States, and our traditional standards of justice, decency, and the dignity and equality of all men."[15] Hawai'i's two House representatives each offered written testimony in support of the immigration reform to House Judiciary Subcommittee hearings. Matsunaga noted that the people of Hawai'i were acutely aware of the shortcomings of U.S. immigration law; although "we have extended our hand out to the peoples of the Pacific," he worried that Hawai'i's extended hand "may appear to be in the shape of a fist . . . in light of our discriminating immigration law."[16]

Another reason that Asian Americans had come to expect fair treatment from Congress is because their experience had proven that Asians could become good Americans. Mike Masaoka identified three fears that fueled the long history of anti-Asian racism. The first fear, Asian unassimilability and disloyalty, he told a Senate Judiciary Subcommittee, was rendered moot by the examples of Senators Fong and Inouye and thousands of other Asian

American veterans who had served, and some of whom had died, for their country during World War II. Masaoka noted that even Japanese American Buddhists, who were seen as highly prone to disloyalty by the U.S. military during World War II, served valiantly during the war. As a veteran and trusted figure on Capitol Hill, Masaoka used himself as an example of Asian American loyalty, saying, "I know the slant of my eyes . . . have nothing to do with the slant of my heart." Beyond military patriotism, he argued that Asian Americans had turned out to be model citizens in terms of their obedience to the law (low delinquency rate), commitment to education (high college rate), and social mobility (higher than average incomes and percentage of professionals). All of this occurred despite the fact that Asian Americans "were subjected to persecution and discrimination on the West Coast" unlike that faced by any other immigrant group.[17]

The second fear, incompatibility of Asian and Western cultures, Masaoka claimed flew in the face of the "Japan boom" in the United States in which, more than any other time, Americans of all races had become fascinated with Japanese people, culture, and traditions. The final fear concerned the now mythic notion of the oriental flood, a tidal wave of migration that would inundate the United States. While the national origins system took care of the possible flood from the Eastern Hemisphere, the fear of being overwhelmed by Asians from Latin America, who faced no immigration quotas, lay behind the creation of the Asia-Pacific triangle. To counteract this fear, Masaoka focused on the assimilation and loyalty of Asians to their countries in Latin America, a fact he assured would prevent the vast majority from coming to the United States. Moreover, he said that flood fears were overblown because in the end there were not more than a million Asians south of the border, which even in the impossible event that they all migrated would not have much impact on a country of 190 million.[18]

The enactment of comprehensive immigration reform in 1965 closed the final chapter of the exclusion debate. During congressional hearings on immigration reform proposals, Asian American advocates including Masaoka and the Hawai'i members of Congress recounted the long history of anti-Asian immigration policy starting with Chinese exclusion and continuing through the Gentlemen's Agreement, the Asiatic Barred Zone, the national origins system, the repeal of exclusion, and the McCarran-Walter Act. Most advocates framed Hart-Celler as the end of the cycle of anti-Asian racism. But Mike Masaoka made clear that even under the new immigration plan, migrants from Asia would remain less favored than those from Europe. He referred to administration projections indicating that within five years, the new quotas would enable over twelve times more Europeans (679,603) than

Asians (53,928) to immigrate to the United States. The imbalance resulted from the high preference for family reunification. Because Asian Americans constituted less than 1 percent of the U.S. population, the absolute number of their relatives coming to the United States was potentially much smaller than their counterparts coming from Europe. This predication was used to calm yellow peril fears by stressing that Hart-Celler, while significantly increasing the number of Asian immigrants, would not change the country's racial proportions and was why Masaoka called it "far from perfect" and noted that Congress still had a way to go to "wipe out the widespread favoritism for Europeans . . . which has existed in our law." In decrying the vestiges of anti-Asian racism, the esteemed Asian American leader had no way of knowing how a new generation of Americans would respond to his call.[19]

Model Minority Debate

The Civil Rights Act (1964) and Voting Rights Act (1965) were for racial minorities what the Wagner Act was for industrial workers; they put the full weight of the federal government behind groups that once had few legal protections. Civil rights reforms, however, did not produce a social revolution. Many racial minorities remained at the bottom of society, and they grew impatient and disillusioned with the slow pace of change. As discrimination was being eliminated from federal policies, riots erupted in working-class black communities in Los Angeles, Newark, Chicago, and Detroit. A young generation of racial activists looked to militant black nationalists like Malcolm X, who encouraged impoverished and subordinated African Americans to grab power "by any means necessary." They also identified with revolutionary movements in Africa, Asia, and Latin America as models for political liberation. The most obvious struggle was in Vietnam, where the United States fought against Communist North Vietnam and its insurgent allies across the border in U.S.-backed South Vietnam. It was during the tumult over black militancy and the Vietnam War that a critical mass of Asian American students began to support Black Power. This activism grew into what would become known as the Asian American movement emanating from college and university campuses along the West Coast. Movement activists joined with other racial minorities in demanding broad and, at the time, radical reforms in higher education, such as the establishment of ethnic studies classes and departments run for, about, and by racial minorities. The first Asian American studies programs began in 1969 at the University of California, Berkeley, and what is now San Francisco State University.[20]

Movement activists were not fighting just for curricular reform. They were seeking to catalyze a mass following by raising the awareness among Asian Americans about the continuing problems of racial prejudice and inequality. This was not an easy task given that the end of anti-Asian policies corresponded with the most significant rise in social economic status and national acceptance for Asian Americans. And then there was the challenge posed by new immigrants and refugees, to whom America was both sanctuary and land of economic opportunity. These new Americans hailed from a broad array of countries, while the stream of Japanese declined significantly. The result was a stunning transformation in Asian American demographics. In 2000, the Chinese were the largest Asian American group, followed closely by Filipinos, South Asians, Koreans, Vietnamese, and then Japanese and many other groups.[21] The new immigrants and refugees knew little, if anything, about the history of exclusionism in the United States. Instead, their memories of hardship were rooted in brutal wars and political persecutions experienced in their homelands, from which they were seemingly rescued by the United States. Thus the movement activists faced an uphill task in convincing thankful recent immigrants and socially mobile Asian ethnics that American society was riddled with racism that victimized them and all Asian Americans.[22]

But the biggest challenge for the activists came from outside their ethnic groups. The sociologist William Petersen proved one of their earliest and most formidable foes. In a widely read article published in the *New York Times Magazine* in January 1966, Petersen argued that Japanese Americans had achieved the American dream despite having suffered wartime internment and some of the most egregious forms of American racism. As such, he applauded them as a "model minority" whose path to success offered an example for blacks and other racial minorities to follow if they were to escape the cycle of poverty and dependence on government aid. Later that same year, *U.S. News and World Report* celebrated high rates of social mobility and low rates of criminality in Chinatowns. "At a time when it is being proposed that hundreds of billions be spent to uplift Negroes and other minorities," the magazine reported, "the nation's 300,000 Chinese-Americans are moving ahead on their own—with no help from anyone else." Soon enough the idea of Japanese and Chinese Americans as model minorities became a fixture in news media, while a thriving area of social science research, led in part by Petersen, sought to explain the stark social disparities between blacks and Asian Americans. Beyond this, the model minority concept resonated with Americans who became threatened by urban black riots and the strident demands made by Black Power advocates that were couched in the aggressive symbolism of Third World revolutions. In this way, model minority discourse tapped into pervasive fears of black unrest and in so doing pioneered an image of Asian Americans that a new generation of conservatives would deploy to limit and roll back the civil rights revolution. In neoconservative hands, the praise of Asian Americans as model minorities became a wolf in sheep's clothing that sought to repeal controversial policies like affirmative action and to discredit minority radicalism.[23]

Asian American movement activists compensated for the conservatism in Asian American communities and attacked the model minority image through ethnic studies scholarship that soundly critiqued the ideology of the American dream. Yuji Ichioka, a historian of Japanese Americans and one of the founders of the Asian American movement, made clear his opinion about the American mainstream through a review of Bill Hosokawa's book *Nisei: The Quiet Americans* (1969). Commissioned by the JACL, Hosokawa's book detailed the story of the nisei's rise from social problem to decorated soldiers to postwar model minority. Ichioka noted three problems with this narrative framing. First, "at no time does [he] . . . allude to possible psychological damages which Nisei may have incurred because of their minority experience and the trauma of World War II." Second, Hosokawa's "success ideology" was said to have biased him toward the experience of high achievers like JACL legend Mike Masaoka, thus leading him to ignore the experience of lower achievers still suffering the effects of racism.[24] Finally, Ichioka denounced Hosokawa's faith in the emancipatory potential of American society by rejecting the goal of assimilation. While Masaoka sought to convince Congress that Asian Americans like himself were thoroughly loyal and assimilated to American standards, Ichioka dismissed this kind of "Americanism" as blind acceptance of the status quo that made it possible for America to fight an unjust war in Vietnam and persecute radical black activists and revolutionaries. He claimed that in 1969, the kind of assimilation that Masaoka idealized "still basically means racism, super-patriotism, and rightwing politics." In a separate review, Ichioka dismissed Petersen's comparisons of Asian Americans and blacks as irrelevant for "breaking new ground in the historical knowledge of Japanese immigrants and their descendants."

Also facing harsh criticism was the founder of assimilation theory, sociologist Robert Park, who in the 1920s led the egalitarian Survey of Race Relations opposing Japanese exclusion. Nowhere was this more apparent than in a 1973 essay by Paul Takagi titled "The Myth of 'Assimilation in American Life,'" which appeared in the ethnic studies journal *Amerasia*.

Takagi's main purpose was to expose the alleged racism of the assimilation framework, which had dominated scholarship on Asian Americans since the 1920s when Park and his colleagues and students at the University of Chicago transformed the study of racial and ethnic groups. The author focused his attack on Park, calling him an "apologist for . . . racial conflicts and race prejudices" and a WASP "concerned about the survival of the Anglo race." Takagi also declared that some of Park's observations about Asian immigrants could be "considered a doctrine for racial oppression."[25]

The critiques of Park, Mike Masaoka, and assimilation theory revealed the formation of an interpretive generation gap preventing appreciation of the kind of egalitarianism that had fueled opposition to anti-Asian racism from the nineteenth century to the enactment of the Hart-Celler legislation. In establishing an intellectual home for Asian American radicalism, ethnic studies scholars opposed the status quo within and outside their ethnic communities and dismissed past egalitarian achievements as irrelevant for truly revolutionizing American race relations. Moreover, they produced scholarship that advanced their cause by exposing the struggles of everyday people and the continued significance of anti-Asian racism, while at the same time they deconstructed the model minority discourse as a neoconservative weapon. In 1989 the Berkeley scholar Ronald Takaki published *Strangers from a Different Shore*, a masterful synthesis of Asian American history that embodied each of these goals. A close reading of this book and Takaki's conception of racism illuminates the public controversies regarding Asian Americans during the late twentieth and early twenty-first centuries.

Strangers from a Different Shore became arguably the most popular history of Asian Americans at the time and remains popular more than twenty-five years later. What distinguished the book was Takaki's poetic language, eloquent storytelling, and inclusion of a comprehensive range of Asian immigrant groups. Most important was that it catered to a generation of Americans that lived through the turbulent 1960s, as well as the subsequent Watergate scandal and loss of the Vietnam War. Disillusionment in the American nation as a liberal force for good was a phenomenon that was not limited to scholars of ethnic studies or radical activists; it was a symptom of a broad crisis of American nationalism in which many people no longer felt they belonged to the same national community. For many, the focus on assimilation was too constraining of one's individual or group identity, and so they embraced a notion of pluralism that held the nation together by respecting the right to be different. Thus arose the symbol of America as a mosaic of irreducible parts (a "nation of nations," as Whitman put it) rather than the former conception of it as a melting pot in which differences were stigmatized and eliminated. The success of Takaki's history of Asian Americans stemmed not just from his talents as a scholar and storyteller but also from its being one of the first and best studies of its kind to capture the nation's pluralistic spirit.[26]

Takaki approached Asian American history as a study of racism rather than of the process of assimilation. As revealed in an earlier book of his, Takaki saw American race relations through the lens of Antonio Gramsci's notion of cultural hegemony. In defining cultural hegemony, he quoted thusly from Gramsci: it is "an order in which a certain way of life and thought is dominant, in which one concept of reality is diffused throughout society in all its institutional and private manifestations, informing with its spirit all taste, morality, customs, religious and political principles, and all social relations, particularly in their intellectual and moral connotations." For Takaki, white supremacy was the "one concept of reality" that continued to govern American society despite the ending of overt discrimination by civil rights law. Here was a very different vision of racism from Mike Masaoka's view of the vestiges of European favoritism in U.S. immigration policy that needed to be further addressed in the next round of legislative reform. From Takaki's perspective, racism could not be eliminated merely through legislation because it was embedded in deep structures of society, culture, and the American psyche, requiring nothing short of a revolution in race relations.[27]

Given his view of racism as a total system of inequality, largely fixed in time, Takaki's history of Asian Americans focused on the heroic, though essentially failed, struggles by minorities for acceptance and dignity within a perpetually racist society. In this way, *Strangers from a Different Shore* played down the Great Transformation and end of the exclusion era, discounting the fact that Asian Americans had made their greatest strides toward full equality and social citizenship since World War II. According to Takaki, cultural hegemony continued in more recent times under the guise of the model minority image, a stereotype that justified racial hierarchy by judging Asian Americans as "better" minorities than blacks and Latinos. He also deconstructed what he called the "model minority myth," arguing that Asian Americans continued to suffer from the lasting effects of racism in terms of income (lower than that of comparable whites), job opportunities (the problem of "glass ceilings"), and hate crimes like the killing of Vincent Chin.[28]

Takaki's view of racism as a system of inequality that persisted despite civil rights legislation blinded him to the significance of the egalitarian opposition to Asian exclusion. While he did not intentionally bury the history of the exclusion debate, his reliance on cultural hegemony foreclosed the opportunity to appreciate egalitarianism as anything but the exception to the rule of exclusionism. Posed after Takaki had died in 2009, historian Gordon Chang asked: "Why did Chinese exclusion take so long?" If Takaki was right and there was one concept of reality in the United States that embodied white supremacy at its core, then how come Chinese immigrants were not restricted in the 1850s, before tens of thousands settled in California? This did not happen, as chapter 1 has shown, because business and political expansionists, as well as religious egalitarians, for over thirty years thwarted calls for restriction in the name of harmonious U.S.-China trade relations. The more than two decades it took to pass Japanese exclusion also can be attributed to the strength of egalitarian forces seeking to promote peace and to prevent war between the United States and Japan. And even the U.S. colonization of the Philippines had an egalitarian component that defended the immigration and integrity of Filipinos despite their eventual exclusion. *Strangers from a Different Shore* addressed none of these aspects of the Asian American past because Takaki was not interested in understanding both sides of the exclusion debate.[29]

A caveat: The point here is not that Takaki's book caused scholars to ignore the story of egalitarianism, because this is too simplistic an explanation. After all, William Petersen and other analysts of the model minority also overlooked the exclusion debate. Rather, both Takaki and Petersen embodied and enacted a sea change in the conception of America as a place where race, ethnicity, and cultures were retained. This pluralistic vision contrasted with the former standard of assimilation and invited a wide range of identity expression, from innocuous "Kiss me, I'm Irish" stickers to assertions of Black Power and pride. Galvanized by ethnic studies, Asian Americans gained confidence to revisit the past with an eye toward righting the many wrongs the group had suffered at the hands of American racism. No issue conveyed the combination of identity politics and the forgetting of egalitarianism more than the campaign to redress the racism of the Japanese American internment.

Redress and Forgetting the Exclusion Debate

During the early 1970s, Asian American activists resurrected repressed memories of the internment camps in the campaign to repeal Title II of the Internal Security Act (1950), which permitted the federal government to intern persons it deemed subversive. At the time, this put in jeopardy antiwar protesters, Black Power advocates, and others who threatened the social order. The success of the Title II campaign, which garnered JACL support, launched the movement to redress the wrong of the World War II internment. To the redress movement activists, it was not enough that Congress, and many of the leading actors involved in the creation of Executive Order 9066—now including Earl Warren—admitted, if privately in Warren's case, that internment had been a mistake. Nor was it enough that the loyalty of Japanese Americans had been broadly established through regular commemorations of nisei soldiers and that the memory of wartime internment had started to become sacralized through "pilgrimages" to the sites of the former concentration camps. Beyond these developments—or because of them—the redress movement sought to hold the federal government accountable for committing a racist act and covering it up under the guise of military necessity. While not part of the initial plans, the idea of monetary reparations became seen as important so as to emphasize the seriousness of the offense, as well as to make up for the gross shortcomings of the Japanese American Evacuation Claims Act (1948), which managed to pay only twenty-five cents on the dollar for claims received. The movement's aggressive posture reflected historian Roger Daniels's stance on government culpability, as expressed in his 1971 study *Concentration Camps, USA*. The historian dismissed the widely held conviction that the mass evacuation was simply a wartime mistake: "Rather than a mistake—which according to the dictionary is an 'error in action, calculation, opinion or judgment caused by poor reasoning, carelessness, insufficient information . . . a misunderstanding or misconception—the legal atrocity which was committed against the Japanese Americans was the logical outgrowth of over three centuries of American experience, an experience which taught Americans to regard the United States as a white man's country in which nonwhites 'had no rights which the white man was bound to respect.'"[30]

Redress activists believed that if the internment was a clear expression of racism and not a mistake in judgment made under the duress of war, then it behooved liberty-loving Americans to obtain justice for this violation of civil liberties. Research by independent scholar Michi Weglyn and historian Peter Irons unearthed documents that seemed to be smoking guns proving that the government covered up key pieces of evidence when it made its case for the internment to the Supreme Court and to the general public under the justification of military necessity. Weglyn's publisher, William Morrow, was not interested in her hard-hitting analysis of the internment decision until after the Watergate scandal generated a readership for books that were extremely critical of the U.S. government. Weglyn's *Years of Infamy*, along with Irons's *Justice at War*, launched a legal strategy that throughout the 1980s led the Court to vacate three landmark decisions it had handed down during the war against nisei who disobeyed the evacuation order. These were cases involving Min Yasui, Gordon Hirabayashi, and Fred Korematsu.[31]

Meanwhile, as Weglyn's book came out in 1976, President Gerald Ford formally rescinded EO 9066. Four years later, Congress established a bipartisan commission to study the facts surrounding the mass evacuation and its effects on Japanese Americans and to make recommendations regarding the nation's proper course of action regarding this controversial action. Senator Daniel Inouye had proposed the idea of the commission to the JACL as a means for achieving redress. He, along with now senator Spark Matsunaga and two co-ethnic congressmen from California, Norman Mineta and Robert Matsui, provided instrumental support for the redress movement. Indeed, Hawai'i statehood and the growing political clout of nisei in the Golden State contributed significantly to the process through which Asian Americans gained direct representation in Congress. No longer did they have to rely solely on the good graces of white American politicians.[32]

The redress commission—formally known as the Commission on Wartime Relocation and Internment of Civilians—held a series of hearings on the West Coast in 1981 that generated a historic outpouring of repressed memories by former internees. Never before had they been invited by government officials to tell their often heartbreaking stories. Commentators at the time referred to the hearings as a moment of catharsis and healing for persons who had long suffered in silence. The ethnic community had found a way to speak to power, and, surprisingly, they were heard. The commission published its findings and recommendations based on their testimony, as well as on interviews with a selection of those responsible for the internment decision (many like FDR and Secretary of War Henry L. Stimson were dead) and examination of countless contemporary documents. The title of the report, *Personal Justice Denied*, revealed its core contention that the internment was not justified by military necessity; rather, its "broad historical causes . . . were race prejudice, war hysteria and a failure of political leadership." The report continued: "Widespread ignorance of Japanese Americans contributed to a policy conceived in haste and executed in an atmosphere of fear and anger towards Japan. A grave injustice was done to American citizens and resident aliens of Japanese ancestry who, without individual review or any probative evidence against them, were excluded, removed, and detained by the United States during World War II."[33]

Personal Justice Denied offered the most thorough analysis to date regarding the causes of the internment decision, but in the end, it mostly confirmed what had already been known by researchers. The report concentrated on the racism of General John L. DeWitt, which predisposed him to distrust the Japanese, and on the legacy of exclusionism, which it cast as a "latent anti-Japanese virus on the West Coast . . . brought to life by the fear and anger engendered by Pearl Harbor." The commission's findings would become the definitive word on the internment decision for scholars, educators, writers, artists, filmmakers, museum curators, and a host of other culture makers. (Takaki, for example, based his analysis of the internment in *Strangers from a Different Shore* largely on *Personal Justice Denied*.) But the report's vast influence did not necessarily mean that Congress would implement the commission's recommendations, especially its most controversial one, which was to have the federal government pay $20,000 to every living survivor of the internment camps as restitution for the injustice they suffered. Opponents of the commission report fought back against its "revisionist history" in hearings held to determine what should be done about the commission's findings and recommendations. This proved to be their last stand before the Civil Liberties Act of 1988 enacted nearly all of the commission's recommendations while giving full government sanction to its view of the internment as an intentional, not mistaken, violation of civil liberties.[34]

The hearings on proposed redress legislation inverted the situation from the Tolan hearings in late February and early March 1942, in which egalitarian witnesses faced the impossible task of testifying against mass evacuation within the context of the military's expressed fear of Japanese American disloyalty, supported by the recent issuing of EO 9066. In the mid-1980s the roles were reversed, as the commission's findings showed clear and convincing evidence of government wrongdoing that put the defenders of internment on the defensive. Adding to their difficulty was the overwhelming support for redress by the audience at the hearings. John J. McCloy, former assistant secretary of war, complained that every time he "tried to say anything in favor of the United States or in favor of the President . . . , there were hisses and boos and stomping of feet, which was disgraceful." In 1948 McCloy had strongly supported the Evacuation Claims Act as an expression of faith in the loyalty of Japanese Americans that was proven by nisei soldiers. But in 1984 he opposed the "revisionists" on the commission "who would have us believe that it was racial prejudice which induced the President's action to institute the relocation process in regard to certain segments of our Japanese descended residents in the militarily sensitive areas along our West Coast, and thus, to counter the deep consequences of the Pearl Harbor disaster to our overall defense system." Rather than the result of racism, he maintained it was "indisputable that the direct and proximate cause of the President's decision was the [Pearl Harbor] attack itself and nothing else."[35]

In challenging the significance of race for the internment decision, McCloy pointed to new evidence seemingly confirming that FDR, Stimson, and DeWitt had military reasons to suspect the disloyalty of an unknowable number of Japanese Americans in the event of a Japanese attack. The evidence came from intercepted and decrypted cables known to U.S. officials under the codename MAGIC, which were brought to light by David Lowman, a former officer of the National Security Agency. Lowman testified that the cables had been sent between the Japanese government and its officials in the United States well before the Pearl Harbor attack. One, in January 1941, directly listed the issei and nisei as targets to be recruited for espionage work, and another sent in May that year confirmed that the Los Angeles consulate had "already established contacts with absolutely reliable Japanese in San Pedro and San Diego area, who will keep a close watch on all shipments of airplanes and other war materials, and report the amounts and destinations of such shipments." The latter cable also stated that the consulate had ties to nisei serving in the U.S. Army and working in airplane plants who would provide information useful for intelligence. According to McCloy, FDR was well aware that the MAGIC cables "gave indication of the fact that there was in existence, in place at that point, along the West Coast, a subversive agency which was set up and which was being boasted of by the foreign office, that it was set in place in case there should be an attack on the United States."[36]

One of the nine members of the redress commission, Congressman Dan Lundgren, sided with McCloy and Lowman, as well as with a leading voice behind EO 9066, Karl Bendetsen, who also testified against redress legislation. Lundgren confessed that the commission had not been aware of the MAGIC evidence until well into its proceedings and therefore did not have adequate time to consider it. But another commission member, Father Robert Drinan, disagreed, emphasizing the fact that Lundgren and everyone else on the commission agreed that the internment was not justified by military necessity. At this point, Mike Masaoka supported the redress cause by exerting his political weight, built up from his war heroism and years of experience lobbying on Capitol Hill. He assured that the commission indeed had considered the new intelligence evidence and still believed that Japanese Americans were loyal and did not warrant mass evacuation. The question, he pointed out, was not whether Japan tried to use issei and nisei as spies. When the "chips were down" at Pearl Harbor, "the real answer of what Japan planned for us doesn't mean a thing" because Japanese Americans responded with complete loyalty to the United States. According to Masaoka, the MAGIC cables or intelligence reports were not nearly as important to the issue of loyalty as the final conclusion of the FBI, which "said there was no need to evacuate us, to remove us, to intern us." In the end, Masaoka and many other redress supporters argued that the new evidence only confirmed what the commission already revealed: that a Japanese spy networked had existed before Pearl Harbor, but there remained no real proof that Japanese Americans were involved in a way that would make them a military threat to the United States.[37]

Congressman Samuel Stratton, in testifying against redress legislation in 1986, commented on the problem of changing historical interpretations of the internment. Those who did not experience the trauma of Pearl Harbor, he said, could not understand the response to it: "So for this 99th Congress—many of its Members who were not even alive when Pearl Harbor was hit—. . . to pass judgment on the wisdom of decisions of military and political leaders in a wartime situation that occurred some 45 years ago is simply an exercise in futility." By saying that redress was an "exercise in futility," Stratton did not mean that Japanese Americans deserved to be interned. Rather, he meant that it was not fair to judge the past based on the standards of a different historical era. In this way, he raised an important point for understanding the changing legacy of the exclusion debate. In early 1942, during a moment of great fear and uncertainty, the standard for Japanese American loyalty was set impossibly high by military and civilian officials so as to prevent any chance that Japan would launch another successful attack—this time against a nearly defenseless West Coast. Yet during the 1980s, after decades of honoring nisei soldiers and celebrating Japanese American achievement and acceptance, the question at issue changed from proving the group's loyalty to asking why their loyalty had been questioned in the first place. In this way, redress advocates turned tables on their foes by casting the spotlight of suspicion on FDR, Stimson, McCloy, DeWitt, Bendetsen, and other architects of the internment order. Amid the conservatism of the Reagan era, which included overt attacks on civil rights achievements, these men were judged for their racial beliefs based on the rather low standards of a time in which charges of racism and "reverse-racism" were ubiquitous in American political life. Race became one of the main channels through which Americans fought over repealing affirmative action, cutting back Aid to Families with Dependent Children, raising educational standards, and getting tough on crime, as well as many other issues in the nation's "culture wars." Needless to say, it was much easier to be criticized and reprimanded for racial bias in 1988, when Congress approved redress legislation, than it was in 1942, when the internment order was issued.[38]

Since 1988, the idea of racially biased government leaders and a system of governance has remained central to mainstream political thought on both sides of the political spectrum. Ethnic studies approaches and institutions have gained broad recognition as valuable features of American multiculturalism. It was during the period after redress when Ronald Takaki transformed from a young radical scholar to a nationally recognized pioneer of multicultural U.S. history and best-selling author. At the same time, critical views of Asian exclusion and the "revisionist" notion of internment became mainstays in higher education courses on U.S. history, literature, and American studies. These perspectives also spread to middle and high school curricula, especially through the teaching of such popular books as Maxine Hong Kingston's *Woman Warrior* and Jeanne Wakatsuki Houston's *Farewell to Manzanar*. And, finally, the critical views of anti-Asian racism became further institutionalized through museum exhibits and historical markers like the one concerning the Chinese massacre placed in Los Angeles's historic center. The vast majority of information available on exclusion or internment has focused on victimizers, victimization, and in some cases resistance. But it goes without saying that the discourse rarely casts the history of anti-Asian racism as a debate between exclusionists and egalitarians.

The institutionalization continued in the recent campaign to obtain congressional apology for Chinese exclusion. During a "Day of Remembrance" in February 2011 to commemorate the sixty-ninth anniversary of EO 9066, U.S. House representative Mike Honda, a third-generation Japanese American, supported calls for Congress to apologize for another "shameful chapter in our country's long history of exclusion." In that year, Judy Chu, the first Chinese American woman elected to Congress, replaced Honda as chair of the Congressional Asian Pacific American Caucus. By June 2012 she was able to secure passage of a House resolution expressing regret for Chinese exclusion, which followed one passed the year before by the Senate. Chu felt it incumbent upon her to lead the drive to secure the apology, while Gary Locke and Steven Chu were well-placed Chinese Americans in President Barack Obama's cabinet who also could be counted on for leadership. In introducing the House measure, the congresswoman remarked on the plight of Chinese immigrants when they were excluded in 1882. "At that time of this hateful law," she said, "the Chinese were called racial slurs, were spat upon in the streets, and even brutally murdered." Chu incorrectly celebrated Senator George Frisbee Hoar for being the *lone* voice on Capitol Hill opposing exclusion at that time, and she painted an overly pessimistic picture of the decline of racial egalitarianism: "When the exclusion laws were first introduced, there was a great deal of debate in Congress over their merits. The U.S. had just abolished slavery. The 14th and 15th Amendments had recently been ratified. Slavery had been defeated, and freedom seemed more certain. The national atmosphere led many in Congress to stand up against the discriminatory anti-Chinese laws. But over the years, those standing for justice almost all disappeared. By the time 1882 came around, Members of Congress were fighting over who deserved the most credit for getting the most discriminatory laws passed and standing against the 'Mongolian horde.'"[39]

This analysis of vanishing egalitarianism, while a moving condemnation of past racism, made better politics than history. After 1882, no egalitarian, except for diehards like Hoar, sought to return to the Burlingame era of free immigration, for they had accepted the exclusionist victory as a political fact connected to the return to power of the Democratic Party and increasingly bipartisan exclusionism. Instead of protesting against the exclusion of Chinese labor migration, egalitarians sought to protect the rights of exempt classes, as well as those of Chinese residents in the United States and the American-born generations. As chapter 3 reveals, these efforts on behalf of Chinese immigration were not always successful; but as exclusionists like Samuel Gompers knew well, the opposition always put up a good fight. Ignoring these efforts by both white and Chinese egalitarians is to simplify the past to meet the political—and perhaps psychological— needs of an interest group. But to what extent do such apologies for past wrongs benefit all Americans, which is their stated intention? What lessons are learned? The conclusion to this book considers what it means to remember, rather than forget, the long-standing struggle between egalitarians and exclusionists.

CONCLUSION

WHY REMEMBER THE
EXCLUSION DEBATE?

||||||||||||||||||||||||||||||||||||||||||||||||||||||||||||||||||||||||||||||||||||||||||||||||||||||||||||||||||||||||||||||||||||||||

The historical marker remembering the Chinese massacre in Los Angeles discussed at the start of this book stands as testimony to the dark side of the Asian American experience. The importance of such institutional memory is obvious given the history of exclusionism as told in these pages. We, as a society, must prevent acts of violence and discrimination meted out to groups based on race, color, culture, national origin, and legal status—and this *still* includes Asian Americans. If this book has raised awareness of the persistence of anti-Asian racism in readers' minds, then I will have achieved something worthwhile. But at what cost? What happens when the memory of anti-Asian racism in historical markers (as well as in scholarship, museums, films, and public policies designed to right wrongs) is not balanced by the context of egalitarianism? Does cropping out the history of egalitarianism justify the noble goal of raising awareness about today's anti-Asian violence and discrimination? These are tough questions that present no easy answers. I can understand why in today's culture that glorifies victims as "morally superior" (think Holocaust survivors) we are tempted to downplay or ignore the history of egalitarianism in order to draw attention to Asian Americans and contemporary antiracist struggles. But if the goal is to see the past in all its complexity, then we cannot be content with remembering exclusionism and forgetting the exclusion debate. It is only through engaging with a complex past—one with no pure and fixed protagonists, antagonists, or moral direction—that we can learn anything approaching "historical lessons." Such lessons cannot be easily conveyed by historical markers or institutional apologies and do not easily lend themselves to political slogans ("never again"). What follows are lessons that I have learned in writing this book that convey five reasons why we should remember *both* sides of the exclusion debate.[1]

To Increase Explanatory Power

Without an understanding of the opposition to exclusionism, we are at a loss to explain crucial aspects in the history of anti-Asian racism. One of these is the timing of Chinese exclusion, a fact made clear by the inability of existing historical interpretations to answer Gordon Chang's question

"Why did exclusion take so long?" Any answer must appreciate the powerful and long-standing support for the China trade in Congress. Such an appreciation can also explain why exclusion legislation targeted Chinese laborers while exempting the more elite classes. Additionally, it explains why restriction at first was not intended to be permanent and was opposed by the State Department and vetoed by two different presidents. In a similar way, understanding the opposition to Japanese exclusion allows us to explain why it also took so long. For the Japanese case, trade relations were important to preventing and modifying exclusion, but efforts to promote international peace proved more powerful factors pushing presidents, the State Department, and a wide variety of internationalists to stave off congressional exclusion for more than two decades.

For migration from the Philippines, understanding the legacy of egalitarianism means appreciating the complex ways in which notions of racial equality were wrapped up with both U.S. colonialism and Filipino nationalism. As with the Chinese and Japanese, the exclusion debate regarding Filipino immigrants was never a simple question of enacting white supremacist restrictions against an Asian group—as much as exclusionists wanted it to be. In addition, the significance of egalitarianism for the Japanese American internment sheds light on the moment of great uncertainty in the months following the Pearl Harbor attack that caused many egalitarians (including nisei leaders) to at least passively support the mass evacuation of Japanese Americans. At the same time, the war also burnished the egalitarian tradition through the nondiscriminatory efforts of both government agencies and nongovernment organizations that propelled the Great Transformation in the history of the exclusion debate. Without an awareness of the long history of opposition to exclusionism, we would err in seeing the Great Transformation merely as war expediency rather than the culmination of the long-term process of increasing Asian-Pacific trade, civil rights, as well as internationalist connections, goodwill, and institutions.

Finally, it is important to realize that the meaning of key terms like "exclusionism" and "egalitarianism" changed across time and space, although they continued to represent different sides of the debate. For instance, after the Immigration Act of 1924 created a secure system of human flood control, exclusionism took on a more racially tolerant and internationally responsible form that was not possible in the nineteenth and early twentieth centuries. Likewise, egalitarianism narrowed after Chinese restriction to focus on protecting the treaty rights and civilizational standing of elite Asian immigrants. In the early twentieth century it took on shadings of radical labor and by the end of the exclusion era was dominated by anticommunist sensibilities. The egalitarianism of cold warrior Patrick McCarran in the 1950s was quite different from that of Institute of Public Relations staff member Frederick Vanderbilt Field, who shared the Communist Party's antiracist position and whom McCarran grilled in July 1951 as part of a congressional investigation into Communist influence in the IPR.

To Connect Asian American Issues with the Broader History of Public Policies

Understanding exclusion as a political debate enables us to better explain the intersection between Asian American issues and the four overlapping policy communities addressed in this book's introduction: immigration and labor, race relations, foreign relations, and national security. While each has played a key role in the exclusion debate, the significance of their impact changed across five major historical eras. Table C.1 summarizes the historical weight of the policy communities during each era, starting with the beginning of Chinese labor migration during the mid-nineteenth century and the subsequent establishment of the liberal Burlingame constituency. The key turning points were Chinese exclusion, Japanese exclusion and the national origins system, World War II, the McCarran-Walter Act, and the Immigration and Nationality Act of 1965. The immigration-labor policy community remained the most important force shaping the rise of anti-Asian federal policies, from the loud cry for Chinese exclusion in the late nineteenth century until Congress closed the door to Japanese immigration. It took decades to exclude the Chinese and then the Japanese because two policy communities (race relations and foreign relations) fortified the egalitarian side. But the rise of the national security community during and after World War I sealed the fate of Japanese immigrants.

The national origins system, which excluded the Japanese and closed the door significantly to all immigration, decentered the hotly contested exclusion debate in the nation's politics. While the AFL continued its harangue about Asian immigrant labor through World War II, its calls to protect workers from "cheap" immigrant labor rang increasingly hollow as unions acquired significant legal protections during the New Deal. From World War II to the early Cold War, two policy communities (foreign relations and national security) replaced the immigration-labor community as the driving force in the exclusion debate. After the McCarran-Walter Act all but ended the exclusion era, the rise of major civil rights legislation, due in part to Cold War exigencies, repealed the national origins system and thus created the conditions for the emergence of a fully fleshed-out Pacific nation, complete with the country's largest and most diverse Asian

Table C.1. Policy community significance by historical era

Era	Period	Dates	Dominant policy stream(s)	Subordinate policy streams
Before exclusion	Start of Chinese migration to Chinese exclusion	1850–82	Foreign relations, race relations	Immigration-labor (national security)
Peak exclusion	Chinese exclusion to Japanese exclusion and the Immigration Act of 1924	1882–1924	Immigration-labor	Foreign relations, national security, race relations
Late exclusion	Japanese exclusion to World War II	1924–42	Immigration-labor	Foreign relations, national security, race relations
Transwar egalitarianism	World War II to McCarran-Walter Act	1942–52	Foreign relations, national security	Immigration-labor, race relations
Civil rights egalitarianism	McCarran-Walter Act to Immigration Act of 1965	1952–2001	Race relations, foreign relations	National security, immigration-labor

American population ever. Since 1965, the race relations community has taken over as the emergence of legal sanctions for a broad range of civil and economic rights from all branches of the federal government propelled the minority and women's rights revolutions. This is when Ronald Takaki and ethnic studies in general exerted their great influence on the writing of Asian American history.

To Encourage Historical Empathy

Many people are aware of the politics of writing history through some version of Winston Churchill's famous line "History is written by the victors." Two generations of historians since Churchill have labored with great success to uncover history from the "bottom up," including attention to immigrants, racial and ethnic minorities, slaves, peasants, women, sexual minorities, and the working classes. This massive literature, which includes most research on Asian Americans, has democratized the way we think about the past and whose history matters. In so doing, we are now able to empathize with a much broader cast of characters. Yet one of the pitfalls with appreciating history's so-called losers is to ignore the equally complex perspectives and experiences of the winners who defeated them. I learned this lesson through researching Chester Rowell, the leading California progressive reformer, journalist, public intellectual, and long-recognized proponent of excluding Asian immigrants. My preliminary research confirmed the conventional view of him as California's "archetypal" anti-Japanese racist. Yet, upon closer look, it became clear that he was not the person I had expected. As a leader of California's Progressive movement in the early twentieth century, he spearheaded the drive to exclude Japanese immigration, and until his death in 1948 he remained convinced that large-scale migration from Asia was inimical to American society. But, at the same time, he joined the movement for Asian American racial justice by opposing anti-Asian racism and denouncing the belief in white superiority. Furthermore, he questioned the need to intern Japanese Americans during World War II while defending the civil rights of all Asian Americans, as well as of blacks and other racial minorities. He backed congressional repeal of Chinese exclusion and, if he had lived long enough, most certainly would have applauded the overall collapse of anti-Asian policies during the early Cold War.

How and why did "winners" like Rowell reject racism in defending Asian American rights? Answering this question requires seeing the world through their eyes—listening to their voices and understanding the historical context in which they made decisions. Such an approach enables one to get beyond the stereotypes and half-truths about whites as a monolithic racial group. Appreciating their full, complex humanity clears the ground for a fresh understanding of well-known purveyors of anti-Asian racism such as Samuel Gompers, Theodore Roosevelt, Henry George, Alfred Thayer Mahan, Henry Cabot Lodge, Paul Scharrenberg, Albert Johnson, V. S. McClatchy, FDR, Earl Warren, Culbert Olson, Fletcher Bowron, and other major players in the exclusion debate. To be sure, these men did damage to Asian subjects by contributing significantly to the exclusionist cause. But in so doing, they sought to benefit the broader American public. Their good intentions did not excuse their anti-Asian racism. But at the same time, their racism should not cause us to discount their good intentions. While the idea of universal empathy may seem like an ethical point, it is really a methodological one. It is my contention that universal empathy is required to truly understand both sides of controversial issues pertaining to racism, discrimination, and social inequality.

To Highlight the Process in Becoming a Pacific Nation

The history of the exclusion debate addresses the dramatic trans-formation of the United States into a nation with a significant presence of peoples, cultures, and networks connecting it with countries in the Asia-Pacific region. Since egalitarians were early advocates of global integration in the Pacific Ocean basin, the exclusion debate sheds light on America's development as a Pacific nation. Recent writing on transpacific history has revealed the web of connections across and within this vast region. Much of this work relies on understanding large bodies of water as not simply for-midable barriers to human contact and interaction. Starting with the Medi-terranean and then extending to the Atlantic, Indian, and now the Pacific Ocean, scholars have shown with impressive sophistication how the Earth's large watery terrains have acted as superhighways for commerce, as well as for the spread of peoples, ideas, culture, and disease. The highway meta-phor is reminiscent of William H. Seward's mid-nineteenth-century vision of commercial empire in which not only would the United States and China engage in trade but their peoples would mix and merge as part of a new global epoch of Pacific civilization. While aware that anti-Asian racism posed a major obstacle for global integration, Seward was convinced that this process was inevitable given the dynamism of the U.S. economy and the resources in East Asia. It turns out that he was right, but it took much longer and was more wrenching and conflict-ridden than he, or anyone else, could imagine. It took the horror of World War II and the prolonged Cold War crisis to inaugurate the true beginning of the Pacific era.

Asian immigrants were at the center of this long process of global inte-gration. As Seward and later egalitarians knew well, the exclusion debate was crucial to building international understanding throughout the Pacific. Egalitarianism stemmed from what can be called humanitarian self-interest. Seward envisioned Chinese workers developing the frontier of the American West; business leaders sought foreign markets and inexpensive labor; missionaries wanted to save souls; and peace advocates, like many IPR members, worked to prevent war. In this way, egalitarians functioned as early adopters of Pacific integration. Exclusionists, on the other hand, re-sisted it for their own reasons of humanitarian self-interest. Craft unions, like the AFL, sought to preserve their position as the "aristocracy of labor" by excluding Asian immigrants; eugenicists sought to maintain what they believed to be a healthy gene pool; and national security hawks sought to protect the nation from suspicious foreigners who might engage in espio-nage or acts of terror. But as opponents of today's globalization know well, it was impossible, over the long run, to stand in the way of global integration when unlimited fortunes and national greatness were at stake. Learning about the eventual triumph of egalitarianism, as well as about the collapse of exclusionism, enables one to appreciate the inexorable power of the global economy to shape political debates and social beliefs.

To Shed Light on Contemporary Problems

It is important to understand any issue today as a debate with two sides and to have empathy for both in order to fully account for complexities in human identity and relations. More specifically, the policy communities framework in this book enables one to see how, since the terrorist attacks on September 11, 2001, national security has become a dominant force that shapes the conception of Asian subjects and other peoples of color, especially those who most closely resemble the perpetrators of the terrorist acts. Much has been made about the similarities between the post-9/11 predicament faced by Arab and Muslim Americans and that of Japanese Americans after Pearl Harbor. The exclusion debate framework can shed light on such a comparison by examining the hard choices made by egalitarians regarding the decision to evacuate and confine Japanese Americans. Certainly, there was intense outrage, fear, and confusion in the wake of 9/11, just like there was following Pearl Harbor. But there was no mass evacuation or internment after the more recent attack. The exclusion debate framework offers two reasons for this crucial difference. First, 9/11 followed a long period in which civil rights was the dominant policy community. During this time, the federal government held redress hearings, published a definitive study of the Japanese internment that blamed it largely on racial prejudice, and backed up these findings with legislation that paid $20,000 to each living survivor of the internment. By the time of the 2001 terrorist attacks, the idea of race-based evacuation and internment was anathema to mainstream sensibilities. Second, the rise of Japanese Americans to become major players in U.S. policy making acted as a key brake against any political momentum for mass evacuation of suspected enemy groups after 9/11. It did matter that nisei Norman Mineta was serving as President George W. Bush's secretary of transportation when the terrorist attacks happened. Bush made it a point to address the secretary's ordeal during World War II in dismissing rumors that the federal government was planning a mass evacuation of enemy aliens. He, and the vast majority of Americans, had learned from the internment that race does not equal loyalty. While very real violations of civil liberties have been committed by military and civilian personnel during the War on Terror, mass incarceration was not one of them.

The influence of Norman Mineta revealed that Asian Americans no longer suffered from the kinds of vulnerabilities that plagued them for much of their history before World War II, and therefore they became important participants in the nation's political process. Asian American voters helped place co-ethnics in public office like Mineta (mayor of San Jose and long-serving member of Congress before joining the Bush administration), Mike Honda, Judy Chu, Daniel Inouye, Hiram Fong, Spark Matsunaga, Patsy Mink, and Gary Locke, who was governor of Washington. And in some cases Asian Americans, like Bobby Jindal, former governor of Louisiana; Nikki Haley, current governor of South Carolina; and Dalip Singh Saund (member of Congress from California, 1957–63), obtained office without substantial backing from their ethnic communities. Since the 1950s, undocumented workers from Mexico and neighboring countries in Central America have replaced Asian immigrants as groups lacking basic rights and legal standing, what one historian calls "impossible subjects."[2] Recall in chapter 6 that during the late 1920s, exclusionists like V. S. McClatchy wanted to exclude all Mexican immigrants but was thwarted not just by the political influence of West Coast growers who needed their labor but also by the legal fact that Mexicans were eligible for U.S. citizenship. The many people who have crossed the U.S.-Mexico border without official papers do not have the same claims on American citizenship and thus exist, much like Asian immigrants before the Great Transformation, as peoples who during times of great social stress and fears have become victimized by public policies that harass, discriminate, and exclude them. Another vulnerable group are incarcerated peoples, whose legal standing and much of their constitutional rights have been stripped as a consequence of their imprisonment. In this way the War on Drugs, begun during the 1980s under President Ronald Reagan and continuing to the present, provides another opportunity to apply lessons learned from the exclusion debate. The massive number of disproportionately working-class African Americans arrested during the nation's crackdown on drug smuggling, selling, and consumption has perpetuated the image of inner-city blacks as one of America's most feared and therefore subordinated groups. These problems—fears of terrorists, undocumented workers, and inner-city drug users—present us with some of our biggest racial challenges today. If Asian subjects no longer pose the dilemmas for Americans that they did in the past, the history of the exclusion debate can help to explain why.

In the end, we all—Americans and peoples around the world who have experienced political conflicts based in race, nation, culture, or immigration—are part of the living legacy of the exclusion debate. We are the exclusionist banning unwanted immigration; the worker angry at labor competition; the native citizen disdainful of newcomers; the nationalist protecting the nation from the outside world; the missionary converting the "heathen"; the majority stigmatizing minorities; the resident fearful of homegrown terrorism; and the vigilante massacring in the name of justice. And we are also the egalitarian opposing the discrimination of immigrants and other subordinated groups; the employer upset at labor unions; the native citizen disdainful of nativists; the nationalist committed to commercial or military empire; the internationalist working to prevent war; the missionary preaching against parochialism; the majority stigmatizing racists; the resident fearful of mob rule; and the vigilante crusading for social justice. We live the legacy of both exclusionism and egalitarianism because they are two sides to the same coin of human behavior. As humans, we act out of fear, anger, greed, righteousness, pride, hunger for power, desire for security, and sense of superiority over groups of people and ways of knowing different from our own. The instruments of government are the tools we use to institutionalize our actions throughout society. The ultimate lesson of the exclusion debate is that, paradoxically, this intense, long-term conflict testifies to the indivisibility of humanity.

NOTES

Abbreviations Used in the Notes

BRO
Barbara Brower Private Collection, Portland, Ore. (copies of cited documents in this collection are in author's possession)

CG
Congressional Globe

CJIC
California Joint Immigration Committee Records

CR
Congressional Record

CU-CEIP
Carnegie Endowment for International Peace Records, Butler Library, Columbia University, New York, N.Y.

FR
Fresno Republican Editorials, Special Collections, University of California, Los Angeles

GOMP Docs.
Samuel Gompers, *The Samuel Gompers Papers*, vols. 4–5, edited by Stuart B. Kaufman, Peter J. Albert, and Grace Palladino (Urbana: University of Illinois Press, 1991 and 1996)

ICPSR
Inter-university Consortium for Political and Social Research, and Congressional Quarterly, Inc. United States Congressional Roll Call Voting Records, 1789–1998. ICPSR00004-v3. Ann Arbor, Mich: Inter-university Consortium for Political and Social Research [distributor], May 6, 2010. http://doi .org/10.3886/ICPSR00004.v3

ICPSR-Cen
Michael R. Haines and Inter-university Consortium for Political and Social Research. Historical, Demographic, Economic, and Social Data: The United States, 1790–2002. ICPSR02896-v3. Ann Arbor, Mich.: Inter-university Consortium for Political and Social Research [distributor], May 21, 2010. http://doi.org/10.3886/ICPSR02896.v3

IN-H (1921)
U.S. Congress, House, Immigration and Naturalization Committee, *Japanese Immigration*, 66th Cong., 2nd sess. (Washington: Government Printing Office, 1921)

IN-H (1930)
U.S. Congress, House, Immigration and Naturalization Committee, *Exclusion of Immigration from the Philippines*, 71st Cong., 2nd sess. (Washington: Government Printing Office, 1930)

IN-H (1933)
U.S. Congress, House, Immigration and Naturalization Committee, *To Return Unemployed Filipinos*, 72nd Cong., 2nd sess. (Washington: Government Printing Office, 1933)

IN-H (1935-1)
U.S. Congress, House, Immigration and Naturalization Committee, *Oriental Veterans*, 74th Cong., 1st sess. (Washington: Government Printing Office, 1935)

IN-H (1935-2)
U.S. Congress, House, Immigration and Naturalization Committee, Extending Time for Voluntary Return of Unemployed Filipinos to the Philippines—Hearings on H.J. Res. 71, unpublished, 74th Cong., 1st sess. February 5–6, 1935

IN-H (1939)
U.S. Congress, House, Immigration and Naturalization Committee, *India-Born Residents Request Naturalization*, 76th Cong., 1st sess. (Washington: Government Printing Office, 1939)

IN-H (1940)
U.S. Congress, House, Immigration and Naturalization Committee, Hearings on H.R. 7239, To Authorize Naturalization of Filipinos Who Are Permanent Residents of the United States, unpublished, 76th Cong., 1st sess., March 28, 1940

IN-H (1943)
U.S. Congress, House, Immigration and

Naturalization Committee, *Repeal of Chinese Exclusion Acts*, 78th Cong., 1st sess. (Washington: Government Printing Office, 1943)

IN-H (1944)
U.S. Congress, House, Immigration and Naturalization Committee, *Naturalization of Filipinos*, 78th Cong., 2nd sess. (Washington: Government Printing Office, 1944)

IN-S (1965)
U.S. Congress, Senate, Judiciary Committee, Subcommittee on Immigration and Naturalization, *Immigration*, 89th Cong., 1st sess. (Washington: Government Printing Office, 1965)

JC-H (1964)
U.S. Congress, House, Judiciary Subcommittee, *Immigration*, 88th Cong., 2nd sess. (Washington: Government Printing Office, 1964)

JC-H (1985)
U.S. Congress, House, Committee of the Judiciary, *Japanese-American and Aleutian Wartime Relocation*, 98th Cong., 2nd sess. (Washington: Government Printing Office, 1985)

JC-H (1986)
U.S. Congress, House, Committee of the Judiciary, *Civil Liberties Act of 1985 and the Aleutian and Pribilof Islands Restitution Act*, 99th Cong., 2nd sess. (Washington: Government Printing Office, 1986)

JC-S (1948)
U.S. Congress, Senate, Judiciary Committee, Hearings on H.R. 3999, To Authorize the Attorney General to Adjudicate Certain Claims Resulting from Evacuation of Certain Persons of Japanese Ancestry under Military Orders, unpublished, 80th Cong., 2nd sess., May 21, 1948

JC-S (1949)
U.S. Congress, Senate, Judiciary Committee, Naturalization of Asian and Pacific Peoples, unpublished, 81st Cong., 1st sess., July 19, 1949

J-DRO
Meiji-Taisho Series, Japan Diplomatic Records Office (Gaiko Shirōkan), Tokyo, Japan

JS (1877)
U.S. Congress, Senate, Joint Special Committee, *Investigate Chinese Immigration*, 44th Cong., 2nd sess., Report 689 (Washington: Government Printing Office, 1877), 1–1281

LAT
Los Angeles Times

LA-Vote
Election Return, Los Angeles County, General Election, November 2, 1920, California State Archives, Office of the Secretary of State, Sacramento, Calif

ND (1942)
U.S. Congress, Select Committee Investigating National Defense Migration, *National Defense Migration*, 77th Cong., 2nd sess., pts. 29–31 (Washington: Government Printing Office, 1942)

NYT
New York Times

SFC
San Francisco Chronicle

SHIB Docs.
Eiichi Shibusawa, *Biographical Materials on Eiichi Shibusawa*, vols. 34–35 (Tokyo: Shibusawa Eiichi Denki Shiryō Kankōkai, 1960)

SU-DSJ1
Jordan (David Starr) Papers, Hoover Institution, Stanford University, Stanford, Calif.

UC-AA
Arthur Arlett Papers, BANC MSS C-B 408, Bancroft Library, University of California, Berkeley

UC-FAIR
Pacific Coast Committee on American Principles and Fair Play Records, BANC MSS C-A 171, Bancroft Library, University of California, Berkeley

UC-HJ
Hiram Johnson Papers, BANC MSS C-B 581, Bancroft Library, University of California, Berkeley

UC-JP1
James D. Phelan Papers, BANC MSS C-B 800, Bancroft Library, University of California, Berkeley, Berkeley, Calif.

UC-JP2
James D. Phelan Papers, BANC FILM 2443, Bancroft Library, University of California, Berkeley

UC-PS
  Paul Scharrenberg Papers, BANC MSS
  C-B 906, Bancroft Library, University of
  California, Berkeley
UH-IPR
  Institute of Pacific Relations Records,
  M004 and M021, Hamilton Library,
  University of Hawai'i at Manoa,
  Honolulu

Preface

1. The terminology for the confinement of 120,000 Japanese Americans during World War II always has been politically charged, with no options that are entirely neutral. I've chosen to use terms with the least amount of contemporary baggage so that the reader can appreciate the diversity of past views, as well as their change over time. In this way, I use "internment" and "confinement" interchangeably, although the former has a better economy of expression in standing in for the entire historical event—the internment. I use "internment camps" or "concentration camps" to refer to the gated and guarded facilities that housed the "internees." For discussion of relevant terminology, see, for example, Roger Daniels, "Words Do Matter: A Note on Inappropriate Terminology and the Incarceration of the Japanese Americans," in Louis Fiset and Gail Nomura, eds., *Nikkei in the Pacific Northwest: Japanese Americans and Japanese Canadians in the Twentieth Century* (Seattle: University of Washington Press, 2005): 183–207; and Greg Robinson, *The Tragedy of Democracy: Japanese Confinement in North America* (New York: Columbia University Press, 2009), vii–viii.

2. Winthrop Jordan as quoted in Eric Foner, *Who Owns History? Remaking the Past in a Changing World* (New York: Hill and Wang, 2002), 10.

3. For the quantitative side to the "new" political history, see Joel H. Silbey, "Congressional and State Legislative Roll-Call Studies by U.S. Historians," *Legislative Studies Quarterly* 6, no. 4 (November 1981): 597–607; Allan G. Bogue, "The 'New' Political History," *Journal of Contemporary History* 3, no. 1 (January 1968): 5–27; and J. Morgan Kousser, "'New Political History': A Methodological Critique," *Reviews in American History* 4, no. 1 (March 1976): 1–14. More recent reflec-

tions on U.S. political history that include the place of quantification include Mark H. Leff, "Revisioning U.S. Political History," *American Historical Review* 100, no. 3 (June 1995): 829–53; and Paula Baker, "The Midlife Crisis of the New Political History," *Journal of American History* 86, no. 1 (June 1999): 158–66.

4. Michael H. Hunt, *The Making of a Special Relationship: The United States and China to 1914* (New York: Columbia University Press, 1983), xi.

5. Two recent comprehensive histories of Asian Americans that include their social experiences and historical agency are Shelley Sang-Hee Lee, *A New History of Asian America* (New York: Routledge, 2014); and Erika Lee, *The Making of Asian America: A History* (New York: Simon and Schuster, 2015).

6. While the scholarly study of Asian Americans began in the early twentieth century, the academic field of Asian American history emerged in the late 1960s as a "people's history" uncovering the experiences of marginalized individuals and groups. The call was to study the past from the "bottom up" by examining what Asian Americans did or wanted to do, rather than what was done to them. This led, in turn, to a combined approach (bottom-up and top-down) that by the late 1980s informed the master narrative for the field. An important call for the bottom-up turn in the historiography is Roger Daniels, "Westerners from the East: Oriental Immigrants Reappraised," *Pacific Historical Review* 35, no. 4 (November 1966): 373–83. These now classic works of historical synthesis established the master narrative of Asian American history: Roger Daniels, *Asian America: Chinese and Japanese in the United States since 1850* (Seattle: University of Washington Press, 1988); Ronald Takaki, *Strangers from A Different Shore: A History of Asian Americans* (Boston: Little, Brown, 1989); and Sucheng Chan, *Asian Americans: An Interpretive History* (Boston: Twayne, 1991).

Introduction

1. For analysis of the Vincent Chin murder, see Helen Zia, *Asian American Dreams: The Emergence of an American People* (New York: Farrar, Straus and Giroux, 2000), 55–81, as well as the documentary film by Christine

Choy and Renee Tajima, *Who Killed Vincent Chin?* (New York: Filmakers Library, 1988).

2. Since the term was coined by sociologist William Petersen in 1966, the model minority concept has generated voluminous literature: Petersen, "Success Story, Japanese-American Style," *New York Times Magazine*, January 9, 1966, 22–26. Analyses of the stereotype are found, for example, in Ronald Takaki, *Strangers from a Different Shore: A History of Asian Americans* (Boston: Little, Brown, 1989), 474–84; and Frank Wu, *Yellow: Race in America beyond Black and White* (New York: Basic Books, 2002), 39–78. The most comprehensive history of it is Ellen D. Wu, *The Color of Success: Asian Americans and the Origins of the Model Minority* (Princeton: Princeton University Press, 2014). The Wen Ho Lee case is covered in Wen Ho Lee with Helen Zia, *My Country versus Me* (New York: Hyperion, 2001).

3. Eric Liu, *Chinaman's Chance: One Family's Journey and the Chinese American Dream* (New York: Public Affairs, 2014), vii–viii.

4. Representative studies include Bruce Cumings, *Dominion from Sea to Sea: Pacific Ascendancy and American Power* (New Haven: Yale University Press, 2009); David M. Pletcher, *Diplomacy of Involvement: American Economic Expansion across the Pacific, 1784–1900* (Columbia: University of Missouri Press, 2001); Jean Heffer, *The United States and the Pacific: History of a Frontier* (Notre Dame: University of Notre Dame Press, 2002); Arthur Power Dudden, *The American Pacific: From the Old China Trade to the Present* (New York: Oxford University Press, 1992); Arrell Morgan Gibson, *Yankees in Paradise: The Pacific Basin Frontier* (Albuquerque: University of New Mexico Press, 1993); and Donald D. Johnson, *The United States and the Pacific: Private Interests and Public Policies, 1784–1899* (Westport, Conn.: Praeger, 1995). For a different approach attuned to transpacific circuits of migration, trade, and disease, see David Igler, *The Great Ocean: Pacific Worlds from Captain Cook to the Gold Rush* (New York: Oxford University Press, 2013); and for a much broader sweep of time, nations, and peoples, see Matt K. Matsuda, *Pacific Worlds: A History of Seas, Peoples, and Cultures* (New York: Cambridge University Press, 2012).

5. As a globally integrated history of an American policy debate, this book responds to Eric Foner's encouragement, given in his presidential address for the American Historical Association, that "even histories organized along the lines of the nation-state must be, so to speak, de-provincialized, placed in the context of international interactions"; see Eric Foner, *Who Owns History? Remaking the Past in a Changing World* (New York: Hill and Wang, 2002), 54. In contrast, recent scholarship has studied Asian exclusion from a global, rather than nation-centered, approach that sees the United States as just one node in a network of exclusionary regimes that stretched around the world. Two examples are Adam M. McKeown, *Melancholy Order: Asian Migration and the Globalization of Borders* (New York: Columbia University Press, 2008); and Matthew Connelly, *Fatal Misconception: The Struggle to Control World Population* (Cambridge, Mass.: Harvard University Press, 2010). These books focus on globally produced systems of thought and border making. They are not rooted in the study of Asian Americans or U.S. politics per se and thus do not address the wide variety and diversity of local and federal anti-Asian policies in the United States, such as alien land laws and Japanese American internment or the repeal of exclusion. Most important, these global approaches have ignored the exclusion debate in American politics. In this sense, while fascinating accounts on their own terms, the books by McKeown and Connelly exemplify Foner's warning that global histories "can be every bit as obfuscating as histories that are purely national" (Foner, *Who Owns History?*, 54).

6. Emphasis added to the definition. The etymology of "egalitarian" begins in the late nineteenth century, from the French *égalitaire* (*égal* means "equal") and from the Latin term for "equal," *aequalis*: *Oxford Dictionaries: Language Matters* (Oxford University Press, 2015), http://www.oxforddictionaries.com/definition/american_english/egalitarian (September 26, 2015).

7. *CR*, 47th Cong., 1st sess., 1516 (March 1, 1882).

8. Theodore Roosevelt, "Sixth Annual Message," December 3, 1906, in *Papers Re-*

lating to the *Foreign Relations of the United States*, 59th Cong., 2nd sess., 1909, H. doc. 1, xlii.

9. Ansel Adams, *Born Free and Equal* (New York: U.S. Camera Book, 1944), 42.

10. Some might object to my use of "egalitarians" to describe an opposition that consisted of some of the richest and most powerful men in the United States. To these critics, it would be better to call them "hypocrites" or, at best, "racial liberals." This last term has been used by scholars to expose the limitations and contradictions of non-discrimination discourse and policies in the United States since World War II. Indeed, some of the actors in this book were racial liberals influenced by the emergence of liberalism during and after the New Deal era. But most were not. There was not one single identity for the diverse individuals and groups who opposed anti-Asian policies from the 1850s to the 1960s, and since scholars have yet to identify them as a community of interest, there does not exist a language to define them. As a result, I have decided to use a name that captures their shared interest that remained constant over time: to treat Asian Americans on *equal* terms with other immigrant or racial groups. Thus I use "egalitarians," but with the caveat that this category should not be seen as a fixed, homogeneous social fact. Likewise, "exclusionists"—a term more acceptable to scholars—also carries the same burden of being fixed as an essentialized category. Both egalitarians and exclusionists were diverse, historically contingent categories, and taken as a pair, they convey the polarized opinion on questions of anti-Asian discrimination. For recent studies of racial liberalism as it pertains to Asian Americans, see Wu, *Color of Success*; and Charlotte Brooks, *Alien Neighbors, Foreign Friends: Asian Americans, Housing, and the Transformation of Urban California* (Chicago: University of Chicago Press, 2009). A more hopeful study of racial liberalism that includes discussion of Asian Americans is Mark Brilliant, *The Color of America Has Changed: How Racial Diversity Shaped Civil Rights Reform in California, 1941–1978* (New York: Oxford University Press, 2010).

11. My conception of the exclusion debate has been influenced by Eric Foner's study of the language of "freedom" in the United States, which underscores both the centrality of this term for American political discourse and its multiple and changing meanings: Eric Foner, *The Story of American Freedom* (New York: Norton, 1999). Equally influential was Gary Gerstle's framing of American nationalism in the twentieth century as a competition between discourses of racial exclusion ("racial nationalism") and racial inclusion ("civic nationalism"): Gerstle, *American Crucible: Race and Nation in the Twentieth Century* (Princeton: Princeton University Press, 2001). Also see the book that Gerstle acknowledges is most similar to his binary model, Rogers Smith, *Civic Ideals: Conflicting Visions of Citizenship in U.S. History* (New Haven: Yale University Press, 1997).

12. For a comprehensive and up-to-date analysis of this literature, see David K. Yoo and Eiichiro Azuma, *Oxford Handbook on Asian American History* (New York: Oxford University Press, 2016). Other studies include Gary Okihiro, *The Columbia Guide to Asian American History* (New York: Columbia University Press, 2005), 193–241; Shirley Hune, *Pacific Migration to the United States: Trends and Themes in Historical and Sociological Literature* (Washington, D.C.: Smithsonian Institution, 1977); L. Ling-chi Wang, "Asian American Studies," *American Quarterly* 33, no. 3 (1981): 339–54; Roger Daniels, "No Lamps Were Lit for Them: Angel Island and the Historiography of Asian American Immigration," *Journal of American Ethnic History* 17, no. 1 (1997): 3–19, and "American Historians and East Asian Immigrants," *Pacific Historical Review* 43 (November 1974): 448–72; and Sucheng Chan, "Asian American Historiography," *Pacific Historical Review* 65, no. 3 (August 1996): 363–99.

13. The master narrative of Asian American history portrays American society and institutions as though they are infected with anti-Asian racism, which exists as a kind of supervirus that remains forever latent in the body politic until activated by historical circumstances. In this scenario, the typical exclusionists are cast as victimizers and Asian Americans as victims who engage in creative and sometimes heroic means to meet their needs under conditions not of their

own choosing. The victimization-agency model discounts factors that limit or transform exclusionism. In this way it ignores the greatest limitation faced by exclusionists: the intelligent, organized, and well-funded opposition. Chapter 8 in this book discusses the formation of the master narrative as expressed in Takaki's *Strangers from a Different Shore*. An insightful but overlooked critique of the master narrative is Sylvia Yanagisako, "Transforming Orientalism: Gender, Nationality, and Class in Asian American Studies," in *Naturalizing Power: Essays in Feminist Cultural Analysis*, ed. Sylvia Yanagisako and Carol Delaney (New York: Routledge, 1995), 275–98.

14. These studies of Asian Americans, many of which are quite recent, are moving beyond the master narrative to address the significance of opposition to exclusionism: Madeline Y. Hsu, *The Good Immigrants: How the Yellow Peril Became the Model Minority* (Princeton: Princeton University Press, 2015); Sarah M. Griffith, "'Where We Can Battle for the Lord and Japan': The Development of Liberal Protestant Antiracism before World War II," *Journal of American History* 100, no. 2 (September 2013): 429–53; Sarah M. Griffith, "Conflicting Dialogues: The Survey of Race Relations in the Trans-Pacific and the Fight for Asian American Racial Equality" (Ph.D. diss., University of California, Santa Barbara, 2010); and Izumi Hirobe, *Japanese Pride, American Prejudice: Modifying the Exclusion Clause of the 1924 Immigration Act* (Stanford: Stanford University Press, 2001). In addition, three recent articles have highlighted the importance of opposition to Chinese exclusion: Gordon H. Chang, "China and the Pursuit of America's Destiny: Nineteenth-Century Imagining and Why Immigration Restriction Took So Long," *Journal of Asian American Studies* 15, no. 2 (June 2012): 145–69; Paul A. Kramer, "Empire against Exclusion in Early 20th Century Trans-Pacific History," *Nanzan Review of American Studies* 33 (2011): 13–32; and Beth Lew-Williams, "Before Restriction Became Exclusion: America's Experiment in Diplomatic Immigration Control," *Pacific Historical Review* 83, no. 1 (February 2014): 24–56. Studies concentrating on egalitarians also include Sandra C. Taylor, *Advocate of Understanding: Sidney Gulick and the Search*

for Peace with Japan (Kent: Kent State University Press, 1984); Bruce A. Abrams, "A Muted Cry: White Opposition to the Japanese Exclusion Movement, 1911–1924" (Ph.D. diss., New York University, 1987); Fred W. Riggs, *Pressures on Congress: A Study of the Repeal of Chinese Exclusion* (New York: King's Crown Press, 1950); Charles J. McClain, *In Search of Equality: The Chinese Struggle against Discrimination in Nineteenth-Century America* (Berkeley: University of California Press, 1994); Jon Thares Davidann, *Cultural Diplomacy in U.S.-Japanese Relations, 1919–1941* (New York: Macmillan, 2007); Jennifer C. Snow, *Protestant Missionaries, Asian Immigrants, and Ideologies of Race in America, 1850–1924* (New York: Routledge, 2007); Joshua Paddison, *American Heathens: Religion, Race, and Reconstruction in California* (Berkeley: University of California Press, 2012); and Mary Roberts Coolidge, *Chinese Immigration* (New York: Henry Holt, 1909).

15. A good example is Claire Jean Kim, "The Racial Triangulation of Asian Americans," *Politics and Society* 27, no. 1 (March 1999): 105–38. A political scientist, Kim suggests that anti-Asian policies emerged from the need for policy makers to position Asian immigrants as better than blacks but lesser than whites. Curiously, her theory does not situate Asian American issues within a field of politics or consider the significance of political institutions such as Congress, political parties, or the State Department. The historical sections of Kim's article rely on highly selective secondary sources that embody the master narrative of Asian American history. In contrast, Andrew Gyory, *Closing the Gate: Race, Politics, and the Chinese Exclusion Act* (Chapel Hill: University of North Carolina Press, 1998), fleshes out the political details and institutional contexts that Kim ignores in arguing that while West Coast racism was essential, national party politics was the "engine fueling and steering [Chinese] exclusion" (Gyory, *Closing the Gate*, 257). Two recent studies of U.S. immigration history by political scientists support and advance Gyory's perspective: Daniel J. Tichenor, *Dividing Lines: The Politics of Immigration Control in America* (Princeton: Princeton University Press, 2002), 87–113; and Aristide R. Zolberg, *A Nation by Design: Immigra-*

tion Policy in the Fashioning of America (New York: Russell Sage, 2006), 187–92. Yet historians of Asian Americans, in general, have major objections to Gyory's book, many of which seem to stem from its disregard for the field's master narrative that sees politics primarily as racialization. See exchange between Gyory and Stanford M. Lyman in Lyman, "The 'Chinese Question' and American Labor Historians," *New Politics* 4, no. 28 (2000), http://nova.wpunj.edu/newpolitics/issue28/lyman28.htm (September 26, 2015); and Andrew Gyory, "A Reply to Stanford Lyman," *New Politics* 1, no. 29 (2000), http://nova.wpunj.edu/newpolitics/issue29/gyory29.htm (September 26, 2015). Critical reviews of Gyory's book also include Mae M. Ngai in *American Journal of Legal History* 44, no. 3 (July 2000): 304–5; Henry Yu in *Law and History Review* 20, no. 2 (Summer 2002): 418–20; and George Anthony Peffer in *American Historical Review* 105, no. 5 (December 2000): 1751–52.

16. An important, though rarely cited, study about the forgetting of diplomatic history in Asian American historiography is Gordon H. Chang, "Asian Immigrants and American Foreign Relations," in *Pacific Passages: The Study of American-East Asian Relations on the Eve of the Twenty-First Century*, ed. Warren I. Cohen (New York: Columbia University Press, 1996), 103–18. Chang's description of the separation between diplomatic studies and Asian American history identifies the timing of this split (after World War II) but does not analyze causation. The larger relationship between immigration and foreign policy is the subject of Donna R. Gabaccia, *Foreign Relations: American Immigration in Global Perspective* (Princeton: Princeton University Press, 2012).

17. Scholarship on the "transnational turn" in the study of Asian American history is addressed in Yoo and Azuma, *Oxford Handbook*, as well as these special journal issues and research forums: Lon Kurashige, Madeline Y. Hsu, and Yujin Yaguchi, eds., "Conversations on Transpacific History," *Pacific Historical Review* 83, no. 2 (May 2014); Erika Lee and Naoko Shibusawa, "What Is Transpacific Asian American History?," *Journal of Asian American Studies* 8, no. 3 (2005); and articles and commentary by various historians in "Asian American History Forum," *Pacific Historical Review* 76, no. 4 (November 2007): 533–614.

18. A word needs to be said about my focus on "policy communities." In studying the exclusion debate, I have paid less attention than is usual to dominant gender and sexual ideologies because, while part of the general racial discourse, they were not the center of a policy community engaged in the exclusion debate. While feminists and women's groups did at times take positions on Asian American issues (usually egalitarian, as noted in this book), their influence was not instrumental to policy formation or outcomes.

19. Scholars have largely neglected Rowell's switching to the egalitarian side. The image of him as California's "archetypical," though moderate, racist began in Roger Daniels, *The Politics of Prejudice* (1962; repr., New York: Atheneum, 1968), 23–24, 49, and 131–32n15; "archetypal" is used in Daniels, "Westerners from the East," 377. Studies that share Daniels's critical impression of Rowell include Spencer C. Olin Jr., *California's Prodigal Sons: Hiram Johnson and the Progressives, 1911–1917* (Berkeley: University of California Press, 1968), 81; Kevin Starr, *Inventing the Dream: California through the Progressive Era* (New York: Oxford University Press, 1985), 260; Neil Foley, *The White Scourge: Mexicans, Blacks, and Poor Whites in Texas Cotton Culture* (Berkeley: University of California Press, 1997), 52; and Eiichiro Azuma, *Between Two Empires: Race, History, and Transnationalism in Japanese America* (New York: Oxford University Press, 2005), 39. The only biographical study of Rowell does not cover his later career when he became outspoken in opposing anti-Asian discrimination: Miles Chapman Everett, "Chester Harvey Rowell, Pragmatic Humanist and California Progressive" (Ph.D. diss., University of California, Berkeley, 1966). In studying Rowell's part in the 1913 controversy over the California alien land law, Everett recognizes the relationship in his mind between Japanese exclusion and antiracism (393–428). More recent studies of Rowell's "moderate" anti-Japanese prejudice during the alien land law crisis are Frank W. Van Nuys, "A Progressive Confronts the Race Question: Chester Rowell, the California

Alien Land Act of 1913," *California History* 73, no. 1 (Spring 1994), 2–13; and Lon Kurashige, "Transpacific Accommodation and the Defense of Asian Immigrants," *Pacific Historical Review* 83, no. 2 (May 2014): 294–13.

20. "Free" targeted indentured servants; "white" implicated free blacks, or mulatto refugees soon fleeing the Haitian Revolution; and "good character" implied paupers, criminals, and poor people "likely to become a public charge." Moreover, while the word "persons" indicated that women who satisfied the other criteria could become citizens, and while the act further granted them the right to pass their citizenship to children born outside the United States, it stipulated that women in themselves could not pass citizenship to their children if the child's father had "never been resident in the United States." Despite the long-standing significance of race, class, and gender in citizenship requirements, Congress's main concerns in debating the Naturalization Act focused instead on qualifications for landholding and requirements for public office, two critical features of the republican experiment. Hence the "white" racial standard for citizenship was not a sticking point in the debate concerning the Naturalization Act. In this way, the act overturned the section of the Northwest Ordinance (1787) that liberally granted citizenship to free blacks and individual Native Americans who were long-term residents of the eponymous territory. For more on the Naturalization Act, see Zolberg, *Nation by Design*, 83–87.

21. Ibid., 94–95.

22. The quoted phrase borrows from this important study of white racial identity in late twentieth-century America: George Lipsitz, *The Possessive Investment in Whiteness: How White People Profit from Identity Politics* (Philadelphia: Temple University Press, 2006).

23. Takaki, *Strangers from a Different Shore*, 15.

24. Matsuda, *Pacific Worlds*, 45–48.

25. Rudyard Kipling, "The Ballad of East and West," in Kipling, *The Works of Rudyard Kipling: One Volume Edition* (Project Gutenberg, 2000), http://www.gutenberg.org/files/2334/2334-h/2334-h.htm (January 19, 2016). For studies of American orientalism dur-

ing the nineteenth and early twentieth centuries, see, for example, John Kuo Wei Tchen, *New York before Chinatown: Orientalism and the Shaping of American Culture, 1776–1882* (Baltimore: Johns Hopkins University Press, 1999); Robert G. Lee, *Orientals: Asian Americans in Popular Culture* (Philadelphia: Temple University Press, 1999); Mari Yoshihara, *Embracing the East: White Women and American Orientalism* (New York: Oxford University Press, 2002); and Emma Jinhua Teng, *Eurasian: Mixed Identities in the United States, China, and Hong Kong, 1842–1943* (Berkeley: University of California Press, 2013). The classic work on the topic is Edward W. Said, *Orientalism* (New York: Vintage, 1979).

26. The loss of economic parity between China and Europe is addressed in Kenneth Pomeranz, *The Great Divergence: China, Europe, and the Making of the Modern World Economy* (Princeton: Princeton University Press, 2000). For an overview of the Opium War and other Western incursions into China, see Johnathan D. Spence, *The Search for Modern China* (New York: Norton, 1991), 143–58.

Chapter 1

1. *CG*, 32nd Cong., 1st sess., 1975–76 (July 30, 1852).

2. Ibid., 1975.

3. Norman A. Graebner, *Empire on the Pacific: A Study in American Continental Expansion* (New York: Ronald Press, 1955). For more recent studies that rely on Graebner's perspective, see David M. Pletcher, *Diplomacy of Involvement: American Economic Expansion across the Pacific, 1784–1900* (Columbia: University of Missouri Press, 2001); and Arthur Power Dudden, *The American Pacific: From the Old China Trade to the Present* (New York: Oxford University Press, 1992). In arguing that the American push for the Oregon Territory was led by non-maritime interests, Donald D. Johnson sees a more complicated process than Graebner: Johnson, *The United States and the Pacific: Private Interests and Public Policies, 1784–1899* (Westport, Conn.: Praeger, 1995), 72.

4. The distinction between Hamiltonians and Jeffersonians used in this book is based on analyses contained in Drew R. McCoy, *The*

Elusive Republic: Political Economy in Jeffersonian America (Chapel Hill: University of North Carolina Press, 1980); and as applied to the mid-nineteenth century in Robert Kelley, *The Cultural Pattern in American Politics: The First Century* (Washington, D.C.: University Press of America, 1979), 160–84.

5. Calhoun quoted in Graebner, *Empire on the Pacific*, 28. For American fantasies about the China trade, see John Haddad, *The Romance of China: Excursions to China in U.S. Culture, 1776–1876* (New York: Columbia University Press, 2006). How such fantasies were connected to the question of Chinese immigration is addressed in Gordon H. Chang, "China and the Pursuit of America's Destiny: Nineteenth-Century Imagining and Why Immigration Restriction Took So Long," *Journal of Asian American Studies* 15, no. 2 (June 2012): 145–69; and Gordon H. Chang, *Fateful Ties: A History of America's Preoccupation with China* (Cambridge, Mass.: Harvard University Press, 2015), 67–72.

6. William Montgomery Meigs, *The Life of Thomas Hart Benton* (Philadelphia: Lippincott, 1904), 309–10.

7. Cushing's mission is covered in Pletcher, *Diplomacy of Involvement*, 16–17; and Haddad, *Romance of China*, 136–59. Analysis of British aggression in China focusing on the Arrow War is found in James Hevia, *English Lessons: The Pedagogy of Imperialism in Nineteenth-Century China* (Durham: Duke University Press, 2003).

8. For Benton, see Alexander Saxton, *The Indispensable Enemy: Labor and the Anti-Chinese Movement in California* (1971; repr., Berkeley: University of California Press, 1995), 21–22; as well as G. Chang, "China and the Pursuit of America's Destiny," 157–58; Arrell Morgan Gibson, *Yankees in Paradise: The Pacific Basin Frontier* (Albuquerque: University of New Mexico Press, 1993), 358–61; and D. Johnson, *United States and the Pacific*, 65–66.

9. Ernest N. Paolino, *The Foundations of the American Empire: William Henry Seward and U.S. Foreign Policy* (Ithaca: Cornell University Press, 1973), 34.

10. Michael H. Hunt, *The Making of a Special Relationship: The United States and China to 1914* (New York: Columbia University Press, 1983), 16–17.

11. Pletcher, *Diplomacy of Involvement*, 46–65; Lawrence H. Fuchs, *Hawaii Pono: A Social History* (New York: Harcourt, Brace and World, 1961), 22. How the sugar industry grew out of the western negotiation of land claims is covered in Carol A. McLennan, *Sovereign Sugar: Industry and Environment in Hawai'i* (Honolulu: University of Hawai'i Press), 52–80. For the perspective of Native Hawaiians, see Lilikala Kame'eleihiwa, *Native Land, Foreign Desires: Pehea La E Pono Ai?* (Honolulu: Bishop Museum, 1992); Jonathan Kay Kamakawiwo'ole Osorio, *Dismembering Lahui: A History of the Hawaiian Nation to 1887* (Honolulu: University of Hawai'i Press, 2002), 44–73; and Noenoe Silva, *Aloha Betrayed: Native Hawaiian Resistance to American Colonialism* (Durham: Duke University Press, 2004), 39–43.

12. The votes were as follows: 74 percent of representatives from coastal states including Pennsylvania opposed killing the bill for transpacific mail service, while 42 percent of those from interior states voted this way. In addition, 73 percent of Free-Soilers voted against killing the bill as opposed to 43 percent of Democrats. ICPSR, vote 531, 31st Cong., House (February 19, 1851).

13. The roll call vote on the Senate measure to establish transpacific mail service was 22–13 in favor of the bill: 73 percent of northeastern senators supported it, compared with only 30 percent of southerners; 83 percent of Whigs supported it, compared with 50 percent of Democrats. ICPSR, vote 206, 33rd Cong., Senate (July 5, 1854).

14. *CG*, 33rd Cong., 1st Sess., 1566, 1569 (June 29, 1854).

15. Eric Foner, *Free Soil, Free Labor, Free Men: The Ideology of the Republican Party before the Civil War* (1970; repr., New York: Oxford University Press, 1995); Saxton, *Indispensable Enemy*, 21–30.

16. Mark Kanazawa, "Immigration, Exclusion, and Taxation: Anti-Chinese Legislation in Gold Rush California," *Journal of Economic History* 65, no. 3 (September 2005): 792–93.

17. Najia Aarim-Heriot, *Chinese Immigrants, African Americans, and Racial Anxiety in the United States, 1848–1882* (Urbana: University of Illinois Press, 2003), 45–47, 58–59.

18. Quoted in Yucheng Qin, *The Diplomacy of Nationalism: The Six Companies and*

China's Policy toward Exclusion (Honolulu: University of Hawai'i Press, 2009), 29, 32.

19. William Speer, *A Humble Plea: Addressed to the Legislature of California* (San Francisco: Sterett, 1856), Speer's requests, 32–36, "interests of California forbid," 5, on China market, 14–15, "spread of the Chinese," 39.

20. Paul Kleppner, *The Third Electoral System, 1853–1892: Parties, Voters, and Political Culture* (Chapel Hill: University of North Carolina Press, 1979).

21. Eric T. Love, *Race over Empire: Racism and U.S. Imperialism* (Chapel Hill: University of North Carolina Press, 2004), 27–72.

22. Paolino, *Foundations of the American Empire*, 22–24. For the broader context of Republican and northeastern dominance over the nation's political economy from the Civil War through Reconstruction, see Richard Franklin Bensel, *Yankee Leviathan: The Origins of Central State Authority in America, 1859–1877* (New York: Cambridge University Press, 1990). The persistence of America's regionally based political economy is the subject of Bensel, *Sectionalism and American Political Development, 1880–1980* (Madison: University of Wisconsin Press, 1984).

23. Favoring the measure were 73 percent of senators from the Northeast, while the senator from the only southern state (Virginia) did not vote; 76 percent of Republicans were in favor as opposed to 50 percent of Democrats. ICPSR, vote 327, 37th Cong., Senate (April 25, 1862).

24. *NYT*, August 29, 1865; *New York Tribune*, February 7, 1867; *Chicago Tribune*, January 15, 1867.

25. Aristide R. Zolberg, *A Nation by Design: Immigration Policy in the Fashioning of America* (New York: Russell Sage, 2006), 168–75; Andrew Gyory, *Closing the Gate: Race, Politics, and the Chinese Exclusion Act* (Chapel Hill: University of North Carolina Press, 1998), 20–26; Daniel J. Tichenor, *Dividing Lines: The Politics of Immigration Control in America* (Princeton: Princeton University Press, 2002), 66–67; E. P. Hutchinson, *Legislative History of American Immigration Policy, 1798–1965* (Philadelphia: University of Pennsylvania Press, 1981), 50–52.

26. Gyory, *Closing the Gate*, 32–33. Also see Moon-Ho Jung, *Coolies and Cane* (Baltimore: Johns Hopkins University Press, 2006).

27. Conness further defended the Chinese as indispensable labor, saying, "They are a docile, industrious people, and they are now passing into other branches of industry and labor. They are found employed as servants in a great many families and in the kitchens of hotels. They are found as farm hands in the fields, and lately they are employed by thousands" on the Central Pacific Railroad: Robert Denning, "A Fragile Machine: California Senator John Conness," *California History* 85, no. 4 (2008): 44–45.

28. My emphasis. For analysis of the amendment as it pertained to the Chinese, see Aarim-Heriot, *Chinese Immigrants*, 89–90.

29. As chair of the Senate Foreign Relations Committee, Sumner had worked closely with Seward the year before to purchase Alaska from Russia: Pletcher, *Diplomacy of Involvement*, 38–45.

30. John Schrecker, "'For Equality of Men—for the Equality of Nations': Anson Burlingame and China's First Embassy to the United States, 1868," *Journal of American–East Asian Relations* 17 (2010): 9–34 (quote on 29). Also see Haddad, *Romance of China*, 210–30.

31. *New York Tribune*, July 16, 1868; *Alta* is quoted in Schrecker, "'For Equality of Men,'" 14.

32. *New York World* and *San Francisco Examiner* as quoted in Schrecker, "'For Equality of Men,'" 18, 15.

33. *Senate Executive Journal*, 40th Cong., 2nd sess., July 24, 1868, 355.

34. The results of Johnson's proposed resolution was 42–106 opposed. ICPSR, vote 43, 41st Cong., House, March 22, 1869; Aarim-Heriot, *Chinese Immigrants*, 141–42.

35. ICPSR, votes 493, 496, 500, 504, 505, 41st Cong., Senate (July 2 and 4, 1870). Sumner's 1870 proposition came as an amendment to a House bill revising the naturalization law prompted by fraudulent elections in the South: *CG*, 41st Cong., 2nd sess., pt. 6, 5123, 5174–75 (July 2, 1870); for a discussion about the differences between African and Chinese immigrants, see 5177. Analysis of the debate and larger connec-

tions between Chinese and blacks is found in Aarim-Heriot, *Chinese Immigrants*, 143–50; and Moon-Ho Jung, *Coolies and Cane*, 136–44.

36. William Henry Seward, *William H. Seward's Travels around the World* (New York: D. Appleton, 1873), 31–33.

37. Ibid., 280–83.

38. Ibid., 28–30.

39. Aarim-Heriot, *Chinese Immigrants*, 159–60, 165–66.

40. Ibid., 158, 169–70. For the case prompting Field's decision, see Charles J. McClain, *In Search of Equality: The Chinese Struggle against Discrimination in Nineteenth-Century America* (Berkeley: University of California Press, 1994), 54–65.

41. Qin, *Diplomacy of Nationalism*, 83. For the history of Chinese female migration and their restriction, see George Anthony Peffer, *If They Don't Bring Their Women Here: Chinese Female Immigration before Exclusion* (Urbana: University of Illinois, 1999).

Chapter 2

1. *CR*, 47th Cong., 2nd sess., 1516, 1518, 1523 (March 1, 1882).

2. ICPSR, votes 303, 347, and 373, 45th Cong., House, and votes 82–83 and 93, 47th Cong., House. The opposition in 1882 counted eight out of nine New England senators and twenty-two out of twenty-five representatives in the House. In 1879 it included seven out of ten senators and fourteen out of nineteen representatives in the House. In sum, 88 percent of the New England delegation opposed exclusion in 1882, and 72 percent did so in 1879.

3. Joshua Paddison, *American Heathens: Religion, Race, and Reconstruction in California* (Berkeley: University of California Press, 2012), 88–92. For a contrasting view of the hearings, see Najia Aarim-Heriot, *Chinese Immigrants, African Americans, and Racial Anxiety in the United States, 1848–1882* (Urbana: University of Illinois Press, 2003), 183–85; and Andrew Gyory, *Closing the Gate: Race, Politics, and the Chinese Exclusion Act* (Chapel Hill: University of North Carolina Press, 1998), 93.

4. JS (1877), 10–11.

5. Ibid., 276–79. George made a clear distinction between the labor market and global trade. Competition in the latter was to be encouraged, while in the former protected from harmful participants like Chinese workers. George believed in Adam Smith's theory of a free global market in which all nations participate to maximize their own competitive advantages, no government regulations or controls needed.

6. Ibid., 287. For George and the Chinese issue, see Alexander Saxton, *The Indispensable Enemy: Labor and the Anti-Chinese Movement in California* (1971; repr., Berkeley: University of California Press, 1995), 92–103. An original analysis of classical economics and the Chinese question can be found in Kashia Arnold, "Alexander Del Mar: Free Trade and the Chinese Question," *Southern California Quarterly* 94, no. 3 (Fall 2012): 304–45.

7. JS (1877), 286–89.

8. Ibid., 11, 39.

9. Ibid., 38–39, 38, 45.

10. Ibid., 35.

11. Ibid., 40–41.

12. Ibid., 667–68.

13. Ibid., 670, 677–79, 686. The story of Crocker, the Central Pacific Railroad, and Chinese workers is told in Alexander Saxton, "The Army of Canton in the High Sierra," *Pacific Historical Review* 35, no. 2 (May 1966): 141–52.

14. JS (1877), 398, 404, 409.

15. Ibid., 399, 469–70, 50–51. For a fuller study of anti-Catholicism by defenders of the Chinese, see Paddison, *American Heathens*, 77–102.

16. JS (1877), 50, 66–67.

17. U.S. Congress, House, Select Committee, *The Causes of the General Depression in Labor and Business; And as to Chinese Immigration*, 46th Cong., 2nd sess., Misc. Doc. 5 (Washington: Government Printing Office, 1879), 338–50.

18. For the nationalization of the Chinese issue, see Gyory, *Closing the Gate*, 76–135. In the presidential election of 1880, the difference between the top two candidates was two percentage points or less in six states, with California being the closest race. Here are the six states with electoral votes in parentheses: California, 0.1% (6); New Jersey, 0.8% (9); Indiana, 1.4% (15); Oregon, 1.6%

(3); New York, 1.9% (35); Connecticut, 2% (6). Data compiled by author from Gerhard Peters and John T. Woolley, The American Presidency Project, http://www.presidency.ucsb.edu/showelection.php?year=1860 (September 28, 2015).

19. Gyory, *Closing the Gate*, 211–18, quote on 216.

20. Chester A. Arthur, "Veto Message," April 4, 1882, online by Gerhard Peters and John T. Woolley, The American Presidency Project, http://www.presidency.ucsb.edu/ws/?pid=68779%20-%20axzz2hY4WXW6z (September 28, 2015).

21. The 1882 law was referred to formally as "an act to revise U.S.-China treaty stipulations." In popular conversation it was known mainly as the Chinese "restriction" act because its focus on laborers fit the Angell treaty's directive preventing the wholesale exclusion of immigrants. For analysis of the distinction between "restriction" and "exclusion," see Beth Lew-Williams, "Before Restriction Became Exclusion: America's Experiment in Diplomatic Immigration Control," *Pacific Historical Review* 83, no. 1 (February 2014): 24–56; and Paul A. Kramer, "Empire against Exclusion in Early 20th Century Trans-Pacific History," *Nanzan Review of American Studies* 33 (2011): 16, 28n12. In recognizing the historical significance of classes exempt from Asian immigration restriction, I have tried to make clear throughout this book that exclusionist policies focused on the exclusion of laborers and not every migrant from a given Asian country.

22. For discussion of the data and analysis for all tables in this chapter see the Bibliographic Essay on sources for Chapter 2.

23. ICPSR, votes 303, 347, and 373, 45th Cong., House. In 1879, 40 percent of Democrats representing New England and 38 percent of Democrats representing the Mid-Atlantic opposed exclusion. This was more than twice the rate for Democrats from the eastern Midwest (11 percent), western Midwest (14 percent), and South (14 percent). For the opposition to Chinese exclusion in Iowa, see Robert R. Dykstra, *Black Radical Star: Black Freedom and White Supremacy on the Hawkeye Frontier* (Cambridge, Mass.: Harvard University Press, 1993), 263.

24. Richard Franklin Bensel, *The Political Economy of American Industrialization, 1877–1900* (Cambridge: Cambridge University Press, 2000), 19–100 (the per capita manufacturing to agriculture ratio is discussed on pp. 21–23, table 2.2).

25. The index was created from census variables regarding value-added manufacturing, patents approved, real estate wealth, mortgage interest rates, and adult male illiteracy. The index is discussed in ibid., 47–54, while tables for the most and least developed counties are on pp. 49 and 52.

26. *CR*, 47th Cong., 1st sess., 2878 (April 14, 1882).

27. *Sacramento Daily Union*, April 17, 1882.

28. *SFC*, April 22, 1882; *San Francisco Bulletin*, April 26, 1882, as reprinted in *NYT*, May 7, 1882.

29. The method for this analysis is based on access to the ProQuest Historical Newspapers database. In the "advanced search" feature, I selected these characteristics: date range between January 1, 1876, and December 31, 1882; document type = editorial. The keyword inputted was "chinese immigra*" (the asterisk wildcard enables selection of any word beginning with the letters "immigra," which enables hits on either "immigration" or "immigrant[s]"). The above search characteristics provided the universe of relevant editorials for each newspaper. In subsequent steps, each keyword listed in table 2.4 was added to the baseline "chinese immigra*" for each of the four newspapers, and the percentage of hits for each keyword combination was recorded. For the three northeast papers, the average percentage of each keyword combination was taken. The difference between East Coast and West Coast was derived by subtracting the percentage of keyword combinations in the *SFC* from the northeast average. ProQuest accessed by author on October 9, 2013.

30. The analysis in this paragraph focuses on differences between exclusionist and egalitarian discourse that since the 1850s were rooted in geography. It makes no claim that the editorial keywords reflected the views of everyone on either coast. It is possible that the keyword differences in the sampled newspapers were less a reflection of geography than of ideological and political positions on Chinese exclusion. My point is

that geography, ideology, and politics were intricately bound together; it is not that one of these was more important than the others.

31. *CR*, 47th Cong., 1st sess., 1643 (March 6, 1882).

32. Ibid.

33. Gyory, *Closing the Gate*, 142–45, 245.

34. The California thesis arose early in the twentieth century in Mary Roberts Coolidge, *Chinese Immigration* (New York: Henry Holt, 1909). Subsequent studies that built on the California thesis include Gyory, *Closing the Gate*; Tichenor, *Dividing Lines: The Politics of Immigration Control in America* (Princeton: Princeton University Press, 2002); Zolberg, *A Nation by Design: Immigration Policy in the Fashioning of America* (New York: Russell Sage, 2006); and Elmer Clarence Sandmeyer, *The Anti-Chinese Movement in California* (1939; repr., Urbana: University of Illinois Press, 1991).

35. Gyory criticizes historians for over-emphasizing the role that labor unions played in the enactment of Chinese exclusion: Gyory, *Closing the Gate*, 11–14. For criticism of Gyory and his rebuttal, see exchange between Gyory and Stanford M. Lyman in Lyman, "The 'Chinese Question' and American Labor Historians," *New Politics* 4, no. 28 (2000), http://nova.wpunj.edu/newpolitics /issue28/lyman28.htm (September 26, 2013), and Andrew Gyory, "A Reply to Stanford Lyman," *New Politics* 1, no. 29 (2000), http://nova.wpunj.edu/newpolitics/issue29 /gyory29.htm (September 26, 2015); and see also Stanford M. Lyman, "Engels Was Right! Organized Labor's Opposition to Chinese in the U.S.: Stanford M. Lyman Responds," *New Politics* 8, no. 1 (Summer 2000): 60–67. The labor approach to Chinese exclusion that Gyory criticizes is found in Saxton, *Indispensable Enemy*; Gwendolyn Mink, *Old Labor and New Immigrants in American Political Development: Union, Party, and State, 1875–1920* (Ithaca: Cornell University Press, 1986); and David Roediger, *Wages of Whiteness: Race and the Making of the American Working Class* (London: Verso, 1991). For the debate among labor historians that prefigured the Gyory-Lyman conflict, see Herbert Hill's critiques of Herbert L. Gutman's analysis of anti-racism in the United Mine Workers union: Herbert Hill, "Anti-Oriental Agitation and the Rise of Working-Class Racism," *Transaction* 10 (January/February 1973): 43–54; Herbert Hill, "Race and Ethnicity in Organized Labor: The Historical Sources of Resistance to Affirmative Action," *Journal of Intergroup Relations* 12 (Winter 1984): 5–49; and Herbert Hill, "Race, Ethnicity, and Organized Labor: The Opposition to Affirmative Action," *New Politics* 1 (Winter 1987), 31–82.

36. ICPSR and ICPSR-Cen. Quantitative analysis based on the author's merger of data from these two sources as discussed in the Bibliographic Essay on sources for this chapter.

37. The racism school of thought regarding Chinese exclusion stresses the fact that anti-Chinese sentiment had purchase throughout the nation, not just on the West Coast. Studies in this vein include Stuart Creighton Miller, *The Unwelcome Immigrant: The American Image of the Chinese, 1785–1882* (Berkeley: University of California Press, 1969); Stanford M. Lyman, *Chinese Americans* (New York: Random House, 1974); Ronald Takaki, *Iron Cages: Race and Culture in the 19th Century* (1979; repr., New York: Oxford University Press, 1990); and Erika Lee, *At America's Gates: Chinese Immigration during the Exclusion Era, 1882–1943* (Chapel Hill: University of North Carolina Press, 2003), 10, 23–30. Popular histories of Chinese immigration typically fit into this last category. See, for example, Iris Chang, *The Chinese in America: A Narrative History* (New York: Viking, 2003).

38. ICPSR and ICPSR-Cen. Quantitative analysis based on the author's merger of data from these two sources as discussed in the Bibliographic Essay on sources for this chapter.

39. ICPSR, votes 123, 298, 300, 292, 207, 341, 250, 83, 47th Cong., House (May 15, 1882; January 15, 1883; January 16, 1883; January 12, 1883; June 19, 1882; March 1, 1883; July 27, 1882; and March 23, 1882). There were fifteen roll call votes in total that exhibited a greater regional division than the twenty-year exclusion bill (vote 83). In addition to seven of these listed in Table 2.5, the others included procedural votes to adjourn and two votes regarding the construction of a new building for the Library of Congress. The regional difference for the latter ten-year

Chinese exclusion bill (vote 93) was 18 percentage points, slightly less than the twenty-year bill but still showing a divide. For the sake of brevity, Table 2.5 does not show the percent of "Yes" votes for each region. This can be calculated easily by subtracting 100 from every figure in the columns for the Republican Northeast and Republican Midwest (e.g., for the patents measure, the Republican Northeast "Yes" vote was 43 percent, Republican Midwest vote was 92 percent). The difference between the "Yes" votes is the same as that listed for the "No" votes.

40. ICPSR, votes, 207 and 292 (June 19, 1882 and January 12, 1883); revenue marine service is discussed in *NYT*, June 19, 1882; for the shipping bill, see ibid., January 13, 1883 (for text of bill and reporting on it).

41. ICPSR, votes, 341, 250, and 298 (March 1, 1883, July 27, 1882, and January 15, 1883); rivers and harbors appropriation bill vote is discussed in *Atlanta Constitution*, March 2, 1883; shipping measure in the *Baltimore Sun*, January 15, 1883; for debate on the railroad measure, see *Chicago Tribune*, July 28, 1882; the Mexican and Indian war pensions procedural vote is discussed in *Washington Post*, January 16, 1883.

42. ICPSR, votes, 123 and 300 (May 15, 1882 and January 16, 1883); *NYT*, May 16, 1882; the courts bill is discussed in ibid., January 17, 1883.

Chapter 3

1. U.S. Congress, Senate, Committee on Education and Labor, *Report of the Committee of the Senate upon the Relations between Labor and Capital and Testimony Taken by the Committee*, 48th Cong. (Washington: Government Printing Office, 1885), 281, 282.

2. Michael H. Hunt, *The Making of a Special Relationship: The United States and China to 1914* (New York: Columbia University Press, 1983), 92; Yucheng Qin, *The Diplomacy of Nationalism: The Six Companies and China's Policy toward Exclusion* (Honolulu: University of Hawai'i Press, 2009), 113.

3. Hunt, *Making of a Special Relationship*, 94. The Burlingame constituency continued to oppose the harsh features of the Geary Act: ICPSR, vote 106, 52nd Cong., House (April 4, 1892). Also see, for example, re-

marks by Republican senators John Sherman and Cushman K. Davis, as well as southern Democrat John T. Morgan, in *CR*, 52nd Cong., 1st sess., 3482–84, 3532, 3564–65 (April 21, 1892).

4. Jean Pfaelzer, *Driven Out: The Forgotten War against Chinese Americans* (Berkeley: University of California Press, 2007), 252–90.

5. For indemnity, see ICPSR, vote 203, 49th Cong., Senate (June 4, 1886); the collapse of the Burlingame constituency is revealed in ICPSR, votes 70 and 72, 57th Cong., Senate (April 16, 1902). Analysis of the Rock Springs Riot and indemnity is discussed in Shih-shan Henry Tsai, *China and the Overseas Chinese in the United States* (Fayetteville: University of Arkansas Press, 1983), 72–78.

6. In 1893 the U.S. Supreme Court upheld the Geary Act registration requirements. For a full account of the boycott, the court case, and Cleveland's actions, see Pfaelzer, *Driven Out*, 291–335; and Gwendolyn Mink, *Old Labor and New Immigrants in American Political Development: Union, Party, and State, 1875–1920* (Ithaca: Cornell University Press, 1986), 130.

7. ICPSR, vote 274, 48th Cong., Senate (July 3, 1884); also see ICPSR, vote 93, 48th Cong., House (May 3, 1884).

8. Erika Lee, *At America's Gates: Chinese Immigration during the Exclusion Era, 1882–1943* (Chapel Hill: University of North Carolina Press, 2003), 138.

9. For the legal history involving Chinese immigrants, including the *Yick Wo* case, see Charles J. McClain, *In Search of Equality: The Chinese Struggle against Discrimination in Nineteenth-Century America* (Berkeley: University of California Press, 1994), 115–26.

10. As quoted in Mink, *Old Labor and New Immigrants*, 109.

11. Gompers quote in "A News Account of an Address in Lowell [Mass.]," February 9, 1898, in GOMP docs., vol. 4, 434.

12. On Powderly, see Mink, *Old Labor and New Immigrants*, 63; as well as Joseph Gerteis, *Class and the Color Line: Interracial Class Coalition in the Knights of Labor and the Populist Movement* (Durham: Duke University Press, 2007), 62–66.

13. Mink, *Old Labor and New Immigrants*, 17. For the concept of the split labor market,

see Edna Bonacich, "A Theory of Ethnic Antagonism: The Split Labor Market," *American Sociological Review* 37 (1972): 547–59.

14. Barbara Miller Solomon, *Ancestors and Immigrants* (Chicago: University of Chicago Press, 1956), 118.

15. ICPSR, votes 148 and 172, 54th Cong., House (February 8 and March 3, 1897). The first vote, to pass literacy test legislation, received 100 percent approval by the New England contingent, while the second vote, to override the president's veto, won 90 percent. For analysis of congressional voting on the literacy test, see Claudia Goldin, "The Political Economy of Immigration Restriction in the United States, 1890–1921," in *The Regulated Economy: A Historical Approach to Political Economy*, ed. Claudia Goldin and Gary D. Libecap (Chicago: University of Chicago Press, 1994), 225–37.

16. William C. Widenor, *Henry Cabot Lodge and the Search for an American Foreign Policy* (Berkeley: University of California Press, 1980), 47.

17. See Solomon, *Ancestors and Immigrants*, 69–77. For a critical view of Walker's views of Native Americans as head of the Bureau of Indian Affairs, see Ronald Takaki, *Iron Cages: Race and Culture in the 19th Century* (1979; repr., New York: Oxford University Press, 1990), 181–88.

18. Aristide R. Zolberg, *A Nation by Design: Immigration Policy in the Fashioning of America* (New York: Russell Sage, 2006), 208.

19. Solomon, *Ancestors and Immigrants*, 79.

20. Henry Cabot Lodge, "The Anglo-Saxon Land-Law" (Ph.D. diss., Harvard University, 1876).

21. Widenor, *Henry Cabot Lodge*, 60–61.

22. Joshua Paddison, *American Heathens: Religion, Race, and Reconstruction in California* (Berkeley: University of California Press, 2012), 177–80.

23. Josiah Strong, *Our Country: Its Possible Future and Its Present Crisis* (1885; rev. ed., New York: American Home Missionary Society, 1891), 54; Dong-Bai Chai, "Josiah Strong: Apostle of Anglo-Saxonism and Social Christianity" (Ph.D. diss., University of Texas–Austin, 1972), 53.

24. Peggy Pascoe, *Relations of Rescue: The Search for Female Moral Authority in the American West, 1874–1939* (New York: Oxford University Press, 1990), 115–18.

25. Another new element emerging at this time was the new immigrants themselves, who would come to influence the immigration debate as voters and radicals. For the movement against them and their response, see, for example, John Higham, *Strangers in the Land: Patterns of American Nativism, 1860–1925* (1955; repr., New Brunswick, N.J.: Rutgers University Press, 1992); Thomas J. Archdeacon, *Becoming Americans: An Ethnic History* (New York: Free Press, 1983); and Desmond King, *Making Americans: Immigration, Race, and the Origins of Diverse Democracy* (Cambridge, Mass.: Harvard University Press, 2000).

26. For the "imperial problem" confronting the United States at this time, see Lanny Thompson, *Imperial Archipelago* (Honolulu: University of Hawai'i Press, 2010).

27. Eric T. Love, *Race over Empire: Racism and U.S. Imperialism* (Chapel Hill: University of North Carolina Press, 2004), 77–78. Also see David M. Pletcher, *Diplomacy of Involvement: American Economic Expansion across the Pacific, 1784–1900* (Columbia: University of Missouri Press, 2001), 60–65.

28. Christen Tsuyuko Sasaki, "Pacific Confluence: Negotiating the Nation in Nineteenth Century Hawai'i" (Ph.D. diss., UCLA, 2011), 56–65.

29. Michael H. Hunt and Steven I. Levine, *Arc of Empire: America's Wars in Asia from the Philippines to Vietnam* (Chapel Hill: University of North Carolina Press, 2012), 10; also see Pletcher, *Diplomacy of Involvement*, 258–87.

30. Walter LaFeber, *The New Empire: An Interpretation of American Expansion, 1860–1898* (1963; repr., Ithaca: Cornell University Press, 1998), 408.

31. For Roosevelt, see Gary Gerstle, *American Crucible: Race and Nation in the Twentieth Century* (Princeton: Princeton University Press, 2001), 14–80; and Gail Bederman, *Manliness and Civilization: A Cultural History of Gender and Race in the United States, 1880–1917* (Chicago: University of Chicago Press, 1996), 170–216.

32. *NYT*, January 30, 1893. "Sandwich Islands" is an earlier name for Hawai'i.

33. Robert Seaver II, *Alfred Thayer Mahan* (Annapolis: Naval Institute Press, 1977), 358.

34. Lawrence H. Fuchs, *Hawaii Pono: A Social History* (New York: Harcourt, Brace and World, 1961), 45; *SFC*, November 4, 1901.

35. Paul A. Kramer, *The Blood of Government* (Chapel Hill: University of North Carolina Press, 2006), 5–7. See also Kimberly A. Alidio, "Between Civilizing Mission and Ethnic Assimilation" (Ph.D. diss., University of Michigan, 2001).

36. Rick Baldoz, *The Third Asiatic Invasion* (New York: New York University Press, 2011), 46.

37. Quoted in Alidio, "Between Civilizing Mission and Ethnic Assimilation," 97.

38. Kramer, *Blood of Government*, 205. For Filipinos at the St. Louis fair, see ibid., 229–84; and Robert W. Rydell, *All the World's a Fair* (Chicago: University of Chicago Press, 1984), 154–83.

39. Veta R. Schlimgen, "Neither Citizens nor Aliens: Filipino 'American Nationals' in the U.S. Empire, 1900–1946" (Ph.D. diss., University of Oregon, 2010), 49–50, 64.

40. Carlos Figueroa, "Pragmatic Quakerism in U.S. Imperialism" (Ph.D. diss., New School for Social Research, 2010), 69.

41. Chai, "Josiah Strong, 271.

42. Figueroa, "Pragmatic Quakerism," 100.

43. Lucy Maddox, *Citizen Indians: Native American Intellectuals, Race, and Reform* (Ithaca: Cornell University Press, 2005), 79–84. For an insightful historical and political biography of Abbott, see Ira V. Brown, *Lyman Abbott: Christian Evolutionist* (Cambridge, Mass.: Harvard University Press, 1953).

44. GOMP docs., vol. 4, 488.

45. Ibid., vol. 5, 10–11.

46. Hunt, *Making of a Special Relationship*, 178.

47. Delber L. McKee, *Chinese Exclusion versus the Open Door Policy, 1900–1906* (Detroit: Wayne State University Press, 1977), 28–36; Lee, *At America's Gates*, 47–74; and Hunt, *Making of a Special Relationship*, 228–29.

48. Hunt, *Making of a Special Relationship*, 232. For Foord and his organization, see James J. Lorence, *Organized Business and the Myth of the China Market: The Ameri-*can Asiatic Association, 1898–1937 (Philadelphia: American Philosophical Society, 1981). The broader history of the Open Door also is addressed in Thomas J. McCormick, *China Market: America's Quest for Informal Empire, 1893–1901* (1967; repr., Chicago: Ivan R. Dee, 1990); and Marilyn Young, *The Rhetoric of Empire: American China Policy, 1895–1901* (Cambridge, Mass: Harvard University Press, 1969).

49. Pletcher, *Diplomacy of Involvement*, 58–59.

50. Floyd William Matson, "The Anti-Japanese Movement in California, 1890–1942" (Ph.D. diss., University of California, Berkeley, 1953), 2–8; also see, Roger Daniels, *The Politics of Prejudice* (1962; repr., New York: Atheneum, 1968), 21–22. The restriction of Japanese laborers is addressed in Raymond Leslie Buell, "The Development of the Anti-Japanese Agitation in the United States I," *Political Science Quarterly* 37, no. 4 (December 1922): 609; and early anti-Japanese animosity in California is also discussed in Eiichiro Azuma, *Between Two Empires: Race, History, and Transnationalism in Japanese America* (New York: Oxford University Press, 2005), 36–40.

51. *FR*, January 1, 1901. Rowell's remarks about the Japanese resonated with W. E. B. Du Bois's famous observation, made two years later, about the importance of the color line for the twentieth century. See Du Bois, *The Souls of Black Folk* (Chicago: A. C. McClurg, 1903).

52. *FR*, September 26, 1900.

53. ICPSR, vote 40, 53rd Cong., Senate (January 30, 1895); for revision of the unequal Anglo-Japanese commercial treaty, from which the U.S.-Japan treaty was based, see Louis G. Perez, *Japan Comes of Age: Mutsu Munemitsu and the Revision of the Unequal Treaties* (Cranbury, N.J.: Associated University Presses, 1999); reference to U.S. revision, ibid., 171.

54. GOMP docs., vol. 4, 52–53; George Gunton to Fusataro Takano, July 7, 1896, accessed on Professor Kazuo Nimura's website, http://oohara.mt.tama.hosei.ac.jp/nk/English/ggtoft070796.html (October 4, 2014).

55. GOMP docs., vol. 5, 436–37.

56. Jordan actually had great respect for the young social scientist and tried his best

to retain him. The Ross affair is detailed in Orrin L. Elliott, *Stanford University: The First Twenty-Five Years* (Stanford: Stanford University Press, 1937), 326–78.

57. Edward McNall Burns, *David Starr Jordan: Prophet of Freedom* (Stanford: Stanford University Press, 1953), 64; David Starr Jordan, *The Days of a Man, Volume Two, 1900–1921* (Yonkers-on-Hudson, N.Y.: World Book Company, 1922), 5, 4.

58. Jordan, *Days of a Man*, 10–11; Jordan, "Japan and World Relations," Women's International League for Peace and Freedom Publications, Fourth International Congress, Washington, D.C., 1924, box 46, folder 42, SU-DSJ1.

59. Jordan, *Days of a Man*, 402; David Starr Jordan, "Relations of Japan and the United States," *Journal of Race Development* 2, no. 3 (January 1912): 219–20; David Starr Jordan, "American Graduates in Japan," n.d., box 42, folder 12, SU-DSJ1; Jordan, *Days of a Man*, 447.

60. Alexandra Minna Stern, *Eugenic Nation: Faults and Frontiers of Better Breeding in Modern America* (Berkeley: University of California Press, 2005), 22. While Stern captures Jordan's overall nativism (p. 133), she ignores the pronounced egalitarianism he displayed toward the Japanese.

61. The role of eugenics in shaping U.S. immigration policy and notions of race is studied in King, *Making Americans*, 65–73, 166–98; Higham, *Strangers in the Land*, 149–57; and Thomas F. Gossett, *Race: The History of an Idea* (1963; repr., New York: Oxford University Press, 1997), 157–74. For the history of eugenics in California, see Stern, *Eugenic Nation*.

62. Spencer's view appeared in *NYT*, January 31, 1904; Burns, *David Starr Jordan*, 61–62, 66–68; quote is from Jordan, *Days of a Man*, 400.

63. David Starr Jordan, *The Human Harvest: A Study of the Decay of Races through the Survival of the Unfit* (Boston: Beacon Press, 1907), foreword; Burns, *David Starr Jordan*, 61–62, 76.

Chapter 4

1. Theodore Roosevelt, "Sixth Annual Message," December 3, 1906, in *Papers Relating to the Foreign Relations of the United*

States, 59th Cong., 2nd sess., 1909, H. doc. 1, xl.

2. Ibid., xli–xliii.

3. Theodore Roosevelt, "First Annual Message," December 3, 1901, online by Gerhard Peters and John T. Woolley, The American Presidency Project, http://www.presidency.ucsb.edu/ws/?pid=29542 (September 30, 2015).

4. Delber L. McKee, *Chinese Exclusion versus the Open Door Policy, 1900–1906* (Detroit: Wayne State University Press, 1977), 66–102; Michael H. Hunt, *The Making of a Special Relationship: The United States and China to 1914* (New York: Columbia University Press, 1983), 233–34.

5. McKee, *Chinese Exclusion*, 103–45. Also see Hunt, *Making of a Special Relationship*, 241–42; Guanhua Wang, *In Search of Justice: The 1905–1906 Chinese Anti-American Boycott* (Cambridge, Mass.: Harvard University Press, 2001), 2.

6. Hunt, *Making of a Special Relationship*, 244–45.

7. Tyler Dennett, *Roosevelt and the Russo-Japanese War* (1925; repr., Gloucester, Mass.: Peter Smith, 1959), 2; Eleanor Tupper and George E. McReynolds, *Japan in American Public Opinion* (New York: Macmillan, 1937), 6; Ira V. Brown, *Lyman Abbott: Christian Evolutionist* (Cambridge, Mass.: Harvard University Press, 1953), 185.

8. Thomas G. Dyer, *Theodore Roosevelt and the Idea of Race* (Baton Rouge: Louisiana State University Press, 1992), 136; "grew so excited," as quoted in Walter LaFeber, *The Clash: U.S.-Japanese Relations throughout History* (New York: Norton, 1997), 82.

9. "Aryan races," as quoted in Dyer, *Theodore Roosevelt and the Idea of Race*, 135–39; Spencer's view is detailed in *NYT*, January 31, 1904, 4.

10. A. T. Mahan, *The Problem of Asia: And Its Effects on International Policies* (Boston: Little, Brown, 1905), 147–50, quote on 150. For Japan as "honorary white," also see Robert Seaver II, *Alfred Thayer Mahan* (Annapolis: Naval Institute Press, 1977), 464–65.

11. Mahan, *Problem of Asia*, 108–9.

12. Seaver, *Alfred Thayer Mahan*, 476.

13. Tupper and McReynolds, *Japan in American Public Opinion*, 17. The authors say the shift from Japanophile to Japanophobia

in the United States was not as sudden as it has been portrayed. For a thorough analysis of the yellow peril concept in the United States, see Richard Austin Thompson, *The Yellow Peril, 1890–1924* (1957; repr., New York: Arno Press, 1978). A recent study of the intellectual and scientific bases of the yellow peril idea is contained in Michael Keevak, *Becoming Yellow: A Short History of Racial Thinking* (Princeton: Princeton University Press, 2011). Other studies include William F. Wu, *Yellow Peril: Chinese Americans in American Fiction, 1850–1940* (Hamden, Conn.: Archon, 1982); and Jack Kuo Wei Tchen and Dylan Yates, *Yellow Peril! An Archive of Anti-Asian Fear* (London: Verson, 2014).

14. Jack London, "The Yellow Peril" (1904), in *Revolution and Other Essays* (New York: Macmillan, 1910).

15. Sidney Lewis Gulick, *White Peril in the Far East* (London: Fleming H. Revell, 1905), 168.

16. Ibid.,168, 173–74 (my emphasis).

17. See Roger Daniels, *The Politics of Prejudice* (1962; repr., New York: Atheneum, 1968).

18. Thomas Andrew Bailey, *Theodore Roosevelt and the Japanese-American Crisis: An Account of the International Complications Arising from the Race Problems on the Pacific Coast* (Stanford: Stanford University Press, 1934), 12–15, 19. On Tveitmoe, see Michael Kazin, *Barons of Labor: The San Francisco Building Trades and Union Power in the Progressive Era* (Urbana: University of Illinois Press, 1988), 72–73.

19. Bailey, *Theodore Roosevelt and the Japanese-American Crisis*, 113–15, 83, 93.

20. Ibid., 113–16, 123–49.

21. Phillip S. Foner, *History of the Labor Movement in the United States*, vol. 5, *The AFL in the Progressive Era, 1910–1915* (New York: International Publishers, 1980), 27.

22. Phelan quote is from Floyd William Matson, "The Anti-Japanese Movement in California, 1890–1942" (Ph.D. diss., University of California, Berkeley, 1953), 8. The rest of the paragraph is based on Daniels, *Politics of Prejudice*, 21; and Kevin Starr, *California and the American Dream* (New York: Oxford, 1986), 249–53.

23. *FR*, May 30, 1910. Also see Lon Kurashige, "Transpacific Accommodation and the Defense of Japanese Immigrants," *Pacific Historical Review* 83, no. 2 (May 2014): 305–8.

24. *FR*, September 20, 1904; May 31, 1905.

25. David Starr Jordan, *The Human Harvest: A Study of the Decay of Races through the Survival of the Unfit* (Boston: Beacon Press, 1907), foreword; see also Edward McNall Burns, *David Starr Jordan: Prophet of Freedom* (Stanford: Stanford University Press, 1953), 61–62, 76; quote in David Starr Jordan, *The Days of a Man, Volume Two, 1900–1921* (Yonkers-on-Hudson, N.Y.: World Book Company, 1922), 450.

26. For the early history of the Japan Society of New York, see Michael R. Auslin, *Japan Society: Celebrating a Century, 1907–2007* (New York: Japan Society, 2007), 9–15.

27. The Carnegie quote is in *NYT*, December 3, 1907, 3; for Carnegie's peace activities see, for example, David Nasaw, *Andrew Carnegie* (New York: Penguin Press, 2006); and Andrew Carnegie, *Autobiography of Andrew Carnegie* (Boston: Houghton Mifflin, 1920).

28. The records for the U.S.-Japan exchange can be found in Japan Education Exchange, 1911–1913, box 488, folder 2, series III.B, CU-CEIP.

29. For McClatchy's role in flood control, see Robert Kelley, *Battling the Inland Sea* (Berkeley: University of California Press, 1989), 302–3. While Kelley provides the larger context of delta flood control issues, the particular concerns about the Japanese are addressed in Michael Meloy, "The Long Road to Manzanar: Politics, Land, and Race in the Japanese Exclusion Movement, 1900–1942" (Ph.D. diss., University of California, Davis, 2004), 105–48. For comparison to a nearby region, see Cecilia Tsu, *Garden of World: Asian Immigrants and the Making of Agriculture in California's Santa Clara Valley* (New York: Oxford University Press, 2013).

30. Daniels, *Politics of Prejudice*, 46–64; see also Spencer Olin Jr., "European Immigrant and Oriental Alien: Acceptance and Rejection by the California Legislature of 1913," *Pacific Historical Review* 35, no. 3 (August 1966): 303–15. For the legislative story of California's Alien Land Law, see Franklin Hichborn, *Story of the Session of the California Legislature of 1913* (San Francisco: James H. Barry, 1913), 213–75.

31. Hichborn, *California Legislature*, 230.

32. *FR*, March 4, 1913. Rowell supported the land law because it represented a unanimous view of Californians and not just the sandlot demagogues that the East Coast saw as behind western anti-Asian movements. Rowell also said the law allowed Hiram Johnson to score points against Wilson and the national Democrats while gaining Democratic and Republican support in California. Rowell defended the act by saying it was fair because Japan had the same type of law.

33. Aside from his academic prestige, Butler was a leading internationalist who had directed the Lake Mohonk conference on international arbitration.

34. Loomis to Butler, November 3, 1913, in Japan Education Exchange, folder 6, CU-CEIP. In his reply, Butler stated, "The Carnegie Endowment is very much embarrassed in participating in this work for the reason that any expenditure of funds bearing Mr. Carnegie's name would be seized upon by the demagogues in California as turned into a movement to oppress American labor by opening the door to the free importation of the cheap labor of the Orient! This at all events is what would be said, absurd and silly though it may be." Butler to Hamilton Holt, December 30, 1913, Correspondence on U.S.-Japan Relations, 1911–1921 (microfilm), vol. 159, document 363, CU-CEIP.

35. Both Loomis and Guy address the importance of a research survey in their respective reports to the Carnegie Endowment and Japanese Ministry of Foreign Affairs. Loomis's views are expressed in Loomis to Butler, November 12, 1913, in Correspondence on U.S.-Japan Relations, CU-CEIP. For Guy, see his letter to Yasutaro Numano (San Francisco consul general), September 18, 1913, in Miscellaneous Files on the Anti-Japanese Issue in the United States, 1919–1925, vol. 5 (3.8.2.288), J-DRO; see also "Guy reports on Loomis" as a friend of Japan who has bought an interest in the *Oakland Tribune*, Guy Report, February 15, 1915, in From the Consulate in San Francisco, vol. 2 (3.8.2.290–1), J-DRO.

36. Loomis to Butler, November 12, 1913, in Correspondence on U.S.-Japan Relations, CU-CEIP.

37. Charles S. Macfarland, *Christian Unity in the Making: The First Twenty-Five Years of the Federal Council of Churches of Christ in America, 1905–1930* (New York: Federal Council of Churches of Christ in America, 1948), 89.

38. Sidney Lewis Gulick, *The American Japanese Problem* (New York: Scribner's, 1914). For analysis of this book and Gulick's immigration plan, see Sandra C. Taylor, *Advocate of Understanding: Sidney Gulick and the Search for Peace with Japan* (Kent: Kent State University Press, 1984), 80–89.

39. Gulick to K. Matsui (Vice Minister of Foreign Affairs), February 2 and February 5, 1915, in Regarding the Pro-Japanese Education Movement Intended for Americans, vol. 4A (3.8.2.287), J-DRO. For analysis of this episode, see Yuji Ichioka, *The Issei: The World of the First Generation Japanese Immigrants, 1885–1924* (New York: Free Press, 1988), 128–45. Ichioka notes that Scharrenberg may have come up with the idea of receiving a Japanese labor delegate (129).

40. Guy Report, July 31, 1915, 266, in From the Consulate in San Francisco, vol. 2 (3.8.2.290–1), J-DRO; also see Guy Report, April 19, 1915, ibid., for Gulick's successful meeting with Scharrenberg.

41. See Ichioka, *Issei*, 103, for the persecution of Socialists and other radical labor leaders in Japan in the early twentieth century.

42. Guy Report, November 15, 1915, in Report of Activities by the Department of the Education Movement (3.8.2.287-3), J-DRO; Guy Report, January 15, 1916, 2–5, ibid; Guy Report, March 6, 1916, 3–4, ibid.

43. Guy Report, March 27, 1917, appendices; Guy Report, May 29, 1916, 2–5, 7–8; Guy Report, August 3, 1916, 3–4; Guy Report, December 13, 1917, 1–3, 18, all in ibid.

44. The racial context during World War I is addressed in Gary Gerstle, *American Crucible: Race and Nation in the Twentieth Century* (Princeton: Princeton University Press, 2001), 81–95.

45. Desmond King, *Making Americans: Immigration, Race, and the Origins of Diverse Democracy* (Cambridge, Mass.: Harvard University Press, 2000), 76. By this time southerners in Congress supported the literacy test and overall immigration restriction: Claudia Goldin, "The Political Economy of Immigration Restriction in the United

States, 1890–1921," in *The Regulated Economy: A Historical Approach to Political Economy*, ed. Claudia Goldin and Gary D. Libecap (Chicago: University of Chicago Press, 1994), 231–37.

46. U.S. Congress, House, Immigration and Naturalization Committee, *Hindu Immigration*, pts. 1–5, 63rd Cong., 2nd sess. (Washington: Government Printing Office, 1914), 44, 76–79.

47. Ibid., 28, 36.

48. Ibid., 82, 167, 171.

49. Ibid., for Patterson, 24–29; for Bose, 7–8, 11, 20; for Bhutia, 161–62.

50. *CR*, 54th Cong., 2nd sess., 152–62, 205–26 (December 11, 1916).

51. William C. Widenor, *Henry Cabot Lodge and the Search for an American Foreign Policy* (Berkeley: University of California Press, 1980), 152–54.

52. Ibid., 253–54, 266, 272, 298; quotation is on 176.

Chapter 5

1. James D. Phelan, "Letter to a Japanese Gentleman," *North American Review* 219, no. 823 (June 1924): 814–22.

2. Quoted in Roger Daniels, *The Politics of Prejudice* (1962; repr., New York: Atheneum, 1968), 104.

3. Lodge quote in Daniel J. Tichenor, *Dividing Lines: The Politics of Immigration Control in America* (Princeton: Princeton University Press, 2002), 143.

4. For the issue of racial equality at the Paris Peace Conference, see Naoko Shimazu, *Japan, Race and Equality: Racial Equality Proposal of 1919* (London: Routledge, 1998); Paul Gordon Lauren, *Power and Prejudice: The Politics and Diplomacy of Racial Discrimination*, 2nd ed. (Boulder: Westview Press, 1996), 82–107; and Marilyn Lake and Henry Reynolds, *Drawing the Global Colour Line: White Men's Countries and the International Challenge of Racial Equality* (New York: Cambridge University Press, 2008), 284–309.

5. Thomas J. Archdeacon, *Becoming Americans: An Ethnic History* (New York: Free Press, 1983), 171–72. For the migration of peoples from the South during this time, see James N. Gregory, *Southern Diaspora: How the Great Migrations of Black and White Southerners*

Transformed America (Chapel Hill: University of North Carolina Press, 2005).

6. Gulick advocated issei naturalization in congratulations to President Wilson for supporting women's suffrage: Gulick to Wilson, June 18, 1918, box 18, Gulick Family Papers, 1916–1923, Houghton Library, Harvard University, Cambridge, Mass. Also see Sandra C. Taylor, *Advocate of Understanding: Sidney Gulick and the Search for Peace with Japan* (Kent: Kent State University Press, 1984), 123.

7. On Shandong, see Eleanor Tupper and George E. McReynolds, *Japan in American Public Opinion* (New York: Macmillan, 1937), 145–50; for discussion of the *Sacramento Bee*'s renewed push for Japanese exclusion in the postwar period, see Michael Meloy, "The Long Road to Manzanar: Politics, Land, and Race in the Japanese Exclusion Movement, 1900–1942" (Ph.D. diss., University of California, Davis, 2004), 149–54.

8. V. S. McClatchy, *The Germany of Asia* (Sacramento: V. S. McClatchy, 1919), 23–26. This publication collects McClatchy's editorials published in the *Sacramento Bee* from January 1918 to July 1919.

9. Motivation for McClatchy's fear of Japan is also discussed in Meloy, "Long Road to Manzanar," 157–58.

10. McClatchy, *Germany of Asia*, 4–5, 24–28. For the actual Japanese proportion of Hawai'i's population in 1920, see Eileen H. Tamura, *Americanization, Acculturation, and Ethnic Identity: The Nisei Generation in Hawaii* (Urbana: University of Illinois Press, 1994), 58.

11. Meloy, "Long Road to Manzanar," 153–54.

12. Siegel's position, revealed in his questioning of K. Kanzaki (secretary of the Japanese Association of America), was that issei faced an impossible situation in which they were not given a chance to become American and yet were criticized for not assimilating: IN-H (1921), 674; R. W. Ryder Report, 9–10, as part of T. Ohta (San Francisco Consul General) to Baron Y. Uchida (Foreign Minister), October 16, 1920, in Miscellaneous Files on the Anti-Japanese Issue in the United States, 1919–1925, vol. 1 (3.8.2.288), J-DRO; Raker's statement in *LAT*, August 9, 1920.

13. All quotes are in Ryder Report, 12–14, J-DRO; also see *SFC*, August 4, 1920.

14. IN-H (1921), 339–40.

15. Jiro Okabe to Irish, September 17, 1896, BRO; John P. Irish, "Shall Japanese-Americans in Idaho Be Treated with Fairness and Justice or Not?" [printed address], January 23, 1921, 7–8, in ibid. For Irish's testimony regarding assimilation at the hearings, see IN-H (1921), 48–49.

16. IN-H (1921), 1214–26, quote on 1215.

17. Ibid., 1214–26 (quotes on 1215 and 1221).

18. Ibid., 1222, 1224.

19. Lebo in ibid., 1274; Woodruff in ibid., 496; Hinman in ibid., 541.

20. Ibid., 1075–76.

21. This paragraph is based on Irish's unpublished document, written circa 1912, in which he argues for Chinese and Japanese labor in California, 5–8, BRO. See also John P. Irish, "Races in the Delta," *Pacific Rural Press*, June 14, 1913, 660; and Irish, "Fruit Growers Open War on Exclusion Law," *San Francisco Call*, December 5, 1907. Irish's views of race are analyzed in Kurashige, "Transpacific Accommodation and the Defense of Asian Immigrants," *Pacific Historical Review* 83, no. 2 (May 2014): 296–301.

22. For the Industrial Workers of the World, see Melvyn Dubofsky, *We Shall Be All: A History of the Industrial Workers of the World* (Urbana: University of Illinois Press, 1969).

23. Ault in IN-H (1921), 1413–38; Myran in ibid., 376, 379; MacManus in ibid., 754. For the American Legion's role in the exclusion debate, also see ibid., 361; and Raymond Leslie Buell, "The Development of Anti-Japanese Agitation in the United States II," *Political Science Quarterly* 38, no. 1 (March 1923): 71.

24. Yuji Ichioka, "Japanese Response to the 1920 California Alien Land Law," *Agricultural History* 58, no. 2 (April 1984): 163. The California Supreme Court, in upholding the guardianship rights of Hayao Yano in 1922, threw out the third feature, making it possible for Japanese immigrants to control agricultural land through their minor children. For the *Yano* decision, see ibid., 166. Other studies of the 1920 alien land law

include Masao Suzuki, "Important or Impotent? Taking Another Look at the 1920 California Alien Land Law," *Journal of Economic History* 64, no. 1 (March 2004): 125–43; Brian J. Gaines and Wendy K. Tam Cho, "On California's 1920 Alien Land Law: The Psychology and Economics of Racial Discrimination," *State Politics and Policy Quarterly* 4, no. 3 (Fall 2004): 271–93; and Robert Higgs, "Landless by Law: Japanese Immigrants in California Agriculture to 1941," *Journal of Economic History* 38, no. 1 (March 1978): 205–25.

25. This was a very different result from the California referendum held on Chinese immigration in 1879, in which less than 1 percent of voters opposed exclusion: Andrew Gyory, *Closing the Gate: Race, Politics, and the Chinese Exclusion Act* (Chapel Hill: University of North Carolina Press, 1998), 174, 300–301n10.

26. Shima to Jordan, November 8, 1920, SU-DSJ1. Shima's letter was most likely composed for him by the bilingual writer and paid consultant for the Japanese consulate Karl K. Kawakami.

27. The analysis broke the fifty-eight California counties into two equally numbered groups, those most supportive of Proposition 1 and those most opposed. The first group showed the most significant correlation between a yes vote and nonwhite farm ownership (.516) and a slightly less strong but still significant correlation for degree of white males (-.394) and degree of nonwhite farm tenancy (.376). The second group showed no significant correlations, suggesting that neither nonwhite farm ownership or tenancy nor the percentage of white males had much of an impact on Proposition 1 voting. Data obtained from California Secretary of State, *Statement of the Vote: General Election Held on November 2, 1920* (Sacramento: State of California, 1920).

28. The Northern California story is covered in Daniels, *Politics of Prejudice*, and in Meloy, "Long Road to Manzanar." For a study of Southern California, see John Modell, *The Politics and Economics of Racial Accommodation: The Japanese of Los Angeles* (Urbana: University of Illinois Press, 1977), 32–46.

29. LA-Vote.

30. The issei, as ineligible aliens, could not cast votes in the election, while given that the average nisei (second generation) was born in 1920, only a small number of them could vote at this time.

31. Relevant studies of Los Angeles in the early twentieth century include Becky M. Nicolaides, *My Blue Heaven: Life and Politics in the Working-Class Suburbs of Los Angeles, 1920–1965* (Chicago: University of Chicago Press, 2002); Douglas Flamming, *Bound for Freedom: Black Los Angeles in Jim Crow America* (Berkeley: University of California Press, 2006); Scott Kurashige, *The Shifting Grounds of Race: Black and Japanese Americans in the Making of Multiethnic Los Angeles* (Princeton: Princeton University Press, 2010); George J. Sanchez, *Becoming Mexican American: Ethnicity, Culture, and Identity in Chicano Los Angeles, 1900–1945* (New York: Oxford University Press, 1993); Charlotte Brooks, *Alien Neighbors, Foreign Friends: Asian Americans, Housing, and the Transformation of Urban California* (Chicago: University of Chicago Press, 2009); and Robert M. Fogelson, *The Fragmented Metropolis: Los Angeles, 1850–1930* (1967; repr., Berkeley: University of California Press, 1993).

32. Kurashige, *Shifting Grounds of Race*, 44–45; Brooks, *Alien Neighbors*, 47–56; Nicolaides, *My Blue Heaven*, 27.

33. The campaign within the black community is discussed in three reports to the Los Angeles Japanese consulate submitted by McKinney on October 9, 1920, by J. B. Bass on October 30, 1920, and after the election by "NDT" on November 5, 1920, in Measures and Agitation against the Enactment of the 1920 California Land Law, vol. 2, part 3 (3.8.2.339-1-7), J-DRO. Opposition to Proposition 1 in the black press appeared in the *California Eagle*, October 15, 1920; *Citizen's Advocate*, October 16, 1920; and *New Age*, October 15, 1920.

34. Grodjia Report, October 15, 1920, in Measures and Agitation against the Enactment of the 1920 California Land Law, vol. 2, part 3 (3.8.2.339-1-7), J-DRO. For more on radical labor unions, see Grodjia Reports for 7, 14, and 27, in ibid. For propaganda activities among white churches, women's clubs, and Jewish organizations, see Kiyo Sue Inui to Ujiro Oyama (Los Angeles Consul-General), November 5, 1920, in ibid.

35. U.S. Census Bureau, Free Schedules, 1920. Schedules, known as the "manuscript census," accessed via Ancestry.com on various dates from March 2012 to January 2013.

36. LA-Vote: Precincts 123, 43, 48, 536, 566, 582, 599, 605, and 679 were those with the weakest opposition to the land law. Precincts 69, 73, 76, 77, 78, 496, 92, 94, 98, 594, 401, 405, 490, 414, and 423 were the ones with the strongest opposition to the land law. The latter were oversampled (15 precincts rather than 9) because most of them were largely African American, and the purpose was to determine representative occupations of white males. California women got the vote in 1911, but this chart looks at white male heads of household reported on the 1920 census as a means of determining occupational status.

37. The bastion of support for both the Socialists and Democrats was east and north of downtown. For a study of radicalism in one of these areas, see George Sanchez, "'What's Good for Boyle Heights Is Good for the Jews': Creating Multiracialism on the Eastside during the 1950s," *American Quarterly* 56, no. 3 (September 2004): 633–61.

38. McClatchy's activities to advance the exclusion cause are detailed in his correspondence with Phelan and Senator Hiram Johnson; see UC-HJ and UC-JP1. For analysis, see Buell, "Development of the Anti-Japanese Agitation in the United States," 68–73; and Daniels, *Politics of Prejudice*, 91.

39. U.S. Department of State, *Report of the Honorable Roland S. Morris* (New York: Arno Press, 1978). McClatchy's attempt to convert egalitarians is detailed in McClatchy to Senator W. H. King, May 24, 1922, and McClatchy to Hiram Johnson, June 12, 1922, part 3, box 57, UC-HJ; and McClatchy to Phelan, December 19, 1922, UC-JP1. McClatchy's attempts to convert prominent egalitarians were unsuccessful.

40. Lothrop Stoddard, *The Rising Tide of Color: Against White World-Supremacy* (New York: Charles Scribner's, 1920).

41. The *Ozawa* and *Thind* decisions are addressed in Ian F. Haney Lopez, *White by*

Law: The Legal Construction of Race (New York: NYU Press, 1996), 79–110; also see Mae M. Ngai, "The Architecture of Race in American Immigration Law: A Reexamination of the Immigration Act of 1924," *Journal of American History* 86, no. 1 (June 1999): 81–88. The term "tribal twenties" is from John Higham, *Strangers in the Land: Patterns of American Nativism, 1860–1925* (1955; repr., New Brunswick, N.J.: Rutgers University Press, 1992), 264.

42. U.S. Congress, Senate, Immigration Committee, *Japanese Immigration Legislation*, 68th Cong., 1st sess. (Washington: Government Printing Office, 1924), 51.

43. Ibid., 11–13, 21, 26.

44. Ibid., 60, 62, 70.

45. For Colt's comments, see Shortridge in ibid., 154–55, 157, 163; McClatchy in ibid., 31.

46. Gulick to Shibusawa, March 25, 1924, in SHIB docs., 160–61.

47. Phelan to unidentified (mostly likely Hiram Johnson), April 19, 1924, carton 29, folder 29, UC-JP1. While this letter has no apparent author, the fact that it was written while aboard the SS *Majestic* is consistent with Phelan's whereabouts at that time. It was written to someone who had intimate information of the Japanese Exclusion League's lobbying efforts on Capitol Hill, and since all the lobbyists are named in the letter (McClatchy and Webb), it stands to reason that Hiram Johnson is the likely intended recipient. For analysis of the congressional politics regarding Japanese exclusion in April 1924, see Toshihiro Minohara, *Hainichi Iminho to Nichibei Kankei* [Immigration Exclusion Act and U.S.-Japan Relations] (Tokyo: Iwanami, 2002), esp. 144–83.

48. Reed's speech is in *CR*, 68th Cong., 1st sess., 6305 (April 14, 1924). Other senators who said that Hanihara's message caused them to switch their vote included Henry Cabot Lodge, George W. Pepper, Frank B. Willis, and William Bruce. Also, see *NYT*, April 15, 1924; and for analysis, see Daniels, *Politics of Prejudice*, 92–105.

49. Tupper and McReynolds, *Japan in American Public Opinion*, 189.

50. ICPSR, vote 95, 68th Cong., House (May 9, 1924); *NYT*, May 9, 1924.

Chapter 6

1. Carey McWilliams, *Factories in the Field: The Story of Migratory Farm Labor in California* (1939; repr., Berkeley: University of California Press, 1999), 324, 80. See also his heroic depiction of the Industrial Workers of the World, 160, 154–58. California labor leaders, McWilliams asserts, made a mistake in vilifying rather than organizing Chinese workers (80).

2. Guy to Davis, November 26, 1923, J. Merle Davis Correspondence, Survey of Race Relations Collection, Hoover Institution, Stanford University, Stanford, Calif., https://collections.stanford.edu/srr/bin/page?forward=home. For comprehensive analysis of the survey, see Sarah M. Griffith, "'Where We Can Battle for the Lord and Japan': The Development of Liberal Protestant Antiracism before World War II," *Journal of American History* 100, no. 2 (September 2013): 429–53, and "Conflicting Dialogues: The Survey of Race Relations in the Trans-Pacific and the Fight for Asian American Racial Equality" (Ph.D. diss., University of California, Santa Barbara, 2010).

3. McClatchy to Japanese American Leader, July 23, 1924, in Miscellaneous Files on the Anti-Japanese Issue in Foreign Countries. (J.1.1.0.J/X1-U1), J-DRO.

4. CJIC, Progress Report, October 30, 1924, UC-JP1; J. Merle Davis, "We Said: 'Let's Find the Facts,'" *Survey Graphic* 9, no. 2 (May 1926): 202.

5. Park's two articles: "Behind Our Masks," *Survey Graphic* 9, no. 2 (May 1926), 135–39; and "Our Racial Frontier on the Pacific," ibid., 192–96. For analysis of Park's views on race, including involvement in the survey, see Fred H. Matthews, *Quest for an American Sociology: Robert E. Park and the Chicago School* (Montreal: McGill-Queen's University Press, 1977), 157–89; Henry Yu, *Thinking Orientals: Migration, Contact, and Exoticism in Modern America* (New York: Oxford University Press, 2001), 19–30; and Cheryl Anne Hudson, "Making Modern Citizens: Political Culture in Chicago, 1890–1930" (Ph.D. diss., Vanderbilt University, 2011).

6. Gordon H. Chang, "A Man of Whom the University Can Be Proud," in *Morning*

Glory, Evening Shadows: Yamato Ichihashi and His Internment Writings, 1942–1945, ed. Gordon H. Chang, 11–50 (Stanford: Stanford University Press, 1997).

7. Chester Rowell, "Western Windows to the East," in *Survey Graphic* 9, no. 2 (May 1926): 175.

8. Rowell's break with Johnson is covered in *NYT*, August 20, 1922; and *LAT*, August 26, 1922. For his earlier disagreement with Johnson on the League of Nations, see Rowell to Arthur Arlett, March 26, 1919, UC-AA. Records for Gulick's National Committee of American Japanese Relations notes that Rowell accepted the committee's invitation to be an honorary member: Meeting Minutes, May 4, 1921, RG 18, box 36, folder 1, Federal Council of Churches of Christ in America collections, Presbyterian Historical Society, Philadelphia, Penn.

9. See Arlett to Rowell, June 3, 1919, box 9, Chester Rowell Papers, BANC MSS C-B 401, Bancroft Library, University of California, Berkeley; and Rowell to Arlett, June 25, 1919, UC-AA.

10. For nisei Americanization and the anti-Japanese movement in Hawai'i, see Eileen H. Tamura, *Americanization, Acculturation, and Ethnic Identity: The Nisei Generation in Hawaii* (Urbana: University of Illinois Press, 1994), 45–88; Tom Coffman, *The Island Edge of America: A Political History of Hawai'i* (Honolulu: University of Hawai'i Press, 2003), 26–31, 67; and Gary Y. Okihiro, *Cane Fires: The Anti-Japanese Movement in Hawaii, 1865–1945* (Philadelphia: Temple University Press, 1992), 82–101, 129–91. For transpacific dimensions to nisei Americanization, see Hiromi Monobe, "Shaping an Ethnic Leadership: Takie Okumura and the 'Americanization' of Nisei in Hawai'i, 1919–1945" (Ph.D. diss., University of Hawai'i, 2004).

11. Coffman, *Island Edge of America*, 26–31, 67; Monobe, "Shaping an Ethnic Leadership."

12. The founding and early history of the IPR is discussed in Griffith, "'Where We Can Battle for the Lord and Japan,'" 445; Tomoko Akami, *Internationalizing the Pacific: The United States, Japan, and the Institute of Pacific Relations in War and Peace, 1919–1945* (London: Routledge, 2002), 46–58; and Paul F. Hooper, *Elusive Destiny: The Inter-*

nationalist Movement in Modern Hawai'i (Honolulu: University of Hawai'i Press, 1980), 105–36. For meetings before the first conference, see "Attendants at Yale Club meeting," March 6, 1925, and "Notes on Conference Discussion," February 22, 1925, HIA-1/2 IPR Pacific Council, Formative Period, UH-IPR; Park's comment is from Park, "Behind Our Masks," 139.

13. On merging the survey and IPR, see Merle Davis to Professor R. D. McKenzie, February 5, 1930, E-13/23 IPR Personal— J. Merle Davis, 1925–31, UH-IPR.

14. Scharrenberg sought to convince labor leaders that the quota would promote their interests in two ways: by restoring good relations with Japanese workers and by keeping the labor movement strong in Asia in order to offset the growth of bolshevism. His message, however, ultimately failed to deliver labor to Alexander's initiative. For the IPR reaching out to Scharrenberg, see Jerome D. Greene (president of the IPR American Council) to Scharrenberg, March 20, 1930, A-8/12 IPR American Council, UH-IPR; egalitarian discussion of the quota plan is contained in Alexander to Shibusawa, October 17, 1930, vol. 35, SHIB docs.; Greene to Scharrenberg, March 20, 1930, and Scharrenberg to William Green (AFL), July 30, 1931, box 1, UC-PS; Alexander to Holden, February 13, 1930, and reply, February 26, 1930, J110.J/X1-U1 v. 6, J-DRO. For analysis of Scharrenberg's involvement in the quota campaign, see Izumi Hirobe, *Japanese Pride, American Prejudice: Modifying the Exclusion Clause of the 1924 Immigration Act* (Stanford: Stanford University Press, 2001), 108.

15. Hirobe, *Japanese Pride*, 123–28.

16. McClatchy to Phelan, May 26, 1930, UC-JP2.

17. See Hirobe, *Japanese Pride*, 149–209.

18. IN-H (1930), 3.

19. Census figures are reported in Brett H. Melendy, "Filipino Americans," in *Gale Encyclopedia of Multicultural America*, ed. Thomas Riggs, 3rd ed. (Detroit: Gale, 2014), 2:122–23.

20. IN-H (1930), 2–3.

21. McClatchy in ibid., 33, 44; Roxas in ibid., 116.

22. Webb in ibid., 69; McClatchy in ibid., 31 (my emphasis).

23. McClatchy in ibid., 35; Webb in ibid., 69.

24. Ibid., 35.

25. Briones in ibid., 127. Around the same time Congress was focused on the problem of antimiscegenation with respect to Filipino immigrants, it returned U.S. citizenship to Americans married to Asians. The Cable Act in 1922 liberalized naturalization law allowing American women to retain their citizenship after marrying a foreigner. Before this time, such international marriages would result in American women losing their U.S. citizenship; the same, however, was not true for American men marrying foreign women. The one exception to the Cable Act liberalization involved marriage to men who were "ineligible to citizenship." Though that act's sponsors were not ardent exclusionists, they feared that the measure might be voted down by a Congress roused by the postwar campaign for Japanese exclusion. By March 1931, those fears were gone as feminists like Emma Wold and Genevieve Allen from the National Women's Party, with Congressman John Cable's support, won repeal of the act's section that caused hundreds of American women to lose their citizenship upon marrying Asian men. Crucial to the success of the repeal was the insistence on the part of its advocates that the issue was about gender equality for a few hundred American women and that it would have nothing to do with Asian immigration issues on the West Coast. A brief history of the Cable Act and its discriminations is contained in U.S. Congress, Senate, Immigration Committee, *American Citizenship Rights for Women*, 72nd Cong., 2nd sess. (Washington: Government Printing Office, 1933), 29–39. For hearings on a measure to eliminate the discrimination, see U.S. Congress, House, Immigration and Naturalization Committee, *Immigration and Citizenship of American-Born Women Married to Aliens*, 69th Cong., 1st sess. (Washington: Government Printing Office, 1926); Senate hearings on the same bill were held on March 24, 1926.

26. Dickstein's comments appear within the testimony of others: for his remarks on Filipino labor, see Welch in IN-H (1930), 5; Dickstein's opposition to the Immigration Act of 1924 is evident in Trevor in ibid., 17;

for Trevor's role in the Johnson-Reed Act, see King in ibid., 191–92, 211–12. Dickstein's views of national origins quotas also appear in "Reminiscences of Samuel Dickstein" (1950), interview conducted by Allan Nevins and Dean Albertson, Columbia University Oral History Research Office, Columbia University, N.Y., December 1949–June 1950.

27. IN-H (1930), 201, 204.

28. Mead in ibid., 206; Parker in ibid., 89. For an earlier testimony by Mead that reveals his paternalism, see Lawrence H. Fuchs, *Hawaii Pono: A Social History* (New York: Harcourt, Brace and World, 1961), 153.

29. IN-H (1930), 102–5, 110–11.

30. Roxas in ibid., 106; Moncado in ibid., 137.

31. McClatchy in ibid., 35; Roxas in ibid., 113. Roxas's comments elicited sympathy from Congressman Box regarding the actions of U.S. soldiers in the Philippines; see exchange with Roxas in ibid., 111–13.

32. McClatchy's comment in ibid., 30; Houston in ibid., 245, 250. For the planter's position and influence on Houston, see Fuchs, *Hawaii Pono*, 235–36.

33. The most thorough analysis of the congressional debate regarding Filipinos is found in Rick Baldoz, *The Third Asiatic Invasion* (New York: New York University Press, 2011), 156–81, 177–78.

34. Ibid., 170, 79; Paul A. Kramer, *The Blood of Government* (Chapel Hill: University of North Carolina Press, 2006), 424.

35. Baldoz, *Third Asiatic Invasion*, 177.

36. Kramer, *Blood of Government*, 351–52.

37. Bruno Lasker, *Filipino Immigration: To Continental United States and Hawaii* (Chicago: University of Chicago Press, 1931), 342–43. Lasker—former editor of the *Survey*, a periodical for liberal social workers—was an IPR researcher with Socialist leanings and a background in settlement work. For Lasker's biography, see "The Reminiscences of Bruno Lasker," interview conducted by Louis M. Starr, Columbia University Oral History Research Office, Columbia University, N.Y., 1957.

38. IN-H (1930), 113.

39. See Lucy E. Salyer, "Baptism by Fire: Race, Military Service, and U.S. Citizenship Policy, 1918–1935," *Journal of American History* 91, no. 3 (December 2004): 847–76; and

Harry N. Naka, "The Naturalization of Japanese War Veterans of the American World War Forces" (M.A. thesis, University of California, Berkeley, 1935).

40. CJIC, press release #417, March 2, 1935, California Joint Immigration Committee Papers, 1924–1936, UC-JP2; see also appendix of IN-H (1935-1), 17.

41. IN-H (1935-1), 7.

42. Salyer, "Baptism by Fire," 870; IN-H (1935-1), 7.

43. V. S. McClatchy, CJIC confidential "Supplementing Report of April 30," August 2, 1934, p. 4, box 2, UC-PS.

44. Baldoz, *Third Asiatic Invasion*, 186–93; and Howard A. DeWitt, *Anti-Filipino Movements in California* (San Francisco: R and E Research, 1976), 74–75. Discussion of those repatriated is covered in Ngai, *Impossible Subjects: Illegal Aliens and the Making of Modern America* (Princeton: Princeton University Press, 2004), 122–26. For a rich analysis of the politics of repatriation, see Veta R. Schlimgen, "Neither Citizens nor Aliens: Filipino 'American Nationals' in the U.S. Empire, 1900–1946" (Ph.D. diss., University of Oregon, 2010), 367–94.

45. IN-H (1933), 4. Sabath joined Dickstein in opposing the Immigration Act of 1924, writing to President Coolidge, as quoted in ibid., 205, "We should restrict immigration along sane, humane, and scientific lines, instead of branding millions of our citizens as inferior and deliberately hurting the pride of nearly all friendly nations."

46. IN-H (1935-2), n.p.; IN-H (1933), 37.

47. IN-H (1933), 7–8. For Mexican repatriation, see George J. Sanchez, *Becoming Mexican American: Ethnicity, Culture, and Identity in Chicano Los Angeles, 1900–1945* (New York: Oxford University Press, 1993), 209–26.

48. IN-H (1935-2), n.p.

49. Osias in IN-H (1933), 36; Guevara in ibid., n.p.; Garsson in ibid., 9, and see 11–12 for the Legionarios letter describing Filipino hardships in Los Angeles and their petitions for help from the federal government; Grasson in ibid., 11.

50. Baldoz, *Third Asiatic Invasion*, 193; Carey McWilliams, "Thirty-Five Thousand New Aliens," *Pacific Weekly*, August 24, 1936,

119–21, 121, 119. How improving economic conditions raised hopes of Filipinos and impeded participation in repatriation is addressed in Schlimgen, "Neither Citizens nor Aliens," 388–89.

51. James R. Green, *The World of the Worker: Labor in Twentieth-Century America* (New York: Hill and Wang, 1980), 151, 158. Also see Robert H. Zieger, *The CIO, 1935–1955* (Chapel Hill: University of North Carolina Press, 1995), 13–20.

52. UCAPAWA is studied in Chris Friday, *Organizing Asian-American Labor: The Pacific Coast Canned-Salmon Industry, 1870–1942* (Philadelphia: Temple University Press, 1994), 136–45. Scharrenberg's conflict with Communists is revealed in Scharrenberg to Gerald P. Nye (U.S. senator), July 29, 1937, and Scharrenberg, "Communists Attack Asiatic Exclusion Laws," *Coast Seaman's Journal*, n.d., carton 4, UC-PS. For the larger story of the dockworkers' strike in San Francisco and rise of the International Longshoremen's Association and then the International Longshoremen's and Warehousemen's Union (ILWU), see Bruce Nelson, *Workers on the Waterfront: Seamen, Longshoremen, and Unionism in the 1930s* (Urbana: University of Illinois Press, 1990), 103–55. The NLRB report is quoted in Coffman, *Island Edge of America*, 38.

53. McWilliams, *Factories in the Field*, 133. For analysis of McWilliams's "political turn," see Peter Richardson, *American Prophet: The Life and Work of Carey McWilliams* (Ann Arbor: University of Michigan Press, 2005), 55–92; and in his own words, McWilliams, *The Education of Carey McWilliams* (New York: Simon and Schuster, 1979).

54. IN-H (1940), 45, 45A, 48, 53A. This and another hearing on Filipino naturalization followed one held on a bill to naturalize Indians in the United States, IN-H (1939).

55. Scharrenberg in IN-H (1940), 41–42; Marcantonio in ibid., 51–52; Dickstein in ibid., 52.

56. Muzumdar in IN-H (1939), 8, 18; Scharrenberg in ibid, 15–16.

57. The Japanese language schools issue is studied in Tamura, *Americanization, Acculturation, and Ethnic Identity*, 146–51; and Okihiro, *Cane Fires*, 134–38.

58. All citations here are in UH-IPR: Kenneth Scott Latourette, "The Status of the Far East on Curriculums in US," n.d., IPR American Council, 1925–29; "Notes of the Meeting of the Textbook Committee," February 11, 1936, in Honolulu Branch of IPR, Textbook Controversy; Meeting notes, Education Committee, April 4, 1935, Honolulu Branch of IPR, Textbook Controversy; Loomis to Pratt, August 9, 1935, in Honolulu Branch of IPR, Textbook Controversy.

59. *Fresno Bee and Republican*, March 28, 1935. Also see report in ibid., March 29, 1935, and the press release CJIC, "Will Hawaii Suppress Investigation of Japanese Propaganda in Public Schools," in Honolulu Branch of IPR, Textbook Controversy, UH-IPR. For analysis of Haan's warning about Japanese Americans in California, see Brian Masaru Hayashi, "Kilsoo Haan, American Intelligence, and the Anticipate Japanese Invasion of California, 1931–1943," *Pacific Historical Review* 83, no. 2 (May 2014): 277–93.

60. *Christian Science Monitor*, April 23, 1935, and May 20, 1935; *Capital Journal* (Salem, Ore.), May 20, 1935; *Sacramento Bee*, June 21, 1935; *San Francisco Examiner*, August 20, 1936;

61. Loomis's quote is found in Samuel Hume to Loomis, May 1935, Honolulu Branch of IPR, Textbook Controversy, UH-IPR; "fanatics" is from Pratt to Loomis, February 13, 1936, ibid; Oren E. Long to Dr. Walter R. Hepner (California Department of Education), April 24, 1935, ibid; Wallace Alexander, *San Francisco News*, April 1, 1935. Hume's egalitarian efforts on behalf of the Japanese are detailed in Hirobe, *Japanese Pride*, 162–66; Long's background is addressed in Fuchs, *Hawaii Pono*, 314.

62. *NYT*, July 14, 1935; for other favorable press, see *San Francisco Examiner*, June 18, 1935. For Hume's egalitarian efforts, see Hirobe, *Japanese Pride*, 162–66.

63. *Honolulu Star-Bulletin*, March 16, 1936. For background of the newspaper, see Coffman, *Island Edge of America*, 27.

64. Field to Riley Allen, January 28, 1937, Honolulu Branch of IPR, Textbook Controversy, UH-IPR.

65. Field's work with Lasker is detailed in Frederick Vanderbilt Field, *From Right to Left: An Autobiography* (Westport, Conn.: Lawrence Hill, 1983), 93–94; Field to McClatchy, September 24, 1936 and September 29, 1937, Honolulu Branch of IPR, Textbook Controversy, UH-IPR.

Chapter 7

1. Commission on Wartime Relocation and Internment of Civilians, *Personal Justice Denied* (1982; repr., Washington, D.C.: Civil Liberties Education Fund, 1997), 55; reaction in Congress is covered in Morton Grodzins, *Americans Betrayed: Politics and the Japanese Evacuation* (Chicago: University of Chicago Press, 1949), 63–64; for the public opinion poll, see Jacobus tenBroek, Edward N. Barnhart, and Floyd W. Matson, *Prejudice, War, and the Constitution* (1954; repr., Berkeley: University of California Press, 1970), 349n42.

2. *SFC*, February 10, January 27, and February 2, 1942.

3. For the Japanese spy cases, see, for example, *LAT*, June 10, 1941; the impact of the Roberts report is covered in Peter Irons, *Justice at War: The Story of the Japanese American Internment Cases* (New York: Oxford University Press, 1983), 40; for Lippmann, see *LAT*, February 13, 1942. Nationally syndicated columnist Westbrook Pegler referred explicitly to Lippmann's credibility in warning about the Japanese American threat: *Washington Post*, February 15, 1942.

4. Stetson Conn, "The Decision to Evacuate the Japanese from the Pacific Coast," in *Command Decisions* (Washington D.C.: U.S. Army Center of Military History, 1990), 144; Grodzins, *Americans Betrayed*, 86; tenBroek, Barnhart, and Matson, *Prejudice, War, and the Constitution*, 349–50n42.

5. Analysis of FDR is found in Greg Robinson, *By Order of the President* (Cambridge, Mass.: Harvard University Press, 2001), 118–23, quote on 122. For the major players behind internment, see Irons, *Justice at War*, 49–63; and Roger Daniels, *The Decision to Relocate the Japanese Americans* (Philadelphia: J. B. Lippincott, 1975).

6. DeWitt's final recommendation is addressed in Irons, *Justice at War*, 58–59; DeWitt's evolving views are covered in Conn, "Decision to Evacuate the Japanese from the Pacific Coast," especially 137; Ennis in U.S.

Congress, House, Committee on Appropriations, *Sixth Supplemental National Defense Appropriation Bill for 1942*, 77th Cong., 2nd sess. (Washington: Government Printing Office, 1942), 395–96.

7. For German and Italian enemy aliens, see Ennis, JC-S (1948), 74; and Conn, "Decision to Evacuate the Japanese from the Pacific Coast," 147–48. The hostages thesis is discussed in Michi Weglyn, *Years of Infamy* (New York: William Morrow, 1976), 54–66; and Brian Masaru Hayashi, *Democratizing the Enemy* (Princeton: Princeton University Press, 2004), 81–84.

8. Tom Coffman, *The Island Edge of America: A Political History of Hawai'i* (Honolulu: University of Hawai'i Press, 2003), 77.

9. Ibid., 60–69, 78–89 (quote on 79); Takashi Fujitani, *Race for Empire* (Berkeley: University of California Press, 2011), 100–101. For more on nisei in and from Hawai'i during World War II, see Franklin Odo, *No Sword to Bury: Japanese Americans in Hawai'i during World War II* (Philadelphia: Temple University Press, 2004); and Dennis M. Ogawa, *First among Nisei: The Life and Writings of Masaji Marumoto* (Honolulu: Japanese Cultural Center of Hawai'i, 2007).

10. McWilliams in ND (1942), 11789; estimated numbers of egalitarian and exclusionist witnesses are given in Grodzins, *Americans Betrayed*, 203–4; and Robert Shaffer, "Cracks in the Consensus: Defending the Rights of Japanese Americans during World War II," *Radical History Review* 72 (1998): 72, 84–120.

11. Bowron in ND (1942), 11643–44; for support for Bowron among Japanese Americans in Los Angeles, see Tanaka in ibid., 11704–06; Bowron in ibid., 11644.

12. "If friction aroused . . ." appears in Bellquist in ibid., 11248; other quotes in Olson in ibid., 11633.

13. Olson in ibid., 11631, 11634.

14. For conflict between Olson and Warren, see Robert E. Burke, *Olson's New Deal for California* (1953; repr., Westport, Conn.: Greenwood Press, 1982), 194–206. Warren's background regarding the Japanese issue and involvement in wartime evacuation is discussed in G. Edward White, *Earl Warren: A Public Life* (New York: Oxford University Press, 1982), 67–74.

15. ND (1942), 10974, 10981, 11011.

16. Ibid., 11013, 11015.

17. Ibid., 11624, 11627, and 11628.

18. Ibid., 11199; *Christian Century*, April 1, 1942.

19. ND (1942), 11184.

20. Ibid., 11790–91.

21. Masaoka in ibid., 11141; Tatsuno in ibid., 11153–54; Slocum in ibid., 11716.

22. Ibid., 11137.

23. A small percentage of the West Coast Japanese ended up in concentration camps run by the Justice Department. These consisted mainly of community leaders and their families. The largest camp in Crystal City, Texas, also housed selected German and Italian aliens, as well as Japanese removed from Peru. See Tetsuden Kashima, *Judgment without Trial: Japanese American Imprisonment during World War II* (Seattle: University of Washington Press, 2003), 104–26.

24. The voluminous literature on the camps is synthesized and condensed in Roger Daniels, *Prisoners without a Trial: Japanese Americans in World War II* (New York: Hill and Wang, 1993). For a different perspective that underscores the egalitarianism of WRA directors as well as the diasporic mentalities of the internees, see Hayashi, *Democratizing the Enemy.*

25. Dillon S. Myer, *Uprooted Americans: The Japanese Americans and the War Relocation Authority during World War II* (Tucson: University of Arizona Press, 1971), 91–107, xv. For Myer's sincere efforts to be seen as a friend of the internees, see Alice Yang Murray, *Historical Memories of the Japanese American Internment and Struggle for Redress* (Stanford: Stanford University Press, 2008), 56. For Myer's view of Japanese Americans as representing a new type of liberal or "polite" racism, see Fujitani, *Race for Empire*, 115–17.

26. Murray, *Historical Memories*, 55. For egalitarian opposition to the internment, see Shaffer, "Cracks in the Consensus"; and Robert Shaffer, "Opposition to Internment: Defending Japanese American Rights during World War II," *Historian* 61, no. 3 (March 1999): 597–620.

27. Cozzens quote is in Kevin Allen Leonard, "Years of Hope, Days of Fear: The Impact of World War II on Race Relations

in Los Angeles" (Ph.D. diss., University of California, Davis, 1992), 226; Hayashi, *Democratizing the Enemy*, 107–47, 22–25, 106. Analyses of the WRA social scientists include Orin Starn, "Engineering Internment: Anthropologists and the War Relocation Authority," *American Ethnologist* 13, no. 4 (November 1986): 700–720; Yuji Ichioka, ed., *Views from Within: The Japanese American Evacuation and Resettlement Study* (Los Angeles: UCLA Asian American Studies Center, 1989); and Lane Ryo Hirabayshi, *Politics of Fieldwork: Research in an American Concentration Camp* (Tucson: University of Arizona Press, 1999). For a useful overview of research in the camps, see Murray, *Historical Memories*, 140–84.

28. Carey McWilliams, *The Education of Carey McWilliams* (New York: Simon and Schuster, 1979), 101–7 (quote is on 104); Carey McWilliams, *Prejudice: Japanese-Americans, Symbol of Racial Intolerance* (Boston: Little, Brown, 1944), 8–13 (quote on 10), 290–91.

29. Fujitani, *Race for Empire*, 100–101; Coffman, *Island Edge of America*, 84–92.

30. Leonard, "Years of Hope," 227. While Leonard's dissertation offers extensive analysis of the WRA antiracism, parts of this analysis appear in Kevin Allen Leonard, *Battle for Los Angeles: Racial Ideology and World War II* (Albuquerque: University of New Mexico Press, 2006), 199–257.

31. Leonard, *Battle for Los Angeles*, 255–56; Murray, *Historical Memories*, 84–99; quote is in Lon Kurashige, *Japanese American Celebration and Conflict* (Berkeley: University of California Press, 2002), 122.

32. Ruth W. Kingman, "A Brief Historical Report," 3, 5, carton 1, folder 4, UC-FAIR. For background on Kingman and her husband, see Harry L. Kingman, "Citizenship in Democracy," interviews conducted by Rosemary Levenson, 1971–72, Regional Oral History, University of California, Berkeley, http://content.cdlib.org/view?docId=kt9199p014&doc.view=entire_text (October 3, 2015).

33. R. Kingman, "Brief Historical Report," 8–9, 10.

34. Ibid., 10; also see Harvey Schwartz, "A Union Combats Racism: The ILWU's Japanese-American 'Stockton Incident' of 1945," *Southern California Quarterly* 62, no. 2

(Summer 1980): 161–76; Scharrenberg to William Green, March 1, 1945, box 1, UC-PS.

35. Mark Brilliant, *The Color of America Has Changed: How Racial Diversity Shaped Civil Rights Reform in California, 1941–1978* (New York: Oxford University Press, 2010), 22–25.

36. For "join in protecting," see *LAT*, December 18, 1944; and Audrie Girdner and Anne Loftis, *The Great Betrayal* (New York: Macmillan, 1970), 404–5; both Kingman and Kenny quotes are in Kingman, "Brief Historical Report," 12, carton 1, folder 4, UC-FAIR; Bowron quoted in *LAT*, January 15, 1945, 7.

37. Memorandum by Assistant Chief of the Division of Far Eastern Affairs of a Conversation with the Minister Counselor of the Chinese Embassy (Liu Chieh), November 13, 1942, U.S. Department of State (publication 6353), *Foreign Relations of the United States: Diplomatic Papers, China 1942* (Washington: Government Printing Office, 1956), 352. For negotiations of the treaty, see ibid., 268–418.

38. *NYT*, November 27, 1943.

39. The relevant book-length study focusing on white egalitarian interest groups is Fred W. Riggs, *Pressures on Congress: A Study of the Repeal of Chinese Exclusion* (New York: King's Crown Press, 1950). Also see Karen J. Leong, "Foreign Policy, National Identity, and Citizenship: The Roosevelt White House and the Expediency of Repeal," *Journal of American Ethnic History* 22, no. 4 (Summer 2003): 3–30; Madeline Y. Hsu, *The Good Immigrants: How the Yellow Peril Became the Model Minority* (Princeton: Princeton University Press, 2015), 81–103; and Jane H. Hong, "Reorientating America in the World: Race, Geopolitics, and the Repeal of Asian Exclusion" (Ph.D. diss., Harvard University, 2013), 41–76.

40. Dickstein's commentary is found in IN-H (1943), 112, 169, 176, 185–86.

41. Haan in ibid., 133–34, 136; translated radio broadcast is in Walsh in ibid., 79. For a wide-ranging study of Walsh and Pearl S. Buck's "critical internationalism," see Robert Shaffer, "Pearl S. Buck and the American Internationalist Tradition" (Ph.D. diss., Rutgers University, 2003); and also see Peter Conn, *Pearl S. Buck: A Cultural Biography* (Cambridge: Cambridge University Press, 1996).

42. IN-H (1943), 80.

43. Ibid., 69–70, 76, 163–65.

44. Ibid., 179–82.

45. Mason in ibid., 173; Magnuson in ibid., 198.

46. IN-H (1944), 9; U.S. Congress, House, Immigration and Naturalization Committee, *To Grant a Quota to Eastern Hemisphere Indians and to Make Them Racially Eligible for Naturalization*, 79th Cong., 1st sess. (Washington: Government Printing Office, 1945), 113–14. For insight into the Indian and Korean struggles to repeal exclusion, see Hong, "Reorientating America in the World," 78–165.

47. Fernandez in U.S. Congress, House, Immigration and Naturalization Committee, Hearings on H.R. 1844, To Authorize the Naturalization of Filipinos Who Are Permanent Residents of the United States, unpublished, 77th Cong., 2nd sess., February 4, 1942, 19; see also Young in ibid., 8, 14; and Yap in IN-H (1944), 16–17.

48. Harry S. Truman, "Remarks upon Presenting a Citation to a Nisei Regiment," Public Papers of the Presidents: Harry Truman, 1945-1953, Harry S. Truman Library and Museum, https://www.trumanlibrary.org/publicpapers/index.php?pid=1666&st=&st1= (October 5, 2015).

49. Validation of Legislative Amendments to the Alien Land Law, in California Ballot Propositions and Ballot Initiatives, UC Hastings Scholarship Repository, http://repository.uchastings.edu/ca_ballot_props/467/ (October 5, 2015).

50. Brilliant, *Color of America*, 23–41. A state appellate judge in *Sei Fujii v. State of California* ruled that the alien land law violated the UN Charter and UN Declaration of Human Rights, which operated as international treaties; see, for example, *Chicago Tribune*, April 25, 1950, 20, and April 27, 1950, 22. The California Supreme Court later on denied that the UN treaties could void state law; see, for example, *NYT*, April 20, 1952, 25.

51. As quoted in Brilliant, *Color of America*, 42.

52. JC-S (1948), 55.

53. McCloy in ibid., 10; Biddle in ibid., 62; Ennis in ibid., 79, 82.

54. Judd in U.S. Congress, House, Judiciary Committee, *Providing for Equality under Immigration and Naturalization Laws*, 80th Cong., 2nd sess. (Washington: Government Printing Office, 1948), 8, 12.

55. For American criticism of Roxas from Asia experts affiliated with the IPR and other "critical internationalists," see Robert Shaffer, " 'Partly Disguised Imperialism': American Critical Internationalists and Philippine Independence," *Journal of American-East-Asian Relations* 19 (2012): 235–62.

56. An insightful study of the conservative internationalism behind congressional backing for Taiwan is Joyce Mao, *Asia First: China and the Making of Modern American Conservatism* (Chicago: University of Chicago Press, 2015). Other studies include Stanley D. Bachrack, *The Committee of One Million: China Lobby Politics, 1953–1971* (New York: Columbia University Press, 1976); and Ross Y. Koen, *The China Lobby in American Politics* (New York: Octagon, 1974). Frederick V. Field's ordeal is told by him in Frederick Vanderbilt Field, *From Right to Left: An Autobiography* (Westport, Conn.: Lawrence Hill, 1983), 208–56.

57. Ennis in JC-S (1949), 99–100.

58. Judd in JC-S (1948), 9; Rusk in JC-S (1949), 54.

59. Mason in U.S. Congress, House and Senate, Joint Subcommittees of Judiciary Committees, *Revision of Immigration, Naturalization, and Nationality Laws* (Washington: Government Printing Office, 1951), 662, 664; for the American Legion's support for the bill, see Watson Mill in ibid., 18, 20–21.

Chapter 8

1. Takaki obituary, in *NYT*, May 30, 2009.

2. Tom Coffman, *The Island Edge of America: A Political History of Hawai'i* (Honolulu: University of Hawai'i Press, 2003), 105–9. Also see Sanford Zalburg, *A Spark Is Struck! Jack Hall and the ILWU in Hawaii* (Honolulu: Watermark, 1979), 69–238; and Moon-Kie Jung, *Reworking Race: The Making of Hawaii's Interracial Labor Movement* (New York: Columbia University Press, 2006), 160–82.

3. Coffman, *Island Edge of America*, 109–11, 148–58.

4. U.S. Congress, House, Committee on

Interior and Insular Affairs, *Hawaii State-hood*, Report No. 32, unpublished, 86th Cong., 1st sess., 1959, 2.

5. Roger Bell, *Last among Equals: Hawaiian Statehood and American Politics* (Honolulu: University of Hawai'i Press, 1984), 192–252; ICPSR, votes 66, 83–84, 80th Cong., House (June 30 and July 21, 1947), and votes 15–16, 97, 108, 110–112, 116, 85th Cong., House (March 11–12 and September 15, 1959, and March 23–24 and April 21, 1960).

6. U.S. Congress, Senate, Committee on Insular and Interior Affairs, *Hawaii State-hood*, 81st Cong., 2nd sess. (Washington: Government Printing Office, 1950), 101. For deeper analysis of the response by conservative internationalists to Hawai'i statehood, see Joyce Mao, "Asia First: China and American Conservatism, 1937–1965" (Ph.D. diss., University of California, Berkeley, 2007), 219–45. Knowland's views are also considered in Gayle B. Montgomery and James W. Johnson, *One Step from the White House: The Rise and Fall of Senator William F. Knowland* (Berkeley: University of California Press, 1998).

7. U.S. Congress, House, Committee of Rules, To Enable the People of Hawaii to Create a Constitution and State Government and to Be Admitted into the Union on an Equal Footing with the Original States, unpublished, 80th Cong., 1st sess., April 17, 1947, 1.

8. For text of Johnson's speech to Congress and Whitman quote, see *LAT*, January 14, 1965. Between 1955 and 1965, fifty thousand Japanese immigrated to the United States, exempted from the national origins system: Mike Masaoka in IN-S (1965), 627–28. For analysis of the Hart-Celler Act, see David M. Reimers, *Still the Golden Door: The Third World Comes to America* (New York: Columbia University Press, 1986); and Mae M. Ngai, *Impossible Subjects: Illegal Aliens and the Making of Modern America* (Princeton: Princeton University Press, 2004), 227–64.

9. Olson in JC-H (1964), 606. For rare opposition to Asian immigration during the congressional hearings, see Rosalind Frame in IN-S (1965), 810–811. ICPSR, vote 135, 86th Cong., House (September 20, 1965): the only member of the California delegation to op-pose the final House vote on the Hart-Celler bill was James B. Utt, a conservative, isolationist Republican from Orange County who campaigned to remove the United States from the United Nations.

10. Rusk in IN-S (1965), 71–73; Carliner in ibid., 440; James Carey (AFL-CIO) in ibid., 468.

11. For an earlier version of Masaoka's written statement, see JC-H (1964), 877–901; Masaoka in IN-S (1965), 620–24 (quote on 621).

12. Masaoka in IN-S (1965), 627–28.

13. Ibid., 623.

14. Ibid., 627. For analysis of Hawai'i statehood and the racial construction of Asian Americans, see Ellen D. Wu, *The Color of Success: Asian Americans and the Origins of the Model Minority* (Princeton: Princeton University Press, 2014), 210–18. The members of Congress from Hawai'i joined Indian immigrant Dalip Singh Saund, the first Asian American in Congress, who served California in the House of Representatives from 1957 to 1963.

15. Fong in IN-S (1965), 45, 72; Fong, *CR*, 88th Cong., 1st sess., 15765 (August 23, 1963).

16. Matsunaga in U.S. Congress, House, Judiciary Subcommittee, *Immigration*, 89th Cong., 1st sess. (Washington: Government Printing Office, 1965), 199. Mink's written testimony is in ibid., 419–20.

17. Masaoka in IN-S (1965), 624–26.

18. Ibid., 624, 626–27.

19. Ibid., 629.

20. For the Asian American movement and its historiography, see Daryl J. Maeda, *Rethinking the Asian American Movement* (New York: Routledge, 2012); Daryl J. Maeda, *Chains of Babylon: The Rise of Asian America* (Minneapolis: University of Minnesota Press, 2009); and William Wei, *The Asian American Movement* (Philadelphia: Temple University Press, 1995).

21. U.S. Census Bureau, Jessica S. Barnes and Claudette E. Bennett, "The Asian Population: 2000," 9 (February 2002), http://www.census.gov/prod/2002pubs/c2kbr01-16.pdf (October 7, 2015).

22. For the political apathy of Asian Americans, see Elaine H. Kim, "'At Least You're Not Black': Asian Americans in U.S.

Race Relations," *Social Justice* 25, no. 3 (Fall 1998): 3–12; Vijay Prashad, *Everybody Was Kung Fu Fighting: Afro-Asian Connections and the Myth of Cultural Purity* (Boston: Beacon, 2001), vix–xii; and earlier publications such as Amy Uyematsu, "The Emergence of Yellow Power in America," *Gidra* (October 1969), reprinted in Amy Tachiki et al., eds., *Roots: An Asian American Reader* (Los Angeles: UCLA Asian American Studies, 1971), 9–13.

23. William Petersen, "Success Story, Japanese-American Style," *New York Times Magazine*, January 9, 1966; William Petersen, *Japanese Americans: Oppression and Success* (New York: Random House, 1971); "Success Story of One Minority Group in the U.S.," *U.S. News and World Report*, December 26, 1966, 73–76. For an example of the range of model minority scholarship, see Thomas Sowell, *Ethnic America: A History* (New York: Basic Books, 1981); Harry H. L. Kitano, *Japanese Americans: Evolution of a Subculture* (Englewood Cliffs, N.J.: Prentice-Hall, 1969); and Edna Bonacich, "A Theory of Middleman Minorities," *American Sociological Review* 38, no. 5 (October 1973): 583–94. Recent studies that historicize the model minority image include Wu, *Color of Success*; Charlotte Brooks, *Alien Neighbors, Foreign Friends: Asian Americans, Housing, and the Transformation of Urban California* (Chicago: University of Chicago Press, 2009); Scott Kurashige, *The Shifting Grounds of Race: Black and Japanese Americans in the Making of Multiethnic Los Angeles* (Princeton: Princeton University Press, 2010); Naoko Shibusawa, *America's Geisha Ally: Reimagining the Japanese Enemy* (Cambridge, Mass.: Harvard University Press, 2006); and Christina Klein, *Cold War Orientalism: Asia in the Middlebrow Imagination, 1945–1961* (Berkeley: University of California Press, 2003).

24. Yuji Ichioka, review of *Nisei: The Quiet Americans*, by Bill Hosokawa, in Amy Tachiki et al., *Roots: An Asian American Reader* (Los Angeles: UCLA Asian American Studies, 1971), 221–22.

25. Ibid.; Yuji Ichioka, "A Buried Past: A Survey of English-Language Works on Japanese American History," in *Counterpoint: Perspectives on Asian America*, ed. Emma Gee (Los Angeles: UCLA Asian American Studies,

1976), 14; Paul Takagi, "The Myth of 'Assimilation in American Life,'" *Amerasia* 2, no. 1 (1973): 152, 155.

26. For the impact of sixties disillusionment on American nationalism, see Gary Gerstle, *American Crucible: Race and Nation in the Twentieth Century* (Princeton: Princeton University Press, 2001), 345.

27. Gramsci as quoted in Ronald Takaki, *Iron Cages: Race and Culture in the 19th Century* (1979; repr., New York: Oxford University Press, 1990), vi–vii.

28. Ronald Takaki, *Strangers from a Different Shore: A History of Asian Americans* (Boston: Little, Brown, 1989). Also see this critique of Takaki's approach: Sylvia Yanagisako, "Transforming Orientalism: Gender, Nationality, and Class in Asian American Studies," in *Naturalizing Power: Essays in Feminist Cultural Analysis*, ed. Sylvia Yanagisako and Carol Delaney (New York: Routledge, 1995), 275–98.

29. Gordon H. Chang, "China and the Pursuit of America's Destiny: Nineteenth-Century Imagining and Why Immigration Restriction Took So Long," *Journal of Asian American Studies* 15, no. 2 (June 2012): 145–69.

30. Alice Yang Murray, *Historical Memories of the Japanese American Internment and Struggle for Redress* (Stanford: Stanford University Press, 2008), xiv; Daniels quote is on 237 in ibid. For the sacralizing of camp memory, see Jane Naomi Iwamura, "Critical Faith: Japanese Americans and the Birth of a New Civil Religion," *American Quarterly* 59, no. 3 (September 2007): 937–68.

31. For Weglyn, see Murray, *Historical Memories*, 244–49; as well as Michi Weglyn, *Years of Infamy* (New York: William Morrow, 1976). Irons's activism on behalf of Yasui, Hirabayashi, and Korematsu is documented in Peter Irons, *Justice Delayed: The Record of the Japanese American Internment Cases* (Middletown, Conn.: Wesleyan University Press, 1989).

32. The origins of the redress commission are discussed in opening statements by Senator Carl Levin and House majority leader Jim Wright in U.S. Congress, House, Committee on Governmental Affairs, *Commission on Wartime Relocation and Intern-*

ment of Civilians Act, 96th Cong., 2nd sess. (Washington: Government Printing Office, 1980), 2–4.

33. Commission on Wartime Relocation and Internment of Civilians, *Personal Justice Denied* (1982; repr., Washington, D.C.: Civil Liberties Education Fund, 1997), 18.

34. On Dewitt, see ibid., 64–67.

35. McCloy in JC-H (1985), 121, 125.

36. Lowman in JC-H (1986), 399, 401; McCloy in JC-H (1985), 122.

37. Lundgren in JC-H (1986), 83–84; Drinan in ibid., 190–91; Masaoka in ibid., 580. For analysis, see Murray, *Historical Memories*, 357–58.

38. JC-H (1986), 72–73.

39. Mike Honda is quoted in "Rep. Mike Honda Calls for U.S. Apology for Chinese Ex-clusion Act," *San Jose Mercury News*, February 20, 2011; Chu's speech is from *CR*, 112th Cong., 1st sess., House, 8431 (June 1, 2011).

Conclusion

1. This understanding of historical lessons has been influenced by Peter Novick, *The Holocaust in American Life* (Boston: Houghton Mifflin, 1999), 239–66. Nothing in this paragraph should be construed as being in sympathy with the deeply disturbed individuals and groups who deny the historical fact that six million Jews were murdered under Nazi rule during World War II.

2. Mae M. Ngai, *Impossible Subjects: Illegal Aliens and the Making of Modern America* (Princeton: Princeton University Press, 2004).

BIBLIOGRAPHIC ESSAY

|||||||||||||||||||||||||||||||||||||||||||||||||||||||||||||||||||||||||||||||||||||||||||||||||||||||||||||||||||||||||||||||||||||||||||||||||

Chapter 1

The analysis of anti-Asian racism—from the start of mass migration from China until the exclusion of Chinese laborers became a national issue—focuses largely on local and state policies in California with some attention to other regions and to nationwide racial discourse. The major studies include Alexander Saxton, *The Indispensable Enemy: Labor and the Anti-Chinese Movement in California* (1971; repr., Berkeley: University of California Press, 1995); Elmer Clarence Sandmeyer, *The Anti-Chinese Movement in California* (1939; repr., Urbana: University of Illinois Press, 1991); Najia Aarim-Heriot, *Chinese Immigrants, African Americans, and Racial Anxiety in the United States, 1848–1882* (Urbana: University of Illinois Press, 2003); Charles J. McClain, *In Search of Equality: The Chinese Struggle against Discrimination in Nineteenth-Century America* (Berkeley: University of California Press, 1994); Andrew Gyory, *Closing the Gate: Race, Politics, and the Chinese Exclusion Act* (Chapel Hill: University of North Carolina Press, 1998); Stuart Creighton Miller, *The Unwelcome Immigrant: The American Image of the Chinese, 1785–1882* (Berkeley: University of California Press, 1969); Mary Roberts Coolidge, *Chinese Immigration* (New York: Henry Holt, 1909); Moon-Ho Jung, *Coolies and Cane* (Baltimore: Johns Hopkins University Press, 2006); and John Kuo Wei Tchen, *New York before Chinatown: Orientalism and the Shaping of American Culture, 1776–1882* (Baltimore: Johns Hopkins University Press, 1999).

The above literature on anti-Chinese racism enabled me to appreciate two important studies that embed Chinese exclusion within the context of U.S.-China relations: Michael H. Hunt, *The Making of a Special Relationship: The United States and China to 1914* (New York: Columbia University Press, 1983), a masterful "research survey," and Shih-shan Henry Tsai, *China and the Overseas Chinese in the United States, 1868–1911* (Fayetteville: University of Arkansas Press, 1983), a more targeted monograph. Also

useful in fleshing out the influence of China fantasies and diplomatic relations on immigration policies are John Haddad, *The Romance of China: Excursions to China in U.S. Culture, 1776–1876* (New York: Columbia University Press, 2006); John Schrecker, "'For Equality of Men—for the Equality of Nations': Anson Burlingame and China's First Embassy to the United States, 1868," *Journal of American–East Asian Relations* 17 (2010): 9–34; and Yucheng Qin, *The Diplomacy of Nationalism: The Six Companies and China's Policy toward Exclusion* (Honolulu: University of Hawai'i Press, 2009). Gordon H. Chang's essay confirmed and clarified issues that I was considering: Chang, "China and the Pursuit of America's Destiny: Nineteenth-Century Imagining and Why Immigration Restriction Took So Long," *Journal of Asian American Studies* 15, no. 2 (June 2012): 145–69. Parts of Chang's essay are reproduced in his recent synthesis of U.S.-China relations: Chang, *Fateful Ties: A History of America's Preoccupation with China* (Cambridge, Mass.: Harvard University Press, 2015).

Analyses of American continental expansion are also important for placing the exclusion debate within the larger political, ideological, and partisan issues of the day. These studies include Robert Kelley, *The Cultural Pattern in American Politics: The First Century* (Washington, D.C.: University Press of America, 1979); Drew R. McCoy, *The Elusive Republic: Political Economy in Jeffersonian America* (Chapel Hill: University of North Carolina Press, 1980); Norman A. Graebner, *Empire on the Pacific: A Study in American Continental Expansion* (New York: Ronald Press, 1955); David M. Pletcher, *Diplomacy of Involvement: American Economic Expansion across the Pacific, 1784–1900* (Columbia: University of Missouri Press, 2001); Jean Heffer, *The United States and the Pacific: History of a Frontier* (Notre Dame: University of Notre Dame Press, 2002); Arthur Power Dudden, *The American Pacific: From the Old China Trade to the Present* (New York: Oxford University Press, 1992); Arrell Morgan Gibson,

Yankees in Paradise: The Pacific Basin Frontier (Albuquerque: University of New Mexico Press, 1993); Donald D. Johnson, *The United States and the Pacific: Private Interests and Public Policies, 1784–1899* (Westport, Conn.: Praeger, 1995); and Bruce Cumings, *Dominion from Sea to Sea: Pacific Ascendancy and American Power* (New Haven: Yale University Press, 2009).

Another key influence for this chapter was my study of twenty-two roll-call votes in Congress, and related congressional documentation, which enabled me to connect policy communities regarding Pacific commerce with the exclusion debate. As a rule for this and every chapter of this book, each roll-call vote was subjected to statistical analysis that cross-tabulated it with variables for party and region, and selected correlation analyses were run for all roll votes in particular Congresses to contextualize the exclusion debate among larger patterns of congressional voting.

Chapter 2

These studies and sources cited in chapter 1 were also helpful in this chapter: Hunt, *Making of a Special Relationship*; Tsai, *China and the Overseas Chinese in the United States*; Aarim-Heriot, *Chinese Immigrants, African Americans, and Racial Anxiety in the United States*; Gyory, *Closing the Gate*; Saxton, *Indispensable Enemy*; Miller, *Unwelcome Immigrant*; and Qin, *Diplomacy of Nationalism*. A significant review of the literature on the exclusion of Chinese laborers is in Gyory, *Closing the Gate*, 6–15. Recent analyses of exclusion by political scientists have focused on state formation: Daniel J. Tichenor, *Dividing Lines: The Politics of Immigration Control in America* (Princeton: Princeton University Press, 2002); and Aristide R. Zolberg, *A Nation by Design: Immigration Policy in the Fashioning of America* (New York: Russell Sage, 2006). For missionaries, see Joshua Paddison, *American Heathens: Religion, Race, and Reconstruction in California* (Berkeley: University of California Press, 2012); Derek Chang, *Citizens of a Christian Nation: Evangelical Missions and the Problem of Race in the Nineteenth Century* (Philadelphia: University of Pennsylvania Press, 2011); and Peggy Pascoe, *Relations of Rescue: The Search for Female Moral Authority in the American West, 1874–1939* (New York: Oxford University Press, 1990).

Studies of the political economy of late nineteenth-century America are particularly rich and rewarding. I came to appreciate the significance of regions as divided between metropole and periphery through these works of Richard Franklin Bensel: *The Political Economy of American Industrialization, 1877–1900* (Cambridge: Cambridge University Press, 2000); *Sectionalism and American Political Development, 1880–1980* (Madison: University of Wisconsin Press, 1984); and *Yankee Leviathan: The Origins of Central State Authority in America, 1859–1877* (New York: Cambridge University Press, 1990). The notion of a regionally based American political economy is also addressed in earlier studies by Walter Dean Burnham, "The End of American Party Politics," *Society* 35, no. 2 (1960), repr. (January/February 1998): 71; Barrington Moore Jr., *Social Origins of Dictatorship and Democracy: Lord and Peasant in the Making of the Modern World* (Boston: Beacon Press, 1966), 111–58; and Frederick J. Turner, "The Significance of the Frontier in American History," in *Frontier in American History*, 1–38 (New York: Henry Holt, 1920). For a historical biography of Turner that pays attention to his views on American regionally based political economy, see Allan G. Bogue, *Frederick Jackson Turner: Strange Roads Going Down* (Norman: University of Oklahoma Press, 1998).

Two congressional hearings were also important in writing this chapter: U.S. Congress, Senate, Joint Special Committee, *Investigate Chinese Immigration*, 44th Cong., 2nd sess., Report 689 (Washington: Government Printing Office, 1877), 1–1281; and U.S. Congress, House, Select Committee, *The Causes of the General Depression in Labor and Business; And as to Chinese Immigration*, 46th Cong., 2nd sess., Misc. Doc. 5 (Washington: Government Printing Office, 1879), 238–65. Analysis of roll-call voting and related congressional documentation allowed me to test theories about the passage of exclusion and also to fit this issue within broad patterns of voting in the 45th and 47th Congresses. The chapter focuses on these votes related to excluding Chinese laborers: votes 303, 347, and

373, 45th Cong., House (January 28, February 22, and March 1, 1879); and votes 82–83 and 93, 47th Cong., House (March 23 and April 17, 1882). See Inter-university Consortium for Political and Social Research, and Congressional Quarterly, Inc., United States Congressional Roll Call Voting Records, 1789–1998, ICPSR00004-v3 (Ann Arbor, Mich.: Inter-university Consortium for Political and Social Research [distributor]), May 6, 2010, http://doi.org/10.3886/ICPSR00004.v3 (ICPSR). The votes in the 45th Congress were to pass H.R. 2423 (303), to table this measure (347), and to pass it over presidential veto (373). In 1882, the votes were to amend S. 71 (82), to pass it (83), and to pass a revised, ten-year version (93). Rather than focus on just one vote for each year, the analysis takes all three into account because in some cases congressmen changed their vote. For each Congress a database was created that grouped all congressmen (based on their voting on the three measures) into these categories: exclusionist, egalitarian, and nonvoter. (Paired votes were removed from the analysis.) The selection followed a two-thirds rule: exclusionists voted at least two out of three times for exclusion; egalitarians voted at least two out of three times against exclusion; and non-voters did not vote at least two out of three times. To highlight the tension between exclusionists and egalitarians, non-voters were excluded from the analysis. There were fifty-nine non-voters in 1879, 20 percent of the total; and fifty-two in 1882, 18 percent of the total (depicted in maps 2.1 and 2.2).

To perform further quantitative analyses, the roll-call data described above were merged with data from ICPSR-Census, 1880, for the vast majority of U.S. congressional districts (as shown in maps 2.1 and 2.2). Because it was not possible to show census data (organized by counties) by congressional districts within the same city, the analysis studied cities as a whole. Congressional district boundaries for the 47th Congress were obtained from Stanley B. Parsons, William W. Beach, and Michael J. Dubin, *United States Congressional Districts and Data, 1843–1883* (New York: Greenwood Press, 1986).

Chapter 3

The analysis in this chapter continues to rely on Hunt, *Making of a Special Relationship*, and Tsai, *China and the Overseas Chinese in the United States*. Equally important for understanding the hardening of exclusion are Delber L. McKee, *Chinese Exclusion versus the Open Door Policy, 1900–1906* (Detroit: Wayne State University Press, 1977), and Erika Lee, *At America's Gates: Chinese Immigration during the Exclusion Era, 1882–1943* (Chapel Hill: University of North Carolina Press, 2003), and particularly helpful for its attention to Gompers and the AFL is Gwendolyn Mink, *Old Labor and New Immigrants in American Political Development: Union, Party, and State, 1875–1920* (Ithaca: Cornell University Press, 1986). Analysis of early Japanese immigration and the exclusion debate is contained in Floyd William Matson, "The Anti-Japanese Movement in California, 1890–1942" (Ph.D. diss., University of California, Berkeley, 1953); Roger Daniels, *The Politics of Prejudice* (Berkeley: University of California Press, 1962); and Eiichiro Azuma, *Between Two Empires: Race, History, and Transnationalism in Japanese America* (New York: Oxford University Press, 2005).

My general understanding of the broader immigration restriction movement is based in these classics: Barbara Miller Solomon, *Ancestors and Immigrants* (Chicago: University of Chicago Press, 1956); and John Higham, *Strangers in the Land: Patterns of American Nativism, 1860–1925* (1955; repr., New Brunswick, N.J.: Rutgers University Press, 1992). In addition, I consulted Thomas J. Archdeacon, *Becoming Americans: An Ethnic History* (New York: Free Press, 1983); Desmond King, *Making Americans: Immigration, Race, and the Origins of Diverse Democracy* (Cambridge, Mass.: Harvard University Press, 2000); Zolberg, *Nation by Design*; and Tichenor, *Dividing Lines*. While mindful of the new perspectives in the study of American imperialism that have lessened the focus on the U.S. drive for markets, I still found influential these classic studies of U.S. expansionism to Asia: Walter LaFeber, *The New Empire: An Interpretation of American Expansion, 1860–1898* (1963; repr., Ithaca: Cornell University Press, 1998); Marilyn Young, *The Rhetoric of Empire: American China*

Policy, 1895–1901 (Cambridge, Mass.: Harvard University Press, 1969); and Thomas J. McCormick, *China Market: America's Quest for Informal Empire, 1893–1901* (1967; repr., Chicago: Ivan R. Dee, 1990).

Racial dimensions of Hawai'i annexation are addressed in Eric T. Love, *Race over Empire: Racism and U.S. Imperialism* (Chapel Hill: University of North Carolina Press, 2004); David M. Pletcher, *Diplomacy of Involvement: American Economic Expansion across the Pacific, 1784–1900* (Columbia: University of Missouri Press, 2001); Lawrence H. Fuchs, *Hawaii Pono: A Social History* (New York: Harcourt, Brace and World, 1961); and Christen Tsuyuko Sasaki, "Pacific Confluence: Negotiating the Nation in Nineteenth Century 'Hawai'i'" (Ph.D. diss., UCLA, 2011). A good comparison of U.S. imperial endeavors at the turn of the twentieth century that includes Hawai'i is Lanny Thompson, *Imperial Archipelago* (Honolulu: University of Hawai'i Press, 2010). Studies rooting early Filipino migration within U.S. colonization of the Philippines are particularly strong: Paul A. Kramer, *The Blood of Government* (Chapel Hill: University of North Carolina Press, 2006); Kimberly A. Alidio, "Between Civilizing Mission and Ethnic Assimilation" (Ph.D. diss., University of Michigan, 2001); Rick Baldoz, *The Third Asiatic Invasion* (New York: New York University Press, 2011); and Veta R. Schlimgen, "Neither Citizens nor Aliens: Filipino 'American Nationals' in the U.S. Empire, 1900–1946" (Ph.D. diss., University of Oregon, 2010).

Much of this chapter is based on primary sources, including Chester Rowell's views of Japanese immigration appearing in editorials for the *Fresno Republican* and David Starr Jordan's defense of Japanese immigrants that is revealed in Jordan (David Starr) Papers, Hoover Institution, Stanford University, Stanford, Calif.; and David Starr Jordan Papers, Special Collections and University Archives, Stanford University, Stanford, Calif., two separate collections at Stanford University. Also important for this chapter were the records of Samuel Gompers as contained in vol. 4, *A National Labor Movement Takes Shape, 1895–98,* and vol. 5, *An Expanding Movement at the Turn of the Century, 1898–1902*, of Samuel Gompers, *The Samuel Gompers Papers*, edited by Stuart B. Kaufman, Peter J. Albert, and Grace Palladino (Urbana: University of Illinois Press, 1991 and 1996).

As in the first two chapters, the analysis benefited from close attention to partisan and regional divisions as revealed in congressional roll-call voting, in this case on post-1882 expressions of Chinese exclusion and U.S.-China relations, as well as on Hawai'i annexation and the debate over claiming the Philippines.

Chapter 4

The sections in this chapter on Chinese immigration and U.S.-China relations benefit again from Hunt, *Making of a Special Relationship*; Tsai, *China and the Overseas Chinese in the United States*; McKee, *Chinese Exclusion versus the Open Door Policy*; and Qin, *Diplomacy of Nationalism*.

The classic works on this era of Japanese American history are Daniels, *Politics of Prejudice*; and Yuji Ichioka, *The Issei: The World of the First Generation Japanese Immigrants, 1885–1924* (New York: Free Press, 1988). I also benefited from these earlier studies: Matson, "Anti-Japanese Movement in California"; Tyler Dennett, *Roosevelt and the Russo-Japanese War* (1925; repr., Gloucester, Mass.: Peter Smith, 1959); Eleanor Tupper and George E. McReynolds, *Japan in American Public Opinion* (New York: Macmillan, 1937); Thomas G. Dyer, *Theodore Roosevelt and the Idea of Race* (Baton Rouge: Louisiana State University Press, 1992); Raymond Esthus, *Theodore Roosevelt and Japan* (Seattle: University of Washington Press, 1967); Charles E. Neu, *An Uncertain Friendship: Theodore Roosevelt and Japan, 1906–1909* (Cambridge, Mass.: Harvard University Press, 1968); and Thomas Andrew Bailey, *Theodore Roosevelt and the Japanese-American Crisis: An Account of the International Complications Arising from the Race Problems on the Pacific Coast* (Stanford: Stanford University Press, 1934).

The essential starting point for the egalitarian defense of Japanese immigrants in this period is Sandra C. Taylor, *Advocate of Understanding: Sidney Gulick and the Search for Peace with Japan* (Kent: Kent State University Press, 1984); but see as well Bruce A.

Abrams, "A Muted Cry: White Opposition to the Japanese Exclusion Movement, 1911–1924" (Ph.D. diss., New York University, 1987). A useful study of anti-Japanese politics in the Sacramento Delta is Michael Meloy, "The Long Road to Manzanar: Politics, Land, and Race in the Japanese Exclusion Movement, 1900–1942" (Ph.D. diss., University of California, Davis, 2004).

The analysis in this chapter benefited from these published primary sources: A. T. Mahan, *The Problem of Asia: And Its Effects on International Policies* (Boston: Little, Brown, 1905); Sidney Lewis Gulick, *White Peril in the Far East* (London: Fleming H. Revell, 1905) and *The American Japanese Problem* (New York: Scribner's, 1914); and U.S. Congress, House, Immigration and Naturalization Committee, *Hindu Immigration*, pts. 1–5, 63rd Cong., 2nd sess. (Washington: Government Printing Office, 1914). This and all subsequent chapters, with a few exceptions, did not benefit from the study of congressional roll-call voting because, unlike with the Chinese, Congress sought to exclude latter migrations of Asian laborers without singling them out by name in its legislation. In this way, the recorded votes applied to immigration more generally and did not target just Asian Americans.

Archival records that fleshed out new dimensions of the exclusion debate during this period can be found primarily in the Carnegie Endowment for International Peace Records, Butler Library, Columbia University, New York, N.Y.; Francis Loomis Papers, Special Collections and University Archives, Stanford University, Stanford, Calif.; Jordan (David Starr) Papers, Hoover Institution; and David Starr Jordan Papers, Special Collections and University Archives. Reports by Harvey Hugo Guy (Meiji-Taisho Series, Japan Diplomatic Records Office [Gaiko Shirōkan], Tokyo, Japan) to the Japanese consul general in San Francisco also offer insight into the strategies and perspectives of egalitarians working to stave off Japanese exclusion.

Chapter 5

Many of the secondary sources used for the last chapter carry over to this one: Daniels, *Politics of Prejudice*; Ichioka, *Issei*; Taylor, *Advocate of Understanding*; Tupper and Mc-

Reynolds, *Japan in American Public Opinion*; and Meloy, "Long Road to Manzanar."

The analysis also benefited from close attention to almost 1,500 pages of testimony in U.S. Congress, House, Immigration and Naturalization Committee, *Japanese Immigration*, 66th Cong., 2nd sess. (Washington: Government Printing Office, 1921). Also see this subsequent hearing: U.S. Congress, Senate, Immigration Committee, *Japanese Immigration Legislation*, 68th Cong., 1st sess. (Washington: Government Printing Office, 1924); and published primary documents related to Eiichi Shibusawa in Eiichi Shibusawa, *Biographical Materials on Eiichi Shibusawa*, vols. 34–35 (Tokyo: Shibusawa Eiichi Denki Shiryō Kankōkai, 1960). Japanese Foreign Ministry records housed in Tokyo (Meiji-Taisho Series, Japan Diplomatic Records Office [Gaiko Shirōkan]) offer a wealth of information on issues relating to Japanese exclusion. I found especially useful reports by R. W. Ryder on the congressional hearings on Japanese immigration, by various Americans on the alien land law proposition in Los Angeles, and by Harvey Guy on the activities of the education campaign. The Hiram Johnson Papers and James D. Phelan Papers at the Bancroft Library, University of California, Berkeley, in addition to revealing the views of each of these exclusionists, hold crucial documents by V. S. McClatchy and the Japanese Exclusion League. Material on the egalitarian John P. Irish is available at the Special Collections and University Archives, Stanford University, and in Barbara Brower's private collection, Portland, Ore. (copies of cited documents in this collection are in my possession).

Statistical analysis in this chapter has benefited from a rare collection of quantitative analyses of Japanese immigration during this period that include Brian J. Gaines and Wendy K. Tam Cho, "On California's 1920 Alien Land Law: The Psychology and Economics of Racial Discrimination," *State Politics and Policy Quarterly* 4, no. 3 (Fall 2004): 271–93; Masao Suzuki, "Important or Impotent? Taking Another Look at the 1920 California Alien Land Law," *Journal of Economic History* 64, no. 1 (March 2004): 125–43; and Robert Higgs, "Landless by Law: Japanese Immigrants in California Agriculture to

1941," *Journal of Economic History* 38, no. 1 (March 1978): 205–25. Like Gaines and Cho, my analysis of the alien land law ballot measure relies on California Secretary of State, *Statement of the Vote: General Election Held on November 2, 1920* (Sacramento: State of California, 1920). No one has studied precinct data for this vote, which I was able to do, with technical, archival, and data-input assistance, for Los Angeles. I conducted the statistical and GIS analysis for all chapters.

Chapter 6

While most studies of Japanese exclusion stop with the passage of the Immigration Act of 1924, these secondary works enable one to appreciate great efforts since then to overturn it or improve the political and racial climate for the Japanese in the United States and Hawai'i: Izumi Hirobe, *Japanese Pride, American Prejudice: Modifying the Exclusion Clause of the 1924 Immigration Act* (Stanford: Stanford University Press, 2001); Gordon H. Chang, "Yamato Ichihashi: A Biographical Essay," in *Morning Glory, Evening Shadows: Yamato Ichihashi and His Internment Writings, 1942–1945*, edited by Gordon H. Chang, 11–50 (Stanford: Stanford University Press, 1997); Sarah M. Griffith, "'Where We Can Battle for the Lord and Japan': The Development of Liberal Protestant Antiracism before World War II," *Journal of American History* 100, no. 2 (September 2013): 429–53; and Sarah M. Griffith, "Conflicting Dialogues: The Survey of Race Relations in the Trans-Pacific and the Fight for Asian American Racial Equality" (Ph.D. diss., University of California, Santa Barbara, 2010). For the Institute of Pacific Relations, see Griffith, "'Where We Can Battle for the Lord and Japan'"; Tomoko Akami, *Internationalizing the Pacific: The United States, Japan, and the Institute of Pacific Relations in War and Peace, 1919–1945* (London: Routledge, 2002); and Paul F. Hooper, *Elusive Destiny: The Internationalist Movement in Modern Hawai'i* (Honolulu: University of Hawai'i Press, 1980). The exclusion debate in Hawai'i is presented in Eileen H. Tamura, *Americanization, Acculturation, and Ethnic Identity: The Nisei Generation in Hawaii* (Urbana: University of Illinois Press, 1994); Tom Coffman, *The Island Edge of America: A Political History of Hawai'i*

(Honolulu: University of Hawai'i Press, 2003); Hiromi Monobe, "Shaping an Ethnic Leadership: Takie Okumura and the 'Americanization' of Nisei in Hawai'i, 1919–1945" (Ph.D. diss., University of Hawai'i, 2004); and Gary Y. Okihiro, *Cane Fires: The Anti-Japanese Movement in Hawaii, 1865–1945* (Philadelphia: Temple University Press, 1992).

The analysis of Filipino exclusion and labor organizing in this chapter benefited especially from studies by Baldoz, *Third Asiatic Invasion*; Schlimgen, "Neither Citizens nor Aliens"; Kramer, *Blood of Government*; Chris Friday, *Organizing Asian-American Labor: The Pacific Coast Canned-Salmon Industry, 1870–1942* (Philadelphia: Temple University Press, 1994); Howard A. DeWitt, *Anti-Filipino Movements in California* (San Francisco: R and E Research, 1976); Bruno Lasker, *Filipino Immigration: To Continental United States and Hawaii* (Chicago: University of Chicago Press, 1931); and Mae M. Ngai, *Impossible Subjects: Illegal Aliens and the Making of Modern America* (Princeton: Princeton University Press, 2004), 96–126.

Primary sources used for this chapter came from the papers of James D. Phelan (BANC FILM 2443, Bancroft Library, University of California, Berkeley), Paul Scharrenberg (BANC MSS C-B 906, Bancroft Library, University of California, Berkeley), Chester Rowell (BANC MSS C-B 401, Bancroft Library, University of California, Berkeley), Arthur Arlett (BANC MSS C-B 408, Bancroft Library, University of California, Berkeley); Survey of Race Relations Collection, Hoover Institution, Stanford University, Stanford, Calif., https://collections.stanford.edu/srr/bin/page?forward=home (October 3, 2015); Japanese Ministry of Foreign Affairs Records (Meiji-Taisho Series, Japan Diplomatic Records Office [Gaiko Shirōkan], Tokyo, Japan); and Institute of Pacific Relations Records (M004 and M021, Hamilton Library, University of Hawai'i at Manoa, Honolulu). Additional primary sources came from U.S. Congress, Senate, Immigration Committee, *American Citizenship Rights for Women*, 72nd Cong., 2nd sess. (Washington: Government Printing Office, 1933); and these hearings by the House Immigration and Naturalization Committee: U.S. Congress, House, Immigration and Naturalization Committee, *Im-*

migration and Citizenship of American-Born Women Married to Aliens, 69th Cong., 1st sess. (Washington: Government Printing Office, 1926); U.S. Congress, House, Immigration and Naturalization Committee, *Exclusion of Immigration from the Philippines*, 71st Cong., 2nd sess. (Washington: Government Printing Office, 1930); U.S. Congress, House, Immigration and Naturalization Committee, *To Return Unemployed Filipinos*, 72nd Cong., 2nd sess. (Washington: Government Printing Office, 1933); U.S. Congress, House, Immigration and Naturalization Committee, *Oriental Veterans*, 74th Cong., 1st sess. (Washington: Government Printing Office, 1935); U.S. Congress, House, Immigration and Naturalization Committee, Extending Time for Voluntary Return of Unemployed Filipinos to the Philippines—Hearings on H.J. Res. 71, unpublished, 74th Cong., 1st sess., February 5–6, 1935; U.S. Congress, House, Immigration and Naturalization Committee, *India-Born Residents Request Naturalization*, 76th Cong., 1st sess. (Washington: Government Printing Office, 1939); and U.S. Congress, House, Immigration and Naturalization Committee, Hearings on H.R. 7239, To Authorize Naturalization of Filipinos Who Are Permanent Residents of the United States, unpublished, 76th Cong., 3rd sess., March 28, 1940.

Chapter 7

This chapter benefited from a wealth of research on the decision to intern Japanese Americans. The literature begins with Commission on Wartime Relocation and Internment of Civilians, *Personal Justice Denied* (1982; repr., Washington, D.C.: Civil Liberties Education Fund, 1997), but also includes Morton Grodzins, *Americans Betrayed: Politics and the Japanese Evacuation* (Chicago: University of Chicago Press, 1949); Jacobus tenBroek, Edward N. Barnhart, and Floyd W. Matson, *Prejudice, War, and the Constitution* (1954; repr., Berkeley: University of California Press, 1970); Peter Irons, *Justice at War: The Story of the Japanese American Internment Cases* (New York: Oxford University Press, 1983); Stetson Conn, "The Decision to Evacuate the Japanese from the Pacific Coast," in *Command Decisions*, 125–29 (Washington D.C.: U.S. Army Center of Military History,

1990); Greg Robinson, *By Order of the President* (Cambridge, Mass.: Harvard University Press, 2001); Roger Daniels, *The Decision to Relocate the Japanese Americans* (Philadelphia: J. B. Lippincott, 1975); Michi Weglyn, *Years of Infamy* (New York: William Morrow, 1976); and Brian Masaru Hayashi, *Democratizing the Enemy* (Princeton: Princeton University Press, 2004).

In addition to many of the above books, these secondary works contributed to my understanding of the WRA camps, formation of the 442nd Regimental Combat Team, and the return of the internees to the West Coast: Takashi Fujitani, *Race for Empire* (Berkeley: University of California Press, 2011); Tom Coffman, *The Island Edge of America: A Political History of Hawai'i* (Honolulu: University of Hawai'i Press, 2003); Alice Yang Murray, *Historical Memories of the Japanese American Internment and Struggle for Redress* (Stanford: Stanford University Press, 2008); Carey McWilliams, *Prejudice: Japanese-Americans, Symbol of Racial Intolerance* (Boston: Little, Brown, 1944); Kevin Allen Leonard, "Years of Hope, Days of Fear: The Impact of World War II on Race Relations in Los Angeles" (Ph.D. diss., University of California, Davis, 1992); Mark Brilliant, *The Color of America Has Changed: How Racial Diversity Shaped Civil Rights Reform in California, 1941–1978* (New York: Oxford University Press, 2010); Lon Kurashige, *Japanese American Celebration and Conflict* (Berkeley: University of California Press, 2002); Audrie Girdner and Anne Loftis, *The Great Betrayal* (New York: Macmillan, 1970); Robert Shaffer, "Cracks in the Consensus: Defending the Rights of Japanese Americans during World War II," *Radical History Review* 72 (1998): 84–120; and Robert Shaffer, "Opposition to Internment: Defending Japanese American Rights during World War II," *Historian* 61, no. 3 (March 1999): 597–620.

The classic study of the Magunson Act in 1943 is Fred W. Riggs, *Pressures on Congress: A Study of the Repeal of Chinese Exclusion* (New York: King's Crown Press, 1950), but this needs to be supplemented by Karen J. Leong, "Foreign Policy, National Identity, and Citizenship: The Roosevelt White House and the Expediency of Repeal," *Journal of American Ethnic History* 22, no. 4 (Summer

2003): 3–30; Madeline Y. Hsu, *The Good Immigrants: How the Yellow Peril Became the Model Minority* (Princeton: Princeton University Press, 2015), 81–103; and Jane H. Hong, "Reorientating America in the World: Race, Geopolitics, and the Repeal of Asian Exclusion" (Ph.D. diss., Harvard University, 2013). Hong's dissertation provides important insight into transnational campaigns to repeal Korean and Indian exclusion. My analysis of the postwar context of conservative, anti-communist internationalism benefited from Joyce Mao, *Asia First: China and the Making of Modern American Conservatism* (Chicago: University of Chicago Press, 2015), as well as from Stanley D. Bachrack, *The Committee of One Million: China Lobby Politics, 1953–1971* (New York: Columbia University Press, 1976); Ross Y. Koen, *The China Lobby in American Politics* (New York: Octagon, 1974); and Frederick Vanderbilt Field, *From Right to Left: An Autobiography* (Westport, Conn.: Lawrence Hill, 1983).

Egalitarian activity in post-internment California is captured by collections of the Pacific Coast Committee on American Principles and Fair Play Records (BANC MSS C-A 171, Bancroft Library, University of California, Berkeley). For the egalitarianism of Ruth and Harry Kingman, also see Harry L. Kingman, "Citizenship in Democracy," interviews conducted by Rosemary Levenson, 1971–72, Regional Oral History, University of California, Berkeley, http://content.cdlib.org/view?docId=kt9199p014&doc.view=entire_text (October 3, 2015).

Finally, this chapter benefited from an abundance of congressional hearings. For those conducted by the House Immigration and Naturalization Committee, see U.S. Congress, House, Immigration and Naturalization Committee, Hearings on H.R. 1844, To Authorize the Naturalization of Filipinos Who Are Permanent Residents of the United States, unpublished, 77th Cong., 2nd sess., February 4, 1942; U.S. Congress, House, Immigration and Naturalization Committee, *Repeal of Chinese Exclusion Acts*, 78th Cong., 1st sess. (Washington: Government Printing Office, 1943); U.S. Congress, House, Immigration and Naturalization Committee, *Naturalization of Filipinos*, 78th Cong., 2nd sess. (Washington: Government Printing Office,

1944); and U.S. Congress, House, Immigration and Naturalization Committee, *To Grant a Quota to Eastern Hemisphere Indians and to Make Them Racially Eligible for Naturalization*, 79th Cong., 1st sess. (Washington: Government Printing Office, 1945). In addition, hearings from these other committees were important: U.S. Congress, Select Committee Investigating National Defense Migration, *National Defense Migration*, 77th Cong., 2nd sess., pts. 29–31 (Washington: Government Printing Office, 1942); U.S. Congress, House, Judiciary Committee, *Providing for Equality under Immigration and Naturalization Laws*, 80th Cong., 2nd sess. (Washington: Government Printing Office, 1948); U.S. Congress, House, Committee on Appropriations, *Sixth Supplemental National Defense Appropriation Bill for 1942*, 77th Cong., 2nd sess. (Washington: Government Printing Office, 1942); U.S. Congress, Senate, Judiciary Committee, Hearings on H.R. 3999, To Authorize the Attorney General to Adjudicate Certain Claims Resulting from Evacuation of Certain Persons of Japanese Ancestry under Military Orders, unpublished, 80th Cong., 2nd sess., May 21, 1948; U.S. Congress, Senate, Judiciary Committee, Naturalization of Asian and Pacific Peoples, unpublished, July 19, 1949; and U.S. Congress, House and Senate, Joint Subcommittees of Judiciary Committees, *Revision of Immigration, Naturalization, and Nationality Laws* (Washington: Government Printing Office, 1951).

Chapter 8

The study of Hawai'i statehood has only recently been connected to Asian American history in Ellen D. Wu, *The Color of Success: Asian Americans and the Origins of the Model Minority* (Princeton: Princeton University Press, 2014), 210–41; and Joyce Mao, "Asia First: China and American Conservatism, 1937–1965" (Ph.D. diss., University of California, Berkeley, 2007), 219–45. The classic work on the politics of statehood is Roger Bell, *Last among Equals: Hawaiian Statehood and American Politics* (Honolulu: University of Hawai'i Press, 1984), while Coffman places it within the context of Hawai'i's longer political history in *Island Edge of America*.

Analyses of the Immigration Act of 1965 (Hart-Celler) are contained in David M.

Reimers, *Still the Golden Door: The Third World Comes to America* (New York: Columbia University Press, 1986); Ngai, *Impossible Subjects*; Tichenor, *Dividing Lines*; and Zolberg, *Nation by Design*. A recent study focusing on the selection of particular types of Chinese immigrants and refugees is Hsu, *Good Immigrants*.

Daryl J. Maeda has written two books addressing the history of the Asian American movement—*Rethinking the Asian American Movement* (New York: Routledge, 2012) and *Chains of Babylon: The Rise of Asian America* (Minneapolis: University of Minnesota Press, 2009)—but still useful is William Wei, *The Asian American Movement* (Philadelphia: Temple University Press, 1995), as well as the primary sources collected in Amy Tachiki et al., eds., *Roots: An Asian American Reader* (Los Angeles: UCLA Asian American Studies, 1971); Emma Gee, ed., *Counterpoint: Perspectives on Asian America* (Los Angeles: UCLA Asian American Studies, 1976); and back issues of the *Amerasia* journal. For Ronald Takaki's writings, see especially his *Strangers from a Different Shore: A History of Asian Americans* (Boston: Little, Brown, 1989) and *Iron Cages: Race and Culture in the 19th Century* (1979; repr., New York: Oxford University Press, 1990), as well as Sylvia Yanagisako's critique, "Transforming Orientalism: Gender, Nationality, and Class in Asian American Studies," in *Naturalizing Power: Essays in Feminist Cultural Analysis*, ed. Sylvia Yanagisako and Carol Delaney, 275–98 (New York: Routledge, 1995). For patterns of racial politics influencing Asian Americans after World War II, see Wu, *Color of Success*; Charlotte Brooks, *Alien Neighbors, Foreign Friends: Asian Americans, Housing, and the Transformation of Urban California* (Chicago: University of Chicago Press, 2009); Scott Kurashige, *The Shifting Grounds of Race: Black and Japanese Americans in the Making of Multiethnic Los Angeles* (Princeton: Princeton University Press, 2010); Naoko Shibusawa, *America's Geisha Ally: Reimagining the Japanese Enemy* (Cambridge, Mass.: Harvard University Press, 2006); and Christina Klein, *Cold War Orientalism: Asia in the Middlebrow Imagination, 1945–1961* (Berkeley: University of California Press, 2003).

The major study of Japanese American collective memory is Alice Yang Murray, *Historical Memories of the Japanese American Internment and Struggle for Redress* (Stanford: Stanford University Press, 2008), but also see Jane Naomi Iwamura, "Critical Faith: Japanese Americans and the Birth of a New Civil Religion," *American Quarterly* 59, no. 3 (September 2007): 937–68. My understanding of historical memory and the lessons it can and cannot teach is especially indebted to Peter Novick, *The Holocaust in American Life* (Boston: Houghton Mifflin, 1999). Also see David W. Blight, *Race and Reunion: The Civil War in American Memory* (Cambridge, Mass.: Harvard University Press, 2001); John Bodnar, *Remaking America: Public Memory, Commemoration, and Patriotism in the Twentieth Century* (Princeton: Princeton University Press, 1993); and T. Fujitani, Geoffrey M. White, and Lisa Yoneyama, eds., *Perilous Memories: The Asia-Pacific War(s)* (Durham: Duke University Press, 2001).

The primary sources for this chapter were mainly from congressional hearings and other government publications. These include U.S. Congress, House, Committee of Rules, To Enable the People of Hawaii to Create a Constitution and State Government and to Be Admitted into the Union on an Equal Footing with the Original States, unpublished, 80th Cong., 1st sess., April 17, 1947; U.S. Congress, House, Committee on Interior and Insular Affairs, *Hawaii Statehood*, Report No. 32, unpublished, 86th Cong., 1st sess., 1959; U.S. Congress, Senate, Committee on Insular and Interior Affairs, *Hawaii Statehood*, 81st Cong., 2nd sess. (Washington: Government Printing Office, 1950); U.S. Congress, Senate, Judiciary Committee, Subcommittee on Immigration and Naturalization, *Immigration*, 89th Cong., 1st sess. (Washington: Government Printing Office, 1965); U.S. Congress, House, Judiciary Subcommittee, *Immigration*, 89th Cong., 1st sess. (Washington: Government Printing Office, 1965); U.S. Congress, House, Committee on Governmental Affairs, *Commission on Wartime Relocation and Internment of Civilians Act*, 96th Cong., 2nd sess. (Washington: Government Printing Office, 1980); Commission on Wartime Relocation and Internment of Civilians, *Personal Justice Denied* (1982; repr., Washington, D.C.: Civil

Liberties Education Fund, 1997); U.S. Congress, House, Committee of the Judiciary, *Japanese-American and Aleutian Wartime Relocation*, 98th Cong., 2nd sess. (Washington: Government Printing Office, 1985); and U.S. Congress, House, Committee of the Judiciary, *Civil Liberties Act of 1985 and the Aleutian and Pribilof Islands Restitution Act*, 99th Cong., 2nd sess. (Washington: Government Printing Office, 1986).

Additional Archival Sources

Arthur, Chester A. "Veto Message." April 4, 1882. Online by Gerhard Peters and John T. Woolley, The American Presidency Project, http://www.presidency.ucsb.edu/ws/?pid=68779%20-%20axzz2hY4WXW6z (September 28, 2015).

Federal Council of Churches of Christ in America Collections. Presbyterian Historical Society, Philadelphia, Penn.

Gulick Family Papers, 1916–1923. Houghton Library, Harvard University, Cambridge, Mass.

Office of the Secretary of the State. Election return, Los Angeles County, General Election. November 2, 1920. California State Archives, Sacramento, Calif.

Roosevelt, Theodore. "First Annual Message." December 3, 1901. Online by Gerhard Peters and John T. Woolley, The American Presidency Project, http://www.presidency.ucsb.edu/ws/?pid=29542 (September 30, 2015).

U.S. Census Bureau. Free Schedules ("manuscript census"), 1920.

U.S. Census Bureau, Jessica S. Barnes, and Claudette E. Bennett. "The Asian Population: 2000." February 2002. http://www.census.gov/prod/2002pubs/c2kbr01-16.pdf (October 7, 2015).

U.S. Congress, Senate, Committee on Education and Labor. *Report of the Committee of the Senate upon the Relations between Labor and Capital and Testimony Taken by the Committee*, 48th Cong. Washington: Government Printing Office, 1885.

INDEX

|||||||||||||||||||||||||||||||||||||||||||||||||||||||||||||||||||||||||||||||||||||||||||||||||||||||||||||||||||||||||||||||||||||||||||||||||||||||||||||||||||||||||||||

Page numbers in italics refer to illustrations.

Emmons, Delos, 176
Empathy, historical, 229–30
Ennis, Edward J., 174, 175, 197–98
Equality, exclusive vs. inclusive view of, in U.S., 4. *See also* Racial equality
Equal protection clause, 27, 65, 197
ESC. *See* Emergency Services Committee
Espionage, fear of, 11, *12*; during World War I, 105; during World War II, 172–73, 176–77, 222–23. *See also* Internment
Ethnic studies, 213, 215–18, 224
Eugenics, 83–84
Europe: vs. Asia, economies of, 10–11; trans-pacific trade and, 14
European immigrants: conscription of, in Civil War, 28–29; as Democrats, 9, 21, 24; exclusion of, 65–69, 106; in Immigration Act of 1917, 106; quotas on, *12*; recruitment during Civil War, 25–26; recruitment in 1900s, 106; as Republicans, 9; as source of labor competition, 62–63, 65–69; from southern and eastern Europe, 62, 65, 113, 154, 160; U.S. citizenship for, 9–10; as white, 57
Evacuation Claims Act of 1948, 198, 221
Everett, Miles Chapman, 241 (n. 19)
Exclusion, perfect storm of, x–xi, 11–12
Exclusion debate: changes in conditions for late period of, 155–57; contemporary relevance of, xii–xiii, 226–34; end of, 12; gaps in scholarship on, 6–7, 218, 226; Great Transformation in, 170–71; nationalization of, 36, 44–45; policy communities in, 7–8, *228*, 228–29. *See also specific groups*
Exclusionists: changes in meaning of term, 227; Democrats as, 45–47, *47*, 60; focus of scholarship on, 6–7; imperialists compared to, 73–74; individuals' transformation into egalitarians from, 8; meaning and use of term, 3–4, 239 (n. 10); Republicans' transformation from egalitarians into, 44–48, *47*, *48*, 114. *See also specific people*
Executive Order 9066, 170, 176–77, 197–98, 220
Expansionism, U.S.: labor union opposition to, 76–77; in late 1800s, 69–77; in mid-1800s, 15–21, 69–70; in Midway Islands and Alaska, 24, 244 (n. 29); and trans-pacific trade, 15–21, 69
Extraterritoriality: in China, 18, 189, 191; in Japan, 20

Factories in the Field (McWilliams), 139, 164, 185
Fair Play Committee, 186–87, 188
Family reunification, 133, 135, 208, 213
Farewell to Manzanar (Houston), 224
Farrington, Wallace, 168
Fatal Misconception (Connelly), 238 (n. 5)
FBI. *See* Federal Bureau of Investigation
Fears, immigration-related: major categories of, 11, *12*; Masaoka on, 211–12
Federal Bureau of Investigation (FBI), 171, 223
Federal Council of Churches, 102–3, 114–15, 190
Fernandez, Leo, 194
Field, Frederick Vanderbilt, 168–69, 200, 228
Field, Stephen J., 32–33
Fifteen Passenger Act of 1879, 45, 47
Fifteenth Amendment, 29–30, 32
Fifth column activity, 171–73, 177–78, 180, 181–82
Filipino-American National Council, 194
Filipino exclusion, 140, 147–57; in California, 148–54; changes in conditions for debate over, 155–57; congressional hearings on Shortridge amendment on, 154; congressional hearings on Welch bill on, 148–54; explanation of timing of, 227; Philippine independence linked with, 152–55; repeal of, 193–94; sexuality in, 150–51, 194
Filipino immigrants: as aliens vs. nationals, 155; assimilation of, 74, 150, 194; exclusion of (*see* Filipino exclusion); in Hawai'i, 148, 151; in labor unions, 163–64; support for, 74–75; unemployed, repatriation of, 159–62; U.S. citizenship for, 155, 164–65, 193–94
Filipinos, 74–77; efforts to uplift, 74–76, 152; free right of entry for, x, 75, 148, 152; migration patterns of, 148; in U.S. military, 74, 157
Finely, John H., 145
Fisher, Galen: in Committee on National Security and Fair Play, 172, 181, 187; on compensation for internment, 197; at Institute of Pacific Relations conference, 145; in Survey of Race Relations, 140–42; in Tolan Committee hearings, 181–82
Fisk, John, 158
Flood, human. *See* Human flood
Flood control, in California, 99
Foner, Eric, 238 (n. 5), 239 (n. 11)

Fong, Hiram, 207, 211
Foord, John, 78, 79, 88
Foran, Martin, 65–66
Foran Act of 1885, 65–66
Ford, Gerald, 220
Ford, Leland, 171–72
Foreign miners' tax, 22, 23
Foreign relations policy community, 7, 228, 229
Fourteen Points, 110
Fourteenth Amendment, 9; Chinese immigrants under, 26–27, 29, 30, 32, 33; equal protection clause of, 27, 65, 197; race in, 26–27
Free-Soilers, 20, 243 (n. 12)
French Canadians, exclusion of, 5, 65, 67
Fresno Republican (newspaper), 95
Fryer, E. R., 185
Fujii, Sei, 197

Geary, Thomas, 64
Geary Act of 1892, 64, 79, 248 (nn. 3, 6)
Gender, in citizenship requirements, 242 (n. 20)
Gender ideologies, 241 (n. 18)
Generation gap, 216
Gentlemen's Agreement, U.S.-Japan: advocates for replacement of, 133, 135–36, 137; creation of, 94; and Immigration Act of 1917, 106; and Immigration Act of 1924, 112, 135; Japanese women in, 98–99; as model for Indian exclusion, 108
Geopolitical interests, as driver of U.S. imperialism, 72–73
George, Henry: and alien land law of 1920, 129; at congressional hearings on Chinese immigrants, 37–38, 245 (n. 5); on land monopolies, 139; *Progress and Poverty*, 43; on single tax, 44–45, 129
German immigrants: as Democrats, 9, 24; labor union opposition to, 62, 65; during World War I, 105, 114; during World War II, 170, 171, 175, 181
Germany: and Japanese imperialism, 115–16; in World War I, 105
Gerstle, Gary, 239 (n. 11)
Gibson, Otis, 41–42, 44, 57
Gilded Age, 35–36, 68
Gleason, George: in Survey of Race Relations, 140–42; in Tolan Committee hearings, 180–81
Goldblatt, Louis, 182, 187

Gold rush, 8, 21–23
Gompers, Samuel: Asian immigrants opposed by, 62–63, 77, 79, 225; European immigrants opposed by, 62–63, 65–66; on imperialism, 77; on Japanese immigrants, 81–82, 94–95, 104
Gramsci, Antonio, 217
Grant, Madison, 84, 133
Grant, Ulysses S., 34, 43
Grasson, Murray, 161
Great Depression, emergence of industrial unionism in, 162
Great Transformation, in exclusion debate, 170–71
Green, William, 187
Gresham, Walter, 65
Gresham-Yang Treaty, 65, 78, 87
Grew, Joseph, 200
Guevara, Pedro, 161
Gulick, Sidney, 91–92; *The American Japanese Problem*, 102; in congressional hearings of 1924 on Japanese exclusion, 134–36; in education campaign on Japanese immigrants, 102–4; on interracial marriage, 120–21; on Japanese threat to Open Door policy, 91–92; on quotas, 102–3, 104, 114, 146; on racism as white peril, 92, 102, 181; Rowell's support for, 143–44; *White Peril in the Far East*, 102
Gullion, Allen W., 174
Gunboat diplomacy, 19
Gunton, George, 81
Guy, Harvey: in congressional hearings on Japanese exclusion, 117; in education campaign on Japanese immigrants, 101–2, 103–4; Japanese Exclusion League and, 133; in Survey of Race Relations, 140, 141
Gyory, Andrew, 240 (n. 15)

Haan, Kilsoo: on IPR textbook on Japan, 166–68, 169; on Korean independence, 199; on repeal of Japanese exclusion, 190–91
Haley, Nikki, 233
Hall, Jack, 206, 208
Hamilton, Alexander, 16
Hanihara, Masanao, 137, 156, 257 (n. 48)
Harada, Tasuku, 145
Harding, Warren G., 112, 130, *131*, 132
Hare, Butler B., 154–55
Harrison, Benjamin, 71
Hart-Celler Act. *See* Immigration and Nationality Act of 1965

power, emergence of, 89, 90; in World War I, 105, 109. *See also* Gentlemen's Agreement; World War II

Japan boom, 212

Japanese American Citizens League (JACL): on alien land law, 196; Asian American movement on, 215; California Joint Immigration Committee on, 158; establishment of, 158; on Hawaiian statehood, 207; on Immigration and Nationality Act of 1965, 209–11; on internment, 177; *Pacific Citizen* of, 197; in Tolan Committee hearings, 182–83

Japanese American Evacuation and Resettlement Study, 185

Japanese American Evacuation Claims Act of 1948, 219

Japanese Americans and immigrants: assimilability of, 120–21, 135, 144–45, 170; in California (*see* California); in congressional hearings on Japanese exclusion, 117; decline in flow of, 214; exclusion of (*see* Japanese exclusion); in Hawai'i (*see* Hawai'i); internment of (*see* Internment); IPR textbook on Japan and, 166–69; land ownership by (*see* Alien land law); as model minority, 214; as national security threat, 87; racial incompatibility of, 80, 111, 115, 135; Roosevelt (Theodore) on equality of, 4; social mobility of, 99; in Survey of Race Relations, 141; U.S. citizenship for, 86, 114–15, 158, 197; U.S. citizenship for, effects of ineligibility for, 9–10; as white, 84; women, surge of, 98–99; during World War I, 105; during World War II, in army, 170, 171, 176, 186–87, 195, 198, 200, 211–12. *See also* Issei; Nisei

Japanese and Korean Exclusion League, 93

Japanese Associations, 118

Japanese exclusion, 111–38; in California (*see* California); Chinese exclusion compared to, 84–85, 114, 138; congressional hearings of 1920 on, 116–23, 133; congressional hearings of 1924 on, 134–37; early debate over, 79–84; explanation of timing of, 227; in Immigration Act of 1917, 106, 109; in Immigration Act of 1924, 111, 135–38; labor unions on, 81–82, 94–95, 103–4, 122–23; as national security issue, 86–87; regional patterns in support for, 97–104; repeal of, 198–202; repeal of, attempts at, 139–40, 146–47; Shandong controversy and, 115–16, 133; and Survey of Race Relations, 141;

U.S. relations with Japan in, 96–103; during World War I, 104–5

Japanese Exclusion League, 132–33, 141. *See also* California Joint Immigration Committee

Japanese Foreign Ministry, 80, 82, 103–4, 117, 129

Japanese studies: at Stanford University, 142–43; at University of Hawaii, 145

Japan Society of New York, 97, 98, 102

Japan Society of Seattle, 147

Jefferson, Thomas, 16, 17, 18

Jewish immigrants: Filipino immigrants compared to, 154; and interracial marriage, 108, 122; from Russia, 113

Jindal, Bobby, 233

Johnson, Albert: in congressional hearings on Japanese exclusion, 117–18; death of, 159; on Filipino exclusion, 148, 156; in Immigration Act of 1924, 135–38; on Japanese citizenship, 134; on quotas for Japanese immigrants, 147

Johnson, Hiram: on alien land law, 100–101, 253 (n. 32); death of, 194; and Immigration Act of 1924, 137; on internment, 173; on League of Nations, 143; and McClatchy (V. S.), 133; Rowell in election of, 96; and Warren, 179

Johnson, James A., 29–30

Johnson, Lyndon, 203–4, 207, 208

Johnson-Reed Act of 1924. *See* Immigration Act of 1924

Jones, William A., 109

Jones-Costigan Act of 1934, 144

Jones Law. *See* Philippine Autonomy Act

Jordan, David Starr, 82–84; and alien land law of 1920, 124; on interracial marriage, 120–21; on Japanese exclusion, 96–97, 135; Japanese Exclusion League and, 133; Japanese studies at Stanford University under, 142–43; racial theories of, 83–84, 251 (n. 60); Ross fired by, 82, 250 (n. 56)

Judd, Walter, 192, 198–201, 208

Justice at War (Irons), 219–20

Justice Department: on German immigrants during World War I, 105; internment camps run by, 262 (n. 23); in internment decision, 174; on Japanese immigrants during World War II, 171

Kawakami, Karl K., 255 (n. 26)

Kawano, Jack, 163, 205–6

Kearney, Denis, 42, 44, 93

New England interests opposed by Republicans of, 58–61, *60*, 247 (n. 39)
Military, U.S. *See* Army; Navy; Veterans
Military necessity: and Japanese internment, 174, 219, 220; and repeal of Chinese exclusion, 191
Mineta, Norman, 220, 232–33
Mink, Patsy, 211
Miscegenation. *See* Interracial marriage
Missionaries, U.S.: arrival in China, 16, 18; Boxer Rebellion and, 78; defense of Chinese immigrants by, 23; immigration restrictions supported by, 68–69; in international organizations, 98; in Japan, 91–92; at San Francisco congressional hearings, 41–42, 44. *See also specific people*
Model minority, 213–18; critique of concept, 215–18; neoconservatives on, 204, 215, 216; as nonviolent racism, 1; origins of concept, 214–15, 238 (n. 2)
Moncado, Hilario, 153
Mongrelization, fear of, 11, *12*
Monopolies, land, 43–44, 139
Monopoly capitalism, regional differences in congressional votes on, 59, 60, *60*
Mormons, 33
Morris, Roland, 145
Morton, Oliver, 36
Most favored nation status, 27, 29, 33
Mott, John, 141, 145
Multicultural history, emergence of field, 203
Multiculturalism, 203–5, 224
Murray, Alice Yang, 184
Muslim Americans, 232
Mutual aid societies: Chinese (*huiguan*), 22, 33; Philippine, 161. *See also* Six Companies
Muzumdar, Hardias T., 165
Myer, Dillon, 184–85, 186, 197–98, 200
Myran, Albert G., 123

Nanking, Treaty of, 18
National Guard, Japanese Americans in, 144
Nationalism, Philippine, 153–54
Nationalism, U.S.: isolationist, after World War I, 112–16; modern crisis in, 216–17; during World War I, 105, 111
Nationalization, of exclusion debate, 36, 44–45
National Labor Relations Board, 162, 163
National Labor Union, 26
National origins system: China included in, 189; end of, 202, 203–4, 208–13; establishment of, 138; in Filipino exclusion debate, 151, 154, 155; in McCarran-Walter Act of 1952, 201–2
Nationals, American, 75; vs. aliens, 75, 155
National security: collective, 110; as driver of U.S. imperialism, 72–73
National security policy community, 7, 228, *229*
National security threats, 11; Japan as, 86–87, 115–16; and Open Door policy, 88–92; racism as, 87, 92, 102; Russia as, 88–89; after September 11 terrorist attacks, 232
National Trades Council, 147
Native Americans, U.S. citizenship for, 9, 75
Native Sons of the Golden West, 132
Nativism: in congressional support for exclusion, 57; nationalism inspired by, 111; among Republicans, 24, 29; after World War I, 111
Naturalization. *See* Citizenship
Naturalization Act of 1790, 9, 242 (n. 20)
Navy, U.S.: in China, 19; Filipinos in, 74, 157; in Japan, 19–20
Neoconservatives: on model minority, 204, 215, 216; vs. progressive egalitarians, 204
New Deal, 139–40; changes in labor unions during, 162–64; Second, 162. *See also specific legislation*
New England: congressional opposition to interests of, 58–61, *60*, 247 (n. 39); congressional views on Chinese exclusion in, 47–57, *48*, *49*, *50*, 67; economy of, 48–54, *51*; transformation of egalitarians into exclusionists in, 67
Newspapers. *See* Press coverage
New York, businesses against Chinese exclusion in, 52–53
New York Board of Trade, 52
New York Times (newspaper), 25, 53, 73, 167–68, *169*
New York Times Magazine, 214
New York Tribune (newspaper), 25, 28, 53
New York World (newspaper), 28
Nimitz, Chester, 176, 208
Nisei (second-generation Japanese Americans): and alien land law of 1920, 256 (n. 30); in Army during World War II, 170, 176, 186–87, 195, 200; differences between issei and, 99; in Hawai'i, Americanization of, 144–45. *See also* Internment
Nisei: The Quiet Americans (Hosokawa), 215
Nitobe, Inazo, 84, 98; *Bushido*, 98
Nitz, Michael, 1

Pratt, Helen Gay, 167–69

Prejudice: Japanese-Americans (McWilliams), 185–86

Presidential elections: California's influence on, 44, 55–56, 245 (n. 18); of 1828, 21; of 1844, 16–17; of 1860, 24; of 1876, 34; of 1880, 56, 245 (n. 18); of 1904, 88; of 1920, 112, 130, *131*, 132; of 1932, 159

Press coverage: of Burlingame Treaty, 28; of Chinese exclusion debate, 53–54, *54*; of congressional hearings on Japanese exclusion, 117, 118; of IPR textbook on Japan, 166–69; of Japan as yellow peril, 91; of transpacific mail service, 25. *See also specific newspapers*

Progress and Poverty (George), 43

Progressive egalitarians, 204

Progressive exclusionists, 69, 95–97

Progressive Party, 96, 100

Propaganda, in World War II: Japanese, 172–73, 181, 185, 190–92; U.S., 186

Proposition 1 (California). *See* Alien land law

Proposition 15 (California), 195–96, *196*

Prostitutes: exclusion of, 32, 33, 34; women missionaries rescuing, 69

Qing government, 45, 63, 64, 77–78, 87

Quotas, immigration: for Asia-Pacific triangle, 199, 208; for Chinese immigrants, 189, 190; Dillingham Commission on, 106, 113, 114; in Emergency Quota Act of 1921, 113; for European immigrants, 12; for Filipino immigrants, 155; in Immigration Act of 1924, x, 11–12, 113; in Immigration and Nationality Act of 1965, 208–13; for Japanese immigrants, 102–3, 104, 114, 136, 146–47; in McCarran-Walter Act of 1952, 201–2, 203, 208–10

Race: biological theories of, 83–84, 139–40, 142; in citizenship requirements, 9, 134, 242 (n. 20); as driver of U.S. imperialism, 72; in eugenics, 83–84; in Fourteenth Amendment, 26–27; internationalism based on, 133–34

Race relations: in Hawai'i, as racial paradise, 166, 205, 207; in Immigration and Nationality Act of 1965, 204

Race Relations, Survey of, 140–47

Race relations cycle, 142–43, 185

Race relations policy community, 7, 228–29, *229*

Race riots, in California, 150

Racial disruption of social order, fear of, 11, *12*

Racial equality: in Burlingame Treaty, 28–29; in Immigration and Nationality Act of 1965, 204, 211; in inclusive vs. exclusive view of equality, 4; in League of Nations, 113, 197; at San Francisco congressional hearings, 41–42; in United Nations, 197

Racial formation, 6

Racial inclusion, in labor unions, 139, 140, 163

Racial incompatibility theories: on Filipinos, 149–50, 153; on Japanese, 80, 111, 115, 135; Masaoka on evidence against, 212

Racial liberals, 239 (n. 10)

Racial segregation, in California: of Asian students, 93–94, 96; residential, in Los Angeles, 126–28

Racial superiority theories: biology of race in, 83–84, 139–40, 142; in Chinese exclusion debate, 57; exclusionists' disavowal of, 153, 156; in Filipino exclusion debate, 149, 153, 156; among imperialists, 74; among missionaries, 68–69; Takaki on reality of, 217–18

Racism: connection between homeownership and, 128; polite forms of, ix; stereotypes as, 1–2; as white peril, 87, 92, 102, 181, 188–89. *See also* Anti-Asian racism

Radical Republicans, 5, 15, 28

Railroad, transcontinental, 19, 24–25, 40–41

Raker, John E., 107, 117–18, 121–22

Ramona (Jackson), 76

Rankin, John, 173–75

Rayburn, Sam, 207

Reagan, Ronald, 233

Recession, after World War I, 113

Reconstruction: end of, 35, 43, 44; federal protections for Chinese immigrants during, 26–27, 30, 32–33

Redress commission (Commission on Wartime Relocation and Internment of Civilians), 220–24

Redress movement, 218–25

Red Scare, 113, 123

Reed, David A., 136, 137

Refugees, in McCarran-Walter Act of 1952, 201–2

Regional patterns: in congressional support for Chinese exclusion, 47–61, *48*, *49*, *50*, 67, 246 (n. 23); in support for Japanese exclusion, 97–104; in U.S. economy, 48–55

Registration system, for Chinese immigrants, 63–64, 248 (n. 6)

Renunciation of Extraterritoriality in China, Treaty for the, 189

Repatriation, of unemployed Filipinos, 159–62

Republicans: in Burlingame Treaty, 27–28; in congressional elections of 1874, 34, 44; in congressional elections of 1920, 132; creation of party, 23–24; European immigrants as, 9; in Hawai'i, 206; in Los Angeles, 130–32, *131*; midwestern, northeastern interests opposed by, 58–61, *60*, 247 (n. 39); nativism among, 24, 29; in presidential election of 1920, 130–31, *131*, 132; Radical, 5, 15, 28; regional patterns in support for Chinese exclusion, 47–48, *48*, 55–61, *60*; slavery opposed by, 24; transformation from egalitarians into exclusionists, 44–48, *47*, *48*, 114; transpacific trade supported by, 15, 24–28. *See also specific people*

Resettlement, of Japanese internees, 186–87, 192

Residential segregation, in Los Angeles, 126–28

Restitution, for internment, 2, 221, 232

"Reverse-racism," 223

"Revisionist history," 221, 224

Rhee, Syngman, 199

Riis, Jacob, *Making of an American*, 76

Riordan, Thomas, 65

Rising Tide of Color (Stoddard), 133–34

Roberts, Owen, 173

Rockefeller, John D., 98

Rockefeller, John D., Jr., 141

Rockefeller Foundation, 98, 140, 145, 185

Roosevelt, Eleanor, 176, 186

Roosevelt, Franklin D.: on Chinese exclusion, repeal of, 170, 189; death of, 195; as egalitarian, 5, 170; Executive Order 9066 by, 170, 176–77; and Hawai'i Territorial Guard, 176; on Japanese American assimilation, 170; on Japanese Americans in army, 176, 186; in Japanese internment, 174, 198, 220, 221, 222; in presidential election of 1932, 159; Second New Deal of, 162; War Relocation Authority established by, 183

Roosevelt, Theodore: autobiography of, 135; on Chinese exclusion, 87–88; death of, 87, 110; as egalitarian, 4, 5, 8; as exclusionist, 8, 87–88; in Gentleman's Agreement, 94, 135; on Japanese exclusion, 8, 86–94; at Lake Mohonk Conference, 75; on land ownership by Japanese, 99; on Nitobe, 98; and Philippine independence, 109; on

Russo-Japanese War, 88–89; State of the Union addresses by, 4, 86, 87, 93, 114; on transpacific trade, 86; and U.S. imperialism, 72, 73, 109; on world government, 97; on World War I, 105, 110

Roosevelt Revolution, 157

Root, Elihu, 97, 98, 102

Ross, Edward Alsworth, 80, 82, 142, 250 (n. 56)

ROTC program, at University of Hawaii, 144

Rowe, James H., 174

Rowell, Chester H.: on alien land law, 100–101, 143, 253 (n. 32); on Americanization of Japanese immigrants in Hawai'i, 144–45; in Committee on National Security and Fair Play, 172; death of, 194; at Institute of Pacific Relations conference, 145; on Japanese exclusion, 80, 96, 116; on Japanese internment, 172–73; on League of Nations, 143; as progressive exclusionist, 95–96; in Survey of Race Relations, 143–45; transformation from exclusionist to egalitarian, 8, 143–44, 230, 241 (n. 19)

Roxas, Manuel: anticommunism of, 199; on Filipino exclusion, 149, 150, 152–53, 156; on Philippine independence, 152–53, 155

Rusk, Dean, 200–201, 209

Russell, Lindsay, 97

Russia: in Russo-Japanese War, 87, 88–91, 96; as threat to Open Door policy, 88–89

Russian Jews, 113

Russo-Japanese War, 87, 88–91, 96

Ryder, R. W., 117, 118

Sabath, Adolf, 159–60, 260 (n. 45)

Sabotage, fear of, 11, *12*

Sacramento Bee (newspaper), 99, 115, 166

Sacramento Daily Union (newspaper), 52

Sandwich Islands. *See* Hawai'i

San Francisco: congressional hearings of 1876 in, 36–43; congressional hearings of 1879 in, 43–44; earthquake of 1906 in, 93; opposition to Chinese immigrants in, 31–32; opposition to Japanese immigrants in, 79–80, 92–96; women missionaries in, 69

San Francisco Alta (newspaper), 28

San Francisco Board of Supervisors, 32

San Francisco Building Trades Council, 93, 94, 95

San Francisco Bulletin (newspaper), 53

San Francisco Chronicle (newspaper), 53–54, *54*, 167, 172

Veterans of Foreign Wars (VFW), 157, 158, 190, 193

Victimization-agency model of racism, 239–40 (n. 13)

Vietnam War, 210, 213

Violence against Asian Americans: Chinatown massacre of 1871 in Los Angeles, 1, 2, 13, 32, 226; contemporary, 1–2, 217; pogroms of 1880s, 64

Virgin Islands, U.S., 24

Voorhis, Martin, 172

Voting rights, African American, 29–30

Voting Rights Act of 1965, 213

Wages, of Chinese immigrants, 37

Wagner Act of 1935, 162

Walker, Francis Amasa, 67

Walsh, John, 192

Walsh, Richard, 191

Wanghia, Treaty of, 18

War bonds, U.S., 105, 123

War Department: in Executive Order 9066, 170; in internment decision, 174–75

War on Drugs, 233

War on Terror, 232

War Relocation Authority (WRA), 171, 183–87

Warren, Earl: alien land law under, 195, 197; in internment decision, 198; Knowland appointed by, 194; regret regarding internment, 219; Scharrenberg in administration of, 187–88; in Tolan Committee hearings, 179–80, 182

Washington, Booker T., *Up from Slavery*, 76

Washington arms limitation treaties, 133

Watsonville (California), race riots in, 150

Wealth, regional patterns in distribution of, 51

Webb, Ulysses S.: on Filipino exclusion, 149, 150, 151, 152, 153, 154; on Japanese exclusion, 136; in Japanese Exclusion League, 132; Warren replacing, 179

Weglyn, Michi, *Years of Infamy*, 219–20

Welch, Richard: Filipino exclusion bill by, 148–54; on Filipino repatriation, 159; in Hawaiian statehood, 207–8

Welles, Gideon, 26

West Coast: congressional hearings on Japanese exclusion in, 116–23; congressional views on Chinese exclusion in, 48, *48, 49, 50,* 53–54; economy of, 51–54; vs. Hawai'i, in transpacific trade, 205; Japanese internment in (*see* Internment)

Western imperialism, in Asia, 10

West Indies, 24

Westward expansion. *See* Expansionism

Whigs: collapse of party, 23–24; on expansionism and transpacific trade, 16–21

White(s): Europeans as, 57; Japanese as, 84; Latin Americans as, 8–9; outmigration from South, 106; U.S. citizenship limited to, 9, 242 (n. 20)

White peril, racism as, 87, 92, 102, 181, 188–89

White Peril in the Far East (Gulick), 102

White supremacy. *See* Racial superiority theories

Whitman, Walt, 208, 216

Wilbur, Ray Lyman, 143, 145–46, 172

Wilhelm (German kaiser), 91

Wilson, Woodrow: and Japanese exclusion in California, 87, 99–101; in League of Nations, 110, 112; and Philippine independence, 109; in presidential election of 1920, 132; and Shandong controversy, 115; in World War I, 104, 105, 109–10

Woman Warrior (Kingston), 224

Women: Chinese, shortage of, 27, 33; Japanese, as picture brides, 99, 118, 135; Japanese, surge of, 98–99; married to Asians, return of U.S. citizenship to, 259 (n. 25); as missionaries in San Francisco, 69; U.S. citizenship for, 242 (n. 20), 259 (n. 25)

Wong Kim Ark, United States v., 65

Woodruff, Mrs. L. S., 121

Workingmen's Party, 44

World government, 97, 110. *See also* League of Nations

World War I, 104–10; Asian immigrants in military during, 105, 151, 157, 158; end of, 110, 112; Immigration Act of 1917 during, 105–9; loyalty of immigrants during, 105, 114, 123, 151–52; U.S. entry into, 105; U.S. isolationism after, 111, 112–16; U.S. neutrality in, 104

World War II, 170–94; Chinese exclusion in, repeal of, 189–93; complex racial nature of, 188–89; Executive Order 9066 in, 170, 176–77, 197; first roundup of Japanese Americans in, 171; Great Transformation in exclusion debate during, 170–71; Japanese Americans in army during, 170, 171, 176, 186–87, 195, 198, 200, 211–12; Japanese attack on Pearl Harbor in, 169, 170–73, 232; Japanese propaganda in, 172–73, 181, 185, 190–92; loyalty of immigrants during, 171–72, 211–12; racism as white peril in,

CPSIA information can be obtained
at www.ICGtesting.com
Printed in the USA
LVHW101649171122
733396LV00004B/404